The Deeds of
POPE INNOCENT III

The Deeds of
POPE INNOCENT III

by an Anonymous Author

Translated with an Introduction and Notes
by James M. Powell

The Catholic University of America Press
Washington, D.C.

The paper used in this publication meets the minimum requirements
of American National Standards for Information Science—Permanence
of Paper for Printed Library materials, ANSI Z39.48-1984.
First paperback edition 2007

∞

Library of Congress Cataloging-in-Publication Data
Gesta Innocentii III. English.
The deeds of Pope Innocent III / by an anonymous author ;
translated with an introduction and notes by James M. Powell.
— 1st ed.
p. cm.
Includes bibliographical references and index.
ISBN 0-8132-1362-2 (cl.: alk. paper)
ISBN 978-0-8132-1488-7 (pbk.: alk. paper)
1. Innocent III, Pope, 1160 or 61-1216.   2. Papacy—History.
I. Powell, James M.   II. Title.
BX1236.G4613 2004
282'.092—dc21
2003004337

Ad memoriam bonorum temporum

Thomas Brown
Michael Markowski
Mary Skinner
Richard Spence

With a special thanks to Richard for his work on the
Gesta Innocentii III

CONTENTS

ACKNOWLEDGMENTS

This project began when I asked Richard Spence to translate the *Gesta* as it appears in the Patrologia Latina. In typical fashion he made a heroic effort before turning the results over to me with his blessing. Though I have not used his translation, I have occasionally consulted his notes on the text. I wish to publicly thank him here. His name also appears deservedly on the dedication page.

Two colleagues and friends, both experts on Innocent III and his period, have invested considerable effort in correcting my mistakes. Brenda Bolton knows Innocent and the *Gesta* in ways that no one else does; John Moore has worked extensively on the registers of Innocent's letters as well as his sermons, and is preparing a biography. Both have read the manuscript in different stages. John has worked tirelessly to correct my mistakes. It is no fault of his if some persist. Alfred Andrea has contributed substantially to our understanding of the Fourth Crusade. He kindly allowed me to see his translation of letters dealing with that topic, which have now been published. If I have not always followed his lead, it is due in part to the fact that I had already translated most of the letters. But I was grateful for the opportunity to improve my work. I also wish to thank Keith Kendall for his help in checking several references.

Christoph Egger, whose work on the registers is merely one facet of his important research on Innocent and late-twelfth-century theology, has been a valuable sounding board. From the time of his arrival in

Syracuse, I have benefitted from Kenneth Pennington's knowledge of canon law and his interest in the *Gesta.* I owe substantial debts to others too numerous to mention, but I wish to express my deepest thanks to the late Leonard E. Boyle, O.P., to Giles Constable, Edward Peters, and, as ever, to James John. They are all in the notes, but even more in my thoughts.

My debt to libraries is obvious but I must thank the staffs of the Syracuse University Library, the Vatican Library, the Mullen Library of The Catholic University of America, and the Cornell University Library. In my career, I have had so much help from librarians that I consider them as ghostly authors. Finally, in this computer age, I must also acknowledge the help of my son, Michael Powell. He is, indeed, an assistant editor, whose expertise with computing has made my task so much easier.

INTRODUCTION

Composed in the years from about 1204 to 1209, the *Gesta Innocentii III*, or *Deeds of Innocent III*, belongs to a genre of biography that has its origins in the classical period, in such works as Plutarch's *Lives*, Suetonius's *Lives of the Twelve Caesars*, and the *Scriptores historiae Augustae*.[1] But the more immediate models were the series of papal biographies collected in the *Liber Pontificalis*, to which were added those written by Cardinal Boso in the second half of the twelfth century.[2] The work as we possess it, however, is not a complete papal biography. Not only is it limited to approximately the first eleven years of Innocent III's eighteen-and-a-half-year reign, but it shows signs that strongly suggest that the author recognized his inability to complete the work

1. See Agostino Paravicini-Bagliani, "La storiografia pontificia del secolo XIII: Prospettive di ricerca," *Römische Historische Mitteilungen* 18 (1976): 45–54; Brenda Bolton, "Too Important to Neglect: The *Gesta Innocentii PP III*," in *Church and Chronicle in the Middle Ages: Essays Presented to John Taylor*, ed. G. A. Loud and I. N. Wood (London: Hambledon Press, 1991), 87–99, esp. 87–88. Also see Giulia Barone, "I 'Gesta Innocentii III': Politica e cultura a Roma all'inizio del duecento," in *Studi sul Medioevo per Girolamo Arnaldi*, ed. Giulia Barone, Lidia Capo, and Stefano Gasparri, I libri de Viella 24 (Rome: Viella, 2001), 1–23, which contains a useful bibliography on 22–23.

2. David Gress-Wright [David Wright], *The 'Gesta Innocentii III': Text, Introduction and Commentary* (Ph.D. diss., Bryn Mawr College, 1981), 34*–35*. Hereafter cited as *GW*. For bibliography, see *GW*, 129*–36*, and Edward M. Peters, "Lotario dei Segni Becomes Pope Innocent III: The Man and the Pope," in *Pope Innocent III and His World*, ed. John C. Moore (Aldershot: Ashgate, 1999), 3–24, as well as the other articles in this volume. See also *Innocenzo III: Urbs et orbis*, ed. Andrea Sommerlechner, 2 vols. (Rome: Società Romana di Storia Patria, 2003).

according to his original plan, which rather closely paralleled that of Cardinal Boso. This change of plan was chiefly reflected in the decision of the author to incorporate the material that he had collected to date and to arrange it in a coherent pattern with useful introductory comments. It suggests a change in career or some other major event that forced the author to turn from this project.[3] At the same time, internal evidence suggests that he worked to provide a series of "conclusions" to the work, culminating in the final section, with its gift list. In this sense, we are confronted with a complete work, rather than one that was abandoned in midpassage.

Previous authors have stressed the unfinished character of the *Gesta*. I prefer to put greater emphasis on the effort of the author to present a coherent picture of major aspects of Innocent's pontificate, even though that pontificate would last about seven more years.

Papal biography was not an isolated form. It had its parallels in royal annals and biographies, all of which flourished in the twelfth century. But it was perhaps more distinctive as a form of collective memory for a group of policymakers and bureaucrats that had emerged around the reform papacy in this period. There is abundant evidence that the papacy, taken collectively, was developing a sense of the importance of the past. Indeed, papal letters often served to remind their readers of past contexts.[4] The registers of papal letters were a source to be mined along with other archival materials for information needed for the expanding papal administration.[5] The *Gesta* was, therefore, primarily an in-house document. Its audience was mostly composed of members of the curia. For this reason, earlier debates regarding its content, point of view, and purpose largely miss the mark when they

3. *GW*, 33*–34*. Also see James M. Powell, "Innocent III and Petrus Beneventanus: Reconstructing a Career at the Papal Curia," in *Pope Innocent III and His World*, ed. John C. Moore, 51–62, esp. 52–53.

4. James M. Powell, "Myth, Legend, Propaganda, History: The First Crusade, 1140–ca. 1300," in *Autour de la première croisade*, ed. Michel Balard (Paris: Publications de la Sorbonne, 1996), 127–41, esp. 135.

5. *GW*, 34*.

view it as a kind of propaganda piece or a straight-out biography aimed at celebrating an important figure.[6] Of course, it reflected the curial point of view and it was supportive of Innocent's initiatives, but that is understandable if we examine Innocent III within the context of an active papal curia rather than as an isolated papal figure.

Indeed, that is the way that he is presented in the *Gesta*. Nor does this detract from his position. Rather it confirms it in the context of papal tradition.

Authorship

The *Gesta* is an anonymous work.[7] We do not know whether or not this was intentional. But the author clearly knew the pope personally, observed him on a regular basis, and was at least for some time a member of the papal curia. In addition, we may add that the author was very knowledgeable concerning affairs in southern Italy and Sicily. He knew a great deal about internal politics both among churchmen and nobles as well as in the cities. He does not, however, provide any evidence regarding his place of origin. He was most likely trained in the law and was a great admirer of Innocent's skill in dealing with complex legal cases. Moreover, there is nothing in this work that, if made public, would have impeded a successful career in the Roman curia and/or the law. On the basis of these points and a couple of other pieces of collateral evidence, I have put forward the name of Peter of Benevento, the compiler of the important collection of Innocent's decretals made in 1209, as the author of the *Gesta*. Given the lack of any specific evidence to tie him to the authorship, however, it would be presumptuous to attribute the work to him, but I do believe that the case for his authorship is a strong one.

---

6. *GW,* 41*. See also note 117 on p. 146*.

7. *GW,* 112*–14*; Powell, "Petrus Beneventanus," 54–62. For another view, see Barone, "Gesta," 20–21.

Overview

The content of the *Gesta* deserves brief consideration not merely for what it deals with but also for what it does not address. The topics treated include (1) Innocent's background and the reasons for his election as pope; (2) his policies vis-à-vis Rome and the papal patrimony (or Papal States); (3) his defense of the Sicilian crown; (4) his reform of the curia and his legal decisions; (5) his defense of Queen Ingeborg against the effort of King Philip II Augustus of France to secure a divorce and his role in other royal marriage cases; (6) concerns over church unity and the crusade, including the Byzantine Empire, the Bulgarians, and the Armenians, especially also the Fourth Crusade; (7) the coronation of the king of Aragon; (8) Innocent's efforts to control heresy and his relations with the Romans; and (8) his works of charity and his gifts. Although this brief list scarcely does justice to the *Gesta*, it is sufficient to indicate the limits of the work. The main omissions are references to his pastoral work. His recognition of the *Humiliati,* groups of clergy devoted to care of the sick and poor, as a religious order, despite its association with heresy since its condemnation by Pope Lucius III in Verona in 1184, was certainly notable. Nor is there any mention of foundation of the Trinitarian order. Only his foundation of the Hospital of the Holy Spirit "in Sassia" finds mention among his charitable activities. In that connection, there is a brief mention of his preaching, supplementing the reference to his sermons at the beginning of the *Gesta.* But even more surprising is the fact that none of his major decretals dealing with issues of church and state, with the exception of "Solitae," included because it was addressed to the Byzantine emperor, Alexius III, and dealt with the crusade and the union of the churches, is mentioned. Yet all of these belong to this period. They include the decretal "Vergentis," dealing with heresy, a topic much discussed in the *Gesta.* Likewise, the controversy over the succession to the imperial throne is treated only peripherally, despite its close relationship to other events under discussion. This fact led David Gress-Wright to consider the possibility that the author of the *Gesta* was familiar with the *Regestum super Negotio Romani Imperii,* a collection of letters dealing with this issue.[8] As noted above, I am inclined to a circumstantial explanation for the form of the *Gesta,* though the lack of treatment of the controversy over the imperial election supports Gress-Wright's argument that the author used the *Regestum* as a model for his use of papal letters. What the omission of various topics may point to is a conscious effort on the part of the author to present a coherent picture of Innocent's pontificate as he understood it. Even his decision to stop writing in 1208/1209 did not prevent him from staying with this plan.

The *Gesta* sets forth a broad vision of Innocent's pontificate rooted in his commitment to church reform, the crusade, the achievement of unity with Eastern churches under papal authority, and bringing an end to internal dissent. Innocent was, as the author presents him, deeply concerned about the security of the papacy. The opening section of the *Gesta* clearly demonstrates his determination to ensure that the popes would be masters in their own house and able to control their neighbors. As the *Gesta* presents this aim, though with a certain degree of hesitation because of its secular nature, it is fundamental to all of the pope's other initiatives, which are definitely aimed at ecclesiastical unity under papal leadership. Indeed, the organizational plan of the *Gesta* flows directly from this assumption. The materials selected by the author lend themselves to this view. Whether in the patrimony (the Papal States), in the Kingdom of Sicily, in questions of law ranging from the papal appellate role involving disputes in particular churches or matrimonial conflicts involving figures like Philip II of France or the kings of Leon and Castile, or in his efforts to promote Christian unity and the crusade, Innocent appears at center stage. Even the concluding section, dealing with his charitable activities, showing him as a model bishop, fits into the broad scheme pursued by the author.

8. *GW,* 34*.

The Translation

This translation is based on four chief sources: the doctoral dissertation prepared by David Gress-Wright under the direction of Charles Brand at Bryn Mawr College and used with the kind permission of David Wright (the form of his name he now prefers); the fourteenth-century manuscript copy of the original from the Vatican Library, Vat Lat 12111; the edition printed in the *opera* of Pope Innocent III in volume 214 of J.-P. Migne's *Patrologia Latina;* and, especially important because of the large number of letters included in the *Gesta,* the Austrian edition of Innocent's registers.

I have not prepared a critical edition of the Latin text for a number of reasons, but chiefly because that task would have unduly prolonged the preparation of the translation. Instead, I have tried to deal with textual problems and questions regarding punctuation, paragraphing, and citation as these have arisen. I have prepared an appendix in which I have noted the more important emendations to the Gress-Wright text as a help to users of the translation. I have tried to stay close to the Latin, but that has sometimes proven difficult, given the length of some sentences in the letters. On the whole, however, I have felt that it was important to retain the structure of the original as much as possible in order to avoid misreading the text. Obviously, despite the advice I have received, the remaining infelicities are my own.

It is my experience that one of the great benefits of a translation, beyond its value as an educational tool, rests with the increased accessibility to scholars that encourages them, with suitable caution, to use the text as a whole rather than consulting sections appropriate to their research. Since the *Gesta,* taken as a whole, is greater than the sum of its parts, the advantage gained for scholarship may contribute to a greater understanding not merely of Innocent III, but of the papacy in the late twelfth and early thirteenth centuries.

The text contains numerous letters, especially those of Pope Innocent III. Not all of these are found in the register of his letters. Where the letter appears in the register, I have compared the text, but have noted only major variations. The Austrian edition has been invaluable for citations, but I have not always listed every reference they have given. Minor allusions have been ignored, as have multiple references, quite common for citations from the New Testament that drew on the Old Testament.

Innocent III: The Pope of the *Gesta*

Modern interpretations of Innocent III are the product of two main currents in the study of the medieval church. From the seventeenth through the first half of the twentieth century and with continuing influence today, historical controversy swirled about the nature of the papal office and, in particular, the relations between church and state.[9] But the medieval papacy had a view of its world and its place in that world that was considerably more complex than its relationship to secular powers. Since the eleventh century, one of the principal goals of the popes was to ensure its position of leadership over local churches. This goal was paramount over and directive of papal attitudes toward secular rule. Thus, there was a dichotomy between the essentially traditional attitudes of popes regarding the internal political structures of secular society and their radical, even revolutionary, view, of the place of the church in this world. On the one hand, they tended to accept the established order and even to oppose change, but, on the other hand, they worked assiduously to protect ecclesiastical institutions from the growing power of secular rulers.

It has been a growing awareness of the limiting nature of earlier historiography that has contributed to an emphasis on the pastoral concerns of medieval popes. Already in such works as the Fliche-

9. James M. Powell, "Innocenzo III: The Making of an Image," in *Innocenzo III: Urbs et orbis*, 2:1363–73.

Martin *Histoire de l'église,* Catholic historians, motivated in large part by apologetic considerations, were stressing the pastoral work of medieval popes.[10] But the full impact of this work only came slowly, particularly as non-Catholic medievalists began to adjust their view of the medieval papacy. That tendency has reached its fullest recent development in work such as Colin Morris's *Papal Monarchy.*[11] In the case of Innocent III, the work of Brenda Bolton has been especially important.[12]

The election of Innocent III as pope was controversial. The author of the *Gesta* singles out disagreements over his youth among the cardinals. At his election Lothar of Segni was only thirty-seven years of age. The *Gesta* counters this problem by stressing Innocent's education and his writings. But scholars have not been entirely satisfied with this treatment. There has been an ongoing effort to identify a rift among the cardinals both before and during Innocent's pontificate.[13] The *Gesta* does mention factions among the cardinals, but gives no specifics. If there was such a difference, it could not have been major, since the cardinals closed ranks immediately and elected Innocent unanimously. Still, there is ample evidence that Innocent's election represented a break with the immediate past. More importantly, and having a more direct bearing on his election, are the events that followed immediately on his election. The friends of reform groups seem to have had a clear message that Innocent was sympathetic to their cause. Within

10. Augustin Fliche and Victor Martin, *Histoire de l'église,* 34 vols. (Paris: Bloud & Gay, 1934–1960). This compendium in many ways marks a turning point in Catholic treatment of the history of the church.

11. Colin Morris, *The Papal Monarchy: The Western Church from 1050–1250* (Oxford: Clarendon Press, 1989), 433–38.

12. See esp. Brenda Bolton, *Innocent III: Studies on Papal Authority and Pastoral Care* (Aldershot: Variorum, 1995).

13. See Werner Maleczek, *Papst und Kardinalskolleg von 1191 bis 1216: Die Kardinale unter Coelestin III und Innocenz III* (Vienna: Verlag der Österreichischen Akademie der Wissenschaften, 1984), 335; Powell, "Petrus Beneventanus," 52; and Ian S. Robinson, *The Papacy, 1073–1198* (Cambridge: Cambridge University Press, 1990), 510–24. But see also *Gesta,* IV.

the first months following his election, he had the opportunity to demonstrate his commitment to the new religious reforms that had gained popularity in the final decades of the twelfth century.[14] He encouraged groups like the Trinitarians, with their concern for the ransom of those captured by Muslims. He canonized Homobonus of Cremona, a merchant-tailor, who devoted himself to the poor as a model for the urban middle class. With Innocent, the idea of reform took on a broader meaning to the papacy than it previously possessed.

During this period the monastic ideal that provided the spiritual and intellectual core to the great reforms of the late eleventh and early twelfth centuries had captured the minds and hearts of many among the laity.[15] These were often persons drawn from the towns, who were acutely conscious of the problems being created by the growth of urban poverty and the increasing gulf between rich and poor. But, even though the issue of poverty was highly visible, it was only one of numerous problems created by the greater mobility of people from the countryside to the city, including dissatisfaction with the way in which the local churches met their responsibilities. The bishops were concerned that they were losing out to the new ruling class of the towns, as well as to lay nobility, and even to the great monasteries. By the late twelfth century, Western European society had entered a critical period. The papacy, preoccupied by political conflicts, had tried to meet some of these problems at the Third Lateran Council in 1179, but the conflict with Emperor Frederick Barbarossa and that between King Henry II and Archbishop Thomas Becket, as well as Pope Alexander III's forced absence from Rome during much of his pontificate, blunted the effort of the papacy to deal with the

14. James M. Powell, "Innocent III, the Trinitarians, and the Renewal of the Church, 1198–1200," in *La liberazione dei 'captivi' tra cristianità e islam: Oltre la crociata e il gihad: Tolleranza e servizio umanitario*, ed. Giulio Cipollone (Vatican City: Archivio Segreto Vaticano; Gangemi editore, 2000), 245–54.

15. Giles Constable, *The Reformation of the Twelfth Century* (Cambridge: Cambridge University Press, 1996), 296–328.

challenges thrown up in this society. The church also found itself on
the defensive against various groups of reformers and heretics. In
1184, in the bull *Ad abolendam*, Pope Lucius III, in Verona, issued a
condemnation of various groups believed to be heretical, including
the *Humiliati*. At the beginning of his pontificate, however, Innocent
III, with a bare mention of the earlier condemnation, recognized the
Humiliati as a religious order composed of both clerical and lay ele-
ments.[16] This move was undoubtedly controversial, but Innocent appointed a group of influential clergy who were clearly prepared to
take a positive position on this question. It was a technique that revealed an important aspect of Innocent's approach: his ability not
merely to anticipate problems but to work effectively to garner support for his position.

The recognition of the *Humiliati* was only one in a number of meas-
ures undertaken in the early years of his pontificate that set its tone.
Along the same lines was his handling of the case of the bishop and
faithful of Metz, where some members of the laity were meeting secretly to read and discuss the Bible in the vernacular.[17] His letter to the
faithful of Metz, clearly meant for public circulation, supported the
bishop and warned the faithful against practices that were inconsistent
with the views of the church. But his letter to the bishop and chapter,
not meant for public circulation, contained strong advice to proceed
cautiously. He made it clear that he could not proceed with a condemnation on the basis of the evidence that had been presented to him by
the bishop and chapter. He advised them to work with the faithful and
to get more information as to the translation of the Bible being used.

Less controversial but indicative of his sympathy with the new
trends in addressing societal needs was his recognition of the Trinitari-

16. Frances Andrews, *The Early Humiliati* (Cambridge: Cambridge University
Press, 1999), 80–98. The initiative for this action undoubtedly came from the *Humiliati* in Lombardy.

17. Leonard E. Boyle, "Innocent III and Vernacular Versions of Scriptures," in
The Bible in the Medieval World: Essays in Memory of Beryl Smalley, Studies in Church
History, Subsidia, 4 (Oxford: Blackwell, 1985), 97–107.

an order, founded by John of Matha, and his support for the Hospital of the Holy Spirit "in Sassia" in Rome. These steps found further confirmation in the canonization of St. Homobonus of Cremona, whose charitable acts and devotion to the church made him the model urban saint. In this instance, Innocent stressed his orthodoxy and his opposition to heresy.[18] In each of these cases, there is evidence that Innocent was known to be sympathetic to the particular cause prior to his election. John of Matha, for example, had been a student in Paris. The Trinitarian rule, as presented in Innocent's letter of December 17, 1198, was supported by Odo of Sully, Bishop of Paris, and the abbot of St. Victor. Moreover, John was active in Rome from almost the beginning of Innocent's reign. The work of Gui of Montpellier, an important figure in that center of medical education, as Innocent was well aware, inspired the foundation of the Hospital of the Holy Spirit for pilgrims near St. Peter's basilica. Gui was brought to Rome specifically because the pope wanted a hospital that was at the forefront of medical treatment. The canonization of Homobonus in January 1199, only two years after his death, was promoted by Bishop Sicard of Cremona, one of the leading figures in the Italian episcopate, a historian and liturgist, and later legate to Constantinople.

Of all of these activities, only the foundation of the Hospital of the Holy Spirit "in Sassia" received any mention in the *Gesta*. There is no explicit explanation for the omission of the others. Although it is unlikely that the author of the *Gesta* was unaware of the recognition of the *Humiliati*, we should note that the dossier of letters dealing with this issue was not included in the register of Innocent III's letters. The only thing we can say with certainty is that the opening years of Innocent's pontificate set a very different tone from those of his predeces-

18. André Vauchez, "Le 'trafiquant céléste': Saint Homobon de Cremone (+1197), marchant et pére des pauvres," in *Horizons Marins: Itineraire spirituels (Ve–XVIII siècle)*," 2 vols. Publications anciennes et Medievales 20–21 (Paris: Publications de la Sorbonne, 1987), 115–20; also see his *La saintété en occident aux derniers siècles du moyen âge* (Rome: École Française de Rome; Paris: Diffusion de Boccard, 1981), 412–14.

sors. Without being revolutionary, but as someone who was closely
tied to recent developments, he may have given some of the cardinals
pause. Discussion of his age may have been a way of airing concerns
about his reform ideas without creating an internal division among
the cardinals and suggests that his election may have been controversial for other reasons.

But the election of Innocent brought youthful energy to the papacy. He was not so much an innovator as he was a motivator. He was almost constantly on the move in this period, especially in his effort to
stabilize the political situation in the Patrimony of St. Peter.[19] Innocent
worked to strengthen the secular authority of the papacy in the patrimony as a means of ensuring its stability. This was no easy task. Rome
itself lay at the heart of the problem. The Romans, like other urban
dwellers, were deeply divided over political issues. The Roman aristocracy, to which Innocent himself belonged, had close ties to the countryside. The rivalries that were endemic in rural areas were easily im-
ported into the city, where they became enmeshed in urban politics.[20]
Some families, like the Frangipani, were losing out in this competition.[21] They sought allies in the city among those dissatisfied with the
policies of Innocent III. Within the city, there was a strong faction that
wanted to establish a commune, that is, a sworn political association
able to rule the city in its own right, virtually without reference to the
pope.

This development was already well under way in many northern
cities and towns. Moreover, those in Rome who supported Roman
dominance of the countryside, a popular position, often allied themselves with those wanting a commune, but this posed a threat to holdings that provided papal income. The seeming confusion of Roman
politics portrayed in the *Gesta* is the result of the rivalries and alliances

19. Daniel Waley, *The Papal State in the Thirteenth Century* (London: Macmillan,
1961), 30–67.
20. See, e.g., James M. Powell, *Albertanus of Brescia: The Pursuit of Happiness in the
Early Thirteenth Century* (Philadelphia: University of Pennsylvania Press, 1992), 16–36.
21. Brenda Bolton, "Terracina," in Appendix III at the end of this volume.

among these various groups and the effort of Innocent, supported by his own family connections, to impose some kind of order and protect papal interests. But, in a realistic way, he showed a desire to find constitutional solutions where and when he could. The discussion of the Senate reveals genuine constitutional concerns on his part. He was deeply concerned about the impact of factionalism on the Senate. His proposal of a single senator, however, revealed a major difficulty, namely, the refusal of faction leaders to accept this arrangement and the resort to military force on both sides. The author of the *Gesta* suggests that the weakness of the senator chosen was responsible for the problem, but it is evident that that was only partly the case. Likewise in the Papal States, Innocent's solution was constitutional. It took the form of a written constitution and revealed the degree to which he was working within the framework that other secular rulers are moving toward: the law-state. In fact, there is evidence of direct influence of his legislation on the later Constitutions of Melfi of Frederick II for the Kingdom of Sicily.[22] As we shall see, this devotion to constitutional approaches also marked his view of the church. From the beginning of his pontificate, he was planning a council to bring the whole church together to face the major issues of church unity, reform, and crusade. In his view, the pope was strongest when he was at the pinnacle of the law.

Innocent was also drawn into the affairs of the Kingdom of Sicily. In 1130, the Norman count of Sicily, Roger II, had secured recognition of his position as king from the anti-pope Anacletus, but it was not until 1139, after he had defeated Pope Innocent II in battle, that the monarchy was firmly established. This brought to its culmination the alliance between the papacy and the Normans against the growing power of the empire in Italy in the twelfth century. After the death of King William II in 1189 without a direct heir, Henry VI, son of the emperor Frederick Barbarossa, who had married William's aunt, Constance, the daughter of Roger II, to Henry, laid claim to the throne. But many

---

22. *Gesta*, XL. Refers to chapter headings in *PL*, 214. See below, n. 70, in text.

among the nobility and the bishops preferred Tancred, count of Lecce, the illegitimate grandson of Roger II. With their support, Tancred managed to rule the kingdom despite the attempt of Henry to conquer it in 1191, but, following his death, Henry's second invasion, in 1194, was successful. Tancred's family was seized and despite an agreement with Henry to allow Tancred's son, William, to enjoy his father's county of Lecce, they were bundled off to Germany, along with some of their major supporters. When Henry died in 1197, leaving a three-year-old son, Frederick Roger, as his heir, his wife, Constance, ruled. But she died in 1198, even as her envoys were concluding agreements with Innocent III over the succession. At her request, Innocent became regent of the kingdom and protector of young Frederick.

The next several years saw Innocent's attempt to defeat the German party in the kingdom, led by Henry's former seneschal, Markward of Anweiler, who claimed to act in his name. The basis for this claim was the Last Will and Testament of Henry. Innocent, however, not only feared Markward's imperial ties, but suspected that he harbored ambitions to become king himself. Moreover, Constance had opposed Markward and his German allies. On his side, Markward sought to gain support from those who had opposed Tancred. Through much of this period the kingdom was in turmoil. Innocent relied chiefly on his own family for military support, especially James the Marshal and his brother Richard. But Markward was more than a match for them. Even after Walter of Brienne, who had married Tancred's daughter, following her escape from Germany, arrived in Italy in order to claim his wife's inheritance and joined the papal side, the situation did not significantly improve. It was only the death of Markward as a result of surgery for kidney stones and the subsequent breakup of the German party that created a more favorable outcome for Frederick. In the period covered by the *Gesta*, however, matters continued to drag on without a clear resolution.

It was, therefore, with a note akin to frustration that the author of the *Gesta* turned from secular affairs to the reform of the church.[23] He

23. *Gesta*, XLI.

described how Innocent regulated the fees to be charged for services by the various functionaries at the papal curia in order to prevent abuses. In a gesture reminiscent of Christ in the Temple, the pope overturned the tables of the money changers in the passageway near of the kitchen of the papal palace. But the author especially emphasized the pope's administration of justice. He had a high regard for Innocent's legal abilities. Innocent had studied in Bologna, the major center of legal studies at this time, but it is not clear to what extent he availed himself of the opportunity to study law. Still, there is ample evidence of his aptitude.[24]

In discussing a series of cases illustrative of the pope's legal work, which involved disputed ecclesiastical jurisdictions, one such was the conflict between the archbishops of Compostella and Barcelona over seven dioceses and between the archbishops of Tours and Dols over the "metropolitan jurisdiction over Brittany."[25] Another famous case involved the desire of the archbishop of Canterbury to build a church in Lambeth, across the river from London, in spite of the opposition of the Canterbury cathedral chapter. The motives behind this effort by the archbishop were well known in Rome. The English monarchy was held in deep suspicion after the assassination of Archbishop Thomas Becket. Indeed, there was strong feeling in Rome that the monarchy was determined to dominate the English church.[26] Innocent was adamant. It is probable that his personal knowledge of the situation in England, gained on a short visit to Canterbury, helped him to make up his mind. Although the pope was successful on this occasion, the issue remained open for the long term.

Another sensitive issue involved the transfer of archbishops and bishops from one diocese to another without papal permission. Innocent took a hard line. Such actions threatened what he regarded as

24. See Kenneth Pennington's essay "The Legal Education of Pope Innocent III" and related work in his *Popes, Canonists and Texts, 1150–1550* (Aldershot: Variorum, 1993).
25. *Gesta*, XLII.
26. *Gesta*, CXXXI.

the essential position of the papacy in the church. He was fond of citing the famous distinction made by Pope Leo I between the *plenitudo potestatis* (fullness of power) enjoyed by the pope and the *pars sollecitudinis* (share of pastoral rule) that defined the role of archbishops and bishops. Episcopal translations without papal approval threatened this distinction. The cases presented, especially that of the bishop of Würzburg, reveal how Innocent viewed the church. In that instance, Bishop Conrad of Hildesheim accepted election to the diocese of Würzburg and refused to obey Innocent's decision prohibiting his transferral for four years. But he was finally forced to yield. This example suggests that Innocent's view on the role of the pope was not entirely accepted by the episcopacy—hence his willingness to take a position that would not alienate the bishops by allowing the possibility that Würzburg might choose the same candidate in a new election that followed his decision.[27] To reenforce this point, the author of the *Gesta* briefly noted that Innocent had the bishop-elect of Gorizia removed because "he had had himself appointed there." But, after a new election, when the bishop followed the procedure of coming to the papacy for permission, the *Gesta* concludes: "So, he learned by experience that both the rod and the manna are contained in the Ark of the Covenant."[28] The point could hardly have been made more clearly. For Innocent, the law was an instrument of policy, serving the interests of the papacy. While this was not new in the early thirteenth century, it had not been applied with such consistency by previous popes.

The meaning of the internal reformation of the church to Innocent III emerges with clarity from the *Gesta's* discussion of these legal cases. It is worth noting that none of them directly involve secular matters or the laity. Thus, the *Gesta* consciously contrasts Innocent's involvement in secular affairs both in the Patrimony of St. Peter, which was under direct papal rule, and in the Kingdom of Sicily, where he was acting as regent for Frederick, with his role as the head of the ecclesi-

27. *Gesta*, XLIV. This case appears to be mentioned again in *Gesta*, CXXX.
28. *Gesta*, XLV.

astical hierarchy of the church and his pastoral concerns. In this way, the author provides a transition to his discussion of the crusade, which involves both the spiritual office of the papacy and secular affairs. The *Gesta* treats three different aspects of papal rule: secular jurisdiction, spiritual jurisdiction, and mixed jurisdiction.[29] In the case of secular jurisdiction, the pope exercised direct authority in the Patrimony, but his position in the Kingdom of Sicily depended on his role as regent for Frederick. The cases presented show that the pope extended his claim to a general supervision of the churches to ensure the papal role in the ecclesiastical order. It is in the area of the crusade and in dealing with secular powers that the most difficult questions confronted Innocent.

Innocent appointed Soffredus, cardinal priest of Santa Prassede, and Peter Capuanus, cardinal deacon of Santa Maria in Via Lata, "on whom he imposed the sign of the cross," as legates to "to invite others to the service of the cross."[30] He ordered the construction of a ship, which he equipped with armaments and loaded with foodstuffs. The ship made it to Messina, where it was forced to remain because of stormy conditions. The cardinals had to sell the foodstuffs to prevent their spoiling. The pope ordered the ship to be given to the Templars and he sent Cardinal Soffredus to Venice, where, according to this letter, the doge and many of the Venetians took the cross.[31] He sent Peter, cardinal priest of Santa Cecilia, and Gratian, cardinal deacon of Saints Cosmas and Damian, to Pisa and Genoa to negotiate peace, but

29. Gress-Wright discusses the *Gesta's* treatment in terms of temporal and spiritual affairs in *GW*, 30*–34*. I believe that the arrangement is closer to that discussed in Innocent's decretal "Per venerabilem," responding to the request of Count William of Montpellier in 1202 for the pope to legitimate his children born out of marriage. See Brian Tierney, "'Tria quippe distinguit judicia . . .': A Note on Innocent III's Decretal *Per Venerabilem*," *Speculum* 37 (1962): 48–59. It was certainly possible that this decretal influenced the author of the *Gesta*.

30. *Gesta*, XLVI.

31. This event has not been widely discussed in treatments of the Fourth Crusade, but may help us to understand Innocent's strong stand against the Venetians.

they were unsuccessful. He then sent Cardinal Peter Capuanus, who was later promoted to be cardinal priest of St. Marcellus, as legate to France to preach the crusade, to make peace between the kings of the Franks and the English, and to reconcile Philip II Augustus with his wife, Ingeborg, "whom he had unjustly deserted."[32] Peter was able to recruit many important nobles to take part in a crusade, including Theobald, count of Troyes, Louis, count of Blois, Baldwin, count of Flanders and Hainault, and Hugh, count of St. Pol. These were members of families who had played a prominent role in earlier crusades and were in a position to bring large contingents with them from their own lands. He also enjoyed some success in bringing about a truce between Philip and Richard Lionheart, despite the mistrust on both sides, but especially that of Richard, who blamed Philip because he had been taken captive by the duke of Austria and held for ransom by Henry VI at Philip's request after his return from the Third Crusade.

The issue of Philip's marriage to the Danish princess Ingeborg, however, proved to be a major sticking point.[33] Like most marriages of the time, it was a political arrangement designed to protect French interests from the expanding influence of the English monarchy in the north. But, for reasons not now known, Philip reacted strongly against Ingeborg even at the wedding and wanted to call it off. His advisers persuaded him to go through with the wedding, but he almost immediately began to press for a divorce.[34] Still, at their insistence, he made some attempt to consummate the marriage, whether successful or not remains in doubt. Ingeborg, however, always insisted that it was. Finally, the royal advisers were pressured into ordering a trial at which they declared the marriage null on the ground that the king was too closely related to Ingeborg. Marriage was forbidden at this time to those who were related within seven degrees of relationship.[35]

32. *Gesta*, XLVII.   33. *Gesta*, XLVIII.
34. Raymonde Foreville, *Innocent III et la France* (Stuttgart: Hiersemann, 1992), 295–312.
35. *Gesta*, XLIX.

Ingeborg, who was not represented, appealed to Rome. Celestine III, who was then pope, heard the appeal and rejected the king's position, but the *Gesta* says that he looked the other way when the king married Agnes, the beautiful daughter of the duke of Meran. On his accession, however, Innocent took a strong line. After trying to negotiate with the king, he ordered the legate to use interdict to bring the king to an agreement. Prudently, the legate left the kingdom and held a council in Vienne, on the Rhone River, but outside the kingdom, at which he promulgated the interdict, forbidding the holding of church services in the kingdom and ordering the archbishops and bishops to enforce it. Innocent backed his legate completely in spite of the retaliatory efforts taken by Philip against the clergy. But, as the pressure mounted against him, the king was forced to enter negotiations again. These made only token progress until Agnes died while giving birth. But Ingeborg gained little. Although nominally queen, she was held as a virtual prisoner at Étampes. Nevertheless, Innocent did make his point when, with the death of the archbishop of Sens, he rejected Philip's choice, the bishop of Autun, who had failed to implement the interdict until forced to, and appointed Peter of Corbeil, bishop of Cambrai, who had been his teacher in Paris.

The case of Ingeborg is followed by discussion of two other marriage cases, involving Conrad of Monferrat's marriage to the queen of Jerusalem and the marriage of the king of Leon to his niece, the daughter of the king of Portugal, both of which were labelled incestuous by the author of the *Gesta*. The king of Leon compounded his problem by entering into a marriage with another niece, the daughter of the king of Castile. These cases show how Innocent dealt with issues involving secular rulers. One of his favorite allusions was that justice should be administered without respect to persons.[36] The *Gesta* emphasizes equality before the law by contrasting Innocent's handling of Ingeborg's case with that of his predecessor and by showing what

36. *Gesta*, LVIII.

he expected of his legates in carrying out his instructions. We may also suggest that the author, in his choice of cases, wanted to avoid any ambiguities that might reflect on Innocent's enforcement of church law in cases where he was dealing only with secular issues.

Two major goals were central to the program pursued by Innocent III: reform of the church and promotion of the crusade. These were closely linked. Innocent's view of reform was not limited to pastoral or institutional concerns involving the Latin Church. He looked out over a landscape that included the churches of the East as well. He was strongly committed to the unity of the church under papal leadership. From our modern vantage point, it is easy to point out flaws in his understanding of the history of the church that seriously affected his approach to the Eastern churches. But there is no question that he was deeply committed to unity. The letters selected by the author of the *Gesta,* whether directed to the Byzantine emperor, the Latin conquerors of Constantinople, the Bulgarian ruler, or the king of Lesser Armenia, show Innocent working assiduously for ecclesial unity and the crusade. But they also show how far Innocent was willing to go in mixing in secular affairs to secure his ends.

On his accession to the papacy, Innocent was already well aware that Emperor Alexius III was vulnerable.[37] He had deposed his brother, Isaac II Angelos, and imprisoned his nephew, Alexius. He moved quickly to gain Innocent's support and the pope responded just as quickly, aiming to take advantage of the situation. He sent low-level messengers calling upon Alexius to "lead the Greek church back to the obedience of the Apostolic See, its mother, from whose *magisterium* it had withdrawn. . . ."[38] His first letter to Alexius, summarized but not included in the *Gesta,* shows that Innocent wanted to recruit him as a leader in his crusade, promising him the same indulgence and privileges as other crusaders.[39] He also wrote to the patriarch of Constan-

---

37. Gerd Hagedorn, "Papst Innocenz III und Byzanz am Vorabend des IV Kreuzzugs," *Ostkirchliche Studien* 23 (1974): 3–20, 105–36, esp. 12.
38. *Gesta,* LX.   39. RI 1:353, 527.

tinople seeking his support. Alexius's response was unsatisfactory. It avoided any commitment on church unity and raised various objections to imperial participation in the crusade, but it did not close the door to further negotiations. Innocent moved quickly to press his advantage. He sent his chaplain, John, as legate, with letters to Alexius and the patriarch. His letter to Alexius focuses chiefly on the crusade and responds to Alexius's efforts to avoid any commitment. Alexius had argued that the liberation of the Holy Land should be left in the hands of God. Innocent uses a barrage of arguments to try to convince Alexius to make a commitment. In this letter, he also treats the subject of reunification of the churches, announcing his intention to summon a council to deal with the issues between the churches. His letter to the patriarch affirms the primacy of Peter and argues for the papal succession. He deals with an issue particularly sensitive at Constantinople, the apostolic foundation of that see by the apostle Andrew, by arguing that Peter was over Andrew "since he is always put first in the listing of the apostles," not because he was first in time, but because he "was first in dignity."[40] He is at particular pains to respond to the argument that Roman primacy was the result of conciliar decisions rather than a matter of divine provision. But he reiterates his intention to summon a general council to bring about the reunification of Constantinople under Rome. Thus Innocent spelled out his price for the support that Alexius was seeking. Neither Alexius nor the patriarch was willing to agree to these terms, but Alexius still did not want to break off negotiations. On his side, Innocent saw in the council the hope that his plans would come to fruition. But he was also working to promote the crusade in the West. This two-track policy contributed to the difficulties faced by the Western leaders of the Fourth Crusade, since the pope apparently left them in the dark about his negotiations with Alexius.[41]

---

40. *Gesta,* LX.

41. James M. Powell, "Alexius III and Innocent III: A Crusade Plan that Failed," in *Experiencing the Crusades,* ed. Marcus Bull and Norman Housley, 2 vols. (Cambridge: Cambridge University Press, 2003), 1:96–102.

The *Gesta* takes a sudden turn from negotiations with Alexius III to negotiations with Kalojan, or Johannitsa, the ruler of the Bulgarians and the Wallachians. This correspondence, which runs from mid-1202 to 1204, presents a somewhat contrasting picture to the frustrations that Innocent met in his dealing with Alexius III.

The land of the Bulgars and Vlachs or Wallachians lay between the Western-oriented Kingdom of Hungary and the Byzantine Empire. Its rulers had long sought recognition as kings from the papacy in order to bring greater legitimacy to their rule. In the early eleventh century, however, the Byzantine emperor, Basil II, conquered the Bulgarians and they remained under Byzantine rule until the late twelfth century. But the success of the Bulgarians under Johannitsa's older brothers, Peter and Asen, in gaining independence revived the Bulgarian quest for political recognition. After the assassination of Asen and the death of Peter, their youngest brother, Kalojan, or Johannitsa, decided to enter into negotiations with Innocent III. He wanted papal recognition of his kingship and was willing to bring the Bulgarian church into union with Rome.

Innocent was cautious, but anxious to seize the opportunity. The placement of this section immediately after the the failed negotiations with Alexius III and before the *Gesta's* treatment of the Fourth Crusade argues that in the mind of the papal curia it was linked to both events. On the one hand, the negotiations with the Bulgarians led to a successful reunion of the churches, at least at the level of the episcopacy. But the crusader conquest of Constantinople and the tensions between the Hungarians and the Bulgarians threatened not merely the union of the churches but Innocent's desire to gain the support of the Bulgarians for the crusade. The correspondence between Innocent and Kalojan, like that between the pope and Alexius, is concerned chiefly, from the papal side, with the union of the Bulgarian church with Rome and the crusade, though the crusade figures less in this correspondence than in that with Alexius III. Likewise, as with the Byzantine letters, Innocent deals directly with the head of the church.

There is no question that the negotiations with Kalojan posed a
major problem for the pope with regard to the Hungarian monarchy.
Implied in this correspondence but not made explicit are reasons why
the Hungarian king, Emicho, opposed the establishment of a Bulgarian monarchy. The existence of territorial disputes raised the issue of
competition for control of these lands as well as the potential for ab-
sorption of still more territories into the Bulgarian kingdom. Bulgarian kingship would, as Innocent was well aware, stabilize the situation
and put the pope in a strong position to mediate conflicts. He viewed
himself as a promoter of peace and it was on this basis that he involved himself in secular matters.

But one of the main values of this correspondence, perhaps even
the reason that it was included at this point, lay in those letters that
reveal Innocent's views on the relations of the Greek Orthodox
Church to the papacy. Since the Bulgarian church had been under
Greek rule since the tenth century, Innocent undertook to set down
clear terms for its acceptance into union with Rome. The letters that
discuss these issues are much more detailed and explicit than those
between Innocent and the patriarch of Constantinople. Indeed, it is
evident that the pope had in mind a substantial degree of Latinization
of the Bulgarian church. But he also chose as his initial negotiator to
the Bulgarians Dominic, archpriest of the Greeks of Brindisi. In this
way, he no doubt hoped to avoid conflict. Still, his letters to the head
of the Bulgarian church provided guidelines concerning papal thinking on this deeply controversial issue.

Innocent was insistent on certain Western practices, such as the
anointing of priests and bishops at their ordination, but was silent on
others. His main concern was the establishment of a hierarchy loyal to
the papacy. For this reason he named the archbishop of Trnovo as primate, but he sidestepped the issue of making him patriarch by claiming that the primacy was its equivalent in the West. We must suspect,
however, that he feared creating yet another breach in relations with
the patriarchs of Constantinople by conferring that title on the head of

the Bulgarian church. Up to this point, Innocent was successful despite the opposition of the Hungarian king. But the correspondence with Kalojan was only interrupted at this point, not completed. The author of the *Gesta* used these two collections of letters to show how the pope was pursuing his plans for the union of the churches and the crusade. He now took up the crusade itself, picking up where he had left off.

With the escape of Alexius, son of the deposed Emperor Isaac, from prison in Constantinople, the pope's negotiations with Alexius III became entangled with his efforts to promote the crusade in the West. What had been two separate initiatives had come together prematurely, for Innocent had not yet succeeded in his negotations with Alexius III either on the reunion of the churches or on aid for the crusade. On his side, Alexius III was increasingly alarmed by the gathering of the crusader army and the threat that it posed to Byzantium. Innocent sought to reassure him of his opposition to any attack on the empire, but he withheld any firm commitment regarding support of the cause of the young Alexius. Instead, he let Alexius III know that he had allowed the young prince to go to the court of his brother-in-law, Philip of Swabia, to lobby for his support.[42] Innocent clearly wanted Alexius III to know that time for him to decide was running out. While he held out hope to the emperor that he would act favorably to his interests, he pointed out that he faced opposition.[43] This letter is important because it shows that Innocent was still strongly committed to his negotiations with Alexius III and, implicitly, to a view of the crusade in which he would play a leading role, this at a time when the crusaders in the West were already gathered in Venice and were confronted by a serious problem: they had neither the numbers nor the resources to fulfill the contract they had entered into with the Venetians for transport.[44]

42. Innocent may well have taken this opportunity to turn up the heat on Alexius III by stating that he permitted the young prince to go to Philip. That fits the tenor of this letter.

43. *Gesta*, LXXXII.

44. See Donald Queller and Thomas Madden, *The Fourth Crusade: The Conquest of*

The *Gesta* provides the background to this agreement just after the pope's letter of November 16, 1202, cited above. Having already noted that the Venetian leadership had taken the cross, it now dealt with the details of the agreement between them and the crusaders. Innocent planned for the crusaders to attack Alexandria and capture that city and the surrounding areas, but part of the army was to go to Syria. Apparently, the plan was to make a major thrust into Egypt, with the goal of forcing a settlement that would provide security for the crusader states and the return of Jerusalem, but part of the army was to defend Palestine against attacks from Syria while this was taking place. This strategy was to influence subsequent crusades in the thirteenth century. It was not new, but was actually a revival of a plan that the Latin kingdom had entered into with the Emperor Manuel. We thus see that Innocent's attachment to his negotiations with Alexius III, and his reference to Manuel in his correspondence with Alexius III, was based on this crusade plan.

So much has been written on the Fourth Crusade that it is surprising that relatively little has been written about Innocent's relations with the Byzantine Empire in the crucial period leading up to that crusade.[45] What has been written seems to attach little importance to the pope's activity in this period. The focus has been and remains on the crusaders, especially figures like Theobold of Champagne and Boniface of Montferrat, as well as the commission that negotiated the agreement for naval transport with the Venetians. In these matters, Innocent was, so far as we know, a peripheral figure. But, as I have suggested above, that does not mean that he saw himself in that role. Far from it. The *Gesta*, with its Roman focus, offers an alternative view of the development of the crusade. Most have regarded it merely as a pro-Innocentian treatise; some have argued that it was nothing

Constantinople, 2nd ed. (Philadelphia: University of Pennsylvania Press, 1997), 40–54.

45. Charles Brand, *Byzantium Confronts the West* (Cambridge, Mass.: Harvard University Press, 1968), 223–31, esp. 228–29.

but a piece of propaganda. As I have endeavored to show, its pro-Innocentian stance can be easily exaggerated, while its role as propaganda misses entirely the fact that it was meant as an internal curial document. In fact, while the author makes no secret of his sympathy with the pope and his identification with papal goals, his selection and presentation of letters, both from the pope and others, established a record of hard choices confronting the papacy and decisions that, under the best of interpretations, had more to do with salvaging benefits to the church and especially to Innocent's goals of church union and promotion of the crusade than making the pope look good. In fact, the *Gesta* selects some letters not found in the papal register that reveal how nearly impossible the situation confronting the papacy could be.

From the beginning, Innocent had to choose whether to support Venice in its effort to recover the Dalmatian city of Zara, which was disputed between Venice and the Hungarian monarchy, or to take a highly principled but risky step of alienating the Venetians by defending the Zarans. He chose the latter course, on the grounds that crusaders must not, without serious cause, attack Christians and that the city of Zara was claimed justly by the Hungarian king, who was also a crusader. This course was not taken lightly. Innocent had to know that it would split the crusader army. In fact, no less a figure than Boniface of Montferrat, acting directly on the advice of the pope and his legate, absented himself from the siege. As the following correspondence makes clear, Innocent did not adopt this position out of a narrow concern for Zara. He would later point out, in a letter to the doge, that he was well aware of Venetian interests in the region. Rather, he was looking eastward to the impact of Venetian expansion not merely on Hungary but also on the Byzantine Empire.[46] Perhaps he was already beginning to think about the churches in the Balkans and even in Bulgaria and Wallachia. In a sense, we may see Zara as a turning point. In-

---

46. *Gesta*, LXXXVI. See also Innocent's letter permitting the crusaders to travel east in Venetian ships in *Gesta*, LXXXVII.

nocent could no longer realistically view that crusade as a cooperative effort between East and West, but he was reluctant to admit defeat. The *Gesta* here turns its attention from this disaster to the appointment of Soffredus, cardinal priest of Santa Prassede, as legate in the Levant, the death of the patriarch of Jerusalem, the effort to elect Soffredus as patriarch, his refusal, and the election, at Innocent's behest, of Bishop Albert of Vercelli. The purpose of this literary diversion, drawing on events that are from a later period, 1202 to 1205, seems to be to show where Innocent's priorities lay. The *Gesta* emphasizes his concern for the Holy Land by including here his letter to the bishop of Vercelli, persuading him to accept the patriarchate of Jerusalem. Innocent argued that even though the church of Jerusalem had been lost to the Muslims, Albert's leadership was needed to recover Jerusalem.[47]

In the aftermath of Zara, however, the crusaders were about to make their argument in favor of the alliance with the young Alexius as a way to ensure the success of the crusade. Clearly they regarded this argument as potentially persuasive of Innocent under the circumstances that had developed. We thus see how adept the crusade leaders were in sensing what was in the papal mind and in adapting their plans to it, while, at the same time, pursuing their own agenda. Innocent, as the *Gesta* makes clear, rejected this alternative. His letter is the harshest of any he wrote to the crusaders and gives full vent to his frustration: ". . . because you have not kept your garments white . . . you are no more fit . . . to see the kingdom of God." Moreover, he makes clear that he chiefly blames the doge and the Venetians for what has happened.[48] He took the position that the crusaders had no right to intervene in the internal affairs of the Byzantine Empire. Unfortunately, we have little to inform us regarding his thinking beyond his letters. What is clear is that he did not quickly put the setback at Zara behind him. Indeed, it would continue to rankle throughout this period.

47. *Gesta*, LXXXVIII.   48. *Gesta*, LXXXIX.

That the *Gesta* is not merely a letter collection, but a carefully constructed piece of literary art, is particularly evident in the way in which the author allows the events of the Fourth Crusade to be narrated by the leaders of the crusade. With virtually no comment, he published their flatteries and convoluted arguments. But he does tell readers what he thought of these writers. On the one hand, he wanted to show that Innocent was not fooled, but, on the other, he wanted to stress the impossible choices that confronted the pontiff.

The letter sent by the crusaders from Constantinople aimed to show how they were really doing what the pope had suggested, namely, trying to remedy their lack of foodstuffs.[49] They even noted that this was necessary to avoid adding to the burden on the Holy Land, where there were shortages. Their trip to Constantinople was, therefore, merely a matter of escorting the young Alexius back home, where, no doubt he would be greeted with enthusiasm, and securing what they needed for their crusade. Imagine their disappointment when the people of Constantinople rejected Alexius and opposed the crusaders. This example demonstrates the way in which papal admonitions were turned into excuses by the leadership. Of course, this was all window-dressing to the restoration of Alexius by force. That accomplished, this letter ended on a triumphal note. The *Gesta* concludes with the request of the doge and the Venetians for absolution from Peter, cardinal priest of St. Marcellus, and his reluctant agreement.[50]

But the moment of triumph did not last. The *Gesta* follows with the letter of the newly elected Latin emperor of Constantinople, Baldwin, count of Flanders and Hainault, explaining how the deal reached with Alexius IV fell apart.[51]

---

49. *Gesta*, XC.

50. In his letter to Cardinal Peter of July 12, 1205, Innocent says that he had "recently" learned that Peter had given absolution to the crusaders and the Venetians. He expressed his strong disapproval. RI 8 (127) (126) from page proof furnished by Christoph Egger.

51. *Gesta*, XCI.

This letter, dated May 16, 1204, almost nine months after the letter of the leaders informing Innocent of the restoration of Alexius, was only composed after the conquest of Constantinople and after all arrangements had been completed for the rule of the empire. In the view presented by the *Gesta,* the pope was confronted with a *fait accompli.* Replete with justification of the actions taken by the crusaders and the Venetians, the main purpose of the letter was to obtain legitimacy. Baldwin was already emperor. He was not seeking recognition. He presented himself as the one fulfilling the papal plan, including the holding of a general council in Constantinople. He does not hesitate to note that ". . . we have now learned that you invited the rebellious Greeks to a council as if you foresaw these things, although we seem to have meanwhile taken different ways. . . ." Baldwin was asserting control of the high ground. He was also signaling the pope that the crusader leaders were aware of his previous negotiations with Alexius III. Should we see this as a complaint against the actions of the pope? That the *Gesta* was aware of Baldwin's tactic is clear from the fact that the author next copied the agreement between the crusaders and the Venetians which had been arrived at in March 1204, prior to the capture of Constantinople. The tone of this agreement was almost demeaning to the pope, since it left to him only the task of ratifying what had been agreed to by the parties. The *Gesta* reveals that, even though the pope was probably livid, he found that he could do little more than try to salvage something from the wreckage. During this same period, Innocent had carried on an extensive correspondence with Baldwin, but the author of the *Gesta* chose to include only a letter directed to Boniface of Montferrat in August or September of 1205. Choice of this letter was most probably determined by the fact that it represented the pope's acceptance of the reality on the ground. Rather than dwelling on this setback, the *Gesta* moves on to the need for an ecclesiastical settlement. On this front, Innocent was determined to make some kind of a stand. The March agreement left the selection of a Latin patriarch of Constantinople to the recently appointed Venetian chapter of Haghia Sophia, ensuring the election of a Venetian as patriarch. In another feat of political legerdemain, they elected Thomas Morosini, a papal subdeacon and a Venetian, to that office, in what was clearly intended to force the pope to do what the Venetians wanted. Although the pope found defects in the election, he accepted Morosini as patriarch. But, when the Venetians imposed an oath on the patriarch, requiring that he ensure that only Venetians could serve as members of the chapter of Haghia Sophia or as archbishops and bishops, Innocent not only rejected this effort, but made clear his intention to prevent its implementation by insisting on the election of Antelmus, a Burgundian, as archbishop of Patras and even commanding the patriarch to consecrate him if necessary. The final letter in this series, directed to Pietro Ziani, who succeeded Enrico Dandolo as doge, is a complete castigation of the Venetians. As we know from his position at the time of the Fifth Crusade, Innocent held them responsible for the failure of the crusade.[52] This animosity toward the Venetians seems best understood if we accept the view that Innocent's initial plan for the crusade had depended on support from Alexius III. He believed that this plan had been seriously undermined at Zara. Small wonder that he rejected the Venetian effort to secure appointment of a Venetian archbishop of Zara at this time.

The last scenes of the Fourth Crusade were anticlimactic. The Byzantines rebelled. They allied themselves with Joannitsa, the Bulgarian king. The Emperor Baldwin was captured. Despite the efforts of Innocent III, Baldwin died in prison. The author of the *Gesta* follows his now familiar technique of moving on to another topic without pausing to analyze the preceding events.

He selected and arranged the correspondence to make his point. Was this a diplomatic move on his part? Was he trying to avoid direct criticism of the pope? Although both of these are possibilities, I am more inclined to the view that he was influenced by his main theme,

---

52. James M. Powell, *Anatomy of a Crusade* (Philadelphia: University of Pennsylvania Press, 1986), 27.

that is, he was attempting to portray the difficulties that confronted the pope when he was dealing with situations in which secular and spiritual concerns were mixed. The letters he presented showed that the pope was strongly committed to spiritual objectives, but that he was constantly frustrated by secular concerns. This point is made clear in the letters dealing with relations with the Armenians.

The *Gesta* opens this section by describing the initiative undertaken by the Catholicos of the Armenians and Leo, king of Lesser Armenia.[53] Innocent's reply was carefully constructed to avoid any conflict with the Armenian church.[54] He says that the Armenians recognize the *magisterium,* that is, the teaching authority, of the Apostolic See. This letter contains an interesting passage regarding the positive role of the Jews in Christian history. After presenting Peter as the successor of Christ, with a major concern for the unity of the church, Innocent cited the famous passage about the stone the builders rejected becoming the cornerstone that was "later put at the top of the corner, making both the Jewish people and the gentile nations one in the unity of the Christian faith, establishing the church from both, without stain or wrinkle. . . ."[55] Although the theology of this statement was not new, its position in this letter, setting forth the nature of Christian unity to the Armenians, is rather striking. In effect, Innocent was affirming a version of Christian history that put the Jews in the mainstream of the church. The tone of this letter makes it one of the most positive, if not the most positive, directed to an Eastern ecclesiastic by Innocent III. Coming after the lengthy correspondence regarding the Byzantine Church and the thorny questions raised by the Latin patriarch, the contrast is such that we must regard its inclusion here (after all, it had been written in November 1199) as a fundamental statement of Inno-

53. *Gesta,* CIX.
54. James D. Ryan, "Toleration Denied: Armenia between East and West in the Era of the Crusades," in *Tolerance and Intolerance: Social Conflict in the Age of the Crusades,* ed. Michael Gervers and James M. Powell (Syracuse, N.Y.: Syracuse University Press, 2001), 55–64.
55. *Gesta,* CIX. This letter is dated November 23, 1199.

cent's views, a kind of reaffirmation despite the problems raised by the Fourth Crusade. The fact that this letter was followed by Innocent's letter of the same time to the Armenian king, Leo, a letter that takes the same tone, merely confirms this view.[56] This correspondence, however, begun on such an optimistic note, soon ran into serious political problems. Leo's nephew, Raymond Rupin, was heir apparent to Antioch, but he was opposed by Count Bohemond of Tripoli, who also claimed the principality. The result was an almost textbook example of the way in which Latins resisted papal intervention, going so far as to assert that the question of the succession lay outside the jurisdiction of the pope. The inclusion of Innocent's letter to Abbot Peter of Lucedio and the abbot of Mount Tabor, and to Berthold of Katzenellenbogen and Gerard de Furneval, not only reveals the frustration of the pope but also shows that he was willing to recognize the need to include members of the laity in the search for a settlement. While the *Gesta* does not provide a solution to the issues between Leo II and Bohemond IV, it does advance our understanding of the policies of Innocent III. At the same time, it serves to reinforce the interpretation implied in the author's selection and arrangement of this correspondence. This point is made clearer by the way in which the *Gesta* next moves on to the arrival of Peter of Aragon in Rome in 1204. This event, here treated out of chronological order and seemingly without relationship to the preceding or succeeding material, fits nicely as a conclusion to this section because it places the pope in an excellent light, accepting the feudal lordship of Aragon, while conferring the symbols of monarchy on its ruler.

The final section of the *Gesta* is more difficult to fit into the schema sketched above. Perhaps these were materials that had been collected to be included in the *Gesta*, but were placed here because the author was not able to continue the work. The fact that topics that had been treated near the beginning of the work were taken up once again,

56. *Gesta*, CX.

while seemingly unrelated subjects were mixed in, confirms, in my view, that this section was done in haste. The inclusion of the gift list, on the other hand, which had to be compiled over time and with considerable care, suggests that it was always meant to be at the end of the *Gesta*. It has the appearance of an ongoing project, one that could easily have been extended to the end of Innocent's pontificate.[57]

The *Gesta Innocentii III* has only recently begun to receive the attention it deserves as a source for the history of the papacy. While it has been widely cited, it has not been sufficiently studied in its entirety. Despite its incompleteness and the obvious difficulties in understanding it, there is good reason to argue that it is still the best window we have on the mind of Innocent III and the papal curia. The Innocent of the *Gesta* does, in fact, come alive in a way that the Innocent of the papal registers rarely does. Even in the extensive collection of letters dealing with the crusade and Christian unity, the author of the *Gesta* has managed to create a kind of papal dialogue with secular rulers that is, I believe, unique in this genre. Innocent was a youthful pope who dreamed great dreams and attempted to realize them. The *Gesta* plays out those dreams against the realities of an often unreceptive world.

Beyond the *Gesta*

Had the author of the *Gesta* continued, he would have found that Innocent remained committed to the main themes that had characterized the earlier years of his pontificate. His commitment to reform never flagged, nor did his support for the crusade. Above all, he realized his early desire to hold a council and he tried, to the degree that he was able, to make sure that it was a general council, including representation of all within the Church, East as well as West. If historians have devoted more attention to his relations with secular rulers, especially to the succession to the empire, the conflict between Philip of

57. Brenda Bolton, "Qui fidelis est in Minimo: The Important of Innocent III's Gift List," in *Innocent III and His World*, 113–40.

France and John of England, and to the crusades against heretics in
southern France, than to the planning of the Fifth Crusade or the
Fourth Lateran Council, their priorities were not shared by Innocent,
who never lost sight of these ultimate goals and who subordinated
much of what he did to those ends.

It may be understandable if some have tried to credit Innocent
with steps he did not take. Certainly, his role in the founding of the
Franciscan Order, as well as the Dominicans, has been exaggerated.
He encouraged both, but did little more. The major work of creation
was left to his successors, Honorius III and Gregory IX, both of whom
were enthusiastic supporters of these new religious movements,
which is not to say that he was opposed or even lukewarm to them.
Rather, the second half of his pontificate is more focused. No longer so
young, more experienced, less inclined to make bold pronounce-
ments, more sure of himself and what he could accomplish, Innocent
was much more effective during this period than earlier. In this light it
may be worth noting that all of his important decretals on church/
state issues belong to the first half of his pontificate. His conclusion of
the dispute with King John over the archbishopric of Canterbury
demonstrates this point. The *Gesta* deals with this dispute, concluding
with the pope's letter to Archbishop Stephen Langton, which all but
assumes that the issue between the king and the church has been settled and that the interdict laid on England for the royal refusal to accept Stephen as archbishop would soon be lifted. That letter was dated
in March 1208; the interdict was not finally lifted until 1213.[58] But,
when it was, Innocent had achieved everything he set out to achieve,
but without trying to make new law. In fact, he was committed to
John to such a degree that he would even oppose Stephen Langton
over his support for the barons and Magna Carta. Moreover, John had
become a crusader. Innocent was unwilling to let anything else stand
in the way of his plan for the crusade. It is this determination that

58. C. R. Cheney, *Pope Innocent III and England* (Stuttgart: Hiersemann, 1976),
147–54, 304–56.

goes a long way to explain his support for Frederick Roger to be German king and emperor-elect against Otto IV, whose own ambitions stood in the way of Innocent's plans.

Council and crusade defined the second half of his pontificate. The first was to be the great achievement of his reign. The second existed chiefly in his plans and hopes. The Fourth Lateran Council was much more than the culmination of earlier papal councils.[59] It was the first Western council to shape the life of both laity and clergy in the Latin Church in significant ways and even to reach beyond toward the Eastern churches. In the process, it set the West on a path of centralized government that was more clearly defined than it had been. Virtually all of the sacraments came out of the council under a body of definition and regulation much different than what existed before.[60] Most notably, the Eucharistic presence of Christ found doctrinal expression in transubstantiation, while Eucharist and penance were linked much more closely than had ever been the case before. The office of preaching assumed greater importance, largely because of the influence of the Paris theologians, and the discipline of the church and clergy was increasingly regulated. Both secular and regular clergy were affected. Innocent's plan for the crusade was set in solid form at the end of the statutes of the council. Efforts were also made at the council to settle the great secular disputes of the day in order to unify the rulers of the West in support of the crusade. The young Frederick and King John were among those who took the crusade vow. But the death of the pope left the crusade in the hands of his successor. Innocent's pontificate was pivotal in the history of the church for the way in which it clarified and advanced the role of the papacy. The *Gesta* shows us that process in formation.

59. Raymonde Foreville, *Latran I, II, III, IV* (Paris: Editions de l'Orante, 1965), 258–306.
60. Foreville, *Latran,* 342–86, esp. Const. 21, 27, 50, 51, 52.

The Deeds of

POPE INNOCENT III

by an Anonymous Author

[Family, Education, Election]

I. Pope Innocent III, the son of Transmundus, from the family of the counts of Segni, and of Clarina, the daughter of a noble Roman line, was a man of penetrating mind and tenacious memory, learned in Divine and secular literature, eloquent in both the vernacular and in Latin, skilled in chant and psalmody. He was of medium stature and proper bearing, moderate in his views on wealth, but more generous in almsgiving and in his table. He was inclined to be more careful in other matters, unless there was a real need. He was hard on rebels and the contumacious, but kind towards the humble and devout. He was strong and firm, magnanimous and wise, a defender of the faith, a foe of heresy, strict in justice, but compassionate in mercy, humble in good times and patient in bad, somewhat impatient by nature but easily forgiving.[1]

II. He sweated out his studies first in Rome, and then in Paris, finally at Bologna, and he surpassed his contemporaries both in philosophy and theology, as his *opuscula*, which he drafted and dictated at various times, demonstrate. For he authored, before his pontificate, books *On the Misery of the Human Condition*, *On Mysteries of the Mass*, and *On the Fourfold Types of Marriages*. After he became pope, he [com-

---

1. I would like to thank John Moore for sending me a copy of his translation of this passage, which I found very helpful. The use of the past tense raises a question about the dating of this passage, suggesting that it may have been written at a later date. Since we have no information about the composition of the work, we can only conjecture regarding this matter. This translation follows David Gress-Wright, *The 'Gesta Innocentii III': Text, Introduction, and Commentary* (Ph.D. diss., Bryn Mawr College, 1981), in his edition based on the manuscripts. I have also used Vat. Lat. 12111 in conjunction with Gress-Wright. I should note that he now prefers to be known as David Wright.

posed] books of sermons, and *Notes on the Seven Psalms,* letters, *regesta* [of his letters], and decretals, which clearly show how expert he was in both Divine and human law.[2]

III. Pope Gregory VIII, of holy memory, ordained him to the subdeaconate, and Pope Clement III promoted him to cardinal deacon at the age of twenty-nine.[3] He appointed him to the church of SS. Sergius and Bacchus, of which Clement himself had been cardinal deacon. He advanced both in age and probity before God and men to such a degree that everyone anticipated and hoped for his advancement [Lk 2:52].

IV. Within two years after he was raised to the cardinalate, with his own money he restored the afore-mentioned church of SS. Sergius and Bacchus, which was in a sorry condition and in such ruins that more crypt than basilica could be seen, building up the walls and putting on a new roof, constructing a new altar on new steps, and making a new enclosure before the choir. Immediately after he was raised to the apex of the apostolate, he ordered a colonnaded porch to be built at the front of the same church from the wealth God had brought to him as cardinal. Many people wondered where he had found so much money in so short a time since he had refused to sully his hands with filthy lucre, not accepting any donation or promise until the business before him was terminated. He didn't exact anything from anyone, always proceeding on the royal road, neither deviating to right or left, conversing with his brethren without quarreling, not joining any faction.

2. The works of Innocent III are found in J.-P. Migne, *Patrologia Latina,* vols. 214–17. The *Misery of the Human Condition* has been edited as *Lotharius Cardinalis De Miseria Humane Conditionis* (Lucca: Biblioteca scriptorum latinorum mediae et recentioris aetatis, 1955) and *De miseria conditionis humane,* ed. and trans. Robert E. Lewis (Athens: University of Georgia Press, 1980). The other treatises are found in Migne, vol. 217. There is no critical edition of the sermons. Regarding the inclusion here of this notice of his "Notes on the Seven Psalms," composed near the end of his pontificate, see *GW,* 45*, and Barone, "Gesta," 10. It is an interpolation.

3. Pope Gregory VIII, Albert of Morra, reigned from October 21, 1187, to December 17, 1187. Clement III, Paolo Scolari, Innocent's uncle, named him cardinal deacon of SS. Sergius and Bacchus at the age of 29, i.e., in 1190.

V. After Celestine died, therefore, when some of the cardinals betook themselves to the Septizodium of the Monastery of Clivis Scauri
so that they could more freely and in greater security carry out there
the election of a successor, he and some others desired to take part in
the funeral of the deceased at the Constantinian basilica.⁴ And after
they had completed these services with due respect, he joined the others at the aforesaid place. Then the Mass of the Holy Spirit was celebrated by the cardinals alone. When they were sitting together to negotiate on the choice of a pontiff, after they had reclined humbly on
the ground, they gave each other the kiss of peace. And, following the
delivery of the exhortation, scrutineers were elected according to the
custom, who, after they had examined the sealed votes of all and written down the results, reported them to their brethren. Because several agreed on him, even though three others had received some votes,
after they argued about his age, because he was then thirty-seven,
they all finally agreed on him. They did so on account of his moral
probity and his knowledge of letters, electing him as supreme pontiff,
while he wept, cried out, and resisted. They called him Innocent, although his name had previously been Lothar. When the election was
made public, he was conducted with hymns and *laudes* by a multitude
of clergy and people, who were waiting below, to the Constantinian
Basilica, and from there to the Lateran patriarchate, where everything
was carried out according to the usual and ancient custom.⁵

VI. But while the election was being celebrated, there appeared a
sign of this kind, namely: three doves came down on the place in
which the assembled cardinals were sitting. When, after his nomination, he was separated from the others, one of the doves, the
whitest of all, flew to him and sat near his right hand. Someone also

4. Pope Celestine III, Hyacinth Bobo (1191–1198), died on January 8. The Septizodium or Septizonium was an ancient Roman ruin in part adjacent to the
monastery of St. Andrew on the Clivis Scauri, an ancient Roman road on the side of
the Coelian Hill. See Barone, "Gesta," 7.
5. The basilica of St. John Lateran, originally the church of the Savior, the cathedral of Rome.

had a vision that showed that he would marry his mother.[6] And many other revelations were made to religious men about him, which we pass over because he did not want predictions of this kind to be known.

VII. His election was celebrated on the sixth day before the ides of January, in the year of the incarnation of the Lord, 1197.[7] Because he was still a deacon, his ordination to the priesthood was delayed until the Fourth Saturday, [or ember day,] the ninth of the kalends of March.[8] On the following Sunday, on which the feast of St. Peter's Chair in Antioch occurred, he was consecrated bishop at St. Peter's and was established on the throne of the same apostle, not without a manifest sign and everyone's admiration.[9] Four archbishops and twenty-eight bishops, six cardinal priests and deacons, and ten abbots were present at his consecration, which he received with much remorse in his heart and a shedding of tears. With all of these, both the Prior with the subdeacons and the *primicerius* with the cantors, as well as with the judges, the seneschal, the advocates, and the senator, and the rest of the scholastics, wearing the crown, he processed through the city from the basilica of St. Peter to the Lateran Palace in the company of the Prefect and Senator, with the magnates and nobles of the city, and many captains and consuls, and rectors of cities. The whole city was decorated, and the clergy with thuribles and incense, the people with palms and flowers, and both singing hymns and canticles, with the usual distribution of presents, marched before him in companies. And having given lauds both before the church of St. Peter and the Lateran Palace, after he entered the greater dwelling, which is called Leoniana, and distributed presents to the clergy according to custom, he celebrated a solemn banquet.

6. I.e., to the Church.
8. February 21, 1198.

7. January 8, 1198.
9. February 22, 1198.

[Rome and the Papal States]

VIII. Immediately after his election, the Roman people began to press him urgently, beseeching and demanding that he receive them in fidelity and grant them the usual gifts. But he could not be persuaded to agree to this before his consecration. After his consecration, when they began to clamor more turbulently, he gave serious consideration to their petition. The situation of the Roman Church was very difficult, because, from the time of Benedict Carushomo, it no longer controlled the senate of the city.[10] Moreover, Benedict, on becoming senator, had made his men justiciars of Marittima and Sabina, while the Emperor Henry had occupied the whole Kingdom of Sicily and the whole patrimony of the church up to the gates of the city with the exception of the Campagna, in which, however, he was more feared than the pope. Therefore, Innocent decided to agree to the petition of the people in order to remedy the bad times and recover the lost patrimony. But before he responded to the people, he wanted to know whether the treasure of the church was sufficient for this purpose, so he took the precaution to order that throughout individual parish churches the individual parishioners should be secretly counted so that he would know their number and worth. When he had thus discovered the truth, he ordered them to be received throughout the individual *rioni*, but he was not able to take sufficient steps to prevent fraud from being committed in many instances.

Moreover, the form of the oath sworn by the people was of this type:[11]

---

10. Benedict Carasomo, or Carushomo, was sole senator from about 1191 to 1193. See Daniel Waley, *The Papal State in the Thirteenth Century* (London: Macmillan, 1961), 26.

11. *Codex Diplomaticus Dominii Temporalis S. Sedis. Recueil des Documents pour servir à l'histoire du Gouvernment Temporel des États du Saint Siège*, ed. Augustin Theiner, 3 vols. (Rome, 1861–1862; reprint, Frankfurt am Main: Minerva, 1964), 1:28–29. I wish to thank Brenda Bolton for calling this reference to my attention.

I, Peter, Prefect of the city, swear that I will faithfully care for the land that the Lord Pope has committed to my care for the honor and profit of the church. I will not sell, rent, infeudate, or mortgage, or in any way alienate any part of it. I will carefully demand and I will receive the justices and accounts, and I will endeavor to recover its rights, and I will preserve and defend those that have been recovered and will hold them, as long as I am in charge. I will guard the street and I will exercise justice. I will show a diligent regard and dispense effective effort for custody of fortifications so that the honor and command of the Roman church may be well preserved. I will not change castellans and sergeants, nor introduce others except at the order of the Lord Pope. I will not receive subjects and vassals of the patrimony of the church into my fidelity and dominion without the special mandate of the Roman Pontiff. I will not order those entrusted in these things to obey me save during my administration. I will not order fortifications built in the land committed to my administration without the special mandate of the Lord Pope. Whenever required by the Lord Pope, his representative, or by his letter, I will faithfully give an accounting of my administration. And whenever ordered by the Lord Pope, or by the Roman Church, I will resign fully and freely. I swear that I will observe all these things without fraud to my ability, save in all the command of the Lord Pope: so help me God and these Holy Gospels of God.

On the day following his consecration, he received Peter, the Prefect of the city, as his liege man, and by the mantle that he gave him invested him publicly with the prefecture.[12] Up until this time he had been bound by an oath of fidelity to the emperor and held the office of prefect from him. Innocent also received the oath of fidelity from some barons of the area, and after he had sent representatives through the whole patrimony of the church, he ordered that everyone should swear loyalty to him. And, with the exception of the justiciars of the senator, who had sworn fidelity to him, he established his own justiciars. And after the selection of a new senator by his mediator, he recovered the patrimony that had been recently lost, both within and outside the city.

12. Peter de Vico was prefect of the city from 1186 to 1223; see RI 1:23, 34–35.

IX. Still, this wasn't enough for him. Immediately after his election, he sent two cardinal priests, Cinthius of St. Lawrence in Lucina and John of St. Prisca, against Markward in the March to recall him to the *dominium* of the church.[13] But Markward sent his messengers, namely, the bishops of Camerino and Venafro, and the nobleman Rambert Monaldi, to the Lord Innocent, asking through them permission to meet with him under a safe conduct. He also expressed his desire to be subject to him in his person, his wealth, and his land.[14] And the aforesaid noble swore accordingly on his soul. For Markward was likewise seneschal of the empire, duke of Ravenna and Romaniola, Marquis of Ancona and Molise. He was subtle and crafty, with much wealth acquired in the Kingdom of Sicily under the Emperor Henry, who had preferred him among all his other familiars and had made him executor of his Last Will. Wherefore, he promised the Lord Pope that, if he would deign to allow him to enjoy his favor, he would exalt the Roman Church more than it had been exalted since the time of Constantine, since that Testament would redound to the great honor and glory of the Roman Church. He asked, however, that, until he approached his presence. and returned to the Marches, the cardinals would not receive the fidelity of the inhabitants of the Marches for the church. The Pope in fact granted that, in the meantime, they would not coerce those who were unwilling, but would accept voluntary submissions. He sent Guido, cardinal priest of Santa Maria in Traste-

13. Cinthius, cardinal deacon of St. Lawrence in Lucina, later cardinal bishop of Porto; see W. Maleczek, *Papst und Kardinalskolleg von 1191 bis 1216: Die Kardinale unter Coelestin III und Innocenz III* (Vienna: Verlag der Österreichischen Akademie der Wissenschaften, 1984), 104–6; John of St. Prisca, John of St. Paul, cardinal priest of St. Prisca in 1193, cardinal bishop of Sabina 1205–1214. In 1209–12l0, he was the chief suporter of St. Francis of Assisi in the papal curia. See Maleczek, *Papst und Kardinalskolleg von 1191 bis 1216, 114*–17.

14. Bishops of Camerino and Venafro; see Conrad Eubel, *Hierarchia Catholica Medii Aevi,* rev. ed., 6 vols. (Münster: Regensberg Library, 1960), 1:161 and 1:519. Rambert Monaldi was a member of the Monaldeschi family, prominent supporters of Henry VI. See Thomas C. Van Cleve, *Markward of Anweiler and the Sicilian Regency* (Princeton, N.J.: Princeton University Press, 1937), 86, 88, 191, n. 15.

vere, to provide him safe conduct into his presence, if he would agree to these terms.[15] But he was unwilling, because the Lord Pope had anticipated and avoided his trick, and he denied that he had sent Rambert Monaldi to swear in the prescribed manner on his soul. And when the pope handed over the letter he had given to him and according to which he had sworn, he replied that he never learned to read and therefore did not know what the notary had written. But the cardinals excommunicated him for the crimes he perpetrated. They accepted the oaths of fidelity of the inhabitants of the Marches, and they returned the land to the domain of the church. When Markward had paid out a large amount of money and recognized that he would not be able to hold onto the Marches, he offered the pope a substantial amount of money with the promise of an annual payment, if he would receive his fidelity and grant the land to him. But since the pope was unwilling to do this, because he suspected fraud, he left the Marches, and entered the kingdom. Therefore, the entire Marches, save for Ascoli, was returned to the domain and fidelity of the church: namely, Ancona, Fermo, Ancarano, Osimo, Camerino, Jesi, Sinigallia, and Pesaro, with all their dioceses.

IX (bis). Therefore, Conrad of Swabia, Duke of Spoleto and Count of Assisi, seeing his land return to the domain of the church in the same way, tried in as many ways as he could to find favor with the pope, offering him ten thousand pounds without restriction, and an annual payment of a hundred silver pounds, as well as the service of two hundred knights for the patrimony of the church from Radicofani to Ceprano.[16] For security, in addition to his homage and fidelity, and the oaths of his men, he promised to hand over his sons as hostages

15. Guido de Papa was cardinal priest of Santa Maria in Trastevere; later he became cardinal bishop of Preneste, 1206–1221. See Maleczek, *Papst und Kardinalskolleg von 1191 bis 1216*, 99–101. He was a member of the same family as Pope Innocent II, the Papareschi or Paparoni.

16. Conrad von Urslingen, duke of Spoleto, was one of the chief supporters of Emperor Henry VI. Cf. RI 1:88, 126–28: "He returned to Germany and then joined Markward of Anweiler in the Kingdom of Sicily. He died there at the end of 1202."

and to pay for the custody of all fortifications at his own cost. Even though, however, the pope thought that arrangement useful, still, because many were scandalized by his seeming to favor the Germans, who had reduced the Italians to such grave servitude by their cruel tyranny, he decided in favor of liberty and did not accept his offer.[17] Since Conrad could not proceed in this way, he surrendered to the pope's command without any agreement and the pope sent Octavian, Bishop of Ostia, and Gerard, cardinal deacon of St. Hadrian, to Narni, and in their presence, before the bishops, barons, and a large crowd, he swore on the Gospel, relics, and the cross to keep all the commands of the pope.[18] Conrad absolved all his vassals, without restriction, of their fidelity, and commanded all to return to the jurisdiction of the Roman Church. He immediately surrendered two fortifications he was holding, namely, Gualdo Tadino and the Rocca [or citadel] de Cesi. Moreover, he ordered the Rocca of Assisi to be returned. But the men of Assisi, who were besieging it, did not allow it to be handed back to the pope, but destroyed it almost completely after its capture. The Roman church, therefore, recovered the Duchy of Spoleto and the County of Assisi, namely, Rieti, Spoleto, Assisi, Foligno, and Nocera, with all their dioceses. But, because the delay of the aforesaid Conrad was quite suspect, at the command of the Lord Pope, he returned to Germany. The Pope also recovered Perugia, Gubbio, Todi, and Civita Castellana, with their *contadi*, after he had received the oath of fidelity from the citizens, the barons, and the captains.[19] Moreover, he ordered the destruction of the *castrum* of Monte Santa Maria, in which

17. This passage certainly shows the viewpoint of the author. Perhaps he was among those critical of Innocent on this issue.

18. Octavian had been cardinal deacon of SS. Sergius and Bacchus since 1182 and became cardinal bishop of Ostia and Velletri in 1189. He died in 1206. He was a Roman and his family later married into that of Innocent III. See Maleczek, *Papst und Kardinalskolleg von 1191 bis 1216*, 80–83. Gerard was cardinal deacon of St. Hadrian from 1182 to 1208. He was from Lucca, where he had been a canon of the cathedral. He probably died in Sicily late in 1208. See Maleczek, *Papst und Kardinalskolleg von 1191 bis 1216*, 78–79.

19. The *contado* was the district around the city and under its rule. For what

his predecessor, Conrad, called "Fly-brain," held Octavian, Bishop of Ostia, captive on his return from France, so that its destruction would leave it to be remembered only as a name.

X (bis). After the celebration of the feast of the Apostles, the Lord Pope left the city, and went for a personal visit to the city of Spoleto, which he had quite recently recalled to the fidelity of the church. He then came to Rieti, where he was received with great joy and honor, and he consecrated the church of St. Eleutherius the Martyr and the church of St. John the Evangelist. After he arrived in Spoleto, he dedicated the cathedral church. There a certain miraculous event occurred. Because the citizens were anxious about the lack of water, they began to search thoroughly around the city where they might by digging find a supply of water sufficient for the needs of a large herd of horses. And suddenly they saw water rushing from the rock under the wall of the city, and it filled the ditches they dug there, flowing so abundantly that there was enough water for all the horses to drink. And it was called the Papal Fountain. Then he proceeded to Perugia, where he consecrated the altar of the chief church [St. Lawrence], and to Todi, where he solemnly consecrated the altar of St. Fortunatus, and he donated precious and subtly worked silk cloths for the decoration of all the altars he consecrated with his own hands. He named a rector in the Duchy of Spoleto and the *contado* of Assisi, and in nearby lands: namely, Gregory, cardinal deacon of Santa Maria in Aquiro, for Amilia, Orte, and Civita Castellana.[20] He returned to the city around the Feast of All Saints.

XI. Moreover, the cities of Tuscany—save for Pisa, which could never be persuaded to join—entered a league, because of the insuffer-

---

follows, regarding Monte Santa Maria and the captivity of Cardinal Octavian, see RI 1:378, 573–74, about October 1–5, 1198.

20. Gregory of the Crescentii had been made cardinal deacon of Santa Maria in Aquiro by Pope Clement III in 1188. He was very familiar with affairs in the Kingdom of Sicily. He died about 1207. See Maleczek, *Papst und Kardinalskolleg von 1191 bis 1216*, 90–92. His nephew, also Gregory of the Crescentii, became a cardinal in 1216. See Maleczek, *Papst und Kardinalskolleg von 1191 bis 1216*, 183–84.

able tyranny of the Germans which had brought them almost to the brink of slavery, and obtained from the Supreme Pontiff permission for the cities of the church in Tuscany and the Duchy of Spoleto to join this league, always reserving in all things the jurisdiction and mandates of the Apostolic See. Therefore, they set up individual rectors for each city, and a prior, who carried on all the business of the league during his term of office. All the rectors and other officials swore that they would preserve the league for the honor and exaltation of the Apostolic See, and that they would defend the possessions and rights of the Holy Roman Church in good faith, and that they would receive no one as king or emperor without the approval of the Roman Pontiff. But they could obtain nothing from him but a letter of this type:

Innocent, bishop, servant of the servants of God, to his beloved sons, the Prior[21] and rectors of Tuscany and the Duchy, greetings, etc. Just as God, the Creator of the universe, set two great lights in the firmament of heaven [Gn 1:14], the greater light to be in charge of the day and the lesser light to be in charge of the night, so he established two great offices for the strengthening of the universal church, which is called by the name of heaven, the greater to be in charge of souls as if of days, and the lesser to be in charge of bodies as if of nights: these are the pontifical authority and the royal power.[22] Still, just as the moon receives its light from the sun, and it is in fact lesser than it both in size and nature as well as in location and effect, so the royal power receives the splendor of its dignity from the pontifical authority, and the more it remains in that presence, to that extent it shines with lesser light, and the more it is separated from that presence, the more it increases in splendor.[23] Indeed, both powers have merit-

21. Acerbo Falseronis, consul of Florence and prior of the Tuscan League. See RI 1:401, 600, n. l.

22. O. Hageneder, "Das Sonne-Mond-Gleichnis bei Innocenz III," *Mitteilungen des Instituts für Österreichische Gestichichtsforschung* 65 (1957): 340–68.

23. This passage has been a source of problems since the early thirteenth century. See RI 1: 401, 600, nn. d and e. The Latin suggests that the imperial power, like the moon, loses its light in the presence of the sun (the spiritual power) and gains light when it is further from the sun. RI reads: ". . . cuius conspectui quanto magis inheret, tanto minori lumine decoratur, et quo plus ab eius elongatur aspectu, eo

ed to obtain the seat of their primacy in Italy, which, by Divine plan, holds dominion over all the provinces. Therefore, although we should carefully oversee all the provinces, still it is especially important for us to provide by our paternal solicitude for Italy, where the foundation of the Christian religion is, through the Primacy of the Apostolic See, and both the priestly and regal dominion hold sway. Moreover, we exercise our office of supervision in a praiseworthy manner if we ensure by the zeal of our solicitude that sons should not become slaves nor the lesser be oppressed by the greater, so that, keeping to a middle course, they so serve that they do not destroy and that they neither refuse to be subjects nor strive to be in command. We desire, therefore, to embrace you in the arms of Apostolic protection as special sons, and propose firmly in our deliberation to demonstrate to you our defense for the glory of the Divine Name and the honor of the Apostolic See, insofar as we can in honesty, against the incursion of oppression and the insolence of injury, so that by the help of the Apostolic protection, you can persevere in the proper state and the peace now achieved may continue to increase among you. We hope and hold for certain that you should always experience the favor of devotion to the Roman Church and the support of the faith so that, while you receive from us the defense of our protection and we receive from you the support of your devotion, something useful may be obtained by both sides. We therefore advise you altogether and we exhort you in the Lord and we command you by Apostolic letter that, keeping a certain and firm trust in us, who intend, as is fitting to the Apostolic dignity, to do more for you than promise, you should desire to do those things which redound to the honor and profit of the Roman Church so that you can be strengthened by the right hand of its favor. Given at the Lateran, Third of the Kalends of November.[24]

XII. After this, he devoted himself to the recovery of Radicofani, Acquapendente, Montefiascone, and Tuscia Romana, which he finally recovered but not without labor and expense. He freed Aquapendente

---

plus proficit in splendore." For discussion, see Hageneder, "Sonne-Mond," 362–68. Innocent returned to this image in late 1201 or early 1202, in his letter to Emperor Alexis III, but he did not include the passage cited above. This argues that it had special relevance to Rome and Italy. I am grateful to Professor James John for his advice.

24. RI 1:401, 599–601. October 30, 1198.

from the Orvietans, who were attacking it vigorously. Besides, he sent messengers and legates to recover the Exarchate of Ravenna, Bertinoro, and the land of Count Calvala. But the Archbishop of Ravenna claimed that the Exarchate had been granted by the Roman Pontiffs in Antiquity to the church of Ravenna and he produced privileges.[25] Also the church of Bertinoro had been granted again by Pope Alexander, while he was visiting Venice.[26] The Lord Innocent therefore prudently yielded on this for the present rather than trying to take up this matter. He allowed the Archbishop of Ravenna to recover and hold Bertinoro, reserving the right of the Apostolic See.

XIII. But when he asked, through legates appointed especially for this purpose, for the land of the Countess Matilda[27] from the cities holding it, even though these cities wanted to recognize and hold that land from the Roman church under certain agreements, still, because those agreements were not suitable, he was unwilling to grant away any of that land save that which he granted to the Bishop of Mantua. He put the matter off for a more suitable time, because he was then gravely concerned about the division within the empire and turbulence in the Kingdom of Sicily and these matters required his complete attention.

XIV. The Lord Innocent held these fortifications in his own hands and ordered them to be guarded by his own castellans: in Tuscia Romana: Radicofani, Montefiascone, and Orte; in the Duchy of Spoleto: Gualdo Tadino and Cesi; in Sabina: Rocca di Anticoli; in the Campagna: Lariano and Castro; in the Marittima: Rocca del Circeo. At the palace of Montefiascone, he ordered a chapel built and the houses behind the palace up to the walls of the *castrum* to be destroyed, constructing walls extending from the palace to those walls, and he made a large gate so that there would be an entrance to the fortification, not

25. Archbishop William of Ravenna, 1190–1201. RI 1:27, 40–41.
26. Pope Alexander III, 1159–1181.
27. These were allodial lands left to the papacy at her death in 1115. This grant was long disputed by the emperors.

only for use of the *castrum* but also particularly for that place. In the Rocca de Radicofani, he ordered the old walls to be razed and new ones built, a moat to be excavated, and the place to be well fortified. Also, he redeemed the Rocca del Circeo from Rolandus Guidonis de Leculo, to whom Odo and Robert Frangipani had granted it in fief, even though they held it from the Roman church solely as custodians.[28] Moreover, he committed the patrimony of the Apostolic See in Tuscany to the rule of various persons at different times, and he ordered that the *fodrum* for cities and *castra* should be collected from them annually.[29] In other regions, however, he took the proper payment.

XV. But two nobles, Guido and Nicholas, gravely offended the Roman church during his times and those of his predecessors by injuring, capturing, and robbing those coming to and returning from it. So, since the pope could not bear it any longer, he ordered the rectors of the Patrimony of Blessed Peter to visit them in Tuscany.[30] If they refused to return willingly to his command after being warned, they should coerce those who were unwilling. They besieged these insolent and rebellious fellows in the *castrum* of Rispampani, laying waste the fields of grain, cutting down trees, leading their flocks away, and causing a loss of more than three thousand pounds. And when they prepared wood, stones, and cement in order to build a high tower to capture this *castrum*, the aforementioned nobles immediately despaired and returned humbly to his command without any condition. They swore to keep the commands of the Lord Pope regarding what was done with regard to Vetralla and Petrognani, to give security about the raising of illegal tolls and the indemnification of churches, and, in addition, they swore to observe peace faithfully for all his subjects, pil-

28. The Frangipani were among the most important families in Rome in this period.

29. *Fodrum* refers to the fodder requisitioned for the needs of the army. See Carlrichard Brühl, *Fodrum, Gistum, und Servitium Regis. Studien zu den wirtschaflichen Grundlagen des Königtums im Frankenreich* (Cologne: Böhlau, 1968).

30. Innocent obviously regarded them as robber barons. They were Frangipani.

grims, and travelers, as well as restoring the fortifications of Castrum Marthae, providing a bond of one thousand Sienese pounds for all of these agreements. Additionally, they swore fidelity to the Lord Pope according to the manner and custom of all his other subjects.

XVI. About the time of his accession, the men of Narni were seriously molesting Otricoli. Although this had been firmly forbidden under threat of interdict and a fine of a thousand pounds, still they seized and destroyed that *castrum* in contempt of this prohibition. Now the pope, just and strong, ordered the army, composed of both Romans and non-Romans, to move against them. As a result, they suffered more grievous losses than they inflicted. And, finally, after the *castrum* was rebuilt, he received a fine of one thousand pounds from them and they swore to keep his commands, paying two hundred pounds for the restoration of the walls.

XVII. But, because it would take too long to explain in each instance how diligent and zealous he was in reforming the patrimony of the church, it is enough to say a few things among many, because the many can be understood from the few. Although he held this concern in some ways abhorrent (which is why he often said: "he who touches pitch will be stained by it" [Eccl 13:1]), especially because the labor was great and the fruit small, men could not easily be coerced because of their increasing malice.

[The Kingdom of Sicily]

XVIII. But the more he wanted to be free of secular business, the more he was enmeshed in worldly cares.[31] After the death of Roger,[32]

31. Although this may be viewed as a conventional statement or even cynically, the author seems to attach more weight to it since Innocent was clearly becoming more deeply involved in secular political affairs in the Norman kingdom.

32. Died 1193. Roger was the son of Tancred of Lecce, the illegitimate grandson of King Roger II, who had been elected king after the death of King William II. The Emperor Henry VI claimed the kingdom on behalf of his wife, Constance, the daughter of King Roger II, referred to here as Roger I, because he was the first to

the son of Tancred, King of Sicily, whom his father had made king during his lifetime and had ordered to be crowned, and who had married the daughter of Isaac, emperor of Constantinople, the father also soon died, it was said, from an excess of sorrow, leaving three daughters and an infant son, named William. His mother ordered that he should be crowned as king. With the kingdom in such a destitute state, the Emperor Henry, who wanted it on behalf of his wife Constance, the daughter of the late King Roger I of Sicily, grandfather of the aforesaid Tancred, gathered a very large army using especially money he extorted for the ransom of Richard, King of the English, who had been wrongfully seized while returning from the Land of Promise and the service of the cross.[33] He, therefore, entered the kingdom and obtained it without a fight, without resistance. But the aforementioned Sibilia, with her son and daughters, and the Archbishop of Salerno and his brothers took refuge in a certain castle in Sicily. The emperor made a peace treaty, and agreed on these terms: that the emperor by oath granted William, her son, and his heirs, the County of Lecce, which his father Tancred had held prior to his kingship and added to it the Principality of Taranto, with a promise to safeguard their persons and properties. Next, however, after he had them in his power, he seized the opportunity and sent them and some others, and some of the nobility of the Kingdom as captives to Germany. He ordered the brothers of the said archbishop and some others to be blinded, but the archbishop, the queen, and her son and daughters were to be held in close custody. Moreover, Philip,[34] the brother of the

---

hold the title king. Usually, his father, Roger, the Great Count of Sicily, is called Roger I.

33. On his return from the Third Crusade, Richard Lionheart was captured by the Austrian duke and turned over to Emperor Henry VI, who kept him prisoner at the behest of King Philip II of France. This action clearly contravened the protection granted crusaders by the papacy.

34. Philip of Swabia, who acted briefly as regent for his brother Henry's son Frederick and then claimed the German kingship and the imperial title for himself. Alexius deposed and blinded his brother Isaac, the father of Princess Irene. He assumed the throne at Constantinople as Alexius III.

emperor, married the widow of the aforementioned Roger, the daughter of the Emperor of Constantinople, whom Alexius, his brother, blinded. He usurped the Empire of Constantinople.

XIX. Therefore, after the Emperor Henry obtained the whole Kingdom of Sicily, despoiling it of gold and silver and precious stones, he returned to Germany in great triumph, working among the princes to elect his son, Frederick, an infant not yet two years old and not even baptized, as king of the Romans, and to get them to swear their oaths of fidelity to him. Philip was among those who swore an oath to him.

XX. When this was done, the emperor again returned to the kingdom and finally, at Messina, in the presence of the empress, he died. After his death, certain of his familiars departed the kingdom: Markward entered the Marches, Conrad returned to the duchy; moreover, Philip, his brother, went to Montefiascone, and from there returned to Germany, occupying the whole patrimony.[35] But some of the Germans remained in the kingdom, William Capparone in Sicily, Frederick in Calabria, Diepold and his followers holding many fortresses in Apulia and the Terra di Lavoro.

XXI. After the death of the emperor, Celestine died within three months and Innocent took his place, as affairs changed one way and another. The Empress Constance returned to Palermo and sent to the Duchess of Spoleto, who was caring for her son in the March, and ordered him to be brought to her for his coronation as king. And she began to reign with him. Moreover, without compulsion, she sent messengers with gifts to the Lord Innocent, devoutly asking him to agree to grant the Kingdom of Sicily, the duchy of Apulia, the principate of Capua, with other adjacent territories, to herself and her son according to the form by which his predecessors had granted it to their predecessors. But the pontiff was very keen-minded and he was well aware that the privilege of the grant made in the first place by Hadrian and later renewed by Clement detracted not only from the Apostolic

---

35. Markward of Anweiler, Conrad of Urslingen, and Philip of Swabia.

dignity but also ecclesiastical liberty in four areas: namely, elections, legations, appeals, and councils.[36] He therefore ordered the empress to renounce completely those parts of the privilege since he would not grant them at all. She tried to change his intention by gifts. But since he was unwilling to do this, she sent honorable ambassadors, Anselm, the Archbishop of Naples, Haimeric, the Archdeacon of Syracuse, Thomas the Justiciar, and the Judge Nicholas. After lengthy negotiations, they obtained the renewal of the privilege with those chapters completely removed, under the usual payment, fidelity, and homage. The privilege never reached her; she had already died.

XXII. But the most conscientious pontiff, mercifully concerned about the liberation of the captives, especially since the Apostolic dignity was so diminished by the detention of the Archbishop of Salerno, immediately after his accession, sent the bishop of Sutri, who was German, and the abbot of Saint Anastasius, a Cistercian, to Germany. The pope wrote to the bishops that they should warn those holding the captives, and if necessary compel them by excommunication against their persons and an interdict on their lands to set them free. He threatened all the princes that, unless they supported this effort in an effective way, he would put all Germany under an ecclesiastical interdict. But, because his predecessor, Pope Celestine, had excommunicated the aforementioned Philip, Duke of Swabia, while he was Duke of Tuscany, on the grounds that he had invaded and laid waste to the Apostolic Patrimony, and he had also ordered that excommunication made known to the Emperor Henry, Innocent gave this form to his absolution to the aforementioned bishops and abbot. He ordered that, because the sentence of a superior could not be lifted by one in a lesser position, and for this reason it was necessary for Philip himself to approach the Apostolic throne for absolution, nevertheless, they could

---

36. The reference is to the so-called apostolic legation of the Norman kings of Sicily. The popes mentioned are Hadrian IV, Nicholas Breakspear (the only English pope), and Clement III. But the grant actually predated the establishment of the monarchy and was the result of the Norman conquest of Sicily from the Muslims.

free him from the labor of the journey if he would free the aforementioned archbishop. Also, after he took an oath according to the form of the church that he would obey the Apostolic mandates in all those matters for which he had been excommunicated, they might grant him the benefit of absolution. They therefore went to Germany and found that Philip had been chosen as king by some of the princes. Philip met them at Worms and brought about his absolution not publicly but in secret, and not by taking the oath according to the form of the church but by a promise made on a priestly stole. Still he willingly freed the archbishop and his brethren. Moreover, after a short time, he proceeded to his anointing and coronation, not at Aachen but at Mainz, not by the Archbishop of Cologne but the Archbishop of Tarentaise, because no German archbishop would attempt it. But none of the bishops who were present at the coronation presumed to put on their pontificals, except for the Bishop of Sutri, who had been appointed for something else. Wherefore, when he returned to the presence of the pope, who learned the truth by his own confession, both about his neglect of the form and the presumption he had committed, Innocent ordered him to remain outside his see for the rest of his life. As for the captives, although they were now free but were still exiles, he asked the empress by messenger sent especially for this purpose to grant the favor of restoring them. But Sibylla, the widow of King Tancred, together with her children, escaped the place of their imprisonment and fled to France, where she married her eldest daughter to Walter, Count of Brienne.

But the Archbishop of Cologne and some of the other princes, both ecclesiastical and secular, seeing that they were slighted of their role in the election of Philip, summoned Otto, Count of Poitou, son of Henry, the late Duke of Saxony, and elected him king in Cologne, and the Archbishop of Cologne solemnly crowned him in Aachen. And thus there occurred a long-lasting division in the empire. For the Archbishop of Cologne and all his suffragans, in addition to the bishops of Kemburg and Paderborn and those subject bishops, as well as the

Archbishop of Bremen, the Duke of Louvain, the Duke of Lemburg, the Count Palatine of the Rhine, the Landgrave of Thuringia, and many counts, adhered to Otto. And so he obtained almost all the land beyond the Moselle, from Kemburg to Denmark. But the rest of the land and the remaining princes submitted to Philip, although they did not adhere firmly to his cause, as will be obvious later.

XXIII. Meanwhile, however, the Empress Constance, recognizing that the perfidious Markward was scheming to invade the kingdom, distrusted him and commanded everyone by her letters to avoid him as an enemy of the king and the kingdom. She also held Walter, Bishop of Troia, the Chancellor of the kingdom, extremely suspect and took the seal away from him, for his brothers had also gone over to Markward. But due to the influence of the pope, she received him back into her favor, so that, when, a little more than a year after the death of the emperor, she was near death, she made him a royal familiar together with the Archbishops of Palermo, Monreale, and Capua. But she entrusted the regency of the kingdom to the pope, to be confirmed on oath, because she looked on him as her principal lord. She decided that every year during his regency he should receive thirty thousand *tari*[37] from the royal income. And if he should incur any expenses for the defense of the kingdom, all of these amounts should be completely repaid. Then she died, leaving the royal orphan in the custody of the familiars.

But Markward returned to the kingdom with the intention of occupying it with all his strength, claiming that, according to the Last Will of the emperor, he ought to be regent for the king and of the kingdom. Immediately, the Lord Pope sent Gregory, cardinal deacon of Santa Maria in Portico,[38] as legate to Sicily to regulate the affairs of

---

37. A Sicilian gold coin.

38. Gregory of Sancto Apostolo, cardinal deacon of Santa Maria in Portico, 1188–1202. See Maleczek, *Papst und Kardinalskolleg von 1191 bis 1216*, 93–94. Gregory was a Roman from the family *de Sancto Apostolo*. This appointment probably arose from his earlier ties to southern Italy.

the kingdom with the royal familiars. On his arrival, he received the oath of regency from them and ordered it to be made known throughout Sicily. But, because the royal familiars, especially the royal chancellor, who disdained to have a superior, were not well inclined toward him, and since they all worked hard not for the royal benefit but for their own, within a short time he returned to the Apostolic See.

But he had first sent messengers with royal letters throughout the kingdom noting that the oath of regency had been sworn by all to the Lord Pope. Next, the pope sent John, cardinal priest of Saint Stephen on the Coelian, and Gerard, cardinal deacon of Saint Hadrian,[39] to the Terra di Lavoro to persuade the cities, counts, and barons to resist the perfidious Markward, who, having gathered an army, aimed first at seizing the monastery of Monte Cassino in order to obtain free access to the kingdom. When, therefore, the Abbot of Monte Cassino sought the help of the Supreme Pontiff in this moment of pressing need, he sent the noble Lando of Montelongo, Rector of the Campagna, and his cousin on his mother's side, with almost fifty knights and a hundred archers at his expense.[40] With the aforementioned cardinals, they were received in the village of San Germano to defend it against Markward's attack. But the men of the village, weak and unwarlike, fled at his coming to Monte Cassino with their children and wives. They deserted the cardinals and the knights. But the cardinals, with a thousand inhabitants, found refuge in the monastery and the knights and archers formed in the valley before the monastery. Markward, after he had captured and sacked the village, besieged them, thinking he would be able to force them to surrender for lack of supplies and other necessities. When he heard this, the Lord Pope was deeply troubled

39. John of Salerno, cardinal priest of St. Stephen in Celiomonte, 1190–1208, was a Benedictine monk from Monte Cassino. See Maleczek, *Papst und Kardinalskolleg von 1191 bis 1216*, 107–9. Gerard, cardinal deacon of St. Hadrian, 1182–1208, was from Lucca. See Maleczek, *Papst und Kardinalskolleg von 1191 bis 1216*, 78–79.

40. Innocent made extensive use of members of his family, especially in Rome, the patrimony, and southern Italy. Jane Sayers, in *Innocent III: Leader of Europe, 1198–1216* (London: Longman, 1994), 33–36, discusses Innocent's family.

and immediately sent Jordan, cardinal priest of Santa Pudenziana,[41] and Octavian, the subdeacon, his cousin from his mother's side,[42] with five hundred ounces of silver to Peter, Count of Celano, in order to arrange, as best they could, at least to support the besieged with food. Peter took the money and distributed it to his knights, considering this more useful than the needs of the besieged. For he provided hardly any amount of grain there. But, those besieged, though they were in much need and fear, continued to resist manfully and with constancy so that, after two months, when they corrupted some of Markward's army with money and drew close to his camp, he raised the siege. There was some use in that evil, for, after he had seized the village and the knights had fled, such terror seized everyone that, if he had proceeded with that other triumph, he would have found almost no one to resist his malice, but, after awhile, their fear receded. They regained their spirits and some of them prepared to resist him. But he employed not only his forces but also trickery to bring his preconceived malice to a conclusion. Although he overcame some by force, he deceived others by tricks, but he could not win since the Supreme Pontiff stood as an obstacle in his every path. Further, he hoped to win the pope with promises with the help of Conrad, Archbishop of Mainz, who was then returning from Jerusalem.[43] He acted secretly and tried cautiously to see whether he could appease him with an offering of gifts. He promised that, if only Innocent would cease his opposition, even if he would not support him, he would unconditionally grant him a thousand ounces of gold and, after he had obtained Palermo, he would give him an equal amount in ounces of gold, would swear fi-

41. Jordan of Ceccano, cardinal priest of Santa Pudenziana, 1188–1206, was from the family of the counts of Ceccano in southern Lazio. He had been abbot of Fossanova. He was related to nobles in the Kingdom of Sicily. See Maleczek, *Papst und Kardinalskolleg von 1191 bis 1216*, 86–88.

42. Later cardinal deacon of SS. Sergius and Bacchus, Innocent's former church. See Maleczek, *Papst und Kardinalskolleg von 1191 bis 1216*, 163.

43. Conrad von Wittelsbach, archbishop of Mainz, cardinal bishop of Sabina, 1166–1200. See Maleczek, *Papst und Kardinalskolleg von 1191 bis 1216*, 67. He died in October 1200.

delity to him, would double the rent, and would multiply the services the Roman pontiffs were accustomed to get from the Kingdom of Sicily. Also, he would hold the kingdom directly from the Apostolic See. He would not oppose the Supreme Pontiff's care of the orphan king, because, as he firmly asserted, that boy was not the son of either the emperor or the empress, but a substitute, as he proposed to prove by witnesses. But the Supreme Pontiff, aware of his evil, judged his promises and offers execrable. Since he could not profit in this way, he turned to another trick, proposing to be reconciled to ecclesiastical unity. But when he got the answer that he should swear an oath that he would obey the Apostolic mandates on all the matters for which he had been excommunicated, he answered that he was prepared to do so absolutely in spiritual matters, but in temporal affairs he would swear with the reservation that he would obey just commands. And when it was explained to him that the usual form of oath could not be changed in any way for his sake, he finally promised in writing that he would swear on all the matters for which he had been excommunicated without any stipulation and that he would obey all apostolic mandates. But, even though the pope had a strong suspicion of fraud, still, because there ought not be an obstacle to one desiring to return to the church, he sent Octavian, cardinal bishop of Ostia, Guido, cardinal priest of Santa Maria in Trastevere, and Hugolino, cardinal deacon of St. Eustachius,[44] to Veroli in Campagna, so that they might receive Markward into their presence according to the form written above. And when he had come, after considerable argument, he swore in the prescribed manner. He asked the aforementioned bishop and cardinals

44. Octavian, cardinal bishop of Ostia, 1189–1206. He had earlier been cardinal deacon of SS. Sergius and Baccchus, 1182–1189, and was thus Innocent III's predecessor in that church. He was a Roman. See Maleczek, *Papst und Kardinalskolleg von 1191 bis 1216*, 80–83. Hugo or Hugolino, the later Pope Gregory IX, was one of the most active members of the papal curia. He was related to Innocent III on his father's side and was created cardinal deacon of St. Eustachius at the beginning of his pontificate. He became cardinal bishop of Ostia in 1206. See Maleczek, *Papst und Kardinalskolleg von 1191 bis 1216*, 126–33.

to go down to the monastery of Casamari, near that city, to conclude the mandate in order that he might hear it in front of his companions, of whom a large number had remained there. He employed this trick so that, since he was going down from a fortified position to one unfortified, they would not dare to proffer him the mandate. The Bishop of Ostia, seduced by the counsel of the nobleman, Leo of Monumento, his cousin on his mother's side, who was mediator of this reconciliation, agreed.[45] And the others, persuaded, but without foresight, by the Bishop of Ostia, unwisely agreed. When they had gone down to the monastery, a banquet was prepared for them at which Markward served them punctiliously and, at the end of the banquet, there was a rumor that he would kidnap them that so terrified them that they dared not carry out the mandate that displeased him. In total confusion, they did not know what to do. But Hugolino, cardinal deacon of St. Eustachius, having regained his courage, produced a writing fortified by the *bulla* of the Lord Pope before all who were gathered there to hear the mandate.[46] In it was contained expressly the mandate which must be administered to him, and he said, "Here is the mandate of the Lord Pope. We can do nothing else." Moreover, the Supreme Pontiff took this precaution both on his own behalf and theirs. He commanded him, therefore, as it was written, under the obligation of the oath that he had sworn, to surrender the regency completely and to cease the invasion and molestation of the kingdom by himself and his men. Also he should not molest in any way the Patrimony of St. Peter. He should restore everything that he or his men had fraudulently seized from the kingdom that he had and those things which were held by others, and he should make a good faith effort if possible to restore him. Moreover, he should make full satisfaction for the losses and injuries suffered by the Roman Church and the Cassinese

45. The reference is to Cardinal Octavian. Leo de Monumento was lord of Anguillara and served as consul in Rome in the 1180s. He was a supporter of Henry VI, who conferred the city and county of Sutri on him in 1186. See RI 1:471, n. 3.

46. *Bulla* refers to the lead seal attached to the letter, hence the term "bull."

monastery according to the decision of the Supreme Pontiff and depending on his own abilities. He should not exercise power over clerics or ecclesiastics nor cause violent hands to be raised against them. He should not despoil or seize the cardinals and Apostolic Legates nor order them seized or even besieged, unless, attacked by them, he was forced to do so in his own defense. Not that the pope would then say to him that this was allowed, but because he did not forbid it as a requirement of the oath.

XXIV. When this mandate was heard, there was a huge tumult among the people. But Markward himself, although deeply disturbed, still did not allow anything dishonorable to be done against the cardinals. Rather he personally led them to Veroli. He suggested that he desired to approach the Supreme Pontiff in order to inform him about certain very secret matters that he would not reveal to anyone else. For this reason, he asked that, in the meantime, they should agree to suspend the mandate. Moreover, he sent a letter fortified with his seal in witness of the fact that he would take the prescribed oath and that he had received the mandate. But returning to his vomit [Prv 26:11] after his absolution he sent letters to the lord pope, in the salutation of which he considered his fraud carefully in that the salutation was of this sort: "To the reverend father and lord in Christ, Innocent, by the grace of God, Supreme Pontiff of the Roman See, Markward, Seneschal of the Empire, etc. greetings and obedience both due and devout." And in another letter he expressed it in this way: "Markward, Seneschal of the Empire, and that which is, by obedience, devoted service"; as though he neither totally suppressed nor manifestly expressed that he was regent and procurator of the kingdom, as he usually referred to himself in his other letters.

He also sent a letter, not only within the kingdom but also outside it, indicating that he was reconciled to the Supreme Pontiff, and had found such favor in his eyes that he had granted him the office of regent of the kingdom, and had appointed two cardinals to compel all to pay heed to him. When the cardinals disputed these matters with him, he wrote openly that neither for God nor man would he observe the mandate the Supreme Pontiff had laid on him. For this reason, the Lord Pope sent messengers and a letter throughout the kingdom, explaining the whole process of the negotiations and making his dishonesty clear. He strictly ordered everyone to avoid him as an excommunicate, a perjurer, an enemy, and a traitor.

When he saw that his aim was frustrated, he began very subtly to plan how he could cross over to Sicily, the more freely to carry out his wickedness. When he had gathered some followers, he crossed over and undertook evil works. He sent out his followers and accomplices in his iniquity, Diepold, Otto, and Sifried, his brothers, Conrad of Sorella, Odo de Laviano, and Federico Maluto, and some others, who held many fortifications this side of the Faro. All of them had joined him out of vanity. When evil began to increase throughout Sicily by his efforts, the loyal familiars began to ask the Supreme Pontiff to send them a protector with a band of warriors. He therefore sent Cinthius, cardinal priest of Saint Lawrence in Lucina, legate of the Apostolic See, and the nobleman, James, his cousin and marshal, with two hundred mercenaries; to them he added the archbishops, Anselm of Naples and Angelo of Taranto, diligent and prudent men, to use their zeal and counsel.[47] After they had set out, they captured Frederick in Calabria, and they devastated the entire province and then arrived at Messina, the most completely faithful city, which never deserted the royal cause during this disturbance.

XXV. But, in the meantime, Walter, Count of Brienne, had married the firstborn daughter of King Tancred, who had returned from prison along with her mother and sisters. A brave, noble, strong, and generous man, he approached the Apostolic See, seeking humbly and immediately for justice to be done regarding the things that belonged to his wife in Sicily. For he took the position that her father, King Tan-

---

47. James was the son of John Odolino and was later count of Andria. See Sayers, *Innocent III,* 36.

cred, had obtained the throne of Sicily and, after him, his son William had been raised to the throne of the kingdom. The Emperor Henry had taken the throne from him during the reign of Pope Celestine. Henry had finally reached an agreement with him by which he granted to him and his heirs the County of Lecce and the Principality of Taranto. He confirmed this grant both by his own oath and that of his men. But after he had mother and sisters in his power, he sent them as captives to Germany, from which finally, shortly after the boy had died in the captivity, his mother and sisters escaped with difficulty as a result of the Apostolic mandate. The Lord Pope, therefore, hesitated over what should be done regarding the petition of the aforesaid count. For the count himself seemed, not without reason, to be suspect to Frederick, the boy-king of Sicily, son of the emperor, as one who intended to avenge the injuries of his family. But, on the other hand, he feared that if the petition of the count was completely rejected, he might join the enemies of the king and so the more recent mistake might be worse than the earlier one. He deliberated diligently, therefore, not only with the cardinals, but also with other prudent men, and on their advice he finally decided that the rights which the wife of the count had from the grant made by the emperor in the county of Lecce and the Principality of Taranto should be recognized so that justice would not be denied. But, in order to avoid suspicion on the part of the king, he received the above-written oath from the count himself in public consistory, in the presence of a large crowd. To prevent the familiars of the king from being scandalized by this before he explained to them the reason why he had granted letters to the count for obtaining the principate of Taranto and the county of Lecce, he first sent letters to them in this manner:

Recently our beloved son, the nobleman, Walter, Count of Brienne, approached the Apostolic See together with the noble lady, Sibylla, widow of the late King Tancred of Sicily, and her daughter, his wife, as well as with knights and many others and he offered a petition on behalf of his wife and her sisters in the matter of the assignment of the Principate of Taranto and the county of Lecce to them, or a just exchange for the county itself, according to the grant which the late Emperor Henry was known to have publicly made to the late King William, the son of the same king, and his heirs, since neither William himself nor his sisters had wronged him in any way, seeing that they have the excuse of their age. We, therefore, have taken into consideration the nobility and power of that count, since many now follow him and more are about to arrive soon. Since our beloved sons, the counts of Champagne and Flanders, are closely related to him, and they have now taken the cross and are about to set out in aid of the Holy Land and in support of the count, we have deliberated what should be done, whether to try to get his support for the king or allow him to take a position hostile to the kingdom. Recognizing, therefore, that from what we understood of these matters his petition was just, we granted our Apostolic favor to him in his petition, lest, if we were to deny him his just claims, he would join the enemies of the kingdom, or would become a stronger enemy of the king in this way, and the most recent mistake would be worse than the earlier one. We have therefore arranged, after we had with diligent zeal deliberated many plans with him, for him to undertake a security sworn on the cross and relics that, neither by himself nor through another would he enter into any scheme against the person of the king, his honor, and the Kingdom of Sicily. Rather, when he obtains the aforementioned principate and county, or a just substitute, he will keep faith with the king at our command and will pay homage to us and will, on the proper oath, obtain the guardianship of the king and the regency of the kingdom, and he will work in good faith to the degree possible against the king's enemies, namely, Markward, Diepold, Otto of Laviano, and their followers. Likewise, moreover, Tancred's wife, her mother, Sibylla, and his daughter have sworn that they will observe this agreement faithfully and will work with the count so that it will be observed inviolably. But if perhaps the count or his wife should try to contravene in any way by their own action or that of another the oath they have sworn, in addition to the crime of perjury, they will incur the sentence of excommunication on their persons and of interdict on their land, and they will lose completely every right if it is appropriate not only in the aforesaid lands but also in the Kingdom of Sicily. That count will provide to us as suitable supporters of the oath as he is able for his faithful observance of all these matters. Desiring, therefore, to defer to your honor before we do justice to him or even order the exchange of the aforesaid principate and county to take place, advising and exhorting your fraternity in the Lord, we ordered that this should be announced to you so that it would not be done outside of your knowledge. We also command by Apostolic letters that you, giving heed to the justice and power of the count, who by himself and his supporters can serve usefully the king and kingdom, and fight their enemies effectively and with energy, as well as the necessity and poverty of the kingdom, which, due to sin, neither suffices to withstand present but also future attacks, will work prudently and carefully to obtain his rights without disturbance. It should be known that we have in our experience understood the count to be a man of industry and prudence and we believe he fears God, and puts the salvation of his soul before all else. He has firmly promised us that he will render so great a service, God granting, to the king and the kingdom against his enemies that not only will he not molest them in these matters, but he will merit to obtain more. But if perhaps it should seem to you that we can be more on our guard regarding the count, you should inform us about this in your letter so that from your counsel, we may require from him and receive as exact a surety as you consider expedient.[48]

But, when Walter, Bishop of Troia, the Chancellor of the kingdom, received these letters in Messina, he was deeply upset and, after he summoned the people, in the heat of passion he began to attack the intention of the Supreme Pontiff however he could, more concerned for himself than the king because, since he and his family had always opposed King Tancred, he feared lest the count, who had married that king's daughter, should he become powerful in the kingdom, would take bitter revenge against him and his family. But the count, having left his wife and mother-in-law, returned to France so that, after he had collected an army, he might return to obtain the above-described land, and to fight the royal enemies.

XXVI. Meanwhile, Markward, having won the Sicilian Muslims and many noble allies over to his side, succeeded to such an extent

48. Walter arrived in Italy in 1201, which suggests that this letter was written in that year and may have been in the lost registers of the third or fourth year of Innocent's pontificate. See Donald Matthews, *The Norman Kingdom of Sicily* (Cambridge: Cambridge University Press, 1992), 300–304.

that, after he had obtained many cities and castles, he arrived at Palermo and strongly invested the city. For this reason, the legate and the marshal of the Supreme Pontiff, who were in Messina with the chancellor, decided to hurry to Palermo. But what happened on their arrival is evident from the letter of Anselm, Archbishop of Naples, who wrote to the Lord Pope. The tenor follows:

I have desired to announce to you, my Lord, the good tidings which, by the merits of your prayers, the Lord has accomplished in these days, as I have witnessed with my own eyes. And so, your Holiness should know that I landed happily in Palermo on the seventeenth of this present month of July with three galleys and one transport of Apulians, who brought me in honor, thanks to you, together with Bartholomew, your scriptor, and my whole *familia*.[49] On this same day and at the same hour, as it pleased God, the lord cardinal with all the lords of the royal court, except the bishop of Catania, and the royal army likewise arrived in Palermo. There was great joy throughout the city, especially because the wicked Markward, who, with the evil Saracens, had closely invested and besieged it for twenty continuous days, seemed now to have labored utterly in vain. On that very day the royal army had erected its camp outside in the city, namely, in the royal garden called *Januardum*, so that on the very next day, there was a battle with the enemy. But this cunning and experienced man, as soon as he learned the army had landed, sent a message of peace by Rainerius de Manente as a trick in order to learn, if he could, about the weaknesses on our side, and meanwhile he increased his strength hour by hour as he waited. He had also known about our lack of money and that delay of the war was risky for us on account of the insolent urging of the complaints of the mercenaries. He, therefore, believed that by delay or deceit he could ensnare us with pleasant words, and he made sufficient promises especially since he would have influenced his audience to agree to his peace, if the Lord, who knew all things before they happened and long considered the thoughts of men, had not intervened against the counsels of the princes. For with all the different and varied tongues which were gathered in the royal army there was a uniform voice and will, so that all joined together and cried out with one voice: "we reject

49. *Familia* here refers to the usual retinue of the bishop: secretaries, notaries, chaplains, and other clergy.

the peace of this excommunicate and we refuse without discussion the agreement of this enemy of God and men." But these words did not cause him to desist in his efforts to press for his peace agreement nor for our negotiators to listen to those things which were proposed and sought by him. And since it was now almost the end, with everyone murmuring that peace should be concluded, and this seemed certainly to be inconvenient for our side and not to look to our honor, Master Bartholomew, your scriptor, who is unable to tolerate injury to us or to the church of God with equanimity, hearing that this agreement would be concluded in hatred and contempt of you, and that it could also be costly to the whole kingdom, produced a letter from you prohibiting it. Whereas, besides your most devoted Lord of Monreale,[50] there were three other lords gathered for the negotiations, indeed for completing the agreement, namely, the chancellor, the lords of Messina and Cefalù, with the aforementioned Rainerius, the ambassador of Markward present, he brought out and handed over your letters, firmly prohibiting them according to their content and by your mandate from making a treaty or an agreement with the very evil Markward. And so it was done both on account of your command and because the tumult and murmuring of the whole army and the people of Palermo was growing. After the fourth day, between Palermo and Monreale, which Markward had seized by force and was holding from the third to almost the ninth hour, there was a strongly fought battle and, finally, just as it pleased those meriting by your holy prayers, after many adverse defeats, mutilations, and withdrawals of our side, by the help of the extraordinary man, the Lord Marshal, who was holding the castle, located in the rear with his forces, indeed, he was the backbone of the army, we had the victory we desired from the enemy. To provide a better explanation: our best troops, who were drawn up in the front line, though they acted valiantly in the front lines, even though they defeated and killed some, still weren't able to hold back the multitude of those who attacked them; twice they were forced to retreat and, blessed by the Lord, twice the Marshal received them and kept them safe, and while the other part of the Germans and Muslims urged and pressed on, the Marshal and his forces, blessed by the Lord, unanimously and courageously gathered in one hour at one point, turned toward the camps, fled, seized, fell on, and killed those following and pursuing until those who had escaped the sword de-

50. I.e., the archbishop of Monreale. This archbishopric, located just outside Palermo, was erected under King William II.

serted the places where they were camped with all their tents and property. They were dispersed among the high mountains, through the depths of
the valleys and the canyons, and fled on the road of perdition. But some
Pisans, about fifty or more in all, it is said, with a certain Benedict in command, were placed along with a large number of Saracens, who with him
were holding the summit of Monreale, to guard the weaker places. But as
soon as the battle was underway, our infantry, with Count Gentile and
Count Malgerius and some other knights, ascended, reached the top, and
very forcefully gained control of the summit and put to the sword almost
all who were found there. Benedict, the commander, is said to have escaped with a few of his men. But a certain Saracen named Magdad who
was the master and commander of all of the Muslims was attacked and
killed there. But it is not known where Markward fled, or with how many
or which of his men. Still we know that that man who was recently a mediator between men and the devil, Rainerius de Manente, was captured
and put in prison along with many others of higher and better status from
Markward's army, whose names I do not know. How many were killed we
do not know. But we know that they were numerous and outstanding.
Their booty was large and precious so that that whole day hardly sufficed
to remove it. This, my Lord, is the day the Lord has made[51] [Ps 117:24],
the day of our desired redemption and joy, the day on which your name is
magnified and blessed, the day, I say, which also brought us victory over
our enemy, on which that distinguished man, the Marshal, along with his
forces acquired eternal fame. Let God bring it about that his good deeds
may accord with his merits, indeed his most famous works. But I do not
commend him to you because his good works recommend him exceedingly with your Magnificence.[52]

XXVII. In his escape, Markward lost all his supplies, and the Testament of the Emperor Henry VI sealed with a golden bull was found in
a certain chest in which, among other things, these matters were contained word for word:

51. Psalm numbers follow the Latin vulgate.
52. This battle took place in June 1200. It was not decisive. Markward remained
active until his death in September 1202 as the result of surgery after an attack of
kidney stones.

The empress our wife and our son Frederick should hand over to the Lord Pope and to the Roman church all the rights which they were accustomed to hold from the kings of Sicily and should provide security to the Lord Pope just as the kings of Sicily were accustomed to do for the Supreme Pontiff and the Roman Church. If our consort should die first, our son would succeed. And if our son should die without an heir, the kingdom of Sicily would fall to the Roman Church. If our son should die first, our beloved consort should hold our kingdom for her lifetime and after her death the Kingdom of Sicily should go to the Roman Church. About the empire, we order that the Lord Pope and the Roman church should confirm it to our son and, in exchange for this confirmation of the empire and the kingdom, we desire that all the land of the Countess Matilda should be restored to the Lord Pope and the Roman Church, in addition to Medesano and Argelata with their appurtenances. And in addition we ordain and desire that the whole territory from Ponte Payle with Monte Fortino to Ceperano should be handed over to the Lord Pope and that the Roman Church should hold Montefiascone with all its appurtenances. Further, we order that our Seneschal, Markward, should receive the Duchy of Ravenna, the land of Bertinoro, the March of Ancona, and Medesano and Argelata, with their appurtenances from the Lord Pope and the Roman Church and he should swear and make his fidelity to him for all these goods as to his Lord. But, on his death, if he should die without an heir, the Duchy of Ravenna, the territory of Bertinoro, and March of Ancona, Medesano and Argelata with all their appurtenances should remain in the dominion of the Roman Church.[53]

XXVIII. The energy and prudence of the Marshal were pleasing and acceptable not merely to the king and his familiars but also to all the counts and barons and all the natives and foreigners to such a degree that, by general agreement and with the support of everyone, the county of Andria was given to him by a royal privilege, sealed with a golden bull on the conveyance of this grant to him. But because the familiars of the kingdom denied necessary expenses to him and his

53. Thomas C. Van Cleve, *The Emperor Frederick II of Hohenstaufen: Immutator Mundi* (Oxford: Clarendon Press, 1972), 45, speaks of "the so-called testament of Henry VI." But Innocent was acting under the testamentary provisions of Queen Constance.

men and because the excessive heat of the summer had now begun to seriously weaken the military effectiveness of his men, he was compelled to rely on his own resources, and the Lord Pope made a large amount of money available both for wages and gifts, and for horses and arms, since, with the exception of certain payments they had made in Sicily, they had received nothing more from the familiars.

XXIX. The Metropolitan See of Palermo was then vacant due to the death of the archbishop, and the chancellor deeply desired it. He worked to obtain it to the point that he caused himself to be postulated as archbishop and arranged for the same postulation to be agreed to by the legate, without further consultation of the Lord Pope. And, though he had not yet received the *pallium*, nor even postulated, he was nevertheless exercising the office of Archbishop of Palermo in fact and in name. But when this fact came to the attention of the Lord Pope, he rebuked the legate in strong terms because he had proceeded in such an important matter about such an important personage before he had sought his approval. Still, in order to defer to him, he granted from an abundant kindness that the same chancellor might exercise both temporal and spiritual administration in the aforesaid Metropolitan See, but that he would continue to refer to himself as Bishop of Troia and, if he wished, as procurator or minister of the Church of Palermo. But, puffed up in the spirit of pride, he refused to accept this favor, instead he would not hold back either his tongue or pen from defaming the Supreme Pontiff about the business of the Count of Brienne.

XXX. Count Walter of Brienne, however, arrived quickly in Rome with the small but effective body of knights he had collected, but some mocked his foolhardiness for planning to enter the kingdom with such a modest force. When Diepold and his allies heard this, they also collected their forces, and worked strenuously to prevent his entry. Still, the Lord Pope recognized that he would not be able to effect entry with such a small force of knights without loss for them and himself both because the force with his enemies was by far larger and because they were holding the fortified places at the entrance to the kingdom. He took pity and granted him fifty ounces of gold out of which he might collect a force of knights with whose aid he might enter the kingdom. He also gave him letters to the counts and barons, the castellans and citizens, asking them to receive and aid him. And after he had gathered the knights, this intrepid man entered the kingdom and, having been received by the citizens of Chieti, when he had taken over their castle, he set out for Capua, but he was not admitted into the city by the Capuans. Therefore Diepold and his allies, having collected a large force, marched around Capua in front of him, hoping to overwhelm him and his men in a single attack. When the battle lines were drawn up by both sides, there was a hard-fought battle, but under Divine protection, the loyal forces put the disloyal followers of the excommunicate to flight. Some were killed and others captured. Then the Capuans went out and plundered the large booty that had been left behind, while the count pursued those fleeing with his forces. As a result, Count Peter of Celano joined him and stayed with him for a month in order to obtain the county of Molise; with his help, he got hold of the larger part of the county. Fear of him struck all who heard about his power and strength and that of his forces. Following the defeat of the Germans, who prior to his coming had freely roamed the kingdom, this man of peace went down to Apulia, and certain cities and towns belonging to the Principality of Taranto were surrendered to him, namely: Matera, Otronto, Brindisi, and several others. He also got Melfi, Barolo, Montepiloso, and certain other cities and towns which submitted to his custody. He also attacked Monopoli and Taranto and some other places that rejected his rule. He also used his power to obtain the Castle of Lecce and, with prudence, he carried forward many grand projects too numerous to single out.

XXXI. But Bishop Walter of Troia, the Chancellor of the Kingdom, seized almost total control over the royal familiars so that he was like a king, conferring and handing out counties and baronies, appointing and removing justiciars and chamberlains, secretaries, and *stratigoti.*[54] He sold and mortgaged the customs duties and the baillies; he took and spent rents and incomes. He also appointed those he wanted as royal familiars. Unmindful of the Apostolic mandate that he and others had sought as follows:

We forbid any diminution of the royal domain, the creation of any obligation under any pretext, save in case of evident and urgent need: to gather an army on land or sea and then, for this reason, you may mortgage rents, and the money obtained may be spent for the royal support by the *secreti.*[55] By the tenor of these presents, we also prohibit any of your supporters, whom you appoint as royal familiars without the general agreement of all parties or at least the major part of sounder counsel, to dare to administer any important business of the kingdom or presume to order anything concerning the fisc. Also, the royal patrimony should in no way be decreased without our prior consent being sought. We also order that none of the *secreti* should give heed in a personal way to any of the royal familiars or pay him anything from the fisc without the assent of all or the willingness of the *maior et sanior* part.[56] We command them to guard carefully the recently recovered treasury. It worries and disturbs us also now that since the perfidious Markward has, with the Lord's help, been destroyed by our own and the king's forces and reduced almost to nothing, some, as we have heard, to the loss of the king and kingdom, contrary to our mandate, endeavor to make peace with him so that he who has been prostrated by a divine judgment, may arise quickly with renewed strength to damage us by this tricky peace. Lest therefore such a fraudulent peace, which could rather be called pernicious, should come into effect, we strictly forbid by Apostolic letters anyone of whatever rank or order of the clergy or of the people to presume to make or enter into peace with the same perfidious individual. But so that now that he has been vanquished he may be conquered completely, the action should be carried out by the majority against him strongly and prudently. But because peace and tranquillity is proven to be valuable for the king and kingdom above all things, we desire and command that if the Saracens provide sufficient security that they will

---

54. The *strategoti* were urban officials in the kingdom of Sicily. See Hiroshi Takayama, *The Administration of the Norman Kingdom of Sicily* (Leiden: Brill, 1993), 75.

55. These were fiscal officials. See Takayama, *Administration,* 13–24.

56. I.e., the "larger and more sound" group, not necessarily a majority.

no longer ally themselves with the king's enemies and that they will persevere firmly and surely in loyalty and supporting him, you should recall
them to royal favor in a fully developed peace, and you will make known
without hesitation to the same Saracens and other traitors of the kingdom
that if they should contravene that and other of our commands, which we
have issued for the royal honor and the safety of the kingdom, we shall
with greater constancy undertake to tame their rebellion and pride, and
we shall order the Christian Princes who are hastening to the Holy Land to
rise up powerfully, with the Lord's support, for their confusion, saving in
all things the authority of the legate and him to whom we have entrusted
our vicarial authority.[57]

XXXII. In order more adequately to satisfy his preconceived malice,
the chancellor craftily arranged for the recall of the legate of the Apostolic See. Moreover, he summoned his brother, Gentile, count of
Monopello, and made him a royal familiar, working ardently for his
promotion, and he began to negotiate with Markward about peace
contrary to his oath and the Apostolic prohibition, despite the opposition of the other Lords in court save those he had created so that they
would favor him. And although he knew that Markward and his supporters were excommunicated and cursed by the Lord Pope, and he
himself out of his own mouth had excommunicated and cursed him
at Apostolic command together with all his followers, still he made an
agreement with him to admit him among the royal familiars, in fact
making him the chief among all the familiars, dividing the kingdom
with him, so that one of them could administer the business of the
king in Sicily and the other in Apulia and ordering under the royal
signature everyone to accept this agreement and, following its terms,
obey Markward, even if it displeased the Supreme Pontiff. But even if
both intended to deceive the rest, they still agreed to firm up the contract by a marriage between the nephew of one and the niece of the
other. Afterwards, when each understood the deception of the other,

57. August Potthast, *Regesta Pontificum Romanorum,* 2 vols. (Berlin: Decker, 1874),
1:106 (1155), October 1200. The author of the *Gesta* does not proceed in chronological order in his account.

the hidden motives were revealed, since Markward made known by his letters and ambassadors throughout the kingdom that the chancellor was plotting in order to raise his brother Gentile to the throne of the kingdom. On the other hand, the chancellor maintained that Markward was trying to usurp a royal crown for himself. Markward began to rebuild his forces and to carry on with more than usual cruelty. But, because the chancellor had now exhausted all the resources in Sicily, and could not find any way to provide for his expenses, he left the king in his brother's custody and crossed over to Calabria and Apulia in order that he might despoil them in the same way as he had Sicily. He destroyed almost all of the ecclesiastical treasures, crosses, chalices, and thuribles, as well as stripping gold and silver cases and icons, sparing no one from whom he could extort money whether by blandishments or threats or by fraud or force. But although he amassed a huge amount in this way, still he consumed it all uselessly, greedy in taking but wasteful in giving it away.

XXXIII. He, therefore, did not cease to defame the Supreme Pontiff in the worst way with profane language over the affair of the Count of Brienne, whom he deeply hated and conspired and plotted against with the counts and barons as well as the cities. For this reason, the Supreme Pontiff, unwilling to endure further his wickedness, promulgated a sentence of condemnation against him, pronounced him a perjurer and excommunicate for many reasons, and removed him both from the the church of Palermo and that of Troia, ordering another administrator to be established in both and commanding throughout the kingdom that no one should give heed to him and no one should be required to obey him by letter sent out by him under the king's name. A remarkable thing: despised by all, he first fell and went through the land as a wanderer and exile, and since he was not obeyed by the royal familiars, he joined Diepold and his followers, so that he could use whatever evil influence he had against the Supreme Pontiff. When the familiars of the king who were his accomplices heard this, they began to be very much afraid. They sent letters of intercession on their own behalf as well as his to the Lord Pope in the name of the king, and he responded to the king in this manner:

If only the Lord inspired you in your tender years with maturity and infused from that age now to keep to that weighty path by which you could differentiate between good and evil and judge between trust and perfidy, and not condemn the trustworthy for disloyalty nor exalt the disloyal for loyalty. Would that you would learn not from experience but from teaching, what we read in the gospel: "Mankind's enemies are found in their own households" [Mt 10:36]. And as a wise man proclaimed: "No plague is more harmful than the enmity of a relative." If only you knew that when you were younger, and even now, when you are established, the Apostolic See received you under its protection when you lost both your parents. And the hand of servants who conspired against you in the kingdom might from outside the kingdom destroy the root of the pestiferous tree if it were not cut down, so the goblet of poisonous drink might dry up at its source. And even in the kingdom our hand did not fail you, in fact we, through our brethren and knights, prevented the attack of the madman Markward, who raged with barbaric fierceness against your trusty men and wanted, not the regency of the kingdom, as some of his admirers lied to you, but to claim the rule of the kingdom by violence, denying that you were the son of the late Emperor Henry and of your mother, the Empress Constance, of happy memory, in order that he might by this circumstance turn both us and others away from your support. But we did not believe his lies, even though he made many grand promises to us, that we might not wish to impede his plan, even though, in order to attack him in Sicily, we underwent considerable worry and expense, difficulties and labors, not only on our part but on that of the persons of our brethren, exposing them to dangers on your behalf. Moreover, after he had returned to Sicily, we sent our beloved son, Marshal James, our cousin, a noble Roman citizen, against him with our army, and he triumphed, with the Lord's help, in a wonderful way together with your army. If some of your familiars had not recalled our knights from following up the attack, you would today have a final peace and the desired tranquility of your kingdom would have been restored. Note that we performed the obligation of guardian, not merely exercising the position of regent, but also caring for you, since no one is forced to fight at his own expense, and from the decision made by the aforementioned empress, our expenditures were to be administered for the needs of the kingdom, still we defeated your enemy at our expense so that our knights received nothing, save a small amount during their stay, either on their arrival or departure. But we ordered the repair of arms and the resupply of horses, save for their wages, to be paid. Moreover, some of these same familiars who were not pursuing the tranquility of the kingdom, put their own interests into unsettling it, believing that it was better to fish in troubled waters so that there should be no lack of unrest in the kingdom, having refused payment to us for the Marshal. They even dared to set up Markward with all his followers and allies under the guise of a peace, which, as its results show, must rather be called pernicious and contrary to the Keys of the Church, which bound these men by the bonds of excommunication, which they even pronounced themselves. They dared to raise this rejected and fallen man up at your head as a royal familiar, conferring almost the whole plenitude of power in the Kingdom of Sicily on him. And so that he would not rise up weaker but stronger from his fall and that he might prevail the more to your loss, they took all the captives they had seized during his escape and restored them to him; they even wanted to gain the favor of the men of the kingdom for him, once the peace, or rather the perfidy, was undertaken, and they commanded the whole kingdom, whether supporting or not supporting us, to observe it inviolably. This is how the royal familiars acted toward us, how they cared about their honor. In order that they might raise up your enemy contrary to the oath of fidelity by which some of them were bound to us and also what they swore about not entering into any agreement without our command, they stirred up persecution, infusing it with the venom of a serpent and putting oil on the fire. Wherefore, we do not see how they can either petition for themselves or how another can intercede for them, since some of them were under obligation to our favor until they made suitable satisfaction, although, out of the kindness of the Apostolic See, we arranged for them to be tolerated. For they have made a complete turnabout or rather they have switched to the wrong side, undermining the decision of the empress by their interpretations, and they have left us the empty title of regent, withdrawing the honor and leaving only the burden; they have usurped everything by their rashness so that now, contrary to our prohibition, they have exhausted almost all your domain for their alleged purposes. They have distributed counties and baronies according to their own judgment in order to increase their own popularity, and although they burdened the kingdom with numerous ex-

actions, they did not use the money collected for the benefit of the kingdom, nor did they restore to us the expenditures we made in accordance
with the constitution of the empress, nor did they undertake to pay either
the rent they owed or what the empress had decided should be paid to us
and our brethren each year, but they enriched their male relatives from
these goods and they gave dowries to their female relatives. We will pass
over in silence the things they kept for themselves when they held the
purse strings.

We also note the fact that, as your letter mentioned, these pious domestics took advantage of your youth, foreigners intruded everywhere,
indeed the man in whom you hoped and who was eating your bread was
planning the undermining of your peace. We refer back to the example of
your parents, and just as he had counseled them we ordered him to counsel you.

For we have learned and known it for a fact that William I, King of
Sicily, of illustrious memory, had sent many nobles of the kingdom into exile. After his death, those who took the care and custody of his
son, William, King of Sicily, of illustrious memory, recalled those who
were exiled, until now through the benefit of recall and restoration, they
strengthened them in fidelity and devotion to the crown so that none of
his ancestors ever lived in peace of this kind. None was so feared and
loved by his subjects, none provided so well for the peace and quiet of the
kingdom. We have, therefore, given heed to the fact that Henry, the late
emperor, with the agreement of your mother, the daughter of the late
King Roger, the Empress Constance, of illustrious memory, when William,
son of her nephew, King Tancred, of illustrious memory, surrendered,
granted the Principate of Taranto and the County of Lecce to him and his
heirs, and he ordered this grant to be reinforced by the oath on his soul of
princes both in the empire and the kingdom. Neither William nor his sisters did anything to invalidate this, since they were excused by reason of
age, on the basis of which we could act contrary to justice or resist the
truth. We could think of no reason since truth should not be abandoned
for a mere suspicion. Still, we have guarded against this kind of suspicion
insofar as we could. For we have publicly taken the oath of the count himself on the cross, the gospel, and relics that neither through himself nor
through another (etc. as in the letter sent to the familiars of the king, up
to:) should be observed inviolably. For he could, if he had wished, have
joined your enemies, and with their help not only secured his right but

other things as well, and the most recent mistake would be worse than the earlier. But we have preferred to persuade him to defend the kingdom, and to strengthen his fidelity to the crown. For this reason, on his recent entry into the kingdom, he carried out his oath, with the army he had brought with him at his own expense from beyond the Alps, against Diepold, who until now had free rein throughout the whole Kingdom of Sicily on this side of the Faro, and, with the Lord's help, he triumphed in a marvelous manner. Now, by the grace of God, through his effort, it was arranged that your loyal subjects, who were afraid to go outside the walls until now, gathered their harvest in security, and those crops the enemy had sown, they harvest. Until now they were afraid of those he might send. The count also made all of those he was able to snatch from the hand of the enemy take an oath of fidelity to you at our command. But to prevent the kingdom from enjoying a much desired peace at this time and to increase its turmoil the more, the Chancellor Walter entered into an agreement with the one who had been conquered and who had fled, and strove to support the losing party. But, since the hand of the Lord was stretched forth in punishment of the same Diepold, the chancellor was unable to support him, nor could he remain with him, but he sank with the one falling to his ruin, who now for a twofold reason incurs, along with some of his supporters, the sentence of excommunication. You see, therefore, who you ought rather to believe, whether us or some of those you call your familiars. Since we are watching over the destruction of your enemies, we strive to tame their rebelliousness by two swords, one by the aforementioned count, and the other by our loyal men. Moreover, they hand the sword over to your chief enemies and confirm them in their evil ways, not without weakening your strength. Of course, if you consider the truth, the Count of Brienne has brought more to you on one day than some who, with your own goods "widen their phylacteries and lengthen their tassels" [Mt 23:5] have profited you as long as they have lived. Lest, therefore, you listen to them, and so that you do not put trust in their contradictions, because they are concerned not with your honor but what is useful to them, and not for you but for themselves, they speak against our arrangements. But, if perhaps they raise this objection against the count, that the late Emperor Henry ejected his wife and her mother and his wife's brother from the kingdom, you should do better to doubt about some of them, whom the empress for good reason held captive for some period of time. If she had not been prevented by death, or our aid had come to her assistance, perhaps she would have exiled him from the kingdom, or she would have kept him in chains until now. Moreover, it is certain that someone more easily neglects the injury of another than his own. Therefore, we admonish and exhort the royal Serenity in the Lord that, insofar as it can be believed about a man, you should have no hesitation about the count. Rather, you should trust in him, because, even if he is not commissioned by you or your familiars, you will find him more truly loyal and devoted than your men (and would that they were yours), and, after God and us, the most powerful defender of you and your kingdom. And do not believe that we say this more for his utility than for your safety and that of your kingdom. Consider therefore prudently, and may your familiars be careful and not, on occasion of this correction and its rejection, turn to those who thirst for your life, since, once the latter have received power over them, they will not judge them according to divine judgment. But if they should want to return to the heart and now finally obey our commands humbly and with devotion, we will admit them to the favor of the Apostolic See for the honor of your Serenity, for the peace of the kingdom, and for their salvation.

Given at the Lateran, V Non. July, in the fourth year of our pontificate.[58]

XXXIV. The Lord Pope, therefore, sent Peter, Bishop of Porto, as his legate into Apulia and the Terra di Lavoro, ordering the counts and barons, castellans and townsmen all to rally to the count at the command of the legate against Diepold and the chancellor.[59] When the legate arrived in Apulia, that miserable man, chancellor in name alone, approached his presence, asking to be reconciled to ecclesiastical unity. After he had sworn a corporeal oath that he would obey all the commands of the Lord Pope, he was absolved by the legate. But when the legate commanded the chancellor not to oppose the Count of Brienne, he responded that if Peter the Apostle, sent by Christ himself, commanded him to do this, he would not obey a command of

58. Potthast, *Regesta Pontificum Romanorum*, 1:128 (1421), July 3, 1201.
59. Peter Gallocia, cardinal bishop of Porto, 1191–1212. Peter was a Roman. He had served as rector of the Campania before being named cardinal deacon in 1188. Innocent as cardinal dedicated his *De miseria humanae conditionis* to him.

this kind, even if he knew that he would be condemned to hell because of it. Putting his mouth toward heaven when he drew his tongue over the ground, he blasphemed the Supreme Pontiff publicly before everyone in the presence of the legate, and he departed to Diepold. When they had gathered all the forces they could, they proceeded to fight against the Count of Brienne at Barletta. But the count was there with a few men, for he had almost none of the subjects loyal to the king with him there. The Barlettans, even though they had sworn on the preceding day to the legate, also saw the multitude with them and the smallness of the count's forces, and they would not allow them to enter. And so, the count, seeing that he was caught in narrow straits, began to be very anxious, especially on account of the legate, who was growing more fearful than he was. Taking comfort in the Lord, he sprang to arms with his men. After he had received the blessing and absolution from the legate, since the legate had also laid a curse on the enemy, the count, calling on St. Peter in the name of the Lord for help, proceeded to battle. When they had begun to struggle bitterly, their enemies turned tail and fled. They all ran away as best they could. Many were captured, several were killed, and more were drowned in bogs and swamps. For they often saw a shining golden cross carried miraculously before the count. And this victory was so great that it seemed that the first had been almost nothing compared to the second. For, among others, Sifried, the brother of Diepold, was captured, as well as Odo of Laviano, who had killed Bishop Albert of Liège, of blessed memory, and Peter of Venere, the nephew of the chancellor, and Master Gerard, who intruded on the see of Salerno, and many other nobles and powerful men. The reputation of the count was, therefore, increased and broadcast at large throughout the kingdom, but the enemy was humbled and downtrodden. But Count Gentile, having received money, as it was said publicly, handed the Torre ad Mare over to Markward and fled to Messina.

XXXV. Markward got Palermo, and took control both of the palace and the king, subjecting almost all of Sicily save for Messina to his power. He had seized the child and would have usurped the crown for himself, save that he feared the count, to whom, with the king dead, the kingdom would come by hereditary right through his wife. Therefore, he began to negotiate with the pope and the count in many different ways so that, after he had received money he would depart the kingdom. But since he could not obtain it, he awaited an opportune time. God, who did not give up the rod of sinners upon the lot of the just [Ps 124:3], began seriously to whip his perfidy in order not to give glory to another. Since he had now been hard-hearted for a long time, he began to be afflicted so violently with an attack of stone that, emitting great cries as a result of the excessive pain, he was tortured with irremediable suffering. When he could no longer stand the pain, he decided to undergo surgery. But he died immediately. Truly what the Psalmist says was fulfilled in him: "I saw a wicked man, raised up stalwart over the cedars of Lebanon; I passed by and, behold, he was not there. I sought him, but he could not be found" [Ps 37:35–36].

XXXVI. William Capparone, racing to Palermo, seized the palace and the king and from then on called himself custodian and Master Captain of Sicily. But some of the accomplices of Markward, of evil memory, indignant at this, established themselves as another party. The chancellor, considering the time opportune for his return, having again given security by oath that he would obey the Apostolic mandates, sought the benefit of absolution. He returned to Sicily, joined the other party, and worked against Capparone. He sent messengers and letters to the Lord Pope to send a legate to Sicily. The pope sent Gerard, cardinal deacon of St. Hadrian, by whom William Capparone got himself absolved, swearing in his hands to support the regency of the Lord Pope and to obey the cardinal, as vice-regent, in all things.[60] The cardinal began to negotiate an agreement between him and the chancellor, which could not be consummated on account of the simultaneous uprisings. He arrived in Palermo and was received honor-

60. For Gerard, cardinal deacon of St. Hadrian, 1182–1208, see Maleczek, *Papst und Kardinalskolleg von 1191 bis 1216,* 78.

ably by Capparone. He began, as regent, to transact the business of the king and kingdom. But when he ordered Capparone on obligation of his oath to make satisfaction to clerics and churches, he, who was always ready with promises, did nothing he promised, making all decisions in his own interest. For this reason, the cardinal, after a brief delay in Palermo, especially on account of the king, who was delighted at his presence and was cheered by his consolation, returned to Messina to await a response from the Lord Pope.

The chancellor also returned to Apulia and was insisting to the Lord Pope through his messengers and letters, putting on increasing pressure by the petitions of the nobles and magnates to persuade him to deal mercifully with him by making him Metropolitan of Palermo or, at least, Bishop of Troia. But the pope, as he was just and consistent, was not willing to listen to petitions of this kind, lest he do injury without cause to Peter, the former Bishop of Mazara del Vallo, who by his command had been appointed as Archbishop of Palermo, or the present Bishop of Troia, whom he had ordered elected and also consecrated. Instead, he sent the *pallium*[61] to the archbishop lest the chancellor should continue to aspire to his office.

XXXVII. In order to show greater favor to the Count of Brienne, the pope sent that nobleman, James, his cousin and Marshal, to Apulia, appointing them both equally Masters and Justitiars of Apulia and the Terra di Lavoro, and he ordered the Castle of Barletta assigned to James's custody. He also ordered the surrender of Montepiloso, which belonged to the County of Andria, which had been granted to him out of royal generosity. He also ordered the Count of Brienne to provide assistance to help him to obtain that county. Moreover, when they were doing many things prudently and effectively, they came to the Campagna to visit the Supreme Pontiff, whom they had learned was ill. They found him at Anagni, so seriously ill that many thought he

61. The *pallium* is a woolen vestment worn about the neck and shoulders by the pope and granted by him to archbishops as a symbol of their authority.

was dead. When the report of his death had spread, many cities rebelled against the count, some expelling his knights, others killing
them. At this time, he lost Matera, Brindisi, and Otranto. The men of
Barletta laid siege to its fortress and forced the castellan, whom the
Marshal had sent out, to hand over the castle.

XXXVIII. Afterwards, when the Supreme Pontiff had begun to recover, the count and the Marshal returned to Apulia. Although they
were unable to get back those places, still they were eager to acquire
many. For the Marshal obtained the cities of Andria and Minervino,
and from that time on called himself the Count of Andria, and he built
a very strong fortress at Andria where the palace of the count had
been earlier. But some sons of Belial, conspiring against him, attacked
him, thinking to kill him with their swords, but, because he was wearing armor under his shirt, they were unsuccessful, especially because
a certain knight got in their way and they killed him in his presence.
Capturing them, he killed them with diverse torments. He seized and
confiscated all their property. The Count of Brienne carried out many
things on a grand scale, which it would take too long to explain individually. He put so much pressure on the Germans that they hardly
dared leave their castles. When they were deprived of all necessities,
everyone hoped that they could not hold out longer. At Salerno, he
got Terracina and kept up a siege against the Torre Maggiore.[62] He got
such results, however, that he was neglecting to protect his own person. When many argued with him about this, he responded arrogant-
ly that armed Germans would not dare to attack unarmed Franks. For
this reason, when he besieged a certain fortress of Diepold, called Sar-
lum, Diepold noted his carelessness and at early dawn attacked the
count and his men without warning, as they were resting naked in
their tents. He killed a large number and captured the count, though
he had fought bravely and was wounded by arrows and lances. He

---

62. Brenda Bolton provides a history of Terracina in this period in Appendix III
to this volume. It is located where the Via Appia reaches the coast south of Rome.

took him captive to the fort. Some days later, after he had received the sacrament of penance and the viaticum, he paid the debt of the flesh. James, Count of Tricarico, married the widow of the Count of Brienne, but he put off consummation of the marriage because she was pregnant. She gave birth to a son, whom she named Walter after his father.

But Diepold began to insist vigorously with supplication and promises that the Lord Pope should agree to receive him and his men. Because Brother Rainier[63] intervened, the pope received him on the condition that he swore to uphold all the commands of the Supreme Pontiff in all matters for which he had been excommunicated by the pope, that he should faithfully obey him concerning the regency of the king and kingdom, that he should make war and peace at his command, and that he should do justice to all under his jurisdiction seeking it, and that he should not provide aid or favor either within or outside the kingdom to Philip, Duke of Swabia, against the Kingdom of Sicily. He therefore sent the aforesaid Brother Rainier and Master Philip the Notary to the Terra di Lavoro, and, at the command of the Lord Pope, they publicly absolved Diepold in the prescribed manner, after they had received his oath and drawn up agreements, and they did the same in the cases of Markwald of Lariano with his men and then Conrad of Sorella with his and so all the Germans both beyond and on this side of the Faro returned to the mandate of the Supreme Pontiff. Diepold went on to Palermo and worked with William Capparone so that he surrendered the king into the hands of the legate and chancellor after he had received security from them, promising also that he would turn the palace over to them, so that king and kingdom might have peace. He brought the king out of the palace and escorted him to the legate and chancellor. He made a banquet and feasted with them. Meanwhile, a rumor circulated that he was perpe-

---

63. Rainier of Ponza, Cistercian monk of Fossanova, perhaps confessor of the pope. He was employed on a number of diplomatic missions. See RI 1:92, 132, n. 1.

trating a fraud, that when he brought them back to the palace he was going to take them all captive by trickery. Many believed that this was a false charge made to create an opportunity for them to seize him. And so he was seized and held, but since he was not closely guarded, he escaped and returned to Salerno, having left his son in captivity. Meanwhile, his brother Sifried traitorously captured Master Philip, the papal notary. The Lord Pope had sent him to Apulia and the Terra di Lavoro at the request of Diepold himself and made him his temporal vicar, so that he might bring about the observance of peace and justice between the Germans and the Latins. Sifried only released him after he had extorted a heavy ransom.

XXXIX. Among all the Germans who had remained as a scourge in the Kingdom after the death of the emperor, the most disloyal was Conrad, Castellan of Sorella, who also held Rocca Arcis on the frontier of the kingdom. He persecuted and afflicted the whole region not only of the Terra di Lavoro but also Campania and the whole Marittima. The Lord Pope often sent messengers and an army against him, not to attack the city of Sora, which that deceitful fellow possessed, but, if possible, to recall him from his perfidy. Conrad occupied a certain nearby *castrum* called Insula, and reduced its lords to such a state that, even though they were nobles, they were reduced to public begging. The Lord Pope, therefore, despised his malice and sorrowed over their poverty. He sent Peter, cardinal priest of Santa Pudenziana, as rector of Campania and Marittima, to aid them and fight against him.[64]

After he gathered a large army, he marched against him and besieged him in the aforementioned *castrum*, laying waste to the surrounding land. Because the siege was protracted, since he could not be persuaded to surrender, they undertook to divide the rushing torrent which was flowing past the *castrum* so that, after they had crossed it, they could lay siege to the *castrum* itself. But the effort was in vain;

64. Peter did not become cardinal priest of Santa Pudenziana until 1206. He succeeded Jordan de Cecccano as cardinal. See Maleczek, *Papst und Kardinalskolleg von 1191 bis 1216,* 64. This appointment places these events after 1206.

the attempt was not without loss to both sides. But they worked such perfidy that after they received the money which the Lord Pope had mercifully lent to the same nobles, he surrendered the *castrum* to them and agreed to a peace on certain terms, which, within a short time, he did not blush to violate. For, he also captured certain Verolese, loyal subjects and vassals of the Lord Pope, who came to visit and honor him about the Feast of the Nativity, as was the custom, and he forced them, by mutilating their members, to pay a very large ransom, not even sparing a certain noble who had accompanied him as a familiar and whom he had invested with a military belt. When, after he was admonished, he was unwilling to make satisfaction, the cardinal rector of the Campagna and Marittima gave up on him. The citizens of Sora had a strong hatred for this tyrant, who afflicted them with unsupportable burdens, and having entered into secret counsel and negotiation with Roffredus, the venerable Abbot of Cassino, introduced him with many armed men into the city of Sora by night and surrendered the city to him at the command of the Lord Pope. The pope sent his brother Richard and Stephen, his Camerarius, ahead to aid the city and, after them, the cardinal. When they had collected an army, they began to fortify the city, especially because Diepold was said to be approaching with a large armed force to help him, and they occupied Planello, the mountain above the city near Sorella, so that they might defend the city from Sorella by using the fort they built there. Finally, as it pleased the Lord, they rushed into the valley at the break of dawn with a loud cry, and while the heavens opened with a huge downpour, with lightning and thunder everywhere, they joined battle and attacked the men of Rocca, and forced them to flee. Since the terrified tyrant thought he had been betrayed by some of the Latins with him in the Rocca of Sorella, he surrendered himself and his men safely into the hands of the aforementioned Richard, brother of the Lord Pope. Thus, miraculously, contrary to everyone's opinion, they seized the impregnable fortress along with a large supply of foodstuffs and arms. They led Conrad and his men captive to Ceprano, so that they might bring about the surrender of the Rocca Arcis, which was held by Conrad's cousin, Hugo. Although he could not be brought to surrender it by threats or persuasion, so that the matter could be settled without injuries or bloodshed, they obtained it peacefully, especially because of the pope's honesty, with promises and the gift of a thousand ounces of gold and twenty horses, as well as freedom for the captives. When the King of Sicily heard this news with wonder and joy, he granted the city of Sora and the Rocca of Sorella, the Castrum Arcis and its Rocca, Broccum and Pesclum-Solidum, all of which were seized from Conrad, to Richard, the brother of the Lord Pope and his heirs in perpetuity by a privilege, appointing him as count, and causing him to be invested with the county by a royal banner which he solemnly sent to him.

XL. The chancellor remained with the king in the city of Palermo. In whatever ways he could he strove to take the palace from William Capparone. When he failed in this, he often sent royal letters and messengers throughout the kingdom in search of support, but almost no one was willing to aid him. When a long dispute broke out between William Capparone and his allies on one side and the chancellor and his supporters on the other, the Saracens of Sicily, who had taken refuge in the mountains, saw their chance and not only withdrew their obedience almost completely from the king, but also came down some distance from the hills and attacked the Christians in various ways. They seized the *castrum* of Corleone and considered how to do worse. The Lord Pope prudently weighed the miserable state of the Kingdom of Sicily. Although his regency was nearly ended, still he took up the task and came down into the kingdom. He called together the counts, barons, and principal men of the cities at San Germano, near the holy monastery of Cassino, and persuaded them to take oaths and provide pledges that they would receive his ordinances on peace and the defense of the kingdom in good faith and would, if they could, bring about its observance. The ordinance he enacted was as follows: namely, that for the support and aid of the king and the peace and defense of the kingdom, they would obey Master Captains that he appointed for this purpose; that whoever received this ordinance should observe peace with one another. If anyone was injured by another, he should not immediately respond to his attack but should submit the quarrel to the Master Captains to bring about a solution according to reason and the custom of the kingdom.[65] Anyone unwilling to accept or keep this ordinance should be considered a public enemy, and should be attacked by the rest. Two hundred knights should be sent to support and assist the king until September 1, to serve for a year at the expense of those by whom they were sent. Moreover, they should be chosen according to the judgment of estimators appointed especially for this task, taking into consideration the services owed and different capabilities of the counts and barons, as well as of the cities. Arrangements also should be made for foodstuffs to be sent to meet their need. The cities, counts, and barons should assign at their own expense a certain number of fighters under the command of the captains should there be war with anyone on account of this. Moreover, the pope will retain in all matters the full power of increasing or decreasing, changing and declaring, as will seem expedient.

He wrote concerning this matter to all the counts, barons, and others loyal subjects of the kingdom in this manner:

Although we have shown the results of the love and favor we have for the king and Kingdom of Sicily quite often in many ways, now, however, we have demonstrated it more clearly and expressly as a result of our work,

---

65. The parallel between this passage and Constitution I, 8 of the Constitutions of Melfi *(Liber Augustalis)* seems not to have been previously noted. See Wolfgang Stürner, *Die Konstitutionen Friedrichs II für das Königreich Sizilien*, MGH, Leges 5 (Hannover: Hahnsche Buchhandlung, 1996), 158–59; and Hermann Dilcher, *Die sizilische Gesetzgebung Kaiser Friedrichs II: Quellen der Konstitutionen von Melfi and ihrer Novellen* (Cologne: Böhlau Verlag, 1975), 91–95. See also James M. Powell, *The Liber Augustalis or Constitutions of Melfi Promulgated by the Emperor Frederick II for the Kingdom of Sicily in 1231* (Syracuse, N.Y.: Syracuse University Press, 1971), 14, for an English translation.

since, on account of the urgent necessity in the kingdom, we have come down in person, having set aside for the most part the rest of the world's business for this one matter only in order, namely, to reform it in peace and justice. By the grace of God, a good beginning has been made and we intend to make further progress in order to reach the best end. Wherefore, we admonish and exhort and command Your Devotion in the Lord by Apostolic letters that just as you hold the Divine, Apostolic, and Royal favor dear, you should receive joyfully and observe effectively the ordinance which we have made on assistance and support of the king, the defense and peace of the kingdom, according to the example of the other counts, barons, and also the cities. Just as this ordinance is expressly contained in the capitulary, sealed with our bull, you should obey the Master Captains, who have been appointed for its execution by our command. If, God forbid, someone should presume to break it, let him incur the penalty established in the ordinance itself, and we will add the weight of our hands against him both spiritually and temporally. Because we cannot, on account of the heat of the summer, personally go to Apulia at present, we have appointed vicars to carry out this business in the persons of our beloved son, Gregory, cardinal deacon of St. Theodore, legate of the Apostolic See, and we have ordered our beloved son, O.,[66] our acolyte, whom we have sent from our personal retinue to join him.

[Spiritual Concerns]

XLI. Although we have digressed here into Innocent's conduct of temporal affairs, we return to the beginning of his pontificate, in order to pursue his spiritual activities.[67] Thus, among all the pestilences, he hated venality the most, and he pondered how he could extirpate it from the Roman Church. He immediately, therefore, made an edict

66. Potthast, *Regesta Pontificum Romanorum*, 1:301 (3488), August 16, 1208. Gregory of G(u)algano was named cardinal deacon of St. Theodore in 1206. See Maleczek, *Papst und Kardinalskolleg von 1191 bis 1216*, 151–53. O., the acolyte of the pope, is not otherwise identified.

67. Here again the author draws a contrast between Innocent's temporal and spiritual concerns, suggesting how much this issue weighed on the members of the papal curia.

that no official of his curia, save for scribes and those who sealed bulls, should exact anything. For them he established a fixed fee and ordered strictly that each individual should exercise his office free of charge, that he should receive graciously anything that anyone freely gave him. He therefore ordered the doorkeepers removed from the chambers of the notaries so that there would be free access to them. Moreover, within the sacred Lateran Palace, there was a money changers' table in the passage near the cistern of the kitchen on which daily were placed gold and silver vessels, a diversity of moneys, and many treasures for sale or purchase. The pope himself, burning with zeal, turned over the tables of the money changers and ordered them removed completely from the palace [Mt 21:12–13]. Three times each week he publicly celebrated a solemn consistory—this practice had fallen into disuse until now—and in it he listened to the complaints of individuals, examined minor cases through others, but heard major cases himself so subtly and prudently that everyone admired his cleverness and prudence. Many quite learned men and legal experts frequented the Roman Church simply to hear him. They learned more in his consistories than they had learned in the schools, especially when they listened to the opinions he promulgated, because he made allegations in such subtle and efficacious ways that each party hoped to win, because each heard him supporting his case, and no lawyer so expert appeared before him who was not very much afraid of his opposing statements.[68] Moreover, he was so just in deciding cases that he never received appeals, never turned from the royal road, and he handed down decisions with much maturity after due deliberation.

XLII. For this reason, so many and such important cases began to be brought for his hearing from the whole world that he decided a larger number of cases in his time than had ever earlier been decided

---

68. The author's appreciation of Innocent's legal skill suggests his own legal background. See James M. Powell, "Innocent III and Petrus Beneventanus: Reconstructing a Career at the Papal Curia," in *Pope Innocent III and His World*, ed. John C. Moore (Aldershot: Ashgate, 1999), 51–62.

in the Roman church. For right after his accession, the Archbishops of Compostella and Barcelona came into his presence on behalf of cases involving them regarding seven bishoprics, namely: Coimbra, Lamego, Vizeu, Guarda, Lisbon, Evora, and Zamora. Although these cases were perplexing and difficult so that large books might have been written about them, and their merits could hardly be made plain, by his oppositions and inquisitions, he finally made what was hidden so clear and decided these matters so prudently and subtly that everyone commended his outstanding intelligence. At the same time, he so prudently examined that old but still unsettled quarrel which concerned the metropolitan dignity over the whole of Brittany between the churches of Tours and Dols, and so subtly decided it that even though it had been decided quite often by his predecessors, still it had never yet achieved a final solution save through his effort. Also he settled, though not without considerable difficulty, the litigation between the Archbishop and the Chapter of Canterbury which had broken out over the church of Lambeth, which the Archbishop, despite the opposition of the chapter, had ordered to be built and endowed with large and numerous rents, establishing secular canons there, noblemen, potent and literate.[69] For the king and the archbishop supported one another in the decision. But the chapter had no supporter, after God, save the Roman pontiff, asserting constantly, that unless he should order that church to be completely demolished, the metropolitan dignity would be for the most part transferred there. But when the Lord Pope heard sufficiently the reasons advanced by the parties, he decreed by the apostolic authority that the Archbishop should destroy the said church at his own expense, completely revoking in anger all that had been done about it. When the Archbishop refused to carry it out, claiming that the king would not allow it to be done, he, with burning zeal, ordered the archbishop strictly by virtue

69. Christopher R. Cheney, *Innocent III and England* (Stuttgart: Hiersemann, 1976), 208–20.

of obedience that he should put it off no longer. Otherwise, he should understand that he would be suspended from his episcopal office and his suffragans would be withdrawn from his obedience. So, despite the efforts and complaints of the king and archbishop, what he ordered was fully carried out.

Also, in a wonderful manner, he brought to an end a controversy between the Archbishop of Milan and the Abbot of Scozula, in the matter of the district and jurisdiction over it and its castellany and the men of Baveno, Gralia, Capurneto, Vesterpeno, Cadempleno, Insula Superiore, Bolgerate, and Lisia. For after a lengthy and profound litigation on all these matters before different judges delegate, and after witnesses and instruments were produced, and the instruments were held to be suspect because, although the wax of the seal from the inner side was very old, the wax which was put on the external side, as if for the conservation of the seal, was recent and soft. In this way, he detected the forgery and he ordered the seals broken in the presence of the parties with their attorneys, the cardinals, and in sight of all. If they were found to be genuine and incorrupt, he would order the instruments to be renewed under the witness of his own seal. But if they were found to be forged or false, he was unwilling that falsity should prevail over truth. And when this had been done, it was found to be certainly true, namely, that under the old seal, the charter was perforated, and through a connector of new wax which had been put outside as if for the conservation of the seal, it was badly joined to the charter itself, and so, with the discovery of this forgery, he published his decision against the monastery, to the admiration of all that he had in such a wonderful way discovered the defect of forgery. Who indeed might have the ability to list the countless number of questions that he decided between different churches and persons upon diverse and doubtful matters, always walking on the royal road, never deviating to right or left, neither making exceptions for persons nor taking gifts?

XLIII. When the Archbishop of Tours presumed to transfer and to consecrate a certain individual who was elected as bishop of Avranches, and who had already administered both the spiritual and temporal affairs of that diocese for some time, to the church of Angers, and later confirmed him by his metropolitan authority, contrary to the authority of the Apostolic See, and the Archbishop of Rouen later freed him from that church, contrary to the mandate of the Apostolic See, and gave him permission to pass over to the other, the very prudent pope, giving heed that this matter had been undertaken to the loss of the Apostolic dignity, which alone was competent to translate bishops, suspended both the archbishops from the confirmation as well as the consecration of bishops and the elect himself from the exercise of the episcopal office, demonstrating both by authorities and by rational arguments that the same law governs the confirmation of bishops-elect as well as consecrated bishops.

For the same reason, he suspended the Patriarch of Antioch from episcopal office, namely: because he dared to tranfer the Elect of Pamiers to be Bishop of Tripoli without the license of the Apostolic See. But when both humbly confessed their ignorance and sought his permission with supplication, he relented and absolved them without delay and difficulty.

XLIV. In a similar case, he also excommunicated Conrad, Bishop of Hildesheim, the Chancellor of the Imperial Court, a man noble, rich and powerful, intelligent, industrious, and clever, because he rashly presumed to transfer to the church of Würzburg, and, after he was admonished, he refused to correct his error, claiming that he had an indult from Pope Celestine to himself that, if invited, he could take on a higher office. But this privilege could not excuse him, since the church of Würzburg, though richer, was not greater in dignity than that of Hildesheim, and it is a greater permission for someone to transfer to an equal rather than for him to ascend to a higher office. And so, when he refused, after a warning, the pope ordered him to resign both churches, because it is provided in the canons that he who transferred to a larger community had to be removed from the other diocese and deprived of his own, so that he should not preside over those whom he despised through pride or those he coveted through greed. Finally he ordered him to be excommunicated and the excommunication published throughout the whole province.

Since everyone avoided him, he tried many times through honorable mediators to see if he could persuade the pope to favor him, using the influence of princes and offering gifts, and since this did not profit him in any way, he finally recognized his own excess. He took an oath first before the Archbishop of Magdeburg and many of the princes and secondly before the Archbishop of Mainz, that he would obey the commands of the Apostolic See. Then, neither avoiding the dangers of the roads, nor the unsettled conditions of the time, he approached the Apostolic See with deep contrition of heart and great humility of body, imploring the benefit of absolution. When he had repeated the oath, he was absolved. Without shoes and *pallium,* with his shoelaces on his neck, he presented himself in the sight of the Pope and throwing himself completely on the ground in the shape of a cross, he raised his hands with great weeping, asking forgiveness and confessing his sin. The heart of the Pope was moved in his behalf, but he would not loose the bindings of ecclesiastical discipline. After considerable deliberation in a large consistory, he ordered him, under the obligation of the oath he had sworn, to resign completely both the church of Hildesheim and that of Würzburg. Although the bishop was confused, he humbly obeyed, making a virtue of necessity, and sent certain gifts to the Pope, namely, beautiful silver vases. The Pope hesitated for a short while whether to take or refuse them. But, so that the bishop would not despair completely of his favor, he accepted the offerings, and so that he would not think that he could be corrupted by the giving of gifts, he sent him by an honorable representative a precious golden cup, of greater value than all those silver vases. Moreover, wishing to pour oil over wine, although he commanded that the church of Hildesheim should provide by a canonical election a suitable bishop for itself, he ordered the ordination to the church of Würzburg to be postponed so that if perhaps the church again asked for him who had been humbled, he would raise up the one rejected, and so after a year, it came to pass as he had foreseen [Ps 119: 22; 1 Pt:2:7].

XLV. But so that he might not deny judgment to any party, he reached a similar decision in the case of the Archbishop of Salzburg, who, as bishop of Brixen, was elected Archbishop of Salzburg, and presumed to transfer to the metropolitan church without the permission of the Supreme Pontiff. He completely quashed his election and ordered him to leave his second church and to return to the first, annulling whatever he had done there. For this reason, he removed the elect of Gorizia from the bishopric of Gorizia, since he had had himself appointed there. But he, terrified by the example of the other, obeyed humbly. When he was later elected, he did not presume to accept the election, but approached the Apostolic See together with his electors, to obtain the favor of a dispensation. So, he learned by experience that both the rod and the manna are contained in the Ark of the Covenant [Nm 17:25–26].

XLVI. Of all these things, he hoped most fervently to aid and recover the Holy Land, considering carefully how he could effectively fulfill this desire. Because some said that by delaying action the Roman Church was imposing serious and insupportable burdens on others and, moreover, she was not willing to raise a finger for it, he chose two of his brethren, namely, Soffredus, cardinal priest of Santa Prassede, and Peter, cardinal deacon of Santa Maria in Via Lata, on whom he imposed the sign of the cross, so that by word and example they might invite others to the service of the cross.[70] He also ordered that all clerics in major and minor orders should pay one-fortieth of

70. Soffredus had been cardinal deacon of Santa Maria in Via Lata from 1182 to 1193, when he was promoted to cardinal priest of Santa Prassede. He became one of the most important legates of the pope in the East during the Fourth Crusade along with Peter Capuanus, an Amalfitan, who was promoted by Innocent to cardinal priest of St. Marcellus in 1200. See Maleczek, *Papst und Kardinalskolleg von 1191 bis 1216*, 73–80, 117–24. Maleczek has devoted a full study to Peter. See Werner Maleczek, *Pietro Capuano, patrizio Amalfitano, cardinale, legato alla quarta crociata, teologo (1214)* (Amalfi: Centro di cultura e storia amalfitana, 1997).

their ecclesiastical incomes in support of the Holy Land. The cardinals, moreover, should pay a tenth part of their incomes. And so what he decreed was done. He ordered a new ship built, on which he spent a thousand three hundred pounds of his own for armaments. He ordered it to be loaded with grain, vegetables, bread, and meat. He also ordered everything to be distributed for needs of the Holy Land by two brothers, one a Templar, the other a Hospitaller, and a third, a monk. But when they set out, they were forced to land at Messina, where they had to remain for a considerable time on account of the turbulence of the sea. Moreover, seeing the grain spoil, and that it was selling for more in Sicily than in Syria, they took careful counsel and sold the grain in Messina and with the difference in the price they divided the whole amount into three shares and assigned one for the repair of the walls of Tyre, which had been ruined by an earthquake, another for the use of the poor, and the third for the salaries of fighters. He ordered the ship to be given to the Templars as a suitable subvention.

He therefore sent Cardinal Soffredus to the Doge and people of Venice, and at his exhortation, the Doge and many of the people received the sign of the cross.[71] Also, the Marquis of Montferrat, the Bishop of Cremona, the Abbot of Lucedio, and many other nobles from the province of Lombardy, along with a countless multitude of people, vowed to serve the Crucified.[72] The more fully and freely to put this into action, he sent two other cardinals, namely, Peter, cardinal priest of the title of Santa Cecilia, and Gratian, cardinal deacon of

71. The loss of Innocent's registers for the third and fourth years of his pontificate makes it difficult to trace this event in detail. We should note, however, that Soffredus's mission took place after the crusaders were gathered in Venice. Moreover, it is grouped with other events, which suggests that the *Gesta* was not dealing with these issues chronologically but topically.

72. Boniface of Montferrat was the leader of the Frankish contingent in the Fourth Crusade following the death of Theobald III of Champagne. Sicard of Cremona was the author of an important chronicle and a legate to Constantinople. Peter Magnano, abbot of Lucedio, was one of Innocent's most trusted agents in the East.

Saints Cosmas and Damian, to Pisa and Genoa to negotiate a treaty of peace between the Pisans and Genoese to support the Holy Land.[73] But because they were not sons of peace, they would not receive the word of peace. He therefore granted a general indulgence to all the crusaders for the remission of their sins and received them with all their goods under Apostolic protection.

XLVII. He sent the cardinal deacon, Peter,[74] whom he afterward promoted to be cardinal priest of St. Marcellus, to the Gauls, ordering and enjoining three things on him, namely: to exhort and persuade the people to aid the Holy Land, to negotiate and conclude treaties between the kings of the Franks and the English, and to admonish and compel, if necessary, the King of the Franks to leave his false wife, and receive his own wife, whom he had unjustly deserted.

The Cardinal set out, in fact, and succeeded, with Divine favor, in the first task, because a countless number both of knights and infantry took the sign of the cross to aid the Crucified on his exhortation. And with them, many bishops and abbots, as well as many other clerics, resolved on the pilgrimage. Among these, the most important were: Theobald, Count of Troyes, Louis, Count of Blois, Baldwin, Count of Flanders and Hainault, the Count of St. Pol, the bishops of Soissons and Troyes, and certain abbots of the Cistercian Order.

With regard to the second task, also, the legate was so successful that Philip, King of France, putting his trust in his hands, promised at his command to enter into peace or truces with the King of England. But Richard, the King of England, raised difficulties. When, however, the legate began to threaten ecclesiastical penalties, he was persuaded by sounder counsel, and agreed. He negotiated a five-year truce be-

73. Peter Dianus was promoted to cardinal priest of Santa Cecilia in 1188 and died in 1206. He had considerable experience in negotiations with Genoa and Pisa and elsewhere in northern Italy. See Maleczek, *Papst und Kardinalskolleg von 1191 bis 1216*, 85–88. Gratian was named cardinal deacon of SS. Cosmas and Damian in 1178. He was a nephew of Pope Eugenius III and came from Pisa. He had worked with Peter in negotiations with Henry VI.
74. This refers to Peter Capuanus rather than to Peter Dianus.

tween the kings, ordering certain castles, which each held firmly against the other, to be demolished.

XLVIII. With regard to the third task, however, it should be noted for better understanding that, after the death of the first wife of Philip, King of the Franks, who had been the daughter of Baldwin, Count of Hannegau, and the niece of Philip, Count of Flanders, who bore him an only son named Louis, the king agreed with Canute, the King of the Danes, that he would marry Canute's sister, Ingeborg. He sent Stephen, Bishop of Noyons, with the royal insignia to bring her and the king awaited her with much anticipation. When sufficient and suitable securites had been given concerning the marriage, her brother sent her with Peter, Bishop of Roskilde, together with a suitable escort. When they had crossed the sea and arrived at Amiens, where the King of France, impatient of delay, awaited their coming, he married her on the same day, and on the next day, he ordered that she should be solemnly crowned before the gathered princes, both ecclesiastical and lay, by William, Archbishop of Reims. But, at the suggestion of the devil, during the very solemnities of coronation, he began violently to abhor, tremble, and pale at her sight, so that, deeply disturbed, he could hardly remain to the end of the solemn undertaking. Immediately, the word divorce was raised, on the grounds of the impediment of affinity, which some said existed between them, saying his second wife was related to his first wife in the fourth or fifth degree of consanguinity. But others asserted it could not be done immediately without a scandal; it must be delayed for awhile. Meanwhile, some suggested to the King that he should try to change his attitude and consummate the marriage. Therefore, the king went to her at Fossé near Paris, where he had ordered her to be taken, and, when he had entered the marriage bed, he quickly left her, conceiving such hatred for her that he could scarcely bear the mention of her in his presence. But the Queen asserted that the King had consummated the marriage. The King, however, maintained that he was unable to consummate the marriage.

XLIX. When the Archbishop of Reims, the legate of the Apostolic See in his province, and several other bishops met, the marriage was tried before them, though the queen herself was totally ignorant of the proceedings. Like one left on her own after her compatriots had left, she was totally ignorant of the French tongue. The question of affinity was intemperately sworn to by certain witnesses and the Archbishop next pronounced the sentence of divorce. When this was explained to the Queen through a certain interpreter, she, more astonished than she could express, wept and lamented and cried out: "Evil France! Evil France!" and she added: "Rome! Rome!." For she did not know how otherwise to protest in French or to appeal the sentence to the Apostolic See. The King, therefore, immediately sent her out of the Kingdom of the Franks, and ordered her confined in a certain convent of nuns outside the kingdom.

L. Many, in fact almost all who feared God and loved justice, were disturbed at this wicked decision. The report, or rather the evil rumor of this fact, came to Celestine, who was then pope. When he learned the truth more fully and certainly from Master Melior, cardinal priest of SS. John and Paul, who returned from France, because the deed was so notorious that it could not be concealed by subterfuge, the Apostolic authority rejected that sentence of divorce, which had been decided without proper procedure and in haste against an ignorant and undefended woman.[75] By his messengers, he forbade the king to enter into another union.

But the more the pope appeared committed in this matter at the beginning, the more lukewarm he was found at the end. Although the King of the Danes, the brother of the queen from the same parents, implored him through honorable messengers to force the King of the Franks to take back his sister, whom he had unjustly dismissed, as queen, as the reason of law required, still he could not obtain this

75. Melior, cardinal priest of SS. John and Paul, died in 1197. See Maleczek, *Papst und Kardinalskolleg von 1191 bis 1216*, 83–85.

from him. Indeed, following his prohibition, he even tolerated the fact that the king married and and kept, not without great scandal, the daughter of the Duke of Meran, who was very beautiful.[76]

LI. But as soon as Innocent succeeded Celestine, he immediately undertook by letter and through the Bishop of Paris to warn the king to separate from her whom he had taken in marriage contrary to the prohibition of the church and to take back into conjugal favor her from whom, after a legitimate marriage, he had separated. The pope provided that, after her restitution, he would not deny the king the right and permission for a hearing, if he should make such a proposal. He also assured him that, to the extent that his action might trouble the king in any way, he would be troubling himself every bit as much. Since he was yet obliged to defer more to the heavenly than to an earthly king, he would proceed without any distinction of persons just as reason required. But, because the same king, despite frequent warnings, was unwilling to obey, he ordered his legate by Apostolic letters that, if perhaps this hardship would bring him to an understanding, having removed the right of appeal, he might subject the whole land to ecclesiastical interdict so that no divine office would be celebrated there save the baptism of children and penance for the dying.

When the archbishops, abbots, and many others had gathered, therefore, for a council in Dijon, the king, sensing beforehand that the legate would desire to proceed against him, ordered through his messengers the case to be appealed to the Apostolic See. But the legate, in order not to avoid the appeal, but to delay temporarily so that he might more conveniently fulfill the Apostolic mandate, after he summoned many archbishops to Vienne, among whom some present were from the Kingdom of the Franks, finally promulgated the sentence of interdict. He ordered by his letters, into which he introduced

76. Agnes of Meran was the daughter of Berthold, duke of Meran. She died in 1201 and her children by Philip were legitimated by the pope in the same year. See *Dictionnaire de Biographie Française* (Paris: Latouzey, 1933–), 1:753–54.

the content of the Apostolic letters, all prelates of churches in the territory of the king of France to observe it and to order that his letters be obeyed. But if perhaps some of the bishops should dare to act contrary to it, they should understand that they were suspended from episcopal office. He also prohibited others, of whatever rank or order, to exercise their offices and benefices. Moreover, he called on all to respond at the Feast of the Ascension, then nearly arrived, concerning disobedience to the Apostolic See.

LII. Therefore, after his letters were received, some began to obey on hearing, like the canons of Sens, the bishops of Paris, of Senlis, Soissons, Amiens, Arras, and some others. They firmly observed the sentence of interdict. But others put off observance of the sentence, like the Archbishop of Reims, the bishops of Laon, of Noyon, of Auxerre, of Beauvais, of Thérouanne, of Meaux, of Chartres, of Orleans, and a few others. They sent messengers to the Apostolic See and gave various excuses, although these were frivolous. But they promised that, if this matter were explained to them, and if it was pleasing to the Supreme Pontiff, they would observe the sentence. When the Supreme Pontiff rejected their excuses with very clear reasons, he ordered them also to obey the sentence of interdict. When they heard this command, they humbly obeyed, and thus the whole territory of the king of the Franks was brought under the strictest interdict, so that with the churches closed, no one could bury the bodies of the dead in cemeteries, but they remained everywhere unburied above ground.

LIII. The king, however, burned with such indignation that he at first ordered the bishops and other clerics who observed the interdict to be violently expelled from their churches and all their goods seized. But when all the people complained, the king could not withstand the rigor of ecclesiastical severity and he sent as messengers to the Supreme Pontiff certain clerics and knights, complaining over and over about the legate, but still offering through his messengers to swear to submit to the judgment of the legates or judges delegate. The most prudent pope responded that there must be a distinction as to whether the king was willing to submit to a judgment already made or to a judgment still to be made. If it was in accordance with the judgment already made, namely, that he would remove the second woman from his marriage bed and accept the aforementioned queen, he would willingly receive his oath. Indeed, no oath would be necessary. If he did this, he would relax the sentence of interdict, as long as the bishops and clergy who had earlier been despoiled received full restitution. But if he meant a future judgment, namely, that the pope would decide the question of affinity according to the law, he would receive the oath offered as long as, once the woman was removed, he would first take the queen back.

But when the king heard this through his messenger, he began to be anxious because he did not want to take her back since he hated her vehemently, and he especially did not want to lose the one he had embraced. But, when some of the princes, both ecclesiastical and lay, met, he began to deliberate with them what should be done in this matter. They responded unanimously that the mandates of the Apostolic See must be obeyed. He asked his uncle, the Archbishop of Reims, who had promulgated the sentence of divorce, whether what the Pope had written to him was true, namely, that the sentence of divorce was not valid, but should be labeled the illusion of a drunkard. When he responded that what the Supreme Pontiff had written was true, the king immediately drew the conclusion, "Therefore, you are foolish and fatuous to have issued such a sentence."

LIV. When, therefore, the messengers left, he insisted, as before, that, after the interdict was relaxed, he should be recognized at law. But, when he could not influence the mind of the Supreme Pontiff, which was founded on justice, by threats, or petitions, or promises, he submitted to his will. The pope sent Octavian, Bishop of Ostia, as legate to France, fixing for him such an approach that before all, he should order full satisfaction for the losses and injuries inflicted on clerics and churches so that those who were oppressed by serious attacks and losses on account of their obedience and reverence of the Apostolic See, might understand for themselves and rejoice that they had received adequate satisfaction through the Apostolic See. Then he should order that the woman who had been introduced to the companionship of the king should be removed both carnally and from his company, that he should order her to be excluded not merely from the royal embrace but also from the boundaries of the kingdom, and that the aforementioned queen should be solemnly taken back by the king himself and treated royally, with a publicly expressed oath of security that he would not send her away without the judgment of the church. Then he might relax the sentence of interdict, reserving to the pope himself the correction of those who had not observed the interdict from the beginning. If, after frequent and diligent warnings and exhortations, the king was not willing to keep the aforesaid queen as his legitimate wife, but preferred to find fault with the marriage, he ordered the legate to fix a period of six months as the peremptory limit for completing the case, within which, if the queen wished, her brother, the king of the Danes, might be advised to send prudent men for her defense, with lawyers and witnesses, and whoever else might be needed, under both Apostolic and Royal security, to a competent place chosen by the free will of both parties. With the agreement of the parties, he associated John, cardinal priest of Santa Prisca, with the Bishop of Ostia to examine and defend the case, enjoining him, with the assistance of religious, literate, and prudent men to take care to examine the case sufficiently, diligently, and patiently, holding themselves such wise in words and deeds and other circumstances that no suspicion could arise about them.[77] In observance of the law in everything, they should bring the case to a conclusion justly providing security and liberty to the queen in all matters.

The Bishop of Ostia set out to the King of the Franks in accord with

77. John of St. Paul, cardinal priest of St. Prisca from 1193 to 1205, when he was promoted to cardinal bishop of Sabina. See Maleczek, *Papst und Kardinalskolleg von 1191 bis 1216*, 114–17.

this approach and was received honorably and devotedly both by him and his magnates. First he commanded that satisfaction should be made in a fitting way to ecclesiastics for their losses and injuries, and that the queen should be brought from the place where she was to a certain royal castle, where, in the presence of the archbishops, bishops, the king, and magnates of the kingdom, together with a great multitude of clergy and people, the king, at the legate's command, received the queen, ordering an oath to be sworn on his soul that he would treat her honorably as queen and would not dismiss her without the judgment of the church. And so the legate relaxed the sentence of interdict, which had lasted for eight months, with much joy and applause.

But some criticized him because he neglected the form of the Apostolic mandate and proceeded in some superficial matters; although he separated the woman from the embraces of the king, he did not exclude her from the boundaries of the kingdom because she was pregnant and about to give birth. But the Lord himself gave judgment in the case, because after she gave birth, she became seriously ill and died.

LV. Since the king, therefore, could not be persuaded to treat the queen with marital affection, certain days and a certain place were appointed for the case at Soissons, in which the parties and both legates before whom the case began to be tried were present. Although the king had many and better lawyers, still the queen did not lack an intrepid spokesman, for the sake of God.[78] But the king realized that, when the proceeding had gone on for several days, he would profit little, and he departed in anger, unwilling to urge his case further before these legates. But, even if the Supreme Pontiff was not able to persuade the king to love the queen, he still never ceased now with soft, now with sharp, words to work on him so that he would arrange

---

78. It is interesting to speculate that this might be a veiled reference to the author of the *Gesta*.

for her to be honored in a royal manner, often sending her letters of consolation and comfort, and sending his messengers to visit her, he left no stones unturned, even if it was rather displeasing to the king. For the queen complained that she was incarcerated rather than restored, since, even if the king made provision for her with food and clothing, he still kept her under close guard in a palace at Étampes, which she was not permitted to leave and only rarely was anyone allowed to visit her, and so she remained completely destitute of solace.

LVI. In the meantime, since the archbishopric of Sens was vacant, the bishop of Autun was unanimously elected by the chapter with the consent of the king. Honorable and solemn messengers were sent to obtain permission for his translation and to ask for the *pallium*. But, the Supreme Pontiff, prudently noting that the Bishop of Autun was one of those who had not observed the interdict from the beginning, and the church of Sens had observed it from the beginning, in order to distinguish between the obedient and the devoted, forbade the postulation in public consistory, since, according to Divine Law, one ought not to yoke an ox and ass together to plow and no one should wear a garment woven with both wool and linen [Dt 22:11]. For this reason, someone next exclaimed: "The Bishop of Autun never acquired as much by singing well as he now lost by singing badly" to all those praising God. He appointed Master Peter of Corbeil, who was his teacher in Sacred Scripture at Paris, and whom he had earlier promoted to be Bishop of Cambrai.

LVII. But because the Supreme Pontiff had reserved the correction of those who did not observe the interdict from the beginning to himself, and they had incurred the sentence of suspension, which the legate issued against those who did not observe the sentence, they were compelled to present their cases in person at the Apostolic See. Therefore, the Archbishop of Reims came, as well as the bishops of Chartres, Orleans, Meaux, Autun, Noyons, and Beauvais, and the procurators of those who because of age or illness were unable to come. Likewise, also, certain abbots came. And those who could not come sent suitable procurators. Moreover, he received an oath publicly from all of them that they would obey the Apostolic See both on their nonobservance of the interdict and the sentence of suspension. And so he absolved them from the penalty of suspension, but he delayed the making of a mandate for security.

LVIII. At that time, a detestable incest had been committed in both the East and the West. For, in the East, one woman was joined incestuously to two men. But in the West, one man dared to join himself to two women through incest. With regard to the incest committed in the East, not only a consensus, but also the authority of the clergy dwelling there, intervened. But, as for the detestable union contracted in the West, even though it had been attempted not perhaps without the consent of certain ecclesiastics, still ecclesiastical authority in no wise intervened. Moreover, God, who desired to avenge the greater sin more quickly, and to deter others from similar acts, killed by the sword both Conrad, Marquis of Montferrat, who earlier had entered into an incestuous relationship with the Queen of Jerusalem, and Henry, Count of Champagne, who succeeded him to some extent both in the sin and in the punishment, and cast both down from the precipice and destroyed them by an unforeseen death. But he has not yet punished the authors of this kind of evil in the West. But the longer he holds off, perhaps the more severe will be his vengeance. Moreover, although the Apostolic See may have seemed to have hidden what happened in the East in this matter because of the malice of the times and the urgent persecution, still to avenge what had been tried in the West, it used the rigor of canonical enforcement. For, when it was learned that the King of Leon had dared to enter an incestuous union with his niece, the daughter of the King of Portugal, the pope excommunicated both the King of Portugal and those who were joined in the incestuous union, and he put both the kingdoms of Leon and Portugal under the sentence of interdict. Wherefore, what had been done illegitimately was completely revoked. True enough, the said King of Leon, reached for even worse things, just like him of whom Sacred Scripture says: "Woe to that man, who drags sin after himself like a long net" [Is 5:18]. "He condemned the impious man when he came into the depth of vices" [Prv 18:3]. He impudently dared to enter into a union with the daughter of the King of Castile, his nephew, namely, his own niece. When this came to the notice of the Supreme Pontiff, he immediately sent Brother Rainier, a man revered equally in knowledge and religion, accepted by God and men in the spreading of knowledge and religion, to Spain so that, according to the word of the prophets, he might dissolve the bonds of impiety and loosen oppressive burdens. And by the grace of God, he refrained from taking any gifts, so that, as it is read, it can truly be said of him: "He was not one who enriched Abraham" [Gn 14:23]. When Brother Rainier arrived in Spain, he diligently warned the King of Leon again and again on behalf of the Supreme Pontiff that he should withdraw from such a detestable and evil union, dissolving all the agreements reached for consummating that union. But since no warnings had helped with him, he assigned a definite day and place for him, and when he had awaited him even beyond that limit, he promulgated the sentence of excommunication against him according to the form of the Apostolic mandate for being contumaciously absent and he bound the Kingdom of Leon with a general interdict. He did not proceed against the King of Castile and his land, since that king answered his mandates and proposed freely that he would take back his daughter, if she was returned to him. Also, he obligated himself by letters to be sent to the Supreme Pontiff. Afterward, the Archbishop of Toledo and the Bishop of Palentia, representing the King of Castile, and the Bishop of Zamora, representing the King of Leon, approached the Apostolic See and sought a dispensation from the Lord Pope for a union of this kind between the King of Leon and the daughter of the King of Castile. On account of this, if that special favor the Lord Pope had for the devotion of the King of Castile had not tempered his attitude, he would have been sure to apply ecclesiastical severity in his case in such a way that no one else during his reign would bring such oft repudiated and condemned petitions. But, finally when the archbishop and bishops understood that they could not only not obtain a license in this matter from the Supreme Pontiff, but could hardly even seek an audience to ask him to raise the interdict he had promulgated in the land of the King of Leon, they asserted that as a result of it, a threefold danger threatened the whole kingdom, namely, from heretics, Saracens, and Christians. From heretics, because, the mouths of pastors in those parts had been closed by the interdict, the faithful could not be instructed by them against the heretics and informed to some degree how to resist them. For this reason, then, and because the King of Leon, asserting that he was oppressed by the Roman church, was hardly resisting them at all, the heretics were gaining strength against the faithful and various heresies were breaking out in the kingdom. From the Saracens, because, since the people of Spain were usually persuaded by the exhortations and the remissions of sins offered by the Church to fight the pagans, with the cessation of the office of preaching, the devotion of the people also grew tepid. Because, as long as the people saw themselves subject to the same punishment as their prince with regard to the interdict or from a fault to which they had consented by silence, they perhaps did not believe themselves immune and for this reason were less fervent concerning the war against the Saracens lest they fall into sin. From Catholics, because, since the clergy could not minister to the spiritual needs of the laity, the laity withdrew temporal support from the clergy: keeping the offerings, first fruits, and tithes. For this reason, since the clergy were accustomed to live for the most part from these in those lands, they were forced not merely to beg, but to favor and assist the Jews to the opprobrium of the church and all Christianity. It seemed, however, difficult for the Lord Pope to accede to their petition and to relax the sentence, which was canonically issued according to mind, order, and cause, without suitable satisfaction. From the mind, because, just as God showed the witness of his conscience, he had not proceeded in this matter without a concern for justice and honesty since a presumption might arise from those opposed against the Lord Pope himself, if he allowed such a detestable deed to be tolerated. From order, because the said Brother Rainier, after legitimate warnings and postponements, finally struck down the contumacious man with an ecclesiastical stricture; from cause, namely by Divine and human example, Divine because, when David had sinned against a multitude of the people, the Lord poured forth sheaves of his anger against the people. For this reason, we read that David confessed his sin to the Lord: "I am the one who has sinned, I am the one who has acted evilly. What did they, who are the sheep, do? Turn your anger, I beg, from your people" [2 Sm 24:17]. From human, because the example was evil; namely, that, if perhaps in some kingdoms it should happen that the Lord Pope promulgated a similar sentence, favor would be sought from him in similar matters. And if perhaps he should deny it, he would seem to making an exception of persons. From this also a suspicion would arise with some concerning the Supreme Pontiff himself, with some presuming that he was influenced in this matter by concealed factors. Although, therefore, it would not seem that this petition should be granted for these reasons, still, because where the multitude is affected, there must be a lessening of severity so that a sincere charity might come to heal greater evils, in this matter he decided in favor of the petition of the archbishop and bishops according to the common counsel of his brethren, from which the impediments set forth might seem to have a better result. Therefore, the Supreme Pontiff relaxed the interdict, not entirely but only in part, and not finally, but temporarily, namely, at his pleasure, and for as long as he might see that it was expedient so that in the meantime the spirits might prove whether they were from God, and whether, as the archbishop and bishops affirmed, the hoped-for utility might result, so that the Divine Offices might be celebrated in the kingdom, but the bodies of the deceased would not be given church burial. Moreover, in this matter, he did a special favor for the clergy, namely, that they might be buried in an ecclesiastical cemetery, without the usual solemnity. And, even though it might seem unsuitable to some, perhaps with the office restored ecclesiastical burial would be denied, because according to the canonical sanctions, we should be in communion with those dead, whom we were in communion with while they were alive. But there is nothing incongruous about this to those who understand it correctly, since, according to the decrees of the Lateran Council, the deceased in tournaments, even if they were reconciled to the church through penance, should still be deprived of Christian burial.[79] In order that he might not be seen to remit the penalty but rather to commute it, he bound the King of Leon, the daughter of the King of Castile, and all their principal councilors and supporters by the chain of excommunication. He commanded that, to whatever city, village, or town they might come, no one might celebrate the divine offices there in their presence. He commanded the King of Castile and the queen, his wife, to work energetically to dissolve that union, otherwise he would promulgate a similar sentence against them and their land. Because the King of Leon was said to have handed over certain castles to the daughter of the King of Castile as a dowry so that, if for any reason he left her, they would remain his, they presented an impediment to the dissolution of the union. He, therefore, commanded these castles to be restored and for this purpose he put the girl herself under the sentence of excommunication, decreeing that if any progeny resulted from such an incestuous and damnable union, he or she should be held spurious and illegitimate, and according to legitimate statutes on no account might they succeed to the paternal estate.

Although they persevered for some time in their refusal, they finally had a change of heart, dissolved the incestuous union and, when they were separated from one another, after they took an oath according to the form of the church, they merited absolution.

LIX. At the same time, he anathematized the apostate, Sverre, who had violently seized the Kingdom of Norway, after setting aside the le-

---

79. Most probably, the reference is to the Third Lateran Council.

gitimate heir.[80] Because the Archbishop of Trondheim was unwilling to consent to his perverse acts, the apostate forced him into exile outside his province. He, by mandate of the Apostolic See, was kindly received by the Archbishop of Lund, while the intruder ended life still in his sin. He returned to his church after his exile.

[The Crusade and Church Unity]

LX. After he had heard of the promotion of the Lord Innocent, Alexius, the Emperor of Constantinople, sent honorable messengers to him with precious gifts, asking him to visit his empire in the person of his legates. The Pope sent Albert the Subdeacon and Albertinus the notary to advise the emperor through them of his intention to aid the Holy Land, to whose cries the emperor among all Christian princes should respond because of the abundance of his wealth and his proximity. He should also lead the Greek church back to the obedience of the Apostolic See, its mother, from whose *magisterium*[81] it had withdrawn, persevering for a long time in its contumacy. And he should know that he could not dissimulate in this matter, but should do his duty, since he would receive the justice of the one to be judged.

Writing on this matter to the Patriarch of Constantinople, he advised him to persuade the emperor to this course of action.

But how the emperor responded to both and in what way the Lord Pope answered through his chaplain, John, who was again sent there, this letter directly to the emperor declares:

To Alexius, illustrious Emperor of Constantinople. "It has brought us a feeling of much exaltation," he said, "that, just as we received letters from your Imperial Excellency, your Imperial Highness humbly received our legates and letters, and has responded kindly and devotedly on those matters that we recall we wrote concerning the unity of the church, even if not sufficiently and clearly. You have replied in writing that your empire

80. King of Norway, 1177–1202.
81. I.e., the teaching authority of the church vested in its hierarchy.

has heeded our exhortations and advice. For he, who is the origin of all power [Rom 13:1], according to the Apostle, the searcher of loyalties as well as hearts [Rv 2:23], Jesus Christ, who holds the heart of princes in his hand [Rv 3:7], who opens and no one closes [Prv 21:1], has opened the ears of your Serenity, and has breathed in a spirit of devotion to you, so that you might hear humbly and accept with a kindly spirit those things that have been written by us, though insufficient, his vicar and the successor of the prince of the apostles, in reply to the letters of your Imperial Magnificence. Although you might believe we reproved your Magnificence for your lack of support for the Holy Land, we have not, however, written to criticize but to advise. Although a reproving tone is not foreign to the pontifical office, as Paul said when writing to Timothy: "Preach the word, insist whether it is convenient or inconvenient, convince, reprimand, reprove in all patience and teaching" [2 Tm 4:2]. But we wonder why your Imperial Prudence has apparently not yet given a sign of a commitment to the recovery of the Holy Land in your letters, because, as can clearly be seen from the detention of his land, that the Lord, who makes those confident of salvation from his mercy, not in the multitude, nor in the ark, but in his virtue, was not yet appeased regarding our sins. For you fear, as your letters show, that, if your Imperial Serenity should wish to anticipate the time foreseen by God for the liberation of this land, you would lament to have labored in vain and you would be blamed by the Lord through the Prophet, who said: "They made rulers, and not through me, they have ruled and not recognized me" [Hos 8:4]. It is true that we speak not so much to criticize as to instruct. If you consider carefully and look to the truth, you might understand finally what must be understood in another way. For the giver of all good things, who gives to each according to his works, who is not pleased with forced service, has granted a free will to man so that, in matters where a human remedy can be found, he might not tempt the Lord. For it has been written: "You shall not tempt the Lord your God" [Mt 4:7; Lk 4:12]. It is, therefore, as a result of the necessity of the Christian people or rather of Jesus Christ, that both you and all washed in the waters of holy Baptism should use free will to aid the Crucified exile. If you wish to await the time unknown to men for the redemption of that land and do nothing by yourself, but leave everything to divine disposition, without your help the Lord's sepulcher could not be freed from the hands of the Saracens. Therefore, through negligence, your Imperial Magnificence would incur a Divine offense, and as a result you would not win the favor of the Lord by your assistance. For have you not understood the Lord's meaning? Are you not his counselor, so that you should, certain of the Divine disposition, then first move your arms against the pagans and work for the liberation of the province of Jerusalem, since the Lord has given us the task to free the unhappy Christian people and his inheritance from the hands of the Saracens? Have you not read of the depth of the riches of the wisdom and the knowlege of God, how incomprehensible are his judgments and how unsearchable his ways [Rom 11:33]? Of course, if you understand the secrets of the Divine mind, and you foresee by the hidden eye of revelation the liberation of the Lord's sepulcher, would there not be merit for you then to set out first to the Holy Land, to aid the Lord in carrying out his Will, which cannot be either prevented or perpetuated by you? And those who think this way are forced to call the prophets foolish when they preached that they should do penance, and God foresaw that their sin was increased by their contempt; so, when Moses warned Pharaoh at God's command to free his people [Ex 5:1–2], his heart was so hardened that he was unwilling to free the people, and he was beaten. It would not even be according to the opinion of such individuals either to cease from vices or to attain virtues, but rather to stand for the Divine will, which has foreseen how each individual will be lost or saved. Your Imperial Excellency has read, as we believe, or has heard, that, because of the sin of the Israelite people the Lord changed the forty days, within which it was promised that they would enter the Promised Land, into the same number of years, and, on the contrary, at the contrition and tears of Ezechiel, the Lord extended his life by fifteen years. From this we can clearly understand that the duration of the Saracens' persecution can also be shortened. We read in the Gospel concerning the persecution of Anti-Christ: "Unless those days were shortened, no human would have been saved" [Mt 24:22]. In addition, among other secret and unknowable causes of the invasion and detention of the Eastern Land, the Lord perhaps foresaw this in his mercy, so that, when they, after they left relatives and friends as well as all the goods they had and, following Christ, took up the saving sign of the cross in defense of that very land, they were crowned with martyrdom. Therefore, triumphant, the church rejoices and grows in heaven, for which reason the church militant seems to suffer and diminish. We are unwilling, however, to dwell longer on these matters, since the truth is apparent to those correctly paying attention and diligently searching. But your Imperial Highness will thus aid the exiled Christ in order to avoid the criticism of detractors and to avoid hearing that Gospel charge of the Last Judgment against yourself: "I was a stranger, and you did not take me in, sick and in jail, and you did not come to me" [Mt 25:43].

But we rejoice that on the subject of the union of the church, for which we especially sent our letters and legates, just as we have received letters from you, you seem to have a ready concern and intend to work diligently for what we have written. For you have replied in your letters, to use your words, that it is the function of our Holiness according to earlier synodal practices to carry out the requisite doctrines. And thus, by the most holy action of our Holiness, which is with you, the church will not delay an agreement. Moreover, although the Apostolic See exists not so much as a result of a conciliar decree as it is the Divine head and mother of all the churches, as should be clear to your Highness from the content of the letter we sent to our Venerable Brother, John, the Patriarch of Constantinople, and a copy of which we sent you, and, therefore, the patriarch should differ neither on account of the disparity of rites nor differences in doctrine, but should obey us kindly and devotedly as his head according to the ancient and canonical constitution, since matters which are certain must not be left in doubt. Moreover, we have decided out of many ecclesiastical necessities, with the Lord as author, to summon a council and to celebrate a synodal meeting, at which, if summoned by us according to your promise, this will occur, since these matters that we have sought by our letters are doctrinal: namely, that the member should return to the head and the daughter to the mother. Obligated by due reverence and obedience to the Roman church, we will admit him kindly and joyfully as a most beloved brother and a special member of the church, establishing concerning other matters those that must be decided by the authority of the Apostolic See and the approval of the sacred council with the advice of him and our other brethren. Otherwise, since we ought not further support the scandal of the church, and we ought also to root out tares and chaff from the fields of the Lord, we cannot pretend but in the same council, if it is granted from above, to proceed in this matter with the counsel of our brethren.

We, therefore, advise your Magnificence and exhort you with a greater concern and we enjoin you on the remission of sins that you should so work that the patriarch, either in person, or, if perhaps he is tied up for a good reason and is unable, through suitable procurators and some of the more important prelates of the churches, will attend the council at the appointed time, that he would subscribe to the obedience and reverence of the Apostolic See beforehand according to the constitution of the canons: if things should worsen, which we do not believe, we would be forced to proceed both against you, who can if you wish, carry out what we order, and against him and the Greek church.

On the other matters, we have, however, instructed our beloved son, John, our chaplain and familiar,[82] the legate of the Apostolic See, an honest and discrete man, valued by us and our brethren for his religion, regarded for his honesty, and devoted to your Serenity. We advise and exhort with greater concern that you should receive him kindly as a legate of the Apostolic See and that you honor and trust him in the matters that he shall propose to you on our behalf; you should know for certain that, if you desire our advice, when the storm has been stilled, tranquillity can come to you. Dated at the Lateran on the Ides of November.[83]

LXI. But he wrote to the Patriarch who had consulted him on the two articles in this way:

To the Patriarch of Constantinople.[84] The primacy of the Apostolic See, which no man, but God, indeed the very God-man, has established, has been proven by much evangelical and Apostolic evidence, from which later canonical constitutions have proceeded. They are in agreement that the Holy Roman church, consecrated to St. Peter, the prince of the apostles, is preeminent over others as teacher and mother. For, when the Lord asked, whom do men say the Son of Man is, referring to other opinions of other men, since Peter had responded first among the others, that he was the Christ, the Son of God, he deserved to hear: "You are Peter and upon this rock I will build my church," and a little later: "I will give you the keys of the kingdom of heaven" [Mt 16:18–19]. For, although first and foremost the foundation of the church is the only-begotten Son of God, Jesus

82. John was a Cistercian monk from the monastery of Casamari. He later became bishop of Forcone and then of Perugia, where he died in 1230. Cf. RI 2:167 (176), 323, n. 3.
83. RI 2:202(211), 394–97, November 13, 1199.
84. The patriarch was John X Camaterus, 1198–1206. In this letter, Innocent presents the Latin view of the issues that separated the Eastern, i.e., Orthodox, churches from Rome, as they were understood in his time.

Christ, according to the words of the apostle: "Because he has put the foundation, save that other that cannot be put, that is Christ Jesus" [Lk 6:48], the second and necessary foundation of the church is Peter, even if not first in time still his authority stands above others. Of them, Paul the apostle said: "Now you are not strangers and sojourners, but you are citizens of the saints and domestics of God, built upon the foundation of the apostles and prophets" [Eph 2:19–20], whom the Prophet David witnesses to be the foundations in the holy mountains [Ps 86:1]. Also, the Truth expressed this primacy himself when he said to Peter: "You will be called Cephas" [Jn 1:42], which even if translated as Peter, still means "head," so that, as the head first obtains leadership among the other members of the body, as that in which the fullness of the senses flourishes, so also Peter excels in rank among the apostles, and his successors among all the prelates of the churches. The others have been called to a share of solicitude [2 Cor 11:28], so that he might lose none of the fullness of power to them. The Lord has committed his sheep to him to be fed with a thrice-repeated word, so that he, who is unwilling to have him as shepherd in the persons of his successors, may be considered separated from the flock of the Lord. For he did not distinguish these sheep from those, but simply said: "Feed my sheep" [Jn 21:17], so that all might know that they were committed to him. For James, the brother of the Lord, who was seen to be a pillar, content with Jerusalem alone, that he might raise up the seed of his dead brother where he was crucified, not only left the governance of the universal church to Peter, but the whole world. And this is also evident from the fact that, when the Lord appeared to the apostles on the shore when they were in the boat, Peter, recognizing the Lord, jumped into the sea and, while the others remained in the boat, hastened to the Lord without benefit of a boat. For since the sea signifies the world according to the word of the Psalmist, "This great and spacious sea, the reptiles there without number" [Ps 103:25], when Peter jumped into the sea, he expressed the privilege that belongs to the Pontiff alone, by which he received the governance of the whole world. The other apostles were content to remain in the boat, because the whole world was committed to none of them, but individual provinces or an appointed church for each. Again, in order that his wonderful walk on the waters of the sea to the Lord might designate him the unique Vicar of Christ, he walked wonderfully on the waters of the sea. For, since the waters are many, many people and congregations of the waters are seas, through this fact, that Peter went upon the waters of the sea, he showed that he has received power over all the peoples. For this reason, the Lord is said to have prayed, speaking at the moment of his passion: "I have prayed for you, Peter, that your faith may not fail, and, once you have been converted, strengthen your brothers" [Lk 22:32]. By this, he clearly indicated that his successors would never in the future deviate from the Catholic faith, but would rather recall others and strengthen the hesitant. By this he granted him the power of strengthening others so that he might impose the necessity of obedience on others. And then Peter began to act when some of the absent apostles returned and said "this is a hard saying," when Jesus said to the Twelve, "Do you also wish to depart?" he alone responded for the others, "Lord, you have the words of eternal life, to whom will we go?" In addition, you have often heard and read said of him: "whatever you bind on earth will also be bound in heaven, and whatever you loose on earth will also be loosed in heaven" [Mt 16:19]. But even if you believe that this was said to all of the apostles, still you know the power of binding and loosing was not granted to the others without him but to him without the others, so that, what others could not do without him, he could do without others from the privilege of fullness of power granted and conceded to him by the Lord. For this reason, it seems not unreasonably to follow that he alone is read to have asked Jesus: "If my brother should sin against me, should I forgive him even seven times?" And to him alone Jesus is read to have answered: "I do not say to you up to seven times, but even seventy times seven" [Lk 17:3–4], because the septenary is indeed the number of wholeness, in that all time is known to be contained in the septenary of days. The septenary number therefore multiplied by itself in this place means the whole universe of sins, because Peter alone can forgive not only all things but the sins of all mankind. Finally, after his passion, the Lord is read to have said to Peter, "You follow me" [Jn 21:19], and this ought to be understood not so much from the sequel of the passion he was to suffer as of the dispensation entrusted to him, since Andrew[85] and some others beside Peter were crucified like the Lord, but the Lord made Peter alone both his vicar in office and his successor in ministry.

For this reason, after the Ascension of the Lord, Peter began to rule the

85. This reference to St. Andrew is an effort to refute the claims of Constantinople to equality with Rome, based on its foundation, according to legend, by St. Andrew.

church as his successor: to fill up the number of the Twelve, appointing and ordering another to be chosen in the place of Judas the liar, from the words of the prophet. After the coming of the Paraclete, he strengthened the disciples by the words of Joel [J l 3:1; Acts 2:14–41], not filled by new wine but enlightened by the grace of the Holy Spirit. He ordered that those who believed should do penance and be baptized. He was the first among the disciples to work a miracle by curing a cripple. As leader and chief among them, he published the sentence of death against Ananias and his wife, Saphira, because they had lied to the Holy Spirit [Acts 5:1]. He cut off the root of the simoniacal pestilence which was spreading against the primitive church with the apostolic sickle. He alone promulgated the sentence against Simon Magus, even though he had not offered money to him alone but to the whole community [Acts 8:19–24].

In addition, when he was in rapture, he saw the heavens open and a certain vessel descending like a large linen cloth hung down from heaven at the four corners of the earth, and it contained all the quadrupeds and serpents of the earth as well as the birds of the air. And, when a voice said to him: "arise, Peter, sacrifice and eat," he answered, "Heaven forbid, Lord, for I have never eaten any unclean or common things." And the voice spoke to him a second time, "What God has purified, you should not call common" [Acts 10:13–15]. Through this, it was manifest that Peter was in charge of all the people, since that vessel signified the world and everything in it, both Jews and gentiles. And, although, he was later, by a Divine revelation, translated from Antioch to Rome, still the primacy granted him was not left behind but rather he transferred the principate of the chair with him, since the Lord in no wise desired to diminish him and He had foreseen that he was to be martyred at Rome. Of course, when afterward the Lord himself, Who suffered in him, saying, "I come," to him, asserted that he would go to Rome to be crucified,[86] he consecrated the Roman church by his own blood, and he left the primacy to his successor, transferring the full plenitude of power to him: for sons were born to him indeed for the father, and the Lord established them as princes over all the earth.

Of course, since the church is represented by the bark of Peter, Peter, at the command of the Lord, led the bark into the deep, casting the net of

---

86. See Jn 13:36 for the ultimate source of this saying which was adapted by St. Ambrose, *Contra Auxentium* (*PL*, 16:1053).

preaching among the prey, when he put the principate of the church there where the height of the secular power flourished and the imperial monarchy resided, to which almost all nations, like the rivers of the sea, paid tributes at certain times. He indeed first converted the Jews to the faith. He was the first to convert gentiles to the faith after the Ascension of Christ so that he might show that he was the primate over both groups of the faithful, since on the very day of Pentecost at his exhortation about three thousand Jews received the sacrament of baptism. Then, at the angelic revelation, he went on to baptize Cornelius the centurion and his family as the first fruits of the gentiles [Acts 10:44–49]. But when there was a great discussion among the apostles, at the consultation of the faithful, whether they should be baptized and should observe the law of Moses, Peter responded quickly with the principal authority: "Why do you tempt God to impose a yoke on the neck of the disciples that neither our fathers nor we could bear" [Acts 15:10]? In conformity with this opinion, James promulgated an Apostolic decree on this question. Paul, also, after he went to Arabia and then returned to Damascus, next, after three years, came to Jerusalem to see Peter, to discuss the Gospel with him, lest perhaps he should run or even already had run in a void. Also, recognizing the singular privilege of his antonomiastic apostolate, he wrote concerning him: "For he who worked in Peter for the apostolate [among the circumcised] has worked for me among the gentiles" [Gal 2:8]. But so that the one the Lord put in charge of the others by the privilege of office, he might also adorn with the privilege of virtue, he conferred so much power on him that the sick were healed in his shadow, that what the Lord said is known to be completed in him: "He who believes in me, he will do the works I do and also greater than these" [Jn 14:12].

But we have not, therefore, set forth these matters so that we, who, although unworthy, have succeeded to the Apostolic Office, might wish to boast about our great accomplishments or to exalt upon ourselves in wonders, since we know that the Lord said: "Everyone who humbles himself will be exalted, and he who exalts himself will be humbled" [Mt 23:12]. For this reason, when the question of greatness was raised among the disciples, he responded: "The one who is greater among you will be the servant, and he who is superior is also a minister" [Mt 10:43–45], proposing himself as an example, because the Son of Man did not come to be ministered to, but to minister. For this reason, also, Peter said: "Do not lord it over those assigned to you, but be examples to the flock" [1 Pt 5:3]. For, also, another scripture says: "So far as you are greater, humble yourself in all things" [Sir 3:29]. And, again: "Make yourself a prince: don't extol yourself; be among them as one of them. For God resists the proud but gives grace to the humble" [Jas 4:6].

But on these accounts and others, as we believe, which your Fraternity ought not ignore, recognizing the *magisterium* of the Apostolic See, you have decided to consult it on certain doubtful matters. We certainly find this pleasing and acceptable, and we therefore commend your Prudence: not that we think we are sufficient in ourselves but our sufficiency is from God, who gives to all abundantly and does not reproach, who makes the tongues of infants speak and opens the mouths of the mute. You have asked, because you are in doubt and desirous to learn the reason we call the Roman Church one and universal in our letters, as it is now divided in certain particular ways; since the shepherd is one and the flock is one, even if there are several pastors appointed under one prince of pastors, Christ.

But we respond thus to your questions. The church is called universal for two reasons. For the understanding of things said must be taken from the reason for speaking, since the thing is not subordinate to the word but the word is subordinate to the thing. The church, which is made up of all the churches, is called universal, which in Greek is called by the word catholic. And, according to this understanding of the word, the Roman church is not the universal church but part of the universal church, namely, first and particularly like the head in the body, since the fullness of power is in it, while some share of the plenitude devolves on the others. And that universal church is called one, which contains all of the other churches under it; and according to this reckoning of the name, only the Roman church is called universal since it alone by the privilege of its singular dignity is in charge of the others. Just as God is called the universal Lord, not as if He is now divided into very special or subordinate types, but because all things are under his dominion. For there is one general church, of which the Truth said to Peter, "You are Peter and upon this rock I will build my church" [Mt 16:18]. And there are many individual churches, of which the apostle said: "My daily concern is solicitude for all the churches" [2 Cor 11:28]. One consists of all, as the general from particulars, and one is preeminent over all, because, since the body of the church is one, of which the apostle says: "We are all one body in Christ" [Rom 12:5], it is the head that excels all the other members.

You have also asked and even strongly asserted, desiring to learn what you may accept as reasonable, without contradiction, since David says in the Psalms concerning Jerusalem: "Mother Sion says man, and man is made in her" [Ps 86:5], namely, where Christ has deigned to dwell, equally to preach and to teach, as well as to work our salvation, we place the foundation of our faith in her, which is why she deserves to be called mother, since from her the doctrine of salvation will come. Why is the Roman church called the mother of all the churches? She received the sacraments of the orthodox faith from the church of Jerusalem, as the apostle also shows clearly, when he says that he preached the Gospel, that had its origin in Jerusalem, even unto Illyricum. But even if we know from the foregoing the answer to this question, since the Roman church is called mother not because of her age but rather because of her dignity—for, even if, according to John, Andrew preceded Peter in the faith, still Peter was over Andrew, since he is always put first in the listing of the apostles, not because Peter was first in time, but because he was first in dignity [Jn 1:35–42]. Still, to remove all doubt, your Fraternity ought to distinguish among the various references of the name between the Roman church and that of Jerusalem, because that church must be called the mother of all the faith, since the signs of faith proceeded from her; indeed, she must be called the mother of the faithful because by the privilege of her dignity, she is in charge of all the faithful. Likewise, just as the synagogue is called the mother of the church, because it, too, preceded the church and the church proceeded from it—as it says in the Canticles, "The sons of my mother fight against me" [Sg 1:5]; and again, "a little while, when I had crossed over, I found one whom my soul loved, I held him and did not let him go until I brought him to the house of my mother" [Sg 3:4]—still, the mother church is general and she always conceives, fertile with new offspring, she bears and nourishes: she conceives by catechizing those she instructs, she gives birth by baptizing those she purifies, she nourishes by communicating those she renews. Of her, the prophet says in the Psalm, "She makes the sterile woman a mother of sons to dwell rejoicing in the house" [Ps 112:9]. And elsewhere, the same prophet: "Lift up your eyes," he says, "and see: all these are gathered, they come to you. Your sons come from afar and your daughters arise from your side" [Is 60:4].

Let us rejoice not a little, moreover, and would that our joy be fulfilled in you and upon you, because you have commended the solicitude of our apostolate for the union of the church of the Latins and the Greeks for its

Divine zeal and a glowing plan which, in a series of your letters, you have said that we have.[87] His Imperial Highness has also written to us about this, that, to use his words, it is according to preceding synodal decisions to require synodal agreement, and so by most holy action of our Holiness, who is the church among you, he will not impede the agreement. But even if, as is apparent from the aforesaid matters, the Roman church is not only by synodal but by Divine Constitution the head and mother of all the churches, you should not delay either on account of disparity of rites or differences in doctrine, but should willingly, kindly, and devotedly obey us as your head according to the ancient and canonical constitution, since certain things must not be left in doubt. Still we have decided on account of many ecclesiastical necessities, under the inspiration of the Lord, to summon a General Council and to celebrate a synodal meeting, to which you should come if summoned by us according to the promise of the emperor himself—since these matters we have investigated in our letters are doctrinal, so that, namely, the member should return to the head and mother, taking into consideration the reverence and obedience due the Roman church. She will willingly and joyfully admit you, brother, as the dearest and special member of the church. By the authority of the Apostolic See, and with the sacred approbation of the council, with your counsel and that of our brethren concerning other matters, we will decide what must be decided. Otherwise, since we should not further sustain the scandal of the church and we should pull out the tares and chaff from the fields of the Lord, we should not avoid but in this council, if God should grant, proceed in this business with the counsel of our brethren [Mt 3:12, 13:24–30; Lk 3:17].

We therefore advise your Fraternity and exhort you in the Lord and we order you by Apostolic Letters that, when summoned, you should come to the council at the appropriate time in person or, if you cannot because you are prevented by good reasons, through suitable procurators and some of the more important prelates of your major churches. You should show obedience and reverence to the Apostolic See according to the constitution of the canons, so that, if anything should be done otherwise, which we do not believe, we should be compelled to proceed both against the emperor, who can, if he wishes, do what we command, and against you and the Greek church.

---

87. Perhaps this refers to the plan to summon a council.

On other matters, we have ordered, however, our beloved son, John our chaplain and familiar, the legate of the Apostolic See, an honest and discrete man, valued by us and our brethren for his religion and honesty, to be sent to his Imperial Excellency. We advise and exhort you carefully to receive him as legate of the Apostolic See and that you honor and trust him without any doubt in those affairs that he shall put before you on our behalf. [Dated at the Lateran on the second of the Ides of November.[88]]

LXII. But when the emperor and the patriarch had received these letters and studied them carefully, they sorrowed not a little about the matters that they had earlier written as penitents, because the emperor recognized that he had obligated himself by his promise that when the Supreme Pontiff would summon a general council, he had to send the Greek church to the council so that it would receive the decrees of the council. But the patriarch, as a result of the papal responses to his queries, recognized that he, both by rational arguments and authorities, was obliged to obey the Roman Pontiff. Therefore, after the emperor had taken lengthy counsel with the Greeks, he at last responded in this way: that if the Roman Pontiff should order the council to be celebrated in Greece, where the four ancient councils were held, the Greek church would send its representatives there. He turned deceptively to treat another matter at length, sending a letter to the Supreme Pontiff in which he tried to prove that the empire surpassed the priesthood in power, to which the Lord Pope responded in this manner:

LXIII. To Alexius, Emperor of Constantinople.[89] With our usual affection for you, we have received the letter Your Imperial Excellency dispatched through the person of our beloved son, I., the Archdeacon of Durazzo, a prudent and loyal man. By your letter we learned that the letter we sent you through the office of our beloved son and chaplain, John,

88. RI 2 (200), 382–89, November 12, 1199.
89. This translation of the decretal "Solitae" has been compared with that by Alfred Andrea, in *The Medieval Record: Sources of Medieval History* (Boston: Houghton Mifflin, 1997), 318–22. I am grateful to Professor Andrea for the opportunity. The text is, however, chiefly my own.

who was then serving as legate of the Apostolic See, had arrived in your empire and was read.

As you intimated to us in your letter, however, Your Imperial Sublimity is astonished that we have seemed to reproach you in some small way, although we remember that we wrote not in a spirit of reproach but rather in the gentle spirit of calling something to your attention. We have gathered from your letter that your understanding of what Saint Peter, the Prince of the Apostles, wrote, "For the sake of God, be subject to every human creature, as much as to the king, who is the preeminent authority, as to the generals, for they are sent by God to punish evildoers and to praise the doers of good" [1 Pt 2:13–14]. Concerning this matter we had reason to wonder what caused your Imperial Highness to place the empire above the priestly dignity and power, and from the authoritative text quoted above to want to draw a threefold argument. The first is based on the text: "be subject." The second is based on what follows that: "to the king, who is the preeminent authority." The third is based on the words that are appended directly to that: "to punish evildoers and to praise the doers of good." You imagine by the first argument that the priesthood is of subordinate status, through the second that the empire has precedence, through the third that emperors have received jurisdictions over priests as well as the laity, in fact, the power of the sword over priests! For since some priests are good and some are evildoers, he, who, according to the Apostle, bears the sword for the punishment of evildoers, can wield the sword of vengeance against priests who dare to deviate into evil-doing, because the Apostle does not distinguish between priests and all others.

Doubtless, had you paid more careful attention to the person speaking these words and the people to whom he was speaking and the meaning of the words, you would not have drawn such an interpretation from the text. For the Apostle is writing to his subordinates, and he was urging on them the virtue of humility. It was in this context that he said "be subject," because he wanted to put the yoke of subservience on the priesthood and to confer the authority of guidance on those persons to whom he urged priests to be subject. It also follows from this that even a slave has received power over priests when he says, "to every human creature." Regarding what follows, however, "to the king, who is the preeminent authority," we do not deny that the emperor is certainly preeminent in temporal matters. But the pontiff has precedence in spiritual affairs, which are as superior to temporal concerns as the soul is to the body. We should also note that the statement was not merely "be subject," but "for the sake of God" was added, nor is the text purely and simply "to the king, who is the pre-eminent authority," but rather the phrase "as much as" is introduced, perhaps not without reason. What follows, however, "to punish evildoers and to praise the doers of good," should not be understood as meaning that the king has received the power of the sword over all, good and evil, but only over those who, by using the sword, are under the jurisdiction of the sword, according to what the Truth said: "All who take up the sword shall perish by the sword" [Mt 26:52]. For no one can or should judge the servant of another, because, as the Apostle notes, a servant stands or falls with his master. On that point, you also introduced the argument that, although Moses and Aaron were brothers in the flesh, Moses was the prince of the people and Aaron had more priestly power, and Joshua, the successor of Moses, received the ruling authority over priests. King David also was superior to the chief priest, Abiathar. But, even though Moses was the prince of the people, he was also a priest, and the prophet recognized the priesthood of Moses when he said: "Moses and Aaron were his priests" [Ps 98:6].

The higher authority entrusted to Joshua that you wrote about should be interpreted more in accordance with the spirit of the text rather than the letter, because, as the Apostle writes: "The letter kills, but the spirit gives life" [2 Cor 3:6]. Joshua, who led his people to the Promised Land, symbolized the person of the true Jesus. Also, although David possessed royal power, he governed the priest, Abiathar, not as a result of his royal dignity but on account of his authority as a prophet [1 Sm 22:23]. Whatever was true long ago in the Old Testament is now otherwise in the New Testament, because Christ became a priest forever according to the Order of Melchizedek and offered himself as a sacrifice to God the Father not as a king but as priest on the altar of the cross by which he redeemed the human family.

With particular regard to him who is the successor of Saint Peter and the Vicar of Christ, you should have been able to understand the nature of the special privilege of priesthood from what was said not by just anyone but by God, not to a king but to a priest, who was not from royal lineage but from a family of priestly succession, namely, from the priest who lived in Anatoth: "Behold, I have placed you over peoples and kingdoms that you uproot and scatter, build and plant" [Jer 1:10]. It is also said in the Divine law: "Do not revile God and do not speak evil of the prince of your people" [Ex 22:27]. These words place priests before kings, calling the former gods and the latter princes.

Moreover, you ought to know that God put two great lights in the firmament of heaven, one greater and one lesser—the greater light to preside over the day, the lesser to preside over the night. Each is great but one is greater, because the church is signified by the word "heaven," according to what the Truth said: "The Kingdom of Heaven is like the human head of a household who gathered workers at the break of day in his vineyard" [Mt 20:1]. We understand the word "day" to mean "spiritual" and "night" to mean "carnal," according to the witness of the prophet: "Day utters the word to day, and night proclaims knowledge to night" [Ps 18:3]. God, therefore, put two great lights into the firmament of heaven, that is, the Universal Church. He instituted two offices: pontifical authority and royal power. The one, however, that rules over days, that is, over spiritual matters, is greater; the one that rules over the nights, that is, over carnal matters, is the lesser. Thus, we understand that the difference between the sun and the moon is as great as that between pontiffs and kings.

If his Imperial Highness carefully considers these matters, he would neither place nor permit our venerable brother, the Patriarch of Constantinople, a truly great and honorable member of the Church, to sit on the left next to his footstool, when other kings and princes reverently rise in the presence of archbishops and bishops as they should, and assign them an honorable seat next to themselves. For, as we believe, Your Prudence is not ignorant of the fact that the exceedingly pious Constantine showed such honor to priests.

For, even though we have not written in rebuke, we may, nevertheless, very reasonably rebuke by way of instruction, as Saint Paul the Apostle is recorded to have written to Bishop Timothy: "Preach, persist both when it is convenient and when it is inconvenient, importune, censure, implore, rebuke with all patience and learning" [2 Tm 4:2]. For our mouth should not be bound, but open to all, lest we be, as the prophet says, "Mute dogs who do not want to bark" [Is 56:10]. For this reason our correction should not annoy you but rather should be accepted because a father chides the son whom he loves, and God censures and castigates those whom he loves. We therefore carry out the duty of the pastoral office when we entreat, accuse, rebuke, and take pains to win over to those things that are pleasing to the Divine Will, when it is convenient and when it is inconvenient, not just all others, but also emperors and kings.

For all Christ's sheep were committed to us in the person of Saint Peter when the Lord said: "Feed my sheep" [Jn 21:17], not making any distinction between these sheep and those in order to show that anyone who does not recognize Peter and his successors as teachers and pastors is outside his flock. Because it is so well known, we need hardly mention what the Lord said to Peter and, in the person of Peter, to his successors: "Whatsoever you bind on earth will be bound in heaven, and whatsoever you loose on earth will be loosed in heaven" [Mt 16:19], excepting nothing when he said whatsoever. In truth, we do not wish to pursue this any longer, lest we seem contentious or attracted to something of this sort, because, should it be advantageous to boast, we would prefer to boast not of some mark of honor but of the onerous burden, not of greatness, but of worry. For this reason, the apostle boasts of his infirmities. We have learned that it is written: "Everyone who exalts himself shall be humbled, and he who humbles himself shall be exalted" [Mt 23:12]. Further, "The greater you are, the more you should humble yourself in all things" [Sir 3:18]; and elsewhere, "God resists the proud but gives glory to the humble" [Jas 4:6]. Because of that we describe our exaltation in humility, and we regard our greatest exaltation to be our humility. For this reason, also, we write and confess that we are the servants, not only of God, but of the servants of God and, in the Apostle's words, we are debtors equally to the wise and the foolish [Jer 10:8].

Your Highness knows whether we have been able to lead Your Imperial Excellency to welcome the good and the useful by our letter and whether we have advised you of proper and honorable courses of action, because we remember that we invited you to nothing other than the unity of the Church and aid for the land of Jerusalem. May he who breathes where he wills and who holds the hearts of princes in his hand so inspire your mind that you acquiesce in our advice and counsel and do that which should deservedly produce honor for the Divine Name, profit for the Christian religion, and the salvation of your soul. We, however, will do what we know is expeditious, no matter what you might do.

Would that you made it a point to imitate in word and deed the devotion to the Apostolic See of your illustrious predecessor, the Emperor Manuel[90] of glorious memory, so that, by his aid and counsel, things might

90. Manuel I Comnenus ruled the Byzantine Empire from 1143 to 1180. Innocent is here referring to Manuel's support for the rulers of the Latin Kingdom of Jerusalem, especially Baldwin III and Amalric I.

go better for you and your empire, as they did for him. Would that you, at least from this time onward, would make up for what you have neglected up to now. The archdeacon, however, can faithfully tell your Excellency what he has heard from us.[91]

LXIV. But after this the emperor beseeched the Supreme Pontiff to force the King of Jerusalem to restore Cyprus, which he maintained belonged to the Empire of Constantinople. The Lord Pope replied to him as follows:

We have received, with fitting kindness, the letters which your Imperial Highness has sent to us by your messenger, our beloved son, B., Prior of the Pisans, and have taken note of all the matters you have desired to make known to our Apostolic ears. You asked, our dearest son in Christ, that the illustrious King of Jerusalem should be forced, on our authority by a sentence of excommunication, to restore Cyprus, which belongs to the Empire of Constantinople and you are prepared to make large payments to him, to the Hospitallers and the Templars, for the aid of the Holy Land under suitable security, since Richard, King of England, of illustrious memory, had invaded it in violation of the peace treaty which he had made with your empire.[92] Although you have arranged to send a strong fleet for its recovery, you have delayed lest you shed the blood of Christians and prevent aid to the Holy Land. We, however, in our deliberations about what should be done in this matter, have learned that that King seized Cyprus from the hands of a certain man who did not answer to the Empire of Constantinople at all. Besides, our western princes asked us, because the support of the Eastern Province is administered to a considerable extent from the island of Cyprus, to advise your Imperial Magnificence by our letter that, given the uncertain status of the Holy Land, you should not molest its king about this island. It might easily happen that, if perhaps he thought you, whom he believed to be a supporter and defender of the province of Jerusalem, an enemy, because he would be less able to repel both imperial power and the violence of the pagans, his concern for the

91. Potthast, *Regesta Pontificum Romanorum,* 1:116 (1278), February 21, 1201.

92. Amalric II, king of Jerusalem and Cyprus, and brother of Guy de Lusignan. Richard I of England had conquered Cyprus and had established Guy as king. See Peter Edbury, *The Kingdom of Cyprus and the Crusades, 1191–1374* (Cambridge: Cambridge University Press, 1991), 2–12.

Holy Land, from which less benefit is derived, would be neglected, and he might employ greater effort in defending that from which he would benefit more. He might think he was more easily able to defend this, and, therefore, Christian territory would be opened up in a way that would not be to the interest of the Empire of Constantinople. For this reason, we have been reminded that we have written to your empire and have assiduously besought the western princes by letters and messengers so that we could give a better response to your request. Since, therefore, we may not fully possess the truth about this, before we can finally respond to your Magnificence about these matters, we need more complete information. To obtain this we must carefully seek it by letters and messengers to the king of Jerusalem as well as the western princes, so that we can then give a more certain response to your request. But upon this matter we commend your Imperial Prudence in the Lord for preferring to cease from warfare which would shed Christian blood or impede the defense of Jerusalem. We admonish and exhort Your Highness more attentively that you do not reject this proposal, because we intend your honor and profit to the degree that we can with honesty."[93]

LXV. Since the Kingdom of the Wallachians and the Bulgars withdrew from the obedience to the Apostolic See a very long time ago, the Lord Innocent, as a Good Shepherd, desired to lead these wandering sheep back into the fold and he sent Dominic, the archpriest of Brindisi, a man expert in Greek and Latin, to Joannitsa,[94] the Lord of the Wallachians and the Bulgars, who had withdrawn from the dominion of the Greeks. He sent a letter by him as follows:

To the noble Joannitsa. The Lord has respected your humility and the devotion, which until now you are known to have held for the Roman Church, and he has not only defended you powerfully amid the tumults of war and military crises, but has also wonderfully and mercifully in-

93. Potthast, *Regesta Pontificum Romanorum*, 1:122 (1332), March–April 1201.
94. Johannitsa ruled from 1197 to 1207. He is usually referred to as Kalojan and was the brother and successor of Peter. Their brother Asen had laid the foundation for Bulgaria and Wallachia (the land of the Vlachs) as a state, with its capital at Trnovo. Kalojan was therefore anxious for recognition as king in order to protect his fledgling state from its powerful neighbors.

creased your power. But when we heard that your ancestors took their origin from the noble stock of the city of Rome, and that you drew from them both generosity of blood and the affection of a sincere devotion for the Apostolic See as though by hereditary right, we decided to visit you right away with our letters and our nuncios. But we were not able to achieve our desire until now because we were prevented by various concerns for the church. But now we take this up along with our other concerns. In fact, we embrace them energetically rather than just taking them up so that we might favor you in a praiseworthy way by our legates and letters and strengthen your devotion to the Holy See.

And, for this reason, we have sent our beloved son, Dominic, archpriest of the Greeks of Brindisi, to you in person, and we admonish and exhort your Nobility in the Lord, and we commend you by Apostolic letters to receive him humbly and with devotion and trust him with honor and kindness, and you may explain through him your devotion to us more fully. For when we get a better grasp of your proposal and the intensity of your devotion through him, we plan to send more important messengers or legates to you to strengthen you and your people in the affection of the Apostolic See and to make you more certain of our good will.[95]

LXVI. Joannitsa, however, on receiving the messengers and letters of the Lord Pope, responded in this way:

To the Venerable and most Holy Father, Supreme Pontiff, I, Kalojan, Emperor of the Bulgarians and Wallachians, send joy and greetings to you. We announce to your Holiness that we have received your sacred letters, which the religious man, the archpriest of Brindisi, brought us, and we have valued them more than gold or any precious stone. Therefore, we have given great thanks to Almighty God, who has visited his unworthy servants according to his ineffable bounty and has respected our humility and led us back to the memory of our blood and the fatherland from which we have descended. And now, Holy Father, both Good Shepherd and head of all faithful Christians, desiring to gather the sons of the Holy, Catholic, and Apostolic See together in unity, you have sought us out, remote in body, and, although my brothers of good memory wanted for a long time to contact your Holiness, still they could not come to you because of considerable opposition. And we, also, trying for a first, second,

95. RI 5:114(115), 224–26, mid-1202.

and third time to get in touch with you, could not bring our desire to fruition. But now, since your Holiness has reached out to our Empire, we send a religious man, our faithful priest, Basil, the elect of Kostolac near Smederevo, together with your faithful messenger, the archpriest of Brindisi, to our most loving father, sending from our side thanks and friendship and service as to a spiritual father and Supreme Pontiff. Most Holy Father, you have shown us by your letters that we did not explain to you what we seek from the Roman church. Our empire seeks this from the Apostolic See so that we may be confirmed in the Roman church as in the fidelity of a mother. First, we ask our mother, the Roman church, for our crown and honor as a beloved son in the manner that our ancient emperors had. One was Peter, another Samuel,[96] and others preceded them in the empire, as we have found it written in our books. But now, if it pleases your Holiness to do it, whatever you command our empire will be carried out to the honor of God and of the Roman church. Lest you wonder that your nuncio has not returned more quickly, that we have mistrusted him, because many come into our empire thinking to deceive us, but we have known well how to guard against everything, but we have been well prepared for and received testimony on his behalf and we have found pleasure in him.

But, if you are pleased, most Holy Father, send us the more important messengers you suggested in your letter, and send him with them, and then we will give security both concerning the first mission and the second. May the Lord grant you many years.[97]

LXVII. Also, Basil, the Archbishop of the Bulgars, sent a letter to the pope in this vein:

To the most honorable and holy Supreme Pontiff, I, Basil, unworthy Archbishop of your Holiness and Pastor of Zagorje ob Savi, send greeting, joy, and adoration to you, our spiritual father. Although we cannot show devotion to you in person, still we do so in the spirit, notifying your Holiness that when we saw Dominic, the archpriest of Brindisi, sent by you, we gave thanks to God, who has not despised us, his humble and unworthy servants, hungering and thirsting for the favor and blessing of the Holy,

---

96. Both of these ruled in the late tenth century. Their mention was clearly meant to lend legitimacy to Kalojan's claim to a royal title.
97. RI 5:114(115), 224–26, mid-1202.

Catholic, and Apostolic see, because our lord emperor and we ourselves have desired for many years to contact you, but we could not, and now, by the will of Almighty God and your Holiness, because you have sent prayers and blessings to our Lord the Emperor, you have done exceedingly well. Moreover, we have learned these things from the emperor, who ordered that we be summoned, and we have raised our hands to heaven with all the people, speaking thus: "The Lord was mindful of us, what we have not thought" [Ps 115:12]. Therefore, we all, small and great, like good sons, petition you as our good father that our lord the emperor may obtain what he has asked of you, because he is worthy of it, because he and his entire empire are indeed devoted to the Roman church, as heirs descending from Roman blood. Likewise, we ask your Holiness that our son and companion, the priest Basil, Elect of Kostolac near Smederevo, should be recommended to you, because our Lord the Emperor Kalojan has committed his secrets to them, and what they and our letter say to you, you may hold firm. And we pray your Holiness that you hasten to send messengers, because then we will be more certain of your mission. May God grant you many years.[98]

LXVIII. When he had received letters from them, the Lord Pope sent his chaplain, John, to them with the following Apostolic letter:

To Kalojan, Lord of the Wallachians and Bulgarians. The Apostolic See over which we, though unworthy, preside, mindful of the gospel in which we learn that it was said to blessed Peter and his successors, "If you love me, feed my sheep" [Jn 21:17], and this demonstrates the pure feeling of affection he had for the Lord, that he tries to feed his sheep and gather together also those that are distant into the bosom of the church so that there may be one sheepfold and one shepherd [Jn 10:16]. For, since she is the general mother of all, she tries to gather them together as one, as the hen gathers her chicks, and she visits them both by legates and letter, so that the shepherd may recognize his sheep and the sheep may also recognize the shepherd [Jn 11:52; Mt 23:37]. With this in mind, we sent nuncios and a letter to your Nobility, so that after we have understood the feeling of devotion you have for the Roman church, your mother, we could then send more important messengers to you, and they might feed you, who say that you have descended from the noble stock of the Romans, and the people living under your rule by word and example, and make you more certain of the good will and favor of the Apostolic See. And, even though your Nobility hesitated at first about our messenger, knowing that the Angel of Satan sometimes changes himself into an angel of light [2 Cor 11:14], still, when you understood the truth of the witness of that noble man, you arranged to receive him kindly and honorably, as your letter to us has indicated. Moreover, you have written to us and humbly suggested through him that you considered our letters more precious than gold and any precious stone [Ps 18:11], and you have given thanks to God that he deigned to visit you. You have also added that you tried to send messengers to us once, twice, and a third time, following the example of your brothers of renowned memory, but you could not carry out your desire. Still now, encouraged by our letter, you send Basil the priest, the elect of Kostolac near Smederevo, together with our messenger, although the elect was not able to get to us because of the risks of travel. But you have asked humbly that the Roman church should grant a crown to you, as you have read in your histories, it granted to Peter, Samuel, and your other ancestors. Therefore, we have made a diligent search of our archives in order to be more certain in this matter, and it seems from this that in the land subject to you many kings were crowned. In addition, we found that in the reign of our predecessor, Nicholas, of happy memory, the king of the Bulgars, to whose requests for advice he often responded, had been baptized at his preaching together with his whole kingdom, and the king asked for an archbishop.[99] Likewise, the legate of Michael, King of the Bulgars, presented royal letters with regal gifts to our predecessor, Pope Hadrian,[100] and asked him to send one of the cardinals to select an archbishop, and after their approbation, on his return to the Apostolic See, he might later consecrate him. When Hadrian sent him a certain subdeacon in the company of bishops, the Bulgars, corrupted by the gifts and promises of the Greeks, received Greek priests rather than those chosen by the Romans. But even though the memory of such inconstancy has, until now, caused us to be cautious, so that we would not send any of our brothers, namely, the cardinals, to your presence, still we ordered our beloved son, John, our chaplain and familiar, legate of the Apostolic See, a man of foresight and discretion, whom we and our brothers embrace be-

99. Pope Nicholas I, 858–867. The king in question was Boris-Michael, 854–889. See RI 5:115(116), 226–28, November 27, 1202, esp. 228, nn. 12–19.
100. Pope Hadrian II, 867–872.

cause of his probity and religion among all of our other chaplains in the
arms of a special love of the Lord, and we have committed to him our office so that in your whole land he may correct those spiritual matters that
he sees are in need of correction and establish what should be established
according to God. We also sent the *pallium* by him, namely, the sign of
episcopal dignity, to the archbishop of your land and we have ordered it to
be conferred on him according to the form we directed under our seal. We
also gave the same legate the mandate that, if anyone should be promoted
to orders or consecrated a bishop in your land, he should ordain those to
be ordained and consecrate those to be consecrated only by neighboring
Catholic bishops. We also order that he should inquire diligently into the
truth about the crown granted to your ancestors by the Roman church
both in your ancient books and other documents and he should negotiate
with you everything that needs to be negotiated so that, when, through
him and your messengers, we are more certain about all these matters, we
may proceed more advisedly and maturely as should be done. We therefore admonish your Nobility and exhort you in the Lord that you should
kindly receive this legate as you would our person and treat his beneficial
advice and decisions honorably, and receive them and order them to be
received and kept by all Bulgarians and Wallachians. For as it is expedient
for you, both for temporal glory and for eternal life, like your race, so also
you and your people may be an imitator of the Romans. You claim descent
from the Romans, you should follow the rules of the Roman church so
that your people may be seen to reflect their ancestry in Divine Worship.
[Dated 5th Kalends of December.[101]]

LXIX. Likewise,

To the Archbishop of Zagorje ob Savi. Because we understand that it
was said to us in the person of Blessed Peter, "And after you have been
converted, confirm your brethren" [Lk 22:32], since, from the countless
cares that burden us, we are converted to the tranquillity of our mind, we
also strengthen those distant brethren and fellow-bishops, who, even if
they are absent in body, we believe to be present in spirit [1 Cor 5:3; Col
2:5] in those matters that pertain to their salvation and the unity of the
church, so that, just as they have been summoned to a share of solicitude,
so also they may be strengthened by our advice. Of course, since the body
of the holy church is one according to the Apostle, "we are all one body in

101. RI 5:115(116), 226–28, November 27, 1202.

Christ" [Rom 12:15], it should not be thought that there are several heads on one body, but, after the Lord, one must be known to be the head of the church of God, the one whom Jesus Christ our Lord appointed to be his vicar and also named as head, saying to Peter, "you will be called Cephas" [Jn 1:42], which also means Peter and head. Of course, since the Lord committed the feeding of his sheep to him, saying, "Feed my sheep" [Jn 21:17], this shows that he who is unwilling to have him as head and pastor is outside the sheepfold of Christ, which is the church. Therefore, we, though unworthy, whom the Lord desired to be his vicar, the successor of the Prince of the Apostles, so that we might demonstrate also through the effect of deed the paternal affection we have for the church of the Bulgarians and the Wallachians, which is said to have descended from the Romans according to flesh and blood, we have ordered our beloved son, the archpriest of Brindisi, to enter the presence of our beloved son, the noble Kalojan, Lord of the Bulgarians and Wallachians, and to strengthen him and the Christian people under his rule in devotion to the Apostolic See and, on his return, to make us more certain of the purity of their faith and the sincerity of their devotion. Moreover, we rejoice and we commend your Prudence in the Lord, because, recognizing the *magisterium* of the Apostolic See, you have written that you thirst for the favor and the blessing of the holy Catholic and Apostolic church. And you give thanks to God that that noble man has merited to receive our letter. We wish, therefore, that you would strengthen more fully now the church committed to you in Apostolic unity; "beloved son, John (as in the letter sent to Kalojan up to "we embrace"), we commanded our beloved son, John, to be sent to you and that noble man, so that he might correct in the whole land of that noble, etc. (up to "to be established"). Through him also the *pallium* to your fraternity, etc. (in almost the same manner up to "to be conferred"). Moreover, you should know that we have given a mandate to our legate that if perhaps in your province, etc. (in almost the same manner up to "we may proceed"). We therefore admonish and exhort your fraternity more attentively and we order you by Apostolic letter that, recognizing the *magisterium* and primacy of the Apostolic See, you should both persist in devotion to us and receive our legate kindly as if he were us, etc. (in almost the same manner to "to be preserved"), so that those who trace their origin to the Romans may follow the institutions of the Roman church.[102]

102. RI 5:118(119), 231–33, November 27, 1202.

LXX. But when John had succeeded, he handed over the *pallium*, the miter, and the ring to the aforementioned archbishop after he had received the oath of fidelity and obedience to the Supreme Pontiff and the Roman church to be given in perpetuity. When he had been received honorably and devoutly by the aforesaid Johannitsa, or Kalojan, the Lord of the Wallachians and Bulgars, with his counsel and agreement he established two other Metropolitan Sees in the kingdom: namely, Valebud [Köstendil] and Prosthlaven,[103] which he subjected to the aforesaid See of Zagorje ob Savi as Primate. At Trnova, one of the nobler cities of that province, he established the primacy. Having accomplished all these matters successfully, Johannitsa subjected himself and his Kingdom to the Roman church by the letter of privilege, whose content follows:

In the Name of the Father, and the Son, and the Holy Spirit, Amen. Since it has pleased our Lord Jesus Christ to make me lord and emperor of all Bulgaria and Wallachia, I have enquired in the writings of our ancients and the books and laws of our predecessors, emperors of blessed memory, how they established the kingdom of the Bulgars and the imperial foundation, and, on careful investigation, we have found in their writings that those emperors of the Bulgarians, Simon, Peter, and Samuel, and our predecessors received the crown for the empire and the patriarchal blessing from the most Holy Roman Church of God and the Apostolic See, Peter the Prince of the Apostles. So, also, my empire has desired to receive the blessing and the foundation of the imperial crown as head of his empire, and the patriarchal blessing from the Roman church and from the Apostolic See, Peter, the Prince of the Apostles, and from our most Holy Father, the universal pope, Innocent III, and the mandate of the Lord Pope shall have been given and granted in the city of Trnovo of my Empire, for the making and consecrating of archbishops, metropolitans, and bishops, and the remaining ecclesiastical sacramental obedience he granted to my empire so that they may have the fullest power in every holding and things belonging to my empire. For all the holdings of the church of my whole empire and my metropolitan patriarch and archbishop and bishops

103. Conrad Eubel, *Hierarchia Catholica medii aevi,* 3 vols. (Padua, 1960), 1:130 and 409. Valebud, now Köstendil, Bishop Anastasius; Preslaven, Bishop Savas.

and all the priests are subject to the Roman church and keep the law and custom and obedience which the emperors of all Bulgaria and Wallachia, our early predecessors, kept, and we follow in their footsteps in the same manner. Moreover, my empire has signed according to the security of its chrysobull that my empire will never depart from the Roman church and the Apostolic See, the Prince of the Apostles, Peter. My other princes of the empire may separate but I will be the beloved son summoned to the holy and Apostolic Roman See of the Prince of the Apostles, Peter. And, finally, whatever lands of Christians or pagans my empire may acquire will be under the power and mandate of the same Roman church and Apostolic See. And so that the present chrysobull of my empire may be kept valid and firm, I have given my empire into the hands of the most reverend man, John, legate of the Holy Roman church and chaplain of the Lord Pope, in which he has also brought our pious and favored-by-God empire under it in the six thousandth seventy and twelfth year, in the seventh indiction.[104]

LXXI. In addition, Joannitsa sent Basil, Bishop of Kostolac near Smederevo, with John, the chaplain, by whom he also transmitted certain gifts as a sign of devotion to the Lord Pope, as well as letters with the following content:

To the most Holy Ruler and Universal Pope, sitting on the See of blessed Peter, and to the Lord Father of my kingdom, Innocent III, Pope of the Apostolic See and the Roman church, and teacher of the whole world. I hope in God the savior of all men that your Holiness is in very good health and that your affairs prosper, together with all those gathered around the throne of your Holiness, the cardinals of the Holy Roman church. Your great Holiness should know that your son, and the son of the Roman church, the emperor of all the Bulgarians and Wallachians, with all the princes of my empire, is quite well through God and your holy prayers. My empire sent messengers to your Holiness many times, but they were not able to go to your Holiness. And so they could not go, because those who were not at peace with my empire controlled the roads. Afterward, in the month of June, my empire sent my archbishop of the whole Bulgarian region and of the holy universal and great church of Trnovo, called pri-

---

104. RI 7:4, 14–15, September 1203.

mate by the men of my empire, and a great man, named Basil, who was
not permitted to proceed to your Holiness when he arrived in Durazzo in
order that your Holiness might fulfill the desire of my empire according to
the custom of our predecessors, the emperors of the Bulgars and the Wallachians, Simon, Peter, and Samuel, my ancestors, and all the other emperors of the Bulgars. But with God's help and through the intervention of
the prayers of your Holiness, the present nuncio of the apostolic chair and
the first See of the Prince of the Apostles and of the holy and universal Roman church, John the Chaplain, came to me and brought me letters at the
command of your Holiness and the Apostolic See and he gave the *pallium*
to the said archbishop and made him primate of all Bulgaria and Wallachia
and brought letters of your Holiness to my empire and he explained what
your Holiness commanded. He filled my heart with great joy, which God
and your Holiness gave to me according to the will of my empire. And I
ask and pray your great Holiness to fulfill the desire of my empire and
send a pastoral staff to gather the sheep, and the other things the patriarch
has by custom, and make the present primate patriarch in the holy and
great church of Trnovo, the first city of all Bulgaria. Let that church have a
patriarch in perpetuity even after the death of that patriarch, at the command of your Holiness. And because it would be difficult to travel to the
Roman church at the death of a patriarch because of the long distance and
the warfare of mankind, it should be granted to the church of Trnovo by
the Roman Church to elect and consecrate a patriarch for itself, so that
that land may not remain without blessing on account of his absence, and
your consecration imperfect, and the sin would redound to your Holiness.
Moreover, we now seek that the chrism for baptism of Christians should
be made at the command of your Holiness in the holy and great church of
Trnovo. Your Holiness should know that when the *Romei*[105] learn that we
have received consecration from your Holiness, they will not give me
chrism. And I ask something else from your Holiness: that you send a cardinal to my empire, either him who came to me or another from the
Apostolic See, and that you give him a diadem and a scepter according to
the blessing of the Apostolic See and the Prince of the Apostles, and that
you send a privilege sealed with a great bull as a copy to be preserved in
perpetuity in the church of Trnovo, and let them give all these things to
my empire, and let them consecrate and crown my empire. Moreover, all

105. I.e., the Byzantines.

these things should be sent to my empire by your Holiness. Let the present messenger, the Bishop of Kostolac near Smederevo, Basil, see that he can refer to what you have written in your own hand. If your Holiness fulfills all these things, I will consider them together with the stock of my empire and of all Bulgarians and Wallachians, as beloved sons of the Holy Orthodox Roman church. And I leave the matter concerning the boundary of Hungary, Bulgaria, and Wallachia to the judgment of your Holiness to direct that business rightly and justly so that no sin should touch the soul of your Holiness, and so that my empire may have the rights of Bulgaria and Wallachia and may cease killing Christians against me and my empire. Moreover, your Holiness should know that five dioceses of Bulgaria, which the King of Hungary has invaded and holds together with the rights of churches and bishoprics, belong to my empire. They have been destroyed, and if this is just, let this be done. Whatever the present messenger of my empire, Bishop Basil of Kostalac near Smederevo, will say to your Holiness, you may hold to be true because he speaks for me.[106]

LXXII. By the same messengers, the Archbishop sent a letter as follows to the Supreme Pontiff:

Many favors and great prayers to the Lord and the most glorious one, and cochair of the Apostolic See, the father of all Christianity, and my lord, Pope Innocent III, Archbishop Basil concerning the lesser and more humble things of all Bulgaria and Wallachia, your perfect blessing. I adore the most merciful God and the most blessed Mother of God that my writing has found your Holiness sound and rejoicing and what my soul has desired for eighteen years, behold, today, what God and your holy prayer has given to us, the blessing of the See of Blessed Peter the Apostle and your Holiness. Your Holiness knows how I have passed my life seeking your blessing. My humility has moved through the month of July the fourth day of the six thousandth seventieth and eleventh [year], in the sixth indiction, to our holy and most glorious father, Innocent, the Roman Pope, and I have spent thirty days in Durazzo by the sea, and when I wanted to board ship to cross over, the Greeks detained me and did not let me pass but held me at Durazzo for eight days, and after many prayers to God and the most blessed Apostle Peter, Prince of the apostles, on my part, and your holy prayers, the Latins freed me. For they took counsel about

106. RI 7:6, 18–20, after September 8, 1203.

casting me into the sea, but God and your holy prayer rescued me. More-over, leaving the city, I returned to a villa called Kavaja,[107] and there I stayed for twenty days, and from there I sent my two good men to your Holiness in Rome, and whether they crossed the sea, God knows, but your letter reached me from my Lord, the emperor, telling me to return quickly because a cardinal arrived here from the Lord Pope. Reading the emper-or's letter and seeing that he was summoning me, I returned and reached Trnovo in the month of September, and I found the holy man, just and right, sent by your Holiness, called John the chaplain, and he gave me all the letters of your Holiness, and they were read to me. For this reason, my soul rejoiced, and I gave thanks to God, raising my hands to heaven, be-cause the Lord has visited his people and our blessed father, the pope, seeking the sheep that was lost that he might lead it back into the holy sheepfold [Jn 10:16]. And just as it said in the letters of your Holiness, so Master John the chaplain carried out the order of your great Holiness. He gave your blessing to me and granted me the *pallium* for the fullness of the pontifical office in the month of September on the eighth day on the feast of the Nativity of the Most Holy Mother of our God. And I, after I received the *pallium* with much humility of devotion, exhibited the obedience of fi-delity in the presence of the bishops who wrote to your Holiness and our prince and many others assisting in the church. And again, Holy Father, I ask your Holiness that you dispose and fulfill the ecclesiastical order and how I should rule the flock that has been committed to me by God and your Holiness. We do not have the holy chrism, nay, rather, we had re-ceived it from the Greeks but for the rest, the Greeks detested both us and you. You should know, my Lord, because all these things remained in your Holiness, that you ought to dispense in all things and teach us about the holy chrism how we should baptize people, and that we may not be a people without holy chrism, and that would be a sin. But you should ad-monish us, your sons, lost and wandering, and send me, good Father, the *pallia* needed for the two metropolitans of Preslav and Valebud.[108] What-ever else your Holiness knows may be needed for the fullness of my pon-tifical office, your Holiness will send it to me.[109]

---

107. Southwest of Durazzo.
108. RI 7:5, 17, nn. 13 and 14.
109. RI 7:6, 15–18, after September 8, 1203.

LXXIII. When the bishop and the chaplain arrived at the Apostolic See, the Lord Pope received them kindly, and at the request of Joannitsa, represented by the bishop, after diligent negotiation, he established him as King of the Wallachians and Bulgarians, sending him Leo, cardinal priest of Santa Croce,[110] as legate of the Apostolic See, and by him, the scepter of the kingdom and the royal diadem, so that, as Vicar of the Supreme Pontiff, he might anoint and crown him as king, having transmitted to him the following Apostolic privilege:

To Kalojan, illustrious King of the Bulgarians and the Wallachians, and his descendants, who will succeed him in perpetuity both in the kingdom and in devotion to the Apostolic See, in Jesus Christ, the King of kings and the Lord of lords, priest forever according to the order of Melchizedech [Ps 109:4], unto whose hands the Father gave all things, subjecting all things beneath his feet, to whom the earth and its fullness belongs, the world, and all dwelling in it, nay, rather, before whom every knee bends, in heaven, on earth, and in the nether world. He established the Supreme Pontiff of the Apostolic See and the Roman church, whom he ordained as his Vicar in blessed Peter, over peoples and kingdoms, conferring upon him the power of rooting out, of building and planting [Jer 1:10], speaking to him in the prophet who was from the priests of Anatoth, "Behold I have set you above peoples and kingdoms that you may root out, destroy, and despoil, and scatter, and build and plant."[111] In order to demonstrate this more clearly, not through another but through himself, when he took on human flesh for mankind, and he stretched out his shoe into Idumea in order to subject the foreigner to him and to bring back his sheep, who were not of this sheepfold, that there might be one sheepfold and one shepherd, he placed the foundation of the universal church in himself, whom God blessed over all in the world, and he conferred his *magisterium* and primacy on Peter, the Prince of the apostles, saying to him: "You are Peter, and upon this rock I will build my church and the gates of hell will not prevail against it, and I will give you the keys of the kingdom of heaven" [Mt 16:10]. Wherefore he also added," Whatever you will bind on earth will also be bound in heaven and whatever you loose on earth will

---

110. Leo Brancaleonis, cardinal priest of Santa Croce in Gerusalemme, 1202–1224. See Maleczek, *Papst und Kardinalskolleg von 1191 bis 1216,* 137–39.

111. Jeremiah was born in the village of Anatoth.

also be loosed in heaven" [Mt 18:19]. After his passion, he also ascended to heaven, committing his sheepfold to him and commending it to him in all things, and he said to him: "Feed my sheep" [Jn 21:17], with the word repeated three times, showing clearly by this that those who would deny contumaciously that they were subject to blessed Peter and committed to him were not sheep that belonged to his sheepfold, and they were not willing to learn his teachings and be subject to his *magisterium*, since the church is the ark on which a few souls, though others perished in the flood, are saved. Wherefore, just as all who the ark did not take aboard perished in the flood so all who shall have been found outside the church will be condemned at the judgment.[112] The church is prefigured in the ark, the deluge prefigures the judgment, and Noah, the pilot of the ark, prefigures Peter, the shepherd of the church. Noah, we read, walked with the Lord, but Peter is said to have come to the Lord on the waves of the sea, which signifies the world.

Also, we note expressly in this that no particular church was committed especially to Peter, but the whole world and the general church. For just as there are many peoples, so the great sea and the spacious world signifies the universe. For this reason, after he had chosen the others for a share of solicitude the Lord chose him for the fullness of power, when he said to him, "You will be called Cephas, which means both Peter and head" [Jn 1:42], so that he might show that Peter was the head of the church, and he would spread over the members like the unguent that ran down from the head of Aaron into his beard, so that nothing at all might be lost, since the fullness of the senses flourished in the head, but some share is spread through the members. In addition, when Peter asked if his brother should sin against him, how many times he should forgive him, even up to seven times, the Lord is read to have answered, "I do not say to you up to seven times, but even seventy times seven" [Mt 18:21–22]. Of course, since all time is included in the number of days, when seventy is multiplied by itself, it means in this context all the sins of all people, since Peter alone was able to forgive not only all sins but also the sins of everyone. For to him and no other is the saying of the Lord directed: "You follow me" [Jn 21:22], that is, in the office of the true shepherd and imitate

112. The idea that those "found outside the church at the time of judgment will be condemned" is used by Innocent here to refer not to pagans, Jews, or Muslims, but to those who have consciously rejected the Roman Church, as the context makes clear.

him in the fullness of ecclesiastical power, because the Lord made him his vicar in office and his successor in the *magisterium*. Thus the Lord transferred the inheritance to Peter's successors so that he could through him and under him make for others as if a partial legacy from his inheritance.

Since, therefore, we, though unworthy, exercise the office of vicar on earth of him who rules in the kingdom of men, and he will give it to whomever he wishes, since through him kings reign and princes rule, we know that it is said to Peter and his successors and us in him, "I have prayed for you to the Father that your faith may not fail, and after your conversion, confirm your brethren" [Lk 22:32]. Since by the command of the Lord we are required to feed his sheep, the Bulgarian and Wallachian peoples, who have for so long been separated from their mother's breasts, we wish to provide by paternal care in spiritual and temporal matters, desiring, confident in his authority, by whom Samuel anointed David as king, to appoint you king over them, and through our beloved son, Leo, cardinal priest of the title of Santa Croce, Legate of the Apostolic See, a man of foresight and honesty, special to us among our other brethren, we send the scepter of the kingdom and the royal diadem to you, to be placed on you as if by our hands, when he receives from you the oath that you will remain devoted and obedient to us and to our successors, and to the Roman church, and you will preserve all the lands and peoples subject to your empire in the obedience and devotion of the Apostolic See. At the petition, moreover, of our venerable brother Basil, Bishop of Kostolac near Smederova, whom you sent to the Apostolic See, we grant you the right of coining public money in your kingdom with your image on it. We also grant the privilege of the primacy to our venerable brother, Basil, Archbishop of Trnovo, over all the lands you rule, and they may, by the authority of the Apostolic See, crown both his successors and yours, after they have received an oath. And they may obtain the primatial dignity in your land, and the metropolitans both of the Bulgarian and Wallachian provinces will be subject to him, and they should show due reverence and honor to the primate according to canonical form. Thus, therefore, dearest son, you should recognize the favor that the Apostolic See, your mother, grants you, so you may repay us for all we have given to you. So you should confirm your kingdom in subjection and devotion to the Apostolic See so that, since it was founded under Peter on the firmness of that rock, of which the apostle spoke. The rock, moreover, was Christ, and the downpour of rains, the pressure of winds, and the assault of rivers did not frighten him. You also, in addition to the help of the Apostolic See that you see in the present to the degree of your devotion, will pass from a temporal kingdom to an eternal kingdom. We decree, therefore, no one, etc., infringe this privilege of our constitution and confirmation to him. But, if anyone, etc. Given at Anagni, by the hand of John, subdeacon and notary of the Holy Roman Church, sixth kalends of March, the seventh indiction, in the year of the Incarnation, 1204, in the seventh year of our pontificate.[113]

LXXIV. By the same legate, he also sent a banner to the king, with a letter as follows:

So that you may glory in the cross of our Lord Jesus Christ, and you should ascribe your triumph not to yourself but to him to whom every knee is bent, who teaches hands to fight and moves fingers to war, and among the various events of war you may feel fortified by his support, to whom the Lord granted the keys of the kingdom of heaven and the power of loosing, in addition to the insignia of the royal office that we sent to your Serenity by our beloved son, Leo, cardinal priest of Santa Croce, legate of the Apostolic See, a man of foresight and honest, we have also ordered to be sent to you by him a banner, which you should use against those who honor the crucifix by their lips, but are far from it in their hearts, at the petition of our venerable brother, Basil, Bishop of Kostolac, near Smederevo. But it increases not without mystery the meaning of the cross and keys that blessed Peter the Apostle took on both the cross of Christ and received the keys from Christ. And so, it represents the sign of the cross, as, on it, Christ, who conquers, reigns, and rules, defeats the powers of the air, and on which, seizing the prize, he captured the booty, dying the death in life, and he seized the Behemoth in his eyes as if in a trap [Jb 40:10]. Moreover, it represents the twin keys, the one of discretion, the other of power, so that you may distinguish between good and evil, light and darkness, as well as the sacred and profane. You should exercise the material sword committed to you for the punishment of malefactors, for the praise of the good, and you should take arms and shield against those who do not place themselves as helpers of God, but confident in their ferocity and in their number press forward to kick against the

---

113. RI 7: 3–6, about February 25, 1204. I wish to thank John Moore for providing me with his translation of portions of this letter.

goad. Therefore, we admonish your royal Serenity and we exhort you carefully and we command you by apostolic letter, that you employ this banner with humility of heart and that you be mindful of the Passion of the Lord between the battle lines, and you recognize his *magisterium*, to whom the Lord himself said, "You are Peter, and upon this rock I will build my church, and the gates of hell will not prevail against it, and I will give you the keys of the kingdom of heaven" [Mt 16:18–19]. For thus your enemies not only cannot prevail against you, but, the Lord granting, they will not remain before your face.[114]

LXXV. He also established the Archbishop of Trnova as Primate of all Bulgaria and Wallachia; and by the same legate, he sent the following privilege:

To the Archbishop of Trnovo, Primate of the Bulgarians and Wallachians and to his successors appointed in perpetuity in devotion to the Apostolic See. The King of kings, etc. (to "Samuel anointed David as king, we appointed our beloved son in Christ, Kalojan, until now their Lord, as king over them by our beloved son" etc.) to he will remain in devotion to the Apostolic See, we appointed you also as primate in the kingdom of the Bulgarians and Wallachians and we granted the authority of the primacy to the church of Trnovo by the present privilege, deciding that you and your successors, who will succeed you in devotion to the Apostolic See, who excel the other metropolitans of Bulgaria and Wallachia by reason of the primacy, and they should show due honor and reverence to them according to the canonical form of the primacy. We want your fraternity to know that among us these two words, primate and patriarch, mean almost the same thing, since patriarchs and primates have the same model, even though their names are different. Also, by the present privilege, we grant you and through you and your successors the full right of blessing and crowning the kings of the Bulgarians and Wallachians, but on your death, the present primate of this church, no one may be appointed with the object of taking any office unless he has been canonically elected to it according to the approved custom. Moreover, the elect should be consecrated solemnly as bishop by the metropolitans and suffragans of the same church who can be present, but the one consecrated should send messengers to the Apostolic See to ask for the *pallium* taken from the body of

114. RI 7:12, 26–27, about February 25, 1204.

blessed Peter, namely, the sign of fullness of the pontifical office. On receiving it, he will swear the oath to us and to our successors and to the Roman church that other primates and metropolitans swear to us according to general custom, and you yourself, on receiving the *pallium*, in the formula we sent signed with our seal as a perpetual reminder, expressing in it that, when they crown anyone king from the successors of the aforesaid king, they should receive the prescribed oath from him. Moreover, when one of the metropolitans, who are subject to you by right of primacy, goes the way of all flesh, you will confirm the canonical election of a suitable person and you will consecrate the person chosen as bishop. But you should send your messengers together with messengers of the church he presides over to the Apostolic See for the *pallium*, and we will freely and happily transmit it to you and through you to the metropolitan bishop, to be conferred according to the form you will receive under our seal, so that, if it happens that a legate or messenger is present, you will pursue it equally with him. But we grant that the chrism and oil of catechumens and of the sick should be made each year on Holy Thursday according to the custom of the Roman church, so that as often as necessary, those to be baptized may be baptized, and those to be confirmed may be confirmed by their diocesan bishops, and neither the consecration of bishops nor the ordination of priests may be either impeded or delayed for a defect of this kind. Although until now, with you, neither in the ordination of priest nor in the consecration of bishops was it the custom to receive anointing, still we wish that hereafter, following not only your rite but the Divine mandate, by which it is prescribed in the law that bishops and priests should be anointed, those to be ordained to the priesthood and those to be consecrated bishops should be solemnly anointed on their hands in the case of priests and on the hands and head in the case of bishops. We also grant your fraternity the license to have, besides the cross, the banner of our Lord's Passion, carried before you throughout Bulgaria and Wallachia. Given at Anagni, sixth of the kalends of March, year seven.[115]

LXXVI. Because, according to the custom of the Bulgarians and the Wallachians, bishops were not anointed either in the order of the priesthood or in consecration, the Lord Pope ordered that the bishop of Kostolac near Smederevo should be anointed in his presence ac-

---

115. RI 7:2, 6–8, about February 25, 1204.

cording to the Latin Rite by John, the Bishop of Albano, with two other bishops assisting, and he commanded that both the Primate and the Metropolitans and all the bishops should receive the sacred anointing, and thenceforward no priests should be ordained or bishops consecrated without anointing, giving his reasons on these matters in the letters he sent to the primate, to whom he also sent freely all the episcopal insignia by the same legate, writing to him as follows:

Since our Venerable Brother, the bishop of Kostolac near Smederevo, approached the Apostolic See, he informed us clearly that he had not received anointing with holy oil at his consecration, since bishops among you are not usually anointed when they are consecrated. Therefore, we have ordered that what was lacking in his case should be supplied, ordering that his head and hands should be anointed with Holy Chrism by our brother, John, Bishop of Albano,[116] with the assistance of two bishops, according to ecclesiastical custom. For the Catholic church holds this not merely by Divine precept but also from the example of the apostles. In Exodus, we read that the Lord commanded Moses to anoint Aaron and his sons so that they might enjoy his priestly office [Ex 30:30]. And Anacletus,[117] originally a Greek, who was ordained to the priesthood by blessed Peter and later succeeded Clement in the Apostolic office,[118] related that bishops on their ordination were to be anointed, according to the custom of the Apostles and Moses, because all sanctification consists in the Holy Spirit, whose invisible power is intermingled with the Holy Chrism. For this reason we wish you to know that there are two kinds of anointing, the exterior, which is material and visible, and the interior, which is spiritual and invisible. The body is anointed visibly with the exterior; the heart is anointed invisibly with the interior. Concerning the former, James said: "If anyone is sick among you, he should bring the priests of the church to pray over him, anointing him with oil in the name of the Lord, and the prayer of faith will heal the one who is sick" [Jas 5:14]. Of the latter, John

---

116. John was bishop of Tuscania in 1188 and bishop of Viterbo-Tuscania after 1192. In 1189 he was named cardinal priest of San Clemente. He was cardinal bishop of Albano from 1199 to 1210/1211. He was from Lombardy. See Maleczek, *Papst und Kardinalskolleg von 1191 bis 1216*, 94–95.

117. Pope Anacletus, 76–88.

118. Pope Clement, 88–97. See RI 7:3, 8–13, esp. 9, n. 6.

the Apostle said: "You who have received anointing from him, let him remain among you and you will not have need for anyone to teach you, but his anointing will teach you all things" [Jn 2:27]. The visible and exterior anointing is the sign of the invisible and interior anointing. But the invisible anointing is not only the sign but also the sacrament because, if one receives it worthily, it either works or increases without doubt what it designates. Therefore, in order to show the exterior and visible anointing, the oil, which is called the chrism of catechumens or of the sick, is blessed and made what it becomes by a mystical cause from oil and balsam. For through oil, the splendor of conscience is meant, as we read: "The prudent virgins brought oil in vessels with their lamps" [Mt 25:4], but by balsam, we mean the odor of reputation, because we read, "Like balsam, when it gives its aroma, I have given off perfume" [Sir 24:15]. Therefore, the bishop should be anointed with chrism not only on his body but in his heart, so that he may have the odor of reputation on the outside as much as the next one. Concerning the splendor of conscience, the apostle says, "Our glory is the witness of our conscience, for all the glory of the daughter of the king is from inside" [2 Cor 1:12]. Concerning the odor of reputation, the same apostle said, "We are the good odor of Christ everywhere, and we are the odor of life for some in life, for others, the odor of death in death" [2 Cor 2:15–16]. For the bishop ought to have good witness, both from those who are inside and from those who are outside, just as the curtain closes the curtain, and he who hears, let him say, "come" [Rv 22:17]. By this anointing, the head and hands of the bishop are consecrated. For, by the head we mean the mind, as in this passage: "Anoint your head and wash your face" [Mt 6:17]. By hands, we refer to works, according to this, "My hands distilled gold."[119] The hands are, therefore, anointed with the oil of piety so that the bishop might do good for all, but especially for the household of the faith. The head, however, is anointed with the balsam of charity so that the bishop may love God with his whole heart, his whole mind, and his whole soul, and his neighbor like himself [Mt 22:37; Mk 12:30; Lk 10:27]. The head is anointed because of its authority and dignity, the hands for their ministry and office. The head is anointed since it shows that it represents his passion, of whom the prophet says: "Like the unguent on his head that descends to his beard, the beard of Aaron" [Ps 132:2]. For Christ is the head of man and he says of himself: "The spirit of

119. Sg 5:5, where the word used is myrrh instead of gold.

the Lord is upon me, and for this he anointed me; he sent me to evangelize the poor" [Lk 4:18]. The hands are anointed so that the bishop may show that he has received the power of blessing and consecrating. Therefore, when the consecrator anoints, he says, "O Lord, deign to consecrate and sanctify these hands by this anointing and our blessing so that whomever they consecrate, may be consecrated and whomever they bless, may be blessed in the name of the Lord."[120] But in the Old Testament, not only the priest is anointed but the king and the prophet, as in the Book of Kings, the Lord commands Elias, "Go and turn your way through the desert to Damascus, and when you arrive there, anoint Aziel king over Syria and Jesi, son of Namsi, king over Israel. But you should anoint Elisea, son of Saphat who is out of Abelmela, as prophet in your place" [1 Kgs 19:15–16]. But Jesus the Nazarene, whom God anointed with the Holy Spirit, as is contained in the Acts of the Apostles, was anointed with oil in front of his brothers. He is, according to the Apostle, head of the church, which is his body. The anointing of the prince was transferred from the head to the arm, so that from that time on, the prince was not anointed on the head, but on the arm or shoulder or shoulder blade. In these things the principate is fittingly designated as we read: "The principate was made on his shoulder" [Is 9:6]. For this reason, also, Samuel caused the designated shoulder to be put before Saul and gave him a place at the head before those who had been invited. But the sacramental portion on the head of the bishop has been preserved; it represents the person of the head in the pontifical office. It is fitting, moreover, to distinguish between the anointing of the bishop and the prince, because the head of the bishop is consecrated with chrism, but the arm of the prince is anointed with oil. This shows the degree of difference between the authority of the bishop and the power of the prince. Because Christ, therefore, made us a kingdom and priest in his blood for our God, which is why Peter the Apostle said: "You are a chosen stock, a royal priesthood" [1 Pt 2:9], and so in the New Testament not only kings and priests are anointed but also all Christians twice before baptism, but with blessed oil, first on the breast, then between the shoulders, and twice after baptism, but with Holy Chrism, first on the top of the head and then on the forehead. The one to be baptized is anointed on the breast so that he will reject error and ignorance by the gift of the Holy Spirit and receive the true faith, because

120. Prayer to be said on anointing the hands of a priest. See RI 7:3, 11, n. 11.

the just man lives by faith [Heb 10:38]. Moreover, the one to be baptized is anointed between the shoulders so that by the grace of the Holy Spirit he will cast away negligence and laziness, and do good work, because faith without works is dead [Jas 2:26], so that by the sacrament of faith there may be cleanness in his breast; by the exercise of work there may be strength of labors in his shoulders to the extent that faith, according to the apostle, is worked through love. But the one baptized is anointed on the top of his head so that he may be ready to give account to any demand of the faith, because by the head is understood the mind, as we read: "The eyes of the wise man in his head" [Eccl 2:14], and the upper part of it is reason, and the lower part sensuality. Wherefore, reason is well understood by the top, which is the upper part of the head, which is the superior part of the mind. The one to be baptized is anointed on the forehead so that he may fully confess what he believes, because in the heart there is belief for justice, but in the mouth let there be confession for salvation; mindful of this, the Lord has said, "He who has confessed me before men, I will also confess him before my father" [Mt 10:32]. Before baptism, indeed, he is anointed with blessed oil, and after baptism with sacred chrism, because chrism is suitable only for the Christian. For Christ is named from chrism, or rather chrism is named after Christ, not according to the form of the name but according to the rationale of faith. Christians are called after Christ, as those anointed are derived from the anointed, so that all of the anointed should participate in the odor of him whose blood was shed. By the anointing of the forehead, the imposition of the hands is designated, and this, by another name refers to confirmation, because, through it, the Holy Spirit is given to increase and strengthen. For this reason, while a simple priest, that is, a presbyter, can administer other anointings, none save the highest priest, that is, the bishop, should confer this, because we read concerning the apostles, whose vicars the bishops are, that they were giving the Holy Spirit by the imposition of hands, as the preaching of the Acts of the Apostles shows. "When the apostles who were in Jerusalem had heard," it said, "that Samaria had received the word of God, they sent Peter and John to them" [Acts 8:15]. And when they arrived, they prayed for them that they might receive the Holy Spirit, for He had not come to any of them, but they had only been baptized in the name of the Lord Jesus. Then they imposed their hands upon them, and they received the Holy Spirit, whose coming is designated by the mystery of anointing, because the dove, in which the Holy Spirit descended upon Christ in baptism in the evening, returned in the cataclysm and brought back the branch of the living olive. And David the prophet, certainly having foreknowledge of this sacrament, predicted that the face would be made joyful in oil [Ps 103:15].

In addition, according to ecclesiastical custom, there are anointings when an altar is consecrated, when a church is dedicated, when a chalice is blessed, not only from the mandate of the Divine Law, but also by the example of blessed Sylvester, who, when he consecrated an altar, anointed it with chrism.[121] For the Lord commanded Moses to make an oil for anointing, with which to anoint the tabernacle and the table with the vessels. And if, perhaps, you have doubts about these anointings, when we have heard from you, we will instruct your fraternity more fully. But the sacrament of anointing makes something else effective and is figured in the New and Old Testaments. For this reason, the church is not judaizing, as some, who do not know the Scriptures or the powers of God, say. Therefore, we admonish your Fraternity and exhort you more carefully by Apostolic letter, and we command you that you also should receive the sacred anointing at the command of our beloved son, Leo, cardinal priest of Santa Croce, legate of the Apostolic See, lest anything should be lacking to the fullness of the sacrament, so that, when you have been anointed with the sacred chrism, you may likewise anoint your archbishops and bishops, and through them you cause the hands of priests to be anointed with blessed oil, keeping that custom for ordaining priests and consecrating bishops and ordering its observance as the Apostolic See observes it, which is at the Lord's disposition, the mother and teacher of all the faithful.

Moreover, we have sent your episcopal ornaments by the same cardinal: shoes, sandals, amice and alb, cincture, undergirdle, napkin, maniple, tunic and dalmatic, gloves and ring, chasuble and mitre. We sent the *pallium* earlier by our beloved son, John, our chaplain, and, although the Roman Pontiff does not use the pastoral staff, both for historical and mystical reasons, still you can use it as do other bishops, and the same cardinal can teach you all the reasons as he learned them from us.[122]

LXXVII. He also sent *pallia* to the two newly created Archbishops by the same legate, to be given to them according to this form:

121. Pope Sylvester I, 314–335.
122. RI 7:3, 8–13, about February 25, 1204.

To the honor of Almighty God and the Blessed Virgin Mary, and of the blessed Apostles, Peter and Paul, and of the Lord Pope Innocent and the Roman Church, as well as the church committed to you, we grant to you the *pallium* taken from the body of blessed Peter, as a sign of the fullness of pontifical office, which you may use in the churches subject to you at the solemnities of Masses, on the Nativity of the Lord, the feast of Stephen the Protomartyr, on the Circumcision of the Lord, the Epiphany, Ash Wednesday, Palm Sunday, the Lord's Supper, Holy Saturday, Easter, *feria secunda* after Easter, the Ascension of the Lord, Pentecost, the three feasts of Saint Mary, the Birthday of John the Baptist, the solemnities of all the Apostles, the commemoration of all Saints, the dedications of churches, the consecrations of bishops, the ordinations of clerics, the principal feasts of your church, and on the anniversary of your consecration. Of course, the Roman Pontiff alone always uses the *pallium* in the solemnities of masses everywhere, because he is possessed of the fullness of ecclesiastical power, which is symbolized by the *pallium*. But others should use it on certain days, not always or everywhere, but in their church in which they have received ecclesiastical jurisdiction, since they are called to a share of solicitude, not to the fullness of power.[123]

He also commanded that he should receive an oath from the Primate and the archbishops:

I, Archbishop of Trnovo, primate of all Bulgaria and Wallachia, from this time on, will be loyal and obedient to blessed Peter and to the Holy Roman Church and the Apostolic See, and to my Lord Innocent and his Catholic successors. I will not act in deed, or counsel, or by assent, so that they may lose life or limb, or may be seized or despoiled, I will not offer counsel to anyone who would believe me, to their loss, within my knowledge. If I should know a certain evil of them, I will endeavor to stop it, but if I cannot stop it, I will take care to inform them as soon as I can. I will defend the honors and dignities of the Roman papacy, and the causes of the Apostolic See, as much as possible, saving my order, against everyone living. When summoned, I will come to a synod unless I have been prevented by a canonical impediment. I will visit the threshold of the apostles every four years in person or by my representative unless absolved by per-

123. RI 7:10, 24–25, about February 25, 1204.

mission. I will devoutly receive a legate of the Apostolic See whom I know for certain to be a legate, and I will assist him in his needs. When I consecrate any of my suffragans as bishops, I will make him swear that he will give obedience and due honor to the Roman Pontiff and the Apostolic See. When I crown anyone king of the Bulgarians and Wallachians according to the indulgence granted me and my successors by the Apostolic See, I will receive his security on oath that he will remain devoted and obedient to him who is then in charge of the Apostolic See and his successors, and to the Roman church, and also he will hold all the lands and peoples subject to his empire in obedience and devotion to the Apostolic See. I will keep all these things in good faith, so help me God and these Holy Gospels in the present and future.[124]

LXXVIII. As the Legate, therefore, passed though Hungary, he was honorably and devoutly received both by the king and the princes. But when he arrived at the borders of Hungary, the king sent messengers after him to prevent his passage. On this matter, the Lord Pope proceeded as his letters sent to the King of Hungary make clear:

Among other Catholic kings and Christian princes, we especially glory in you, dearest son, that you are loyal to God and devoted to us, so that you may merit to be glorified in order that you may obtain the special grace and favor of the Apostolic See just as from this not only several judgments but also examples prove. For, on his return to the Apostolic See, John, then our chaplain but now bishop of Forcone,[125] suggested to us again and again that, after he was received by you with great honor and devotion, he mercifully obtained not only what he asked about the business of Kulin[126] from your royal Highness, but also asked for free passage through your kingdom for himself and other messengers and legates of the Roman church and on their return to Bulgaria and Wallachia. You, also, if we remember well, have suggested that it pleased your serenity that the *Meggaiuppanus* of Serbia[127] should show due and devoted reverence and obe-

124. RI 7:11, 25–26, about February 25, 1204, but without date.
125. John became bishop of Forcone (after 1256, Aquila) in the spring of 1204. He was promoted to bishop of Perugia ca. 1206. See RI 2:167(176), 323, n.3.
126. See RI 7:126, 199, n. 4. "Banus" of Bosnia, 1180–1204.
127. Vukan, prince of Serbia, was installed by King Emmerich of Hungary in place of his brother, Stephen.

dience to the Apostolic See and that he should receive a crown from us, saving your right in the temporals of kings. Wherefore, we have remembered that we ordered the carrying out of this matter by our brother, the Archbishop of Kalocsa. We have been persuaded not only by these general reasons but also by special ones and we, therefore, ordered our beloved son, Leo, cardinal priest of the title of Santa Croce, legate of the Apostolic See, to be sent to Bulgaria and Wallachia by way of your kingdom for the propagation of the Christian faith. He, as he has intimated in his letters to us, was honored by your Royal Highness even more than he would have believed so that, you, as if you had set aside the whole royal burden, tried to bring about those things that would please him, after you had earlier, with all joy, given passage to the messengers he had ordered sent to Bulgaria. Often he gave the kiss of peace and made a mutual promise of special friendship with great joy and gave gifts. He not only obtained permission for passage but you also ordered your messengers to guide him to Bulgaria with honor, promising that you would send him your letter at the border, which he could keep with him secretly and work faithfully for the reestablishment of peace according to its terms. Proceeding, therefore, with your messengers, he arrived at the boundary of the kingdom at a *castrum* called Kovin, where the Kingdom of Hungary is separated from the province of the Bulgarians only by the Danube, with many from the other side awaiting him with desire, but after the hour of one day, he unexpectedly received messengers, and they, coming with greatest haste, ordered that his passage and that of the Bulgarian bishop should be prevented.

The messengers proposed on the king's behalf that he should return to a certain fortress of yours that was now three days' journey in the rear and remain there while he asked the lord of the Bulgarians through messengers to come quickly to a certain island on the border in order that he might first understand more fully the controversy which existed between you and bring it to a proper conclusion, otherwise he would not allow him to pass. But the cardinal himself, among many things, responded that he ought not to act in this way, but, because if he were to receive him on his return to the breasts of his mother with agreements of this kind, and he would be involved in this matter not only in secular but spiritual business, it would appear that a kind of simoniacal depravity was involved, because he could not force him to do anything until he was tied to the Apostolic See by a special bond. For this reason, since the king was unwilling to retreat from his undertaking, he next issued an edict by the count of the fort that whoever dared to sell anything to him and his party or even the bishop or to show any of the comforts of humanity, would incur a penalty against their persons and property, and the cardinal himself with the bishop was guarded by at least three hundred surrounding armed retainers, who put such pressure on him that they observed the rooms of the enemy, if they could be called rooms, so that we should be silent about those things which overwhelmed them and their men in the worst way concerning the necessities of nature. Alas, alas, dearest son, where is the royal clemency, where the Christian religion, where the special devotion you claim to have for us and the Roman church? The finest color has been changed and gold had been made worthless. Therefore, let God attend to them, who seduced your soul with evil counsel and desired to sow discord between the kingdom and the priesthood! But we certainly hope that you will now correct these mistakes either personally or that you would make such changes at our admonishing that injury may become honor and offense may be returned to favor. Therefore, we ask your Royal Serenity more attentively about what we trust fully, and we advise you to make satisfaction so as to abolish the injury to the cardinal, indeed, actually more to us than to him, but rather directed against the Lord Jesus Christ in us, so that we can experience your devotion in this and are not forced on this account to do anything that can be injurious to you, because, insofar as an injury to us would be an injury to you in anything, we cannot permit such bad example to be uncorrected and still pursue our project with God as its author.[128]

We have written to you more meekly and kindly than the present matter might require lest someone looking at our letter think that the Apostolic See had withdrawn from you and would not be supportive of your utility and honor, because there are many deeds carried out in your kingdom which, if they were reduced to a file, would require more serious correction, not only concerning your vow, fraternal deception, and election of prelates, but also about many other things which we have not gone into lest you should be too upset at present. May you, therefore, provide for yourself, lest you get into difficulty in this matter, which you do not have the power easily to carry out.[129]

128. RI 7:126, 201 inserts the following statement in the text: "Hec cedula fuit interclusa in litteris ad prefatum regem transmissis." This means that what follows was a secret message to the king.

129. RI 7:126, 199–202, about September 15, 1204.

LXXIX. But the King sent a certain knight with a letter of explanation to the Lord Pope, and the Lord Pope responded through him as follows:

We have received the letter of your Royal Highness sent to us by your beloved son, the noble man, E., knight, and we have carefully noted what you meant by it. We respond to the first point, therefore, that, certainly your predecessors of pious memory from whom the Kingdom of Hungary attained the unity of the Catholic faith by the diligence of blessed Stephen the king,[130] and all who descended from his progeny, by the precedence of Divine grace, were held in high regard at the Apostolic See, just as in the kingdom, they likewise succeeded in showing reverence to them and to the successors of blessed Peter, especially your father, King Bela,[131] of distinguished memory, who desired to honor the Apostolic See throughout his life, whom you, succeeding both in the kingdom and in devotion, have desired to do whatever might bring him comfort and honor. Further, just as we recognize the things that have been said to be true without any doubt, so you should without doubt recognize those things that must be said to be true. For, although our predecessors desired to love and honor your ancestors among all the other kings with a special favor, trying to favor them according to God in every necessity, the Apostolic See took care especially to promote your father of distinguished memory in all his struggles so that, when, as we believe, for certain reasons known to you, he could not obtain the royal crown, our predecessor, Alexander,[132] of happy memory, after many exhortations, commands, and warnings delivered to the Archbishop of Esztergom,[133] to confer the royal crown on him, since he could not persuade him, finally ordered the Archbishop of Kalocsa[134] to crown him as king without any prejudice to the church of Esztergom, and thus obtained his coronation at the mandate of the Apostolic See. Also, so far as it could, the Apostolic See took care to support you at the beginning of your reign, which was quite disturbed by the dissensions of many, and showed the result of affairs which finally through its legate, appointed especially for this purpose, brought you and your party and your brother

130. Stephen, king of Hungary, 1000–1038.
131. Bela III, king of Hungary, 1172–1196.
132. Pope Alexander III, 1159–1181.
133. Archbishop Lukas Bánffy, 1158–1174.
134. Archbishop Chemma of Kalocsa. See RI 7:127, 203, n. 6.

and his followers from the other party to peace, and although it was agreed to and signed, still would that it were better observed!

We respond to the second point in this way: that you indeed granted our messengers wishing to go through your land into the land of Joannitsa, lord of the Bulgarians and Wallachians, safe conduct and free passage, dismissing the army you had gathered against him at the request of our legate, after their goods were destroyed for no reason. Upon these matters we refer them to your Serenity for full favorable action.

But you have written that Joannitsa occupies the land that your father gave in dowry to your sister, the empress of the Greeks,[135] and he has cruelly laid waste to the land of Serbia, subject to your crown, with a large multitude of pagans so that besides those who are party to his tyranny, many Christians have been led into captivity by pagans. And, at a time when, especially persuaded by our pleas, the king of Bohemia[136] withdrew from his alliance with Philip and joined King Otto, you sent a strong army against him on the king's behalf. You knew very certainly that whatever was attempted to your injury and loss would be exceedingly injurious to us. So that he would make suitable satisfaction to you, we diligently work for the fulfillment of your desire and for an efficacious result.

We respond to the third point in this way, that if you have written that Joannitsa is not by right lord of any land, even though he may have occupied some part of your kingdom and some part of the kingdom of another for a time, for which reason you wonder why we would propose so immediately to crown such a manifest enemy of yours as king without consulting you, still it is from a certain point of view that we speak, saving your peace, since you do not know the full truth in this matter. For, of old, many kings were successively crowned in Bulgaria by Apostolic authority, like Peter and Samuel and several others after them. For, also, at the preaching of our predecessor, Pope Nicholas,[137] of holy memory, the king of the Bulgarians, to whose consultation he very often responded, merited to be baptized with his whole kingdom, but then, with the prevalence of the Greeks, the Bulgarians lost the royal dignity, and indeed were forced under a heavy yoke to serve the emperor of Constantinople, until recently

135. Margaret, daughter of King Bela III, married the Byzantine emperor Isaac II Angelos in 1185.
136. King Otokar of Bohemia changed sides from Philip of Swabia to Otto of Brunswick in 1202.
137. Pope Nicholas I, 858–867.

two brothers named Peter and Joannitsa, descendants of the stock of the earlier kings, began not only to occupy but also to recover the land of their fathers, with the result that they obtained a wonderful victory on one day from great princes and numberless peoples. Therefore, we do not deny that they violently invaded some foreign lands, but we assert constantly that they have recovered a major share of the land by hereditary right. For this reason, we intend to crown him king not over a foreign land but over his own in the manner of our predecessor. We also desire him to restore the land he holds unjustly and that the land held unjustly by others should be restored to him, since he asked this of us: that in the matter of lands that were invaded, we would work to bring about justice to both parties, you and him. Since, therefore, you should grant not only free passage but also safe conduct to our messengers to him and his messengers to us, we do not think that he would be a very unsafe enemy for you, even if through the desire of our solicitude, with the reason for enmity removed, you could make friends of your enemies. We did not advance the completion of this business, since frequently we have taken care to send messengers to him with letters on account of this, in order to recall the daughter to her mother and lead the member back to the head, so that there would be one flock and one shepherd. But also we could not delay in this case because, since the nobleman, Stephen, *meggaiuppanus* of Serbia, asked us humbly through our messengers to send a legate to his land to lead it back into the obedience of the Roman church and grant him a royal crown. And we, after discussions with our brethren, decided to agree to his request, appointing as legate, our venerable brother, John, Bishop of Albano. With the understanding finally that this might be rather displeasing to your Royal Sublimity, we abandoned the undertaking, not without a certain confusion on our part, out of favor for you. But after you fought Serbia, when Stephen was removed and Vukan replaced him, you intimated through our messengers that you wanted to lead that land back to the obedience of the Roman church and you were likewise in agreement that, with your rights in temporal matters safeguarded, said Vukan should receive the royal crown from the Apostolic See. For this reason, we ordered that this business concerning the counsel of your messengers should be entrusted to the Archbishop of Kalocsa. But when two years went by, we saw no progress.

We respond now to the fourth point in this way: that, although you received and honored carefully our beloved son, Leo, cardinal priest of the title of Santa Croce, so that you made him depart kindly with the kiss of peace to be conducted to the frontiers of the kingdom, so that now there was nothing left but the passage of the Danube from Hungary to Bulgaria, still, because, in the words of the poet, "The stranger is worse off when he is thrown out than when he is denied entry,"[138] we wonder not a little and we are rather concerned more for you than for ourselves, that you next ordered him to be brought back, since it would have been less indecent not to have allowed his entry than not to permit his departure after he was admitted. As to the reason you gave in your letter on this affair, it would suffice to give that Solomonic response: "In vain is the net cast before the eyes of birds" [Prv 1:17], save that it behooves us to respond to it that you asked strongly in your letter that we would either give up entirely the project for the coronation or at least hold off awhile until the discord between you could be settled by judgment or by arbitration, since you are prepared to appear for judgment or arbitration by our legate. Therefore, we give a very few reasons about several matters lest too much of a response disturb you too much. For when the aforementioned cardinal made a long delay in your kingdom and was received with openness but also honored magnificently by you and others, he could not immediately be an impartial mediator to establish an agreement or an equal judge for settling the controversy, unless he would be received in an equal way by him in his own land so that every suspicion might removed. Besides, he could not compel him to make peace or to render justice before he received the yoke of apostolic discipline and would be subject to our *magisterium* and commands. Since the same legate proceeded to this point to propagate the sacrament of the Christian faith and promote the honor of the Apostolic See, you would, if you prevented him, immediately incur Divine indignation and merit our anger, and you would make him more your enemy and would profit nothing, because we could carry out our project in another way. Nevertheless, give careful heed how you finally decide and understand what we are thinking. If we wish to prevent it, the son of your flesh might not be crowned king. If you try to prevent our spiritual son from being crowned a king, a prodigal son, I say, who formerly dissipated his substance in luxurious living with harlots, but finally found himself and returned to his father, who running to him, embraced his son who returned and ordered his servants to put the best garment on

138. Ovid, *Tristia*, V, 6, 13.

him and put a ring on his hand and shoes on his feet, and to kill the fatted calf and hold a feast, because his son was dead and returned to life, was lost and has been found [Lk 15:11–32]. The gospel parable teaches us how a father should deal with the anger of the elder son. We wish you to imitate its lesson both in this and in other matters. But if, perhaps, you are afraid that after he has received a crown, the one raised up will immediately become more insolent, you should know for certain that not only would he not profit from the trickery he pulled insofar as he would lose out by his lies, and we say less to you so that you should through yourself know more.

We respond to the fifth point that, even if you should write that after two years you have not been able to obtain justice with the help of the Roman church, under our security against the trickery of your enemies, who destroyed Zara, until now such an irreparable loss, and treated lightly the opinion of the Apostolic See, and, for this reason, [you think] you may never obtain justice with the help of the Roman church if you permit Joannitsa to be crowned before the discord between you and him is settled, we want you to be aware, dearest son, that we have taken care to bind both the Venetian fleet and the army of the Franks by the chain of anathema because of the destruction of Zara. And when the leaders of the Gallican army[139] sought absolution, they could not be absolved unless they swore to keep our mandates and obligated not only themselves but also their heirs through authentic and patent letters to obtain satisfaction for this excess at our command. But because the Venetian Doge and his men have not yet requested the grace of absolution, we have already proceeded against them in such a way that we have refused to consecrate their beloved son, the patriarch-elect. Indeed, when he approached us in person, we sent him back in disorder, not without much shame. We also made known to you that at Zara, which until then was subject with its whole province to the Patriarch of Grado,[140] you should order a canonical election of a suitable person to be held and send the one elected to us for consecration and the *pallium,* so that we might thus begin to punish the pride of the Venetians. In the same way, Joannitsa would be punished if, after receiving a crown, he was unwilling to appear for the arbitration and judgment of our legate on the discord that exists between you, and his

139. I.e., the Frankish crusaders.
140. Benedict Falier, patriarch-elect of Grado.

most recent situation would become worse than his earlier, his most recent error worse than his former. But, because, as much as we love Joannitsa, we love you incomparably more, we now believe we have found an agreement by which provision can be made for your honor and right, just as you should know from the letter we have sent on this matter. Therefore, we ask your royal Serenity more carefully and we admonish you, that giving glory to God and honor to us, you do not impede the propagation of the Christian faith, whose fruitful counsel you will no doubt experience.[141]

LXXX. Moreover, by that word contained in the previous letter, "what finally would you think if we should wish to prevent the son of your flesh from being crowned as king," the King was deeply terrified because, since he had commanded a solemn court to meet so that he might order the coronation of his little son as king, he was vehemently afraid lest the Pope would command that his coronation be prevented. When, therefore, the aforesaid cardinal sent messengers to the papal court, he finally obtained permission for passage from the King. When the legate had set out, he accomplished everything as it had been decided and on his return he carried letters from the King and the Primate of the Bulgars and Wallachians as follows:

From Kalojan, king of all Bulgaria and Wallachia, to the one raised by God, the most holy, the beloved in Christ and most honored father of my kingdom, Innocent III, the very sacred Pope of Rome and successor of the Prince of the Apostles, the apostle Peter. The legate of the Apostolic See, the Lord Cardinal Leo, brought the writing of your holiness to my empire, learning also about his soundness and safety, I have glorified almighty God and his most holy mother. And, hopefully, my imperial letter will find your Holiness living and flourishing with all joy and delight. My empire, by the grace of almighty God and the blessed Mother of God, and through the intercession of your Holiness, is safe and very well with all joy and exultation. But, your Holiness, the spiritual father of my kingdom, the Lord Pope, should know that the Lord Leo, legate of the Apostolic See, came to

141. RI 7:27, 202–8, September 15, 1204. This letter is contained in a letter of this date addressed to Cardinal Leo of Santa Croce.

my empire, bearing the crown, and blessing it he placed it on the head of my empire, and he put in my hands the scepter and the banner. He blessed the most holy patriarch of my kingdom and of all Bulgaria at the command of your Holiness, and we have especially glorified God and the blessed Mother of God, as well as the consideration of your Holiness in that your Holiness fulfilled our every desire according to our request. And all Bulgaria and Wallachia, and all the parts of my empire, have glorified exceedingly and magnified your Holiness. Moreover, I also write you concerning the Hungarian, since my empire does not have any association of regions or any business with him, nor does it injure him; indeed, he holds in contempt and injures the territories of my empire. And the Lord Leo saw and he will announce to your Holiness what is just or unjust by my empire or if I hold Hungary in contempt. And your Holiness should write to him that he should stay away from my kingdom because my empire neither has contempt for him nor does it invade his lands. But if he should come against the lands of my empire, and God helps so that he is conquered, your Holiness should not hold my empire suspect but I should be free. I also write your Holiness about the Latins who entered Constantinople so that you may write them to keep their distance from my empire and, just as my empire does them no harm, neither should theirs do evil to us. But if perhaps they try to attack my empire and hold it in contempt and they are killed, your Holiness should not hold my empire suspect, but all should be free. Moreover, I have sent two boys to your Holiness, one is named Basil, the other Bethlehem, and it is my command that they should learn Latin letters in the schools because we do not have grammar teachers who can translate the letters you have sent us, and after they learn, they should be sent back to my empire. Moreover, I have now sent as a token of remembrance two pieces of velvet; one is red and the other white, and a camel. But when I send legates to your Holiness, I will be ever mindful of your Holiness.[142]

LXXXI. Many favors and much good health from me, Basil, humble primate of the Bulgarians and Wallachians, to the father of all and my lord and father, the most magnificent and most holy Pope Innocent. We pray to almighty God and the most holy Mother of God and the most blessed Apostles, Peter and Paul, that the letter of my Humility may find you in good health and safety, and by the magnificence of your Lordship, I live,

---

142. RI 7:230, 409–11, November 8–15, 1204.

also, I, enveloped in great sins, live by the grace of God. Be it known, therefore, to your great Holiness that Cardinal Leo, sent by your Holiness and the Apostolic See, arrived safe and sound. He reached our great city of Trnovo on the fifteenth of October, and brought the complete fullness of the patriarchal dignity and all the raiment that was sent to me by your great Holiness; he handed over the ring and privilege, and the letters and instructions, and he anointed me with chrism and blessed me at the command of your Holiness. He consecrated me at the command of your Holiness, and he consecrated me as patriarch on the seventh of November, namely, on the feast of St. James, the brother of the Lord, and on that day, I anointed the metropolitans and other bishops with great joy and the Cardinal blessed both of the metropolitans and gave them the *pallium* and the miters, and he put the miters for the others on their heads.[143] Moreover, on the eighth day of the same month, namely, on the Feast of St. Michael, he crowned and blessed the Emperor Kalojan, Lord of all the Bulgarians and Wallachians, and he placed on his head the royal crown and put the scepter in his hands. He completed and accomplished all these things according to the will of your Holiness, and blessing us, he departed from us on the fifteenth of November. Meanwhile, your great Holiness should know that, at the command of the lord emperor, I am sending two boys to you. One is the son of the priest, Constantine, the other of the king, so that they may learn Latin letters from the command of your Holiness. And whatever you think worthwhile to the honor of the emperor, do it. For may God preserve your Holiness for many years and a long life.[144]

LXXXII. Alexius,[145] the son of Isaac, the former emperor of Constantinople, escaped prison and came to the Supreme Pontiff, laying a

---

143. Despite Innocent III's effort to avoid granting the patriarchal dignity to Basil, this letter makes clear that he regarded himself as patriarch.

144. RI 7:231, 411–12, November 8–15, 1204.

145. He would reign as Alexius IV. He sought support in the West and gained the imperial throne with the help of the crusaders, despite Innocent's opposition. He failed to provide promised support to the crusaders and provoked a rebellion in Constantinople led by Alexius V Ducas, who murdered him on the night of February 8–9, 1204. For a discussion of these events from the Byzantine point of view, see Charles Brand, *Byzantium Confronts the West, 1180–1204* (Cambridge, Mass.: Harvard University Press, 1968), 250–52. For a more general account, see Warren Treadgold, *A History of the Byzantine State and Society* (Stanford, Calif.: Stanford University Press, 1997), 659–66.

serious complaint about his uncle, Alexius,[146] Emperor of Constantinople, namely, that he had cruelly blinded his father, Isaac,[147] whom he should have honored as brother and lord, and violently seizing the throne, he had imprisoned both him and Alexius himself, his son, bound them with iron chains. He, therefore, sought justice concerning him, against whom the same emperor had sent his ambassadors and letters to the Supreme Pontiff, whose content is explained in his Apostolic letter responding to the emperor. He also dealt with other matters upon which the same emperor had written him:

We have received the letter and ambassadors of the Imperial Dignity in the proper manner, and we have diligently considered both those matters which the ambassadors desired to propose and those contained in the same letter. Your ambassadors explained further to us and your letter also contained word that, since the army of the Christians, which is about to come to the aid of the Holy Land proposed to invade the land of your Greatness and to use weapons against Christians, it was fitting to our office that we should recall them from such a plan, lest perhaps befouling their hands with the murder of Christians, they then both offend God and to no small degree weaken their attack on the enemies of Christ. In addition, on the part of your Highness, they added that we should in no way show favor to Alexius, the son of Isaac Angelus, the former emperor, who approached Duke Philip of Swabia so that he could, with his help against you, obtain the throne, because the throne ought not to come to him for any reason, since it is conferred not by heredity but by election of the nobles, unless perhaps he was begotten after the height of the imperial dignity had been achieved, and Alexius could not claim this, since he was born before his father was promoted to the emperorship. Because his father was then a private person in the empire he could not claim something as a right for himself. But we responded to your imperial Prudence in the following manner, that the aforesaid Alexius some time ago approached our presence and in our presence and that of our brethren, with many noble Romans there, proposed a serious question, asserting that you seized his father unjustly and against his will, caused him to be blinded, and handed

146. Alexius III, to whom the following letter is addressed.
147. For Isaac II, see Treadgold, *Byzantine State*, 656–59.

them over to be detained in prison. Because he had no recourse to a superior, and we were, according to the apostle, debtors to both the wise and the foolish, we were required to do justice to him. When we responded to him as we saw was useful, he departed from us and hastened quickly to his brother-in-law, Philip, with whom he carried on deliberations so that Philip sent his ambassadors to the princes of the Christian army without any delay, asking and petitioning them that, because he and his father had been wrongfully despoiled of the imperial throne, they ought to enter the kingdom of Constantinople with him, and give counsel and show favor to recover it for him. He promised that he was prepared to help them magnificently in all things both in aid of the Holy Land and in expenses and gifts and to stand by all our commands, and that he wanted to honor the Holy Roman church in all ways that he could and carry out those things which would be pleasing to our will. But after the princes had deliberated, they responded that since they could not and ought not proceed in such an arduous business without our authority and mandate, they wished to consult us on these matters and then to await the pleasure of our will. They persuaded our beloved son, Peter, cardinal priest of Saint Marcellus,[148] who had taken passage with them, to return to our presence and seek our will upon all these matters. Indeed, the cardinal approached our presence and took care diligently to propose everything to us, and when your ambassadors come into our presence, we will discuss these matters with our brethren and make a decision that should be pleasing to your merit, although several persons assert that we ought to show kindly favor to a request on his behalf, because the Greek Church is less obedient and devoted to the Apostolic See.[149]

LXXXIII. When massive preparations for aid to the province of Jerusalem were undertaken both in Italy and Gaul, the crusader counts of the Gauls sent their ambassadors to Italy to the doge and people of Venice to obtain suitable transport ships for themselves. They also agreed to enter equally into a *societas*,[150] and afterward, under certain agreements they reached, there was a provision that in ad-

---

148. I.e., Peter Capuanus. See Maleczek, *Papst und Kardinalskolleg von 1191 bis 1216*, 117–24.

149. RI 5:121(122), 239–43, November 16, 1202.

150. A *societas* was a common type of commercial contract.

dition to those headed at some time to Syria, the rest would go to
Egypt to capture Alexandria and the surrounding areas, and thus the
Holy Land might be more easily freed from the hands of the pagans.
When, therefore, the Franks and the Venetians signed a *societas,* they
both sent ambassadors to the Apostolic See asking the Supreme Pontiff to confirm by his Apostolic authority the agreements they had
made for the aid of the Holy Land. But sensing what was to come, he
responded cautiously that he would order those agreements to be
confirmed in such a way that they would not injure Christians, unless
perhaps they wrongfully impeded in their journey, or for some other
just and necessary reason they could not act otherwise, but only with
the approval of the legate of the Apostolic See. But the Venetians were
unwilling to accept the confirmation on these terms. For this reason,
their intention was certainly understood by the result of their deeds
when it later became clear. Meanwhile, it happened that Theobald,
Count of Troyes,[151] who had prepared himself magnificently for the
journey of pilgrimage, paid the debt of the flesh. The rest of the counts
and barons, with the advice of the King of France, therefore, called on
Boniface, Marquis of Montferrat,[152] and made him the leader of the
Christian army, handing over most of the money that the count had
collected for the aid of the Holy Land. He, indeed, made a trip from
France through Germany, where he was said to have held negotiations with Philip, Duke of Swabia, who was acting as king, so that he
might obtain the aid of the Christian army to bring Alexius, his brother-in-law, the son of Isaac, the former emperor of Constantinople,
whose sister Philip himself had married, who had fled to him from
prison, back to Constantinople to obtain the Empire of Romania.
When the marquis approached the Supreme Pontiff on this same mission, he began to negotiate from afar. But when he understood that

151. Theobald III, count of Champagne, member of a distinguished family of
crusaders, was one of the chief leaders of the Fourth Crusade.
152. Boniface was member of a family with extensive ties to the East, including
the Byzantine Empire.

the pope's mind was unfavorable to this matter, after he had discussed the business of the cross, he returned to his territories.

LXXXIV. How diligent and solicitous, committed and prepared Innocent was in supporting the needs of the Holy Land so that he might inflame the Christian army is clearly evident from the letters he sent about this business. Since there are many and diverse examples of these, I have felt that this one should be included here:

To the archbishops, bishops, and other prelates of churches constituted in the Kingdom of France. Both we and you, indeed all, summoned to the lot of the Lord, must fear lest the men of Nineveh [Mt 12:41] rise up in judgment with us and with our clerics and condemn you since they did penance at the preaching of Jonah, but you, until now, not only did not open your hearts but did not want to open your hands at our oft repeated command to aid the poor Jesus Christ, to relieve the disgrace to which he is continuously exposed by the enemies of our faith. For, behold, once more is the Crucified nailed to his cross, once more is he cut down by blows, beaten, again the hate of the haters falls upon him, when his enemies say: "if you are the son of God, save yourself" [Mt 27:40]. Indeed if you can, free the land of your birth from our hands and restore your cross to its worshipers. But we have chiefly learned and sorrowed that often when we asked again and again, you would not give a small drink of cold water so that now, the laity, whom you invited to the support of the cross not with deeds but with words, take up that evangelical saying: "They make heavy burdens for the shoulders of their subjects, but they are themselves unwilling to lift even a finger" [Mt 23:4]. Now you are reproached by the laity that you would more willingly support actors than Christ, you consume more in feeding dogs and birds than you are willing to pay for his aid, abundant deeds for others, miserliness or, as we more truly say, avarice for them. Is this what you give him for what he has given to you? Is this how you love him? Is this the way you respond to his manifold benefits?

So you should show more clearly how you lay down your souls for the sheep [Jn 10:11], you who are not willing up to the present to pay even the fortieth share of your incomes for him; when some of you are required to pay not only a fortieth according to the terms of our mandate but a thirtieth, according to the promise made at the Council of Dijon for such a pious need. We, therefore, advise all of you as a group and exhort you in the Lord, and we command by Apostolic writings, and from the side of God almighty in the power of the Holy Spirit, under the threat of Divine judgment, we strictly command that, according to the terms of our earlier letters, you and all the clergy subject to your jurisdiction, should pay for the support of the Holy Land at least a fortieth of all ecclesiastical rents and incomes, even before you have deducted interest, whose payment cannot be avoided, and you, brother archbishops and bishops should put that fortieth, collected and exacted faithfully, immediately in a safe place.

For this purpose, individuals among you, having associated with them two brethren, one from the Hospital of Jerusalem and the other from the Knights of the Temple, with the counsel of the noblemen, Matthew de Lallio, Conon of Béthune, and Milo of Bremont, as well as Walter of Guyonville, and other discrete men, should provide suitable stipends from the same sum, with a suitable security taken from them, to knights or other warriors who have taken the sign of the Lord's cross so that they may remain in defense of the Holy Land for a year or more depending on the amount of the subsidy. If they should turn back from the road, God forbid, after they have received it, they may not convert the subsidy to other uses, but should rather restore it for the stipends of warriors. Also, those on their return will not be absolved from the granted security before they show you royal letters or letters of the patriarch, the masters of the Hospital, the Knights of the Temple, or even of our legate, providing testimony concerning their delay. But, so that the Apostolic mandate may be more easily and better fulfilled, you should take care to convene in the individual provinces, in the metropolitan church, or if this can not be done there because of hostility or some other clear impediment, in two or three places of the province without delay, and negotiate among yourselves, according to the form of the Apostolic mandate, about support for that land, and after their return, each of you should without delay convoke a council on our authority in his diocese, commanding abbots and priors, both exempt and others, archdeacons and deans, and the whole clergy in his diocese to tax their rents and incomes according to a true estimate. Within three months of having made a report on them, they should without delay send the fortieth share of their value with the bishop himself as witness and a number of religious men, supported for security by some faithful and discrete laity, to a suitable place in the same diocese. We make an exception from these general rules for the hermits of Grandmont and the Carthusians, the Cistercian monks, and the Premonstratensian Canons, for whom we have enjoined a special mandate regarding this matter.[153] We order that a trunk should be put in individual churches for this purpose, with three keys consigned, the first to the bishop, the second to the priest of the church, the third to be kept by some religious layman, so that the faithful may be advised, as the Lord will inspire their minds, to put their alms with a firm purpose for the remission of their sins. Once a week in all the churches mass will be sung publicly for the remission of sins, especially for those making offerings on a certain day that the priest will announce to the people. On the days falling between the solemnity of the masses, at the sounding of the bell, let the "O God, the gentiles have come into your inheritance" [Ps 78:1], with the usual prayer, be said. Moreover, we grant to you, our brother archbishops and bishops, that you can, with the counsel of discrete men, taking into consideration the quality of the persons and the amount of their goods, and having, nevertheless, weighed the level of their devotion, commute the work of the enjoined penance into the making of an alms from those who desire to aid the Holy Land with their goods. Also, you should know that we have ordered our beloved brethren the bishops of Paris and Soissons and our beloved sons, the abbots of Valserne and St. Victor, strictly by Apostolic writings, that they should compel, after due warning, by Apostolic censure without right of appeal, those who met in the council at Dijon summoned by our beloved son, Peter, cardinal priest of the title of St. Marcellus, then legate of the Apostolic See, who promised freely the thirtieth of their incomes for the aid of the Holy Land, to pay at least the fortieth. Indeed, how meritorious the service of the cross may be, how praiseworthy, when they have left their own possessions behind, to aid the Holy Land with the rest is clear enough from the gospel reading. For those who, having taken on the sign of the cross, should not hesitate to go to the aid of the Holy Land and be seen to fulfill the gospel literally: "If anyone wishes to come after me, let him deny himself, and take up his cross and follow me" [Lk 9:23]. And those who would become true followers of Christ, hated father, mother, wife, daughters, brothers and sisters even more than their own soul, according to the Word of truth [Mt 19:29]. For would they not appear to

---

153. These orders, all products of the twelfth-century reform of monastic life, enjoyed Innocent's special favor.

have hated father, mother, wife, sons, brothers, and sisters, who have put aside carnal affection in purity of spirit for the king of kings? Would those who did not fear to lay down their lives in order to avenge the Crucified, not hate their own soul, with the privilege of procuring his love, about which the Truth is proclaimed in the Gospel: "No one has greater love than he who lays down his life for his friends" [Jn 15:13]. Such individuals, seeking if they can drink the chalice for the Lord, which he himself was about to drink, confident in the grace of Christ, might say certainly with the sons of Zebedee: "We can" [Mk 10:35–45]. Those confident of Christ's grace might say securely with Peter: "See how we have left everything and have followed you. What, therefore, will be our reward" [Mk 19:27]? For would not he who left behind kingdoms, principalities, counties and great wealth not assuredly use this word which Peter used when he had left only boat and net. Therefore, we, though unworthy, who take his place on earth, for whom such men vow their service, following in the footsteps of our predecessor of holy memory Pope Gregory,[154] establish by the authority of these presents, that their goods and those of like persons from whom they have received the cross, with their families, should remain under the protection of the Holy Roman church, and of us, as well as archbishops, bishops, of other prelates of the church of God, and shall remain safe and at peace until their return or their death is known with absolute certainty. But if anyone should presume to act to the contrary, each of you in his diocese may compel him by Apostolic censure without right of appeal. Desiring in addition to defer to the petition of the crusaders in this way on the sentence of interdict,[155] laid on the land of our dearest son in Christ, Philip, King of the Franks, so that the sinew of ecclesiastical discipline may not be dissolved, we command your discretion by Apostolic letter that, if they should desire to hear the Divine Liturgies, you should make this possible without the ringing of bells and by celebrating in a quiet voice, having excluded others who are not crusaders. If any of them are perhaps bound by the sentence of excommunication, they may request to be absolved after you have received the security of an oath and granted them absolution.

We do not deny that you may demand the established money from them according to the custom of the land and receive what has been ex-

154. Gregory VIII, 1187.
155. Interdict prohibited almost all religious services and was therefore a powerful tool in bringing pressure to bear on those who refused to obey.

acted. But after it has been received you should give it back to them for the aid of Holy Land to support their pilgrimage, counting it as part of the fortieth, if perhaps it should be a burden for you, which we do not believe, on the stipends of those who are not able to cross with their incomes. In addition, following in the footsteps of our predecessors so that clerical crusaders can mortgage their rents for a period up to three years, we grant, desire, and command that you not impede them in this in any way by your own effort or permit them to be impeded by others. Also, for our part, you should take care strictly to restrain the lords of the crusaders lest they burden them unduly or presume to injure them with unaccustomed exactions. But because those who commit themselves to the service of the Divine must abstain from illicit things and use the licit sparingly lest the licit become illicit, if done lasciviously or illicitly, we desire and command that you take care to advise them more diligently on our behalf and persuade them that, on those days on which they ought not eat meat, save for certain sauces, or also on fast days, they should not take more than two courses and those in moderation, unless perhaps a third course, popularly known as a "break," is given to the counts, barons, and other nobles beyond that given to their familiars. They should not wear ermine, but only coarse gray cloth until they fulfil their pilgrimage vow.[156] We desire that both clergy and laity, and also women required to cross over to fulfill their vow or those who have followed their husbands on their pilgrimage, should follow the same instructions. Likewise, you should persuade those who are armed, as well as other servants, in a diligent and effective manner as far as you can, not to wear colored garments but to be content with other suitable clothing.

But, because the noblemen, the counts of Boulogne and Beaumont and many others, as we have learned, become more licentious or delay in fulfilling their vow in the malice of their souls and cast aside the sign of the cross they have affixed to their shoulders, by our Apostolic writings, we strictly command your fraternity, that, regardless of an indulgence they have obtained by deception so that they may receive the sign of the cross and the fact that they may accompany the others at the appointed time, after they have been warned, after appeals have been heard, you should compel them by sentences of excommunication and of interdict on their lands. Wherever such individuals shall come, you should prohibit

---

156. These instructions closely parallel contemporary penitential practices among the laity.

the celebration of the Divine liturgies in their presence. But if perhaps
some indulgence is presented to you which seems doubtful or difficult, so
that you cannot easily judge its merits, you should send it to our presence.
You should undertake to advise diligently and to persuade your parish
clergy that they should not presume to convene tournaments for at least
five years, laying against the persons of those who dare to act in a contrary
manner sentences of excommunication and interdict on their lands, after
annulling the obstacle of appeal, and forbidding the Divine liturgy to be
celebrated in their presence wherever they come. You should not relax
earlier sentences against them, and they should solemnly abjure tournaments for the aforesaid period. Moreover, we, from the mercy of God, and
trusting in the authority of the blessed apostles Peter and Paul, from that
power which God has granted us, though unworthy, of binding and loosing, grant to all who will undergo the labor of this journey in their own
persons and at their own expense a full indulgence of all their sins, for
which they will require penance of heart and mouth, and we promise in
return for their just actions an increase of eternal salvation. Moreover, we
grant full remission of their sins to those who do not go there personally
but only send suitable men, to remain there for at least a year at their own
expense, depending on their status and capacity, and likewise to those
who, even at the expense of another, fulfill the labor of taking up the pilgrimage in their own persons. We also desire that everyone who gives a
fitting subvention for that land from their own goods should share in this
remission according to the amount of their support and the strength of
their devotion. In addition, we have taken the persons and goods of those
who have taken the cross under the protection of St. Peter and ourselves,
as well as under that of the archbishops and all the prelates of the church
of God. If anyone defies this, he should be compelled by ecclesiastical censure with the right of appeal set aside. But if, indeed, those setting forth
have been forced by the oath to assume usury, you, our brother archbishops and bishops, throughout your dioceses, may absolve them from their
oaths and force their creditors by the same legal action, with the obstacle
of appeal set aside, to desist from further exactions. But if any of the creditors force them to pay usury, you will compel him to make restitution by
the same legal measure, with the obstacle of appeal set aside. We command that Jews should be forced by the secular power to remit usury,[157]

---

157. I.e., to forego interest on loans. There was an increasing anti-Jewish tone in

and until they remit it, we order that all contact by the Christian faithful of any kind in merchandising and other matters be completely forbidden them. Nevertheless, we also desire and command that if any of the crusaders are burdened by so much debt that their income is not sufficient to pay for the expenses of the pilgrimage, you should work diligently to advise and persuade their creditors, whom family poverty does not excuse, to delay the terms of payment for a period of up to three years. Moreover, we appoint as our delegates in all these matters our brethren, the bishops of Paris and Soissons and our beloved sons, the abbots of Valserne and of St. Victor as executors of these regulations which we order to be carried out under ecclesiastical jurisdiction and they should exercise the office of admonishment in those matters for which we order that some persons should be admonished.[158]

LXXXV. At the appointed time, the crusader army, both large and strong, devout and feared, arrived in Venetian territory, so that without doubt one might believe that by it the Lord would renew the miracles of the past, and not only would the province of Jerusalem be recovered, but the kingdom of Babylon[159] would also be captured. For the Venetians had prepared such a magnificent fleet, that hardly ever had such great naval preparations been seen or heard of. The Lord Pope, therefore, sent Peter, cardinal priest of the title of Saint Marcellus, legate of the Apostolic See, to the army gathered at Venice so that he might set out with it in the name of the Redeemer. The Doge and the counselors of the Venetians, fearing lest he get in the way of their plan of laying siege to Zara, which they had evilly conceived, said that if he wanted to go with them, they would allow him but he could not exercise the office of legate but only that of preaching. Otherwise he should return. Although this displeased the Franks, still he returned dishonored by the Venetians, explaining in the clearest terms their evil intention to the pope. He sent letters to all crusaders, strictly for-

---

this period. In this instance, we should note that Jews were not subject to ecclesiastical jurisdiction, hence Innocent's appeal to secular rulers to enforce his decision.

158. Potthast, *Regesta Pontificum Romanorum*, 1:97(1045), April–May 1200.

159. A medieval name for Cairo, hence Egypt as a whole.

bidding them to attack the lands of Christians, and by name, Zara, which the king of Hungary, who was also a crusader, held in his possession. Otherwise, they should know that they would be bound with the chain of anathema, and he ordered this prohibition and excommunication to be made more certain to them by the abbot of Lucedio.[160] The Marquis of Montferrat, who had been forbidden in this matter by the oral command of the pope, prudently absented himself; he did not make the journey with them to attack Zara.

LXXXVI. The letter which the pope sent them shows to what extent he was angered at the way they went about destroying Zara:

We sorrow not a little and are disturbed that in those matters in which we were accustomed to weigh out the grace of forgiveness and to promise an increase of eternal retribution, now that we do not speak without much sorrow, we are forced to deny the encouragement of our salutation and the protection of Apostolic benediction. For behold, gold has been changed to a base metal and the silver has almost completely rusted, since, departing from the purity of your plan, you have turned in envy from the path, as though you have withdrawn your hand from the plow and have looked back with Lot's wife [Gn 19:26]. For when you should have hastened in flight from Egypt to the land flowing with honey and milk, you wandered away into the solitude [Ex 3:8]. You led your mind back to where you sat in the fleshpots in Egypt, where you are not only hungry for garlic and exotic foods but thirst after the blood of your brethren. Of course, mindful of the serpent of old, how God put enmities between the seed of the woman and it after the fall of the first human beings, because it could not prevail in the head, crawling on its belly [Gn 3:14], it hid itself in the road so that it could strike the hooves of the horses and throw the rider to the ground together with the horse. It arranged by its usual slyness in trickery and accustomed malignity in injuring to corrupt the whole mass of the leaven and all you have done. You lose the merit of your entire labor when you offend in one thing. Heeding further the ancient enemy who is the devil and Satan, who seduces the whole world, that no one has greater love than that someone lays down his life for his friends [Jn 15:13], that he might deprive you of the affection and mercy of such love, he has caused

160. Peter of Magnano, from Vercelli.

you to make war on your brethren and to deploy your banners first against peoples of the faith so that you will pay him the first fruits of the pilgrimage and shed your blood and that of your brethren. You, having the pretext of not going to Jerusalem but rather of descending into Egypt, have descended from Jerusalem to Jericho and have thereby fallen among thieves [Lk 10:30], who have also despoiled you of the mantle of your virtues and imposed the stripes of sins on you after you have been despoiled. And they still did not want to depart until now nor to leave you half alive, since now plots are hatched among you by evil angels so that you both alter your course to the islands for your necessities and convert the spoils of Christians for your incomes, as we recently learned that you have done at Zara.

For when this fleet arrived there, raising your banners first against the city, you put up your tents for the siege and surrounded the city on all sides and undermined their walls, but not without considerable bloodshed. When the citizens wanted to undergo a trial with the Venetians in our court, and they could not even find mercy in you, they hung images of the cross around their walls. But you, to the injury of the Crucified, nonetheless fought against the city and the citizens and forced them to surrender by violence. Moreover, either reverence for taking the cross or devotion of the most beloved in Christ our dear son Emmerich, King of the Hungarians, and the noble duke Andrew his brother, who for the support of the Holy Land assumed the sign of the cross, or at least the authority of the Apostolic See, which took care to prohibit you strictly lest you try to invade and injure the lands of Christians, unless they either wickedly impeded your journey or perhaps some other just or necessary reason should occur, on account of which you could act with the counsel of the legate, should have deterred you from your very wicked plan. Lest our prohibition was not clearly heard, if anyone dared to act contrary to it, we announced that they would be bound by the chain of excommunication and deprived of the benefits of the indulgences which the Apostolic See granted to crusaders. But although our beloved son, Peter, cardinal priest of Saint Marcellus, legate of the Apostolic See, took care to explain the terms of our prohibition to some of you, and finally our letter was publicly presented to you, you paid no attention to God or to the Apostolic See but forced the miserable Zarans to surrender. The Venetians, therefore, subverted the walls of the same city in your sight, despoiled its churches, destroyed its buildings, and divided the spoils of Zara with you.

Lest, therefore, you should add sin to sin and fulfill in yourselves what we read: "The sinner values little when he arrives in the depth of vices" [Prv 18:3], we admonish your whole group and we exhort you more energetically and we command by Apostolic letter, and under the terms of the anathema we strictly order that you should neither destroy Zara further than it has been destroyed up to this point nor cause it to be destroyed, or as much as you can control, but arrange to restore all that has been taken to the ambassadors of the same king. Otherwise you should know that you will be subject to the sentence of excommunication and deprived of the grant of remission promised you.[161]

LXXXVII. But the princes of the Franks, recognizing their excess, swore in the hands of their bishops that they would obey the commands of the Lord Pope in this matter, and as a result, they were absolved by the bishops. They sent the Bishop of Soissons to the Apostolic See in order to mitigate the anger of the Supreme Pontiff and they advised him how they would proceed in this matter. But he ordered by his letter that they, worthily penitent for such an excess and in order to make suitable satisfaction for sin, should return everything that had come to them from the spoils of the Zarans and should, for the future, abstain completely from similar things. But because no one could relax the sentence of the Apostolic See save on papal authority, he authorized certain discrete men to receive the oath to obey the Apostolic mandates from those who had not yet sworn. Moreover, they should require those who had taken the oath to recognize how they had sworn in their presence and then they should grant absolution to all according to the form of absolution of the church, enjoining on the counts and barons, under the obligation of the oath, that they and their heirs should be required by letters patent to the Apostolic See to make satisfaction concerning such presumption at his command. They should also command everyone for the future to abstain from similar affairs, save for other commands that he might order about this. Still the counts and barons obligated themselves as they

161. RI 5:160(161), 315–17, December 15–31, 1202.

were required and so all were absolved. But the Venetians, like those
who celebrate when they have done something wrong and rejoice in
the worst things, were neither willing to do penance nor to seek absolution. To the issues raised by the Franks, the Lord Pope wrote again
in this manner:

If you are truly sorry for what you have done and propose to make full
satisfaction for your sin, we believe, indeed, we now know, that God is
pleased with you. If the Venetians could be persuaded to make satisfaction
and should merit to receive the benefit of absolution, you could certainly
set sail with them and with them fight the Lord's battle. But if they are unwilling to make satisfaction or to be absolved, like those who are said not
to sorrow but to rejoice in what they have done, we permit you to cross by
ship with them into the land of the Saracens or to the province of
Jerusalem, depending on what has been decided or will be decided between you and them. For this period of time you can maintain communi-
cation with them, but with sorrow and in bitterness of heart and under
the hope of forgiveness. For since they have received the largest amount
of the money for passage and they cannot be persuaded or even forced to
restore it, if it should happen otherwise, we see that you would suffer a
loss from your penitence and they would obtain a reward from contumacy, since they continue to be obligated to pay this debt to you and what is
owed can be exacted and received from those who have been excommunicated. Moreover, it is a certainty in law that if anyone should travel
through the land of heretics or any excommunicated persons, he can buy
and receive necessities from them. In addition, if the head of the household should be excommunicated, his family is excused from participation.
Although, therefore, the Lord Doge of the Venetian fleet remains excommunicated like the head of a house, you, like his family, will be excusable
by God as long as you are in those ships. His excommunication will not af-
fect you if you are in the ships of the excommunicates with sorrow of
heart and you are in contact with those who have been excommunicated,
whose contact you cannot avoid, under hope of their penitence.

But when you leave the ships either in the land of the Saracens or in
the province of Jerusalem, if the Venetians have not been persuaded or
compelled to make satisfaction according to the form of absolution of the
church, you should not dare to fight the battle of the Lord with them lest,
if you raise up those having something of the anathema against the ene-

mies of the cross, you do not prevail against them, but turning your backs, instead, you run away and perish. For we read in the Book of Joshua that when Achan, the son of Carmi [Jos 7:1–25], stole a scarlet mantle of great value and two hundred shekels of silver and a gold bar weighing fifty shekels of Jericho, the Lord of Israel was angered. Wherefore, when three thousand soldiers marched against the city of Ai, they were immediately struck by the men of Ai and fled, and thirty-six men fell. Their enemies pursued them from the gate to Sabirim and they killed those fleeing until evening, and no sooner did the Lord hand the city of Ai over to Israel than the people stoned Achan and consumed all of his goods by fire [Jos 8:1; 7:25–26]. In Paralipomenon, also, when Josaphat, King of Judah, had made a treaty with Ochosia, King of Israel, whose works were very evil, and they made ships to go to Tarsus, we read that Eleazer, the son of Do-dacus of Maressa, prophesied to Josaphat and said, "Because you have a treaty with Ochosia, the Lord has struck at your works, and your ships are destroyed and cannot go to Tarsus" [2 Chr 20:35–37]. In the book of Mac-cabees, we read that when Judas ascended against Gorgia, the governor of Idumea, with three thousand infantry and four hundred cavalry, few were destroyed in the battle [2 Mc 12:32–34]. When afterward, Judas wanted to put the slain bodies in their paternal tombs, he found beneath the tu-nics of those killed votive offerings of idols which were at Iamnia and which were forbidden by Jewish law. Therefore, it was made clear to everyone why those who had perished had been destroyed [2 Mc 12:39].

But lest they should lack supplies, we have written to our beloved son, the emperor of Constantinople, that just as he promised us in his letters he should cause foodstuffs to be furnished to you. But if perhaps he deny these things, since you are still vowed to the common support of the Cru-cified, to whom the land and its fullness belong, the world and all who dwell in it, and it would not seem absurd for the emperor of the land, who controls security by civil law, if his army has a need for food, to take it from anywhere, so you can also with fear of the Lord, but under the plan of making satisfaction for need, take these things without injury to any persons. We also find in the Book of Judges that, when Gideon immedi-ately pursued Zebah and Zalmunna, the kings of Midian, and he first asked for bread from the men of Succoth and secondly from the inhabi-tants of Penuel for the people who had come with him and were now al-most starving. Because they denied him what he asked for, after he re-turned as victor he brought the elders of the city of Succoth both the thorns of the desert and thistles and he afflicted them and he crushed the men of Succoth; he also undermined the tower of Penuel, killing the inhabitants of the city [Jgs 8:5–9, 13–17]. For necessity, especially when it is applied to a necessary work, excuses much and in many things. For when the Lord passed through the cornfields on the sabbath and his disciples wanted some ears and, rubbing them in their hands, they ate them, and some of the pharisees called out to the disciples: "What you are doing is not allowed on the Sabbath." We read that Jesus answered them: "Have you not read what David did when he and those who were with him were thirsty, how he came into the house of God and took the loaves of offering that only the priests were allowed to eat" [Mk 2:26–28]? And he further added that "the son of man is also the Lord of the Sabbath." But both this and battle of the Lord that you intend to fight are also the business of the son of man [Lk 6:1–5]. We have drawn these holy *exempla* from scripture, not to make a concession to wrongdoing but to tolerate what cannot be avoided out of serious necessity without great expense. But you should provide prudently and with security that, if perhaps the Venetians seek some opportunities to break up the army, you will take care to overlook it for a time and to tolerate it until you arrive at the appointed place, when with the opportunity at hand, you may restrain their malice as is useful.[162]

LXXXVIII. And so the Lord Pope sent Soffredus, cardinal priest of the title of Santa Prassede, ahead to the province of Jerusalem to exercise the office of legate. He ordered him to be given a thousand two hundred pounds to distribute for the necessities of his company and for the use of the Holy Land, as he might think best. He also sent Peter, cardinal priest of the title of St. Marcellus, after him so that, if possible, he might join the crusaders, or if that was not possible, that he might cross over to Syria, and he gave him the same amount of money for the same reasons. Both, however, crossed one after the other to the province of Jerusalem, by way of the island of Cyprus, and carried out those things they had been ordered to do. Soffredus went first and he found the Patriarch of Jerusalem near death. A few days later, he

162. RI 6:102, 165–68, about June 20, 1203.

died, and the legate was elected as patriarch by the clergy, on the petition of the people, with the assent of the king and the support of the suffragan bishops. Ambassadors were sent by general advice to the Apostolic See to obtain his appointment to the patriarchate, and after that had been agreed to, to send him the *pallium*. The Supreme Pontiff decided that the cardinal might be persuaded, if possible, but that he should not be forced, if he was unwilling, to accept the patriarchate. And he sent the *pallium* to the other cardinal so that he might confer it on him if he agreed. But he was not at all willing to consent. For this reason, he obtained an agreement to negotiate for the election of someone else. And they all settled on the Bishop of Vercelli, a man distinguished in his life, in his knowledge, and in his reputation, and the pope wrote to him in this fashion:

In order that the only-begotten Son of God, Jesus Christ, might repair the fall of humankind, when he was in the shape of God, he emptied himself, as the apostle says, taking on the form of a slave, made in the likeness of man and discovered in habit like man, and he chose Jerusalem for his passion, made obedient to God the Father even to the death of the cross. He carried our sins in his body on the cross, he was crucified with evil men and thieves. Unless, therefore, the useless slave should wish to be condemned of the vice of ingratitude, he will not refuse to undergo either the yoke or slaughter for the Lord, since the Lord handed himself over to the most awful death like a slave. Of course, in order that the Lord might raise up every occasion for us and might not hold back any place to make excuses in the sin of negligence, whatever the slave might suffer for the Lord, the Lord had already suffered for the slave. Who, therefore, would not leave all earthly things for the one he knew had come down from heaven to the earth? Who would not lay down his life for him, who gave up his spirit for him on the cross? If not that we should give him something for all that he has given to us, neither tribulation nor anxiety nor death nor the sword should retard us, unless necessity requires and utility demands, from tasting the chalice of the passion for him. For however he walked, we should walk and follow his footsteps, and we should not in any way fear the hatred of those who hate, the betrayals of the enemy within, or the power of the savage enemy. But we should walk in his ways and direct our feet on his road, suffering for the present in order to reign with him in eternal happiness.

For we know and hold for certain both from the prophets and from the teachings of the Gospel, that his heart held its reproach when the tongues of those cursing him expressed their hatred, calling him the son of a carpenter, a drunkard and friend of publicans. We know that the one who ate his bread raised his heel against him. We know how, covered with spit, struck with blows, crowned with thorns, he bore patiently the tyranny of Pilate, at last to be crucified and pierced with a lance. Would you, therefore, deny yourself to your Maker in order to refuse to take up the burden of the church of Jerusalem, which he consecrated with his blood? If he has deigned to choose you as in some way his heir, should you not enter into his inheritance, and arouse the seed of the dead brother, who put down his life for you in the land of pilgrimage and propagated the seed of the Gospel of his preaching? Away with avoiding labors, sorrows, and fears, with fleeing poverty, anxiety, and necessities, that you should not endure that burden for which you have been called by the Divine plan! Away with avoiding labors for him, who asserts through the prophet that he has labored for you, saying in the Psalm, "I have labored for sustenance" [Is 1:4], and concerning whom the evangelist has witnessed that he was sitting almost at the sixth hour at the well worn out from his journey! God forbid that you should avoid sorrows for him who has not hesitated to suffer for you, as he says in the Prophet, "O all you, who pass by the way, stop and see if there is any sorrow like my sorrow" [Lam 1:12], and he who protests concerning himself in the Gospel, "My soul is sad even unto death" [Mt 26:38]. Perish, if you should avoid fears for him whom we read in the psalm said of himself, "Fear and trembling came upon me" [Ps 54:6], and of whom he says in the Gospel that he began to tremble and to be disgusted [Mk 14:33]! Do not flee poverty for him who was made poor for you, as it is said in the Prophet, "I am poor and sorrowing" [Ps 68:30], and in the Gospels, "The foxes have their lairs and the birds of the air have their nests, but the son of Man has nowhere to lay his head" [Lk 9:58]. Perish the thought that you should flee from anxieties for him in whose person the prophet spoke thus, "My spirit is anxious within me and my heart is disturbed in me" [Ps 142:4]; and who says of himself, "I have to be baptized in baptism and I am pressed until it is completed" [Lk 12:50]! Away with the notion that for him you should flee necessities, he who brought the necessity on himself for you in hunger and thirst, that we may be silent in other things, as we read in the prophet, "They put gall in my food and they gave me vinegar to drink" [Ps 68:22], and just as the evangelist witnesses concerning him that when he had fasted for forty days and forty nights, he later ate [Mt 4:2], and when he called out "I thirst" [Jn 19:28], on the cross he drank the acid, or wine mixed with myrh or even with gall, from the right hand of those crucifying him.

If perhaps this should move you to take on the prelacy of that church, whose possessions you cannot at present approach since they are almost all now held by the enemy, you may lead the eyes of your mind back to that time when James, the brother of the Lord, received Jerusalem to govern [Gal 1:19; Acts 12:17], not indeed promoting himself but rather refusing since those who were holding power at that time had also crucified the Lord outside the city and later killed James himself around the temple [Acts 12:2]. And, although John and Thaddeus were brothers of the Lord according to the flesh, still James is particularly called his brother since he who marries the widow of a dead brother so that in accordance with the law of Moses she might receive his seed, is also, not unfittingly, called the supplanter, since in a certain way he took the place of the apostles. Although he was not first among the others, still he snatched the place of the firstborn, because he received the governance of the firstborn church, concerning which, namely, the prophet witnesses that the law went out of Sion and the word of the Lord out of Jerusalem [Is 2:3]. This is the city of the great king of which many glorious things have been said, and this especially is added, "Mother Sion knows man and man is made in her and the Most High founded her" [Ps 86:5].

In addition, although part of that church that we sorrowfully speak of was captured and butchered by our enemies in the decline of the Holy Land, the part which escaped the hands of the enemy, indeed even that church, which is renewed by a new shoot, seeks and waits for you as its pastor. You should not dispute about the place, since you have persons whom you govern, because the name of the church refers more to persons than to place, although you should ask this in a spiritual manner so that you may work with all your strength solicitously for the recovery of the place and the reintegration of the land of the Nativity of the Lord. For the prior and canons of the Sepulcher of the Lord approached our presence and both orally and in the letters they brought to us humbly suggested that our beloved son, Soffredus, cardinal priest of the church of Santa Prassede, the legate of the Apostolic See, could not be persuaded to consent to his election to the church of Jerusalem, and gathering together [Ps 47:5; 2 Cor 11:20], they unanimously postulated you as their patriarch. And our beloved son, Amalric,[163] illustrious King of Jerusalem, gave his assent and the archbishops and bishops agreed by their letter to us, asking that we should deign not only to persuade but also to order you to agree humbly to their postulation. Likewise, also, the cardinal priest of Santa Prassede, and Peter, our beloved son, cardinal priest of St. Marcellus, legates of the Apostolic See, suggested through their letters to us that, when the suffragans of the church of Jerusalem maintained that they had a voice in the election, the prior and the canons of the Sepulcher of the Lord denied it; finally it was done so that with two persons nominated, they might confer their votes and voices on them devoutly so that they might choose as patriarch the one they believed the more suitable. Likewise, the prelates of the province, in case they had any right in the election, agreed on them. Therefore, after they deliberated concerning the two persons named, they decided rather to choose you as pastor for the same church.

Although you are exceedingly necessary to us in Lombardy, since we have committed our vicariate to you in difficult negotiations, still out of urgent necessity we advise and exhort your discretion, and we enjoin you on the remission of sins, entreating you on the blood of Jesus Christ [1 Pt 1:2], that, consenting to the Divine summons on the desires of all the above-mentioned persons, you should accept your election. If you should act otherwise, you may seem to resist the Divine Will, which, however, is always fulfilled whether by the willing or the unwilling. You should pay careful attention lest, if a less suitable person or even someone unworthy might gain that church by the desire of some persons, the result cannot be laid at your door because of your refusal. Nor should you flee that labor as if you are unable to complete what you desire, because God does not reward only the completion but the labor, as the Apostle says, "Each will receive his own reward according to his labor" [1 Cor 3:8], and elsewhere scripture witnesses, "God renders a reward for their holy works" [Wis 10:17]. Wherefore, the apostle has said cautiously, "I have labored more for all" [1 Cor 15:10], and he has not said to complete more for all, although from your labors we would hope that sufficient profit will come. You should, therefore, obey this Apostolic mandate for God and because

163. Amalric II, king of Jerusalem

of God, so that we will not have to show a hand of more rigid severity.
For, even if, according to the canonical statutes, no one is compelled to accept promotion, still according to legitimate sanctions some are drawn unwillingly to public office. It is in the interest of both the Apostolic See and
the church in general as well as of everyone as a whole and individually of
the faithful of the Crucified that a suitable person should be appointed as
pastor. You should not take it to be more an honor than a burden since today that church has more about it of a burden than an honor. Nor should
you worry or rationalize why the cardinal priest of Santa Prassede did not
accede to the postulation of himself made by the canons of the Sepulcher
of the Lord because, perhaps just as Sara was reserved for Tobias [Tb 6:11],
and she was reserved to the husband of another by Divine Judgment, or
perhaps he was induced to refuse this burden, because, since he was in
those parts, he might seem to have sought his own promotion. And from
this especially he might get the reputation for ambition, so that, when at
his removal of a certain perverse person, who was unworthily nominated
by the same church, as was his duty, whether opportunely or unoppor-
tunely, the person removed would insist that this was done that he might
later receive the postulation of himself.[164]

LXXXIX. The Bishop of Vercelli humbly approached the Apostolic
See and acquiesced, and, having been raised to the patriarchate, received not only the *pallium* but also the office of legate to be exercised
for four years in his province. He then departed Genoa and sailed to
Syria.

But just as Philip had met with the Marquis of Montferrat, he sent
Alexius, his brother-in-law, namely, the son of Isaac, the former emperor of Constantinople, and under the clever mediation of the same
Marquis, an agreement was reached between him and the Christian
army that the army would take him back to Greece and would aid
him to obtain the empire of Constantinople. He would pay them the
promised money and he would keep the other agreements reached
with them after he obtained the empire. But when this news came to
the Supreme Pontiff, he wrote to them in this vein:

164. RI 7:222, 393–95, February 17, 1205. Letter to Albert, bishop of Vercelli.

Since with a strong hand and extended arm [Dt 5:15] you have gone out
from Egypt in order to offer yourselves in sacrifice to the Lord, we have
been not a little pained and are sorry that until now Pharaoh pursues you
as you flee, or rather you follow the Pharaoh [Ex 14:8], who puts pressure
on you under a certain kind of necessity and a veil of piety to subject
yourselves to servitude under the yoke of an ancient sin. We have sorrowed, moreover, just as we have set forth earlier and we sorrow for ourselves equally and for the entire Christian people. For ourselves, because,
what we have sowed in tears [Ps 125:5], through legates and our letters to
you and others, often not without a certain bitterness of heart and anxiety
of body, setting forth energetically the word of the Lord and exhorting
Christians to avenge the injury of the Crucified, we have believed that we
would be harvesters in exaltation [Ps 125:5] so that unknown to us an enemy of our harvest has sown cockles and spoiled the seeds so that the
wheat would seem to have degenerated into tares [Mt 13:25]. On your
behalf, however, because, when you have purged the old leaven [1 Cor
5:7], you believe that you have put off the old man with his acts, still a tri-
fle of leaven, even a little, corrupts the whole mass and, because you have
not kept your garments white, as if you have again put on an old mantle,
withdrawing your hand from the plow, and looking back with the wife of
Lot [Gn 19:26], you are no more fit to see, according to the apostle, the
kingdom of God [Lk 9:62]. Moreover, we have sorrowed and we continue
to sorrow for the Christian people, because it is made more humble by
what it is believed to be exalted.

For since many, who preceded you in support of the Holy Land, on
hearing that you have not boarded ships, despairing about your proximate
passage, have returned home. The Saracens, doubtful about your arrival
and unconcerned about their departure, arose against Christian souls to
see how (and we are unwilling to say how, because of sin, since it would
become known almost everywhere) they might prevail against them.
Moreover, we rejoice that, after the receipt of our letter, understanding
your excessive wandering, you have carried out the Apostolic mandate
with devotion and humility and, having sworn or certified on oath, you
have received the benefit of absolution, taking on the obligation for yourselves and your heirs, sons, counts, with two Frankish barons, to do satisfaction according to our mandate in the matter for which you have incurred the sentence of excommunication. Moreover, we hope that your
penance will be genuine, that you will repent for what you have done so

that you may avoid similar things in the future, because he who acts unrepentant is not a penitent but a deceiver, and just as dogs return to vomit the penitent returns to sin [Prv 26:11; 2 Pt 2:22]. Also, a sin is more serious, when once committed, it is repeated later. Thus none of you should rashly flatter himself that it is licit to occupy the land of the Greeks or to prey upon it for himself, on the grounds that it is less subject to the Apostolic See and that the Emperor of Constantinople, because he deposed and blinded his brother, usurped the empire. Of course, insofar as in this and other matters, the emperor and the men committed to his jurisdiction did wrong, it is still not your business to judge their crimes. You did not take up the cross in order to avenge this injury, but are rather appointed in obedience especially to avenge the shame of the crucified.

For this reason, we warn your nobility and exhort you more firmly and we order you by Apostolic letter that you should neither deceive yourselves nor allow yourselves to be deceived by others so that under the guise of piety you may do those things, which, God forbid, redound to the injury of your souls. Rather, you should cease frivolous opportunities and pretended necessities, and cross over to the aid of the Holy Land, and avenge the injury of the cross. You should take from the spoils of the enemy those things that you would perhaps wrest from your brothers if you delayed in the regions of Romania. Otherwise, because we neither can nor should, we do not promise the favor of remission to you. Moreover, we want you to keep in mind the terms of our prohibition, by which we forbade you under threat of excommunication to invade or attempt to injure the lands of Christians, unless they either impeded your journey in a wrongful manner or some other just and essential reason should intervene, for which reason you should consult with our legates about what is to be done. We warn you not to go against it lightly. So that the fault of the Doge and the Venetians may not redound to your punishment, we desire and order that you should send our letter, which we ordered to be sent to them and to be sent to the same persons who are known to be with you so that they may not find in them an excuse for their sins.[165]

XC. Nevertheless, they sailed to Greece and arrived at Constantinople, where their letter sent to the Lord Pope by them set forth what they had done:

165. RI 6:101, 163–65, about June 20, 1203.

How much the Lord has accomplished for us, indeed, not for us but for his name, how much glory he has bestowed in these days, we will briefly relate as well as we can, noting at the beginning that we set out from the city of transgression, for thus we call Zara, whose destruction we looked upon with sorrow indeed, but we were forced by necessity [Ps 65:16; Mk 5:19]. We have remembered that nothing was ordained among us that pertained generally to the utility of the army save that Divine Providence might change it for the better and taking everything on itself might make our wisdom foolish [Rom 1:22; 1 Cor 1:20]. This is why, of the things we did gloriously, we reject all their glory for ourselves. Indeed we brought very little to the work and nothing to the planning. For this reason, if anyone should wish to glorify us, he should glory in the Lord, not in himself or another [1 Cor 1:31].

Therefore, after the treaty of Zara was confirmed with the illustrious Alexius, the son of the former Emperor Isaac, we, who were in need of foodstuffs and other things, realized that the burden of the Holy Land would rather be increased, just as was the case with the others, who had gone ahead of us, rather than bringing any increase in help, nor, in such a state of poverty, did we think that we had the power to attack the land of the Saracens. Indeed, persuaded by similar rumors and arguments that the royal party in the city and the majority of the empire strongly longed for the coming of Alexius, whom it had elevated by a proper election to the imperial crown in a solemn agreement; contrary to the usual situation in that season, with a favorable breeze and the winds and sea obedient to the Lord beyond all hope, we landed happily in a short time at the royal city [Mt 8:27]. But our arrival did not go unnoticed. We found about sixty thousand knights in addition to infantry in the city. Passing rapidly through the safest places, the bridges, towers, and rivers, without loss of our men we laid siege to the city and the tyrant by land and sea. He, after he had committed parricide against his brother, had defiled the imperial office by a lengthy illegal possession. Contrary to the opinion of everyone, we found the minds of the citizens set against us and the city with its walls and military machines likewise raised against their Lord, as if infidels, who proposed to pollute the holy places and to tear out completely the Christian religion, had come. That most cruel possessor of the Empire, the depriver and betrayer of his lord and brother, the emperor, who had condemned him to prison perpetually without having committed any crime, likewise would have done the same to his son Alexius if he had not fortunately escaped his hands into exile. Afterward, he held a detestable meeting with the people and infected the powerful and the commoners with poison words whereby he maintained that the Latins had come to subvert their ancient liberties and that they would hasten to restore the place and the people to the Roman Pontiff and subject them to the laws of the Latins. When this business was completed, he likewise motivated and armed everyone against us in such a way that everyone seemed to have taken an oath both against us and our exile. Very often through our ambassadors, as well as through our exile himself and our barons, we demanded to be heard by the citizens. But we were not able to explain the reason for our coming nor the nature of our request. As often as we offered by land or by sea to speak to those standing on the wall, we got spears instead of words. We realized, therefore, that everything had happened beyond our expectation. Impelled by necessity we were immediately forced either to perish or to conquer, since we could not reasonably extend our siege more than fifteen days. The unbelievable shortage of all foodstuffs made this necessary. Thus, we were ready to expose ourselves to danger and incredibly to prevail in all things, and we began to cry out for war not indeed from desperation but inspired by a certain faith in Divine Providence. Quite often when we were drawn up on the field of battle, we forced a countless multitude in ignominious flight back into the city.

In the meantime, therefore, with suitable warlike instruments by land and sea we entered the city on the eighth day of the siege. Fire broke out. The emperor put his battle lines in a field against us, and we came prepared to demonstrate our constancy. Astonished at our fewness, still he ignominiously retreated back into the burning city. That very night he fled the city with a few men. He deserted his wife and infant daughter. Unknown to us, when they learned this, the leading members of the Greek aristocracy gathered in the palace and solemnly celebrated the election, or rather the restoration, of the exile, which was announced, and copious lights testified to unexpected joy in the palace. In the morning a large number of the Greek nobles came out to the camp and sought their elect with joy and maintained that liberty had been restored to the city. They showed the returning son, who had been raised to the imperial throne, that his father, the former emperor Isaac, had been released from prison. And so those things that were necessary seemed to be preordained, the new emperor was led in solemn procession to the church of Haghia

Sophia, the imperial crown was restored to our exile with the fullness of power without any contradiction.

After these things had been accomplished, the emperor moved to fulfill his promises and he increased them with things; he offered foodstuffs for a year to be given to us for the service of the Lord; he went on to pay us two hundred thousand marks and he prolonged the Venetian fleet in his service for a year; and he bound himself with an oath that he would raise the royal banner with us and set out with us on the March passage for the service of the Lord with as many thousands of troops as he could and he included under the same promise that he ought to show reverence to the Roman Pontiff, just as his imperial predecessors, the Catholic emperors, were known to have shown to his pontifical predecessors, and that he would also try to influence the eastern church for this purpose as much as he could, and for the whole of his life he would provide fifty knights at his expense to serve the Lord in the Holy Land.[166]

Then finally the Doge and the Venetians who were in Greece sent ambassadors to Peter, cardinal priest of Saint Marcellus, the legate of the Apostolic See, begging him for the benefit of absolution. He sent the treasurer of Nicosia in Cyprus to them with his letter and, after he had received from them the oath in the form prescribed by the church, he ordered them to be absolved, although, up to this time, they had done nothing to make satisfaction for what they had done.[167] He preferred to have them imperfect rather than dead, especially that they might not spread their contagion to others.

XCI. Therefore, after Alexius, with Isaac, his father, had been restored to the Empire of Constantinople, and did not keep faith with the Latins, the letter transmitted to the Lord Pope describes how the city of Constantinople was captured and how Baldwin, the count of Flanders, was raised to the Empire.

---

166. RI 6:210(211), 358–61, about August 25, 1203. I have compared my translation to that by Alfred Andrea, *Contemporary Sources*, 80–84. My special thanks to Prof. Andrea for his assistance.

167. But cf. Innocent's letter to Peter, RI 8 (127) (126), of July 12, 1205. Innocent says that he had only recently learned that Peter has granted absolution to the Venetians.

XCI. "To our most Holy Father in Christ," he said, "the dearest Lord Innocent, by the grace of God, Supreme Pontiff, Baldwin, by the same grace,
Emperor of Constantinople and ever August, Count of Flanders and Hainault, his knight, kisses his feet with a constant devout desire to serve.
Since by the zeal of paternal solicitude and with a special love for our
community, your Holiness desires to know those things which have been
done around us, we have decided to relate to you as they happened how
the divine clemency has used us in wonderfully new ways, although it
will confer glory to be wondered at by all ages not on us indeed but on his
name. More marvels succeeded constantly his wonders around us [Ps
113:9] so that there should be no doubt even to unbelievers that the hand
of the Lord was the agent of these things, since nothing we hoped for or
foresaw earlier occurred, but then, at last, the Lord provided new help for
us since no human plan seemed adequate. Indeed, if we remember correctly, we related by our letter to your Paternity the progress and the situation to the point when the populous city was violently seized by a few.
After the tyrant fled and Alexius, the son of Isaac, was crowned, he promised and arranged our delay for the winter so that, if any should seem to
resist Alexius, they might be resisted effectively.

   And now we briefly undertake to relate those things which happened
later to us, with this addition, that, just as these attacks on the Greeks
were not the works of men but of God, so they were not the works of God
but of demons which Greece meted out to us with the new Greek emper-
or and through all things with their usual perfidy. But, to avoid by our
customs against foreigners laying tinder to the discord between us and the
Greeks, we departed from the city and camped in the port lying opposite
the city at the request of the emperor. By an unexpected or innate malice,
or having been seduced in his mind by the perfidy of the Greeks, the emperor, to whom we brought so many benefits, abandoned us. He was, with
his father, the patriarch, and most of the nobles, a perjurer and liar and he
committed perjuries as often as he swore oaths to us. Wherefore, rejecting
our help, he attempted in vain to attack us and tried to burn the fleet that
had brought him and raised him to the throne, but with God's protection
he was prevented from such a cruel purpose. His situation became worse
and slaughter, fires, and destruction overcame his people. With the battle
outside imminent, he was inwardly consumed by fear that, with the
Greeks preparing a rival emperor, he would have no opportunity for our
help. When his only hope of escape remained with us, he sent a man,

Mourtzouflos[168] by name, sworn to him and related by blood, of whom he was confident because of the benefits he had given him beyond all others, to our army and he promised the palace of Blachernae in pledge to us under his own oath and that of the emperor until all the emperor had promised us was paid. The noble marquis went to receive the palace; Alexius mocked him and, having scorned the hostages he had already given to us, he did not shrink from his usual perjuries. On the following night, Mourtzouflos, traitor to his master and to us, revealed to the Greeks the secret plan for surrendering the palace to us, and declared that their liberty was to be taken from them forever by this means and that it would all happen thus unless Alexius was deposed. By reason of this betrayal, a third emperor was raised up in the city, and he despatched a force against the sleeping emperor, who was unconscious of the affair, and put him back in prison. He also imprisoned a certain Nicholas, the third emperor, who had recently usurped the imperial regalia at Haghia Sophia. He was handed over to him by the treachery of the Greeks, who had created him emperor. After the death of Isaac, who, before all others, as they say, had turned his son's mind against us with the support of the Greek clergy and people, so that he might be raised from the ground, in short, with the Greeks thirsting only for our blood, the aforesaid traitor launched attacks against us. He fortified the city with machines and ramparts of a type that no one had ever seen before. The wall was of marvellous width and constructed with rubble, with cement of great durability and strength. Rising exceedingly high, it had high towers with a little more or less than about fifty feet distant between each two on the sea-side, from which our attack was feared, with wooden towers erected on the wall in three or four places, containing a large number of armed men. Nevertheless, between each two towers, petraries or mangonels were also built. Wooden towers six stories high were built above the existing towers, and on the top floor, platforms were extended against us, containing ramparts on each side at a height somewhat less than a bow could shoot an arrow from the ground. Also a lower wall surrounded this wall and it was double ditched to prevent any engines, under which sappers could hide, from being brought up to the walls.

Meanwhile, by land and sea the perfidious emperor tested us, but the

168. Alexius Ducas, who overthrew Alexius IV and assumed the throne as Alexius V.

Lord always protected us [2 Mc 10:1] and frustrated his efforts. For, because of our need for provisions, the emperor attacked up to a thousand
men with a great crowd of fighters and he was completely routed on his
first attack. After many were killed and captured without loss to us, he
took to his heels ignominiously, threw away his shield, cast off his arms,
and left the imperial standard for us, as well as the noble icon he ordered
to be carried before him, which the victors handed over to the Cistercian
order. Again and again he attacked our fleet with fire, and in the silence of
the dead of night, with the south wind blowing strongly against our ships,
he sent sixteen fire ships with sails expanded on high and fastened together below at the prow, but with the Lord's help and hard work on our part
we were kept safe. The burning ships, rudders held fast with hooks and
bound with chains, were dragged out to sea by our rowers and we were
freed from imminent danger of death by the Lord. We therefore provoked
him to a land battle, and when he crossed the bridge and stream that separated our army from the Greeks, we waited in formation before the gate
of the royal city and the imperial palace, which is called Blachernae. With
the living cross preceding the battle-lines of Israel, we were ready to meet
the Greeks in battle if they wished to come out. And, in fact, in a skirmish,
our infantry killed a certain noble who came out. Thus, when we returned
to camp, we were often provoked by land and by sea, but with divine
help, we were always victorious. And the perfidious imperial interloper
sent legates of a false peace to us and sought a meeting with the Doge.
And when the magnanimous Doge objected that there could be no peace
agreement with one who had put his Lord in prison, had violated his oath,
as well as his fealty, and an agreement binding even among infidels, and
snatched the empire for himself, the Doge counseled him in good faith
that he should restore his lord and humbly seek pardon. He promised our
support for him and that we should deal, if he wished, mercifully with the
same Lord. And we would impute whatever he had done evilly against us
to age or to poor counsel if he would return to our agreement. He answered with empty words because he had no reasonable response. Moreover, he now rejected obedience to the Roman church and his support for
the Holy Land which Alexius had agreed to by oath and in an imperial letter, so then he chose to lose his life and to ruin Greece rather than allow
the Oriental church to be subjected to Latin bishops. On the following
night he secretly strangled his Lord in prison with a noose. On that very
day that Judas had eaten supper with him [Mk 14:20; Lk 22:21; Jn 13:26]

and with unheard of cruelty, he tore apart the ribs of the dying man with an iron hook that he held in his hand. He made up the story that the life he had destroyed with the noose was the result of an accident and he granted him an imperial funeral to conceal the crime which was known to everyone behind the honor of a funeral.

So the whole winter passed for us until, after our ships were fitted with flying bridges and war machines, we and our forces, taking to our ships, moved on the city on April 9, that is on the Friday before the Passion of the Lord. With one mind, we attacked for the honor of the Holy Roman Church and the support of the Holy Land and on this day we suffered so much but without shedding much of our blood that we retreated from our enemies in shame. On that day, part of them proved superior so that now we were forced by the Greeks to leave our war machinery which we had drawn up on the land and with this loss we were forced to return to the opposite shore. On this day, it seemed we were totally worn out. Greatly disturbed, therefore, and fearful, but still strengthened in the Lord, after we considered the matter, we again went into battle. On the fourth day, April 12, that is the Monday after the Passion of the Lord, with a north wind, we again attacked the walls with the ships' flying bridges laid on the platforms of the towers by the great efforts of our men and despite much resistance by the Greeks. But when they began to feel our swords in hand-to-hand combat the outcome did not remain long in doubt. Two ships, whose names were Paradise and Lady Pilgrim, tied together, which carried our bishops of Soissons and Troyes, first attached the platforms of the towers to their bridges, and with good fortune they carried the pilgrims fighting for Paradise to the enemy. The banners of the bishops were first to reach the walls and victory was granted first to the ministers of heavenly secrets. Our attackers, with divine assistance, defeated a multitude with a very few and, with the Greeks running away, our men bravely opened the gates to the knights. At their entry, the emperor, who was standing armed not far from the walls in his tents, immediately left the tents and fled. Our men were occupied with the slaughter. The populous city was taken. The Greeks fled from our swords. Our men gained entry to the imperial palaces. After much killing of Greeks our men regrouped on that evening, and worn out, they put their arms aside after the attack on the palaces to resume it on the morrow. The emperor gathered his men together and exhorted them to fight on the next day, asserting that he now had our men in his power within the seven walls. But secretly by night, the conquered men fled. When the stunned Greek populace learned this, they discussed finding a new emperor and while they proceeded in the morning to the nomination of a certain Constantine, our infantry without waiting for the advice of the leaders, attempted an attack and the Greeks fled one of the strongest and best fortified palaces, and in a short time the entire city was in our hands. A huge number of horses were seized. Of gold and silver, silks, precious vestments, gems, and all the things men account as riches, such an inestimable abundance was found that the whole Latin world would seem not to possess as much. Those who denied us a few things, lost everything to us by Divine judgment so that we can say with certainty that never did history speak of greater marvels as a result of wars, so that the prophecy might seem to be fulfilled in us which says that one of you will pursue a hundred foreigners [Lv 26:8] because if we share the victory among individuals, each of our men has besieged and conquered no fewer than a hundred. Now, however, we do not claim victory for ourselves because the right hand of the Lord [Ps 97:1] saved that for himself and the arm of his power is revealed in us. This was done by the Lord and it is a wonder above all wonders in our eyes [Ps 117:23].

When, therefore, we had arranged diligently the things that the outcome required to be taken care of, we proceeded unanimously and with devotion to the election of an emperor, and, with all ambition set aside, we appointed as electors of our emperor under the Lord's direction, with six Venetian barons, the venerable bishops of Soissons, Halberstadt, Troyes, and the Lord of Bethlehem, who had been appointed by the Apostolic Authority for us in *Outremer*,[169] the Bishop-elect of Acre and the Abbot of Lucedio. They, after a preliminary prayer, as was proper, celebrated 'Misericordia Domini Sunday'[170] and by the mercy of the Lord unanimously and solemnly chose our person, though unmerited, with the clergy and people alike proclaiming the divine praises. On the following Sunday on which the 'Jubilate' was sung according to the command of the Apostle Peter to honor and obey the king [1 Pt 2:1] as a superior, the gospel announced that no one would take our joy from us with huge honor and transports of joy, also, with even the Greeks applauding in their manner, the bishops, to the applause and pious tears of all, gloriously elevated to the imperial dignity him who had been crowned by God and humanity, to the honor of God and the Holy Roman Church and for the re-

169. The Lord of Bethlehem, i.e., the bishop.
170. May 9, 1204.

lief of the Holy Land. There were many present from the Holy Land and with joyful congratulations, they asserted and showed gracious service to God, as if the holy city was restored to Christian worship, because, to the confusion of the enemies of the cross, the royal city so long in opposition and an adversary of both has dedicated itself to the Roman Church and land of Jerusalem [Phil 3:18]. For this city, which, in the very filthy rite of the gentiles, sucking blood as a sign of the fraternal union you have drunk from alternate bloods, often dared to make friendships with infidels and its very full breast has nourished them and has exulted in worldly pride in serving their arms, ships, and foodstuffs. What, on the contrary, it did for the pilgrims, examples rather than words suffice to inform the whole Latin people. This is the city that, in hatred of the Apostolic See, could hardly bear to listen to the name of the prince of the Apostles, and did not grant a single Greek church to him who had received dominion over all the churches from the Lord himself. This is the city that forgot that Christ should be honored in pictures. Among the evil rites which, rejecting the authority of Sacred Scriptures, it had fashioned, it often presumed to make even saving baptism something to be repeated. This is how it called all Latins not by name of men but of dogs, the shedding of whose blood they considered almost meritorious and lay monks, who possessed the power of binding and loosing in contempt of the priesthood, did not punish it with any penance that required amendment. After their iniquities were complete, sins that disgusted the Lord himself [Mt 17:6; Mk 9:18; Lk 9:41], Divine justice, with our ministry and with fitting vengeance, struck the oppressive absurdities of this kind which no letter could explain, and expelled these people who hated God and loved themselves, gave the Land to us, a land flowing with an abundance of all goods, grain, wine, and oil, rich in fruits, and beautiful with its woods, waters, and pastures, most spacious for living and in which there is no better climate in the world. But our desires in these matters will not cease nor will we allow the royal banner to be removed from our shoulders until we, after that land has been made safe, visit the regions across the sea and, with God's help, complete our plan of pilgrimage. For we hope in the Lord Jesus Christ that he who began a good work in us may complete, confirm, and strengthen the perpetual defeat of the enemies of the cross to the praise and glory of his name [Phil 3:18].

Therefore, we pray your Paternity more readily in the Lord to agree to be prince and leader of that glory, victory, and desired hope whose great gate has been opened to us, and you will do honor to your pontificate and its works, if you inflame by your salutary advice those devoted to your Apostolic Holiness, especially those dwelling in the West, nobles and commoners, of whatever condition or sex, burning with desire for true and abundant riches, both temporal and eternal, to be obtained by all those coming with Apostolic indulgence to serve us and our empire faithfully either temporarily or permanently. For, with God's help, we will furnish all whom zeal for the Christian religion shall bring to us, according to their status and natural diversity, an opportunity to increase their riches and grow in honors. But especially your Paternal solicitude should persuade ecclesiastics, loveable in God's eyes, of any order or rite, to hasten in large numbers to come to preach publicly and, burning with powerful words and teaching by example in the most pleasant and fruitful places, not now flowing with blood but in much liberty and peace and in all good, to plant the church, saving always that they should have canonical license from their superiors.

No believers should doubt that it would pertain to the praise and glory of the Redeemer and the perpetual honor of your Holiness and the special utility of the whole church, if your Paternity were to summon a general council in Constantinople, a city honored by ancient councils, confirmed by the presence of your holy person and your Paternity, might join the new Rome with the old by sacred sanctions to be perpetually valid. For we have now learned that you invited the rebellious Greeks to a council[171] as if you foresaw these things, although we seem to have meanwhile taken different ways, either on account of the rebellion of the Greeks, or for the utility of the world and various occupations. Now is the acceptable time, Holy Father, behold now is the day of salvation [2 Cor 6:2]. The Lord seems to have thought thoughts of peace in your times, and he made your enemies your footstool [Jer 29:11]. Sound the priestly horn in Zion [J 12:15], we beseech you, most beloved Father, summon the assembly, gather the people, collect the elders and nursing mothers, make holy the acceptable day to the Lord [Is 58:5], the day for establishing unity and peace, and that we observe for the Lord, so that our fortitude may be confirmed. For however much we may be insufficient we dare to hope in the Lord that the joy of the Lord may be our strength to erase the scandal to

---

171. See Innocent's letter to Alexius III above. The tone here is accusatory, making clear that the crusaders had not been informed of Innocent's plans earlier.

the cross and to subject every adversary raising up power in those lands against the Lord and against his Christ [Gal 5:11]. You are mindful, Holy Father, of your predecessors, whose souls rejoice in heaven and whose glorious memory lives on earth, John, Agapetus, and Leo,[172] and the others, who we read, as is recorded in the Apostolic archives, have personally visited for various reasons the church of Constantinople and you will find manifestly, if they who claim they have read it do not deceive us, the fact that any of them would have come there for far lesser reasons. If indeed we acted from burning desire beyond what was proper, from your accustomed kindness, Reverend Father, overlook it, and look more to the result of this business than to our words. But we ought not be silent that the reverend bishops and abbots and the venerable clergy of lesser status acted so magnificently, and honorably held themselves so honestly among us and fought for God with powerful arms so constantly and triumphantly that they should expect the crown of victory from the hand of the Lord, and their memory has merited to be forever blessed and they should not lack any grace of Apostolic favor, and the full measure of favor for such well-merited acts. We commend to your Paternity for the merit of his probity, the illustrious man, Enrico Dandalo, Doge of the Venetians, beloved to us and beloved for his merit, together with all our Venetian friends and companions whom we have found to be faithful and diligent in all circumstances."[173]

XCII. But before the Franks and Venetians proceeded to the conquest of Constantinople, they entered into an agreement with one another as follows:

In the name of the Eternal God, Amen. We, Boniface of Monferrat, Marquis, and Baldwin of Flanders and Hainault, Count Louis of Blois and Clermont, Count Hugh of St. Pol, for our party, order the following to be observed with you, Lord Enrico Dandolo, Doge of Venice, Dalmatia and

172. Pope John I, 523–526, headed a delegation sent by Theodorich the Ostrogoth to Emperor Justin. Pope Agapitus I, 535–536, deposed Patriarch Antimos of Constantinople. Pope Constantine I (708–715) met Emperor Justinian II in Nicomedia. He has been in Constantinople previously as the representative of Pope Leo II. See RI 7:152, 253–62, esp. 261, n. 41.
173. RI 7:152, 253–62, after May 16, 1204. See Andrea, *Contemporary Sources*, 110–12.

Croatia, and with your party, on the strict oath of both parties so that unity and agreement between us can be harmonious and to avoid all matters of scandal with the assistance of him who is our peace and has made us both one [Eph 2:1]. First of all, after we have invoked Christ's name, we should attack the city with armed force, and if, with the power of Divine assistance we enter the city, we should remain under the rule of those who have been chosen as leaders of the army, and follow them as ordered. All treasure found in the city by any leader at all should be put in common in the place designated. From that treasure, three parts must be paid to you and the Venetians in place of that which Alexius, the former emperor, was required to pay to you and us. We ought to keep the fourth part for ourselves as long as we shall be co-equals in its liberation. But if anything is left, we should divide it half and half between you and us until you have been paid in full. But if there is not enough to pay the aforementioned debt, regardless of the treasure acquired earlier, we should apply the same arrangement to it, saving however, foodstuffs to be stored and divided equally between your men and ours, so that both parties can be suitably maintained. But what remains to be shared should be divided in another treasure in the aforementioned manner.

Also, you and the Venetians ought to have freely and absolutely without any controversy all the honors and possessions that you were accustomed to have formerly both in spiritual and temporal things, and all the accounts and customs, either written or unwritten. Also six men should be elected from each party, who, bound by a strict oath, should choose the person in the army whom they believe knows better and can better hold and better know how to organize the land and the empire to the honor of God and of the Holy Roman Church and of the empire. And if they are in agreement we should have as emperor him whom they agree to choose. But if six should agree on one party and six on another, they should agree to cast lots, and we should have as emperor the one on whom the lot should fall, and if several agree on one party rather than another we will have as emperor the one on whom the majority agree. But if there are more than two parties, the one on whom the majority agree will be emperor. That emperor should hold a complete fourth part of the empire acquired as well as the Blachernae Palace and the Bucoleon Palace. The remaining three parts are to be divided equally between us and you.

Also, it should be known that clerics who are not of the party from whom the emperor is elected will be in charge of the church of Haghia

Sophia and will elect the patriarch to the honor of God and of the Holy Roman church and of the empire. But clerics of both parties should administer those churches that belong to their own party. But from the possessions of churches so much should be provided to clerics and churches as is needed for them to live and be supported honorably. The remaining possessions of churches ought to be divided and shared according the previous agreement.

In addition, both parties must swear that from the last day of March we will remain for a whole year to support the empire and the emperor for the honor of God and of the Holy Roman church and the empire. Finally, all who remain in the empire should be bound to the emperor by an oath according to good and reasonable custom and those who will then remain in the empire, as has been said, should swear that they will keep firm and fixed the shares and divisions that were made. But it must be known that twelve men, or more, strictly bound by oath, should be chosen from each side to distribute fiefs and honors among the men and to assign the services they ought to perform for the emperor, as it will seem good to them and will appear convenient.

They ought to possess freely and absolutely the fief assigned to each by hereditary right both in the male and female lines and have full power of disposition however they wish, saving the rights and service due the emperor and the empire. But the emperor ought to perform the remaining services that should be performed save those that they, who will possess the fiefs and honors, will perform according to the orders enjoined on them. Also, it is established that no man of any nation which shall be in open war with you and your successors or the Venetian people may be received in the empire until the war has been ended. Also both parties shall be required to work in good faith so that they may be able to ask the Lord Pope that if anyone contravenes this agreement he will be excommunicated. In addition, the emperor ought to swear that he will keep irrevocably firm and fixed the divisions and terms which have been made according to the plan set out above. If, however, anything is to be added or diminished, let it be done in your power and discretion and that of your six counselors and of the lord marquis and his six counselors.

Also, it must be understood that you alone, Lord Doge, do not owe the aforesaid lord emperor who shall be elected or the empire an oath for any services to be done for any gift or fief or honor which should be assigned to you. They or he whom you appoint in your place upon these matters, however, which have been assigned to you, should be held by an oath to perform all service to the emperor according to the plan set forth above. Given in the year of the Lord 1204 in the month of March, the seventh indiction.[174]

XCIII. Since, therefore, the Lord Innocent was aware that many illicit things were contained in this agreement, especially those which concerned the status of churches and clerics, and that many crimes were perpetrated in the conquest of Constantinople and that the crusaders had been forbidden to attack Christian lands, unless perhaps their journey was wrongly impeded, and it did not seem to be a sufficient excuse to make it legal for men to attack the Greeks on the ground that they had withdrawn themselves from the obedience of the Apostolic See and they were not willing to aid the Holy Land, even though they were warned by the same Lord Pope on both matters, and the fact that Emperor Alexius occupied the empire that he wrongfully seized from his brother, since they received no power from above to punish, he began very vehemently to doubt what he should do in so important a business. But after he had held diligent discussion not only with the cardinals but also with archbishops and bishops and other prudent men of whom there were then many from diverse parts at the Apostolic See, he wrote to the noble Marquis of Montferrat who was consulting the Apostolic See on this matter from common counsel in this way:

We commend your prudence and devotion in the Lord that among diverse cares and mundane occupations, which are not only manifold but urgent, you are solicitous and desirous about the salvation of your soul. For what does it a profit a man if he should gain the whole world, but suffers the loss of his soul [Mt 16:26]? Or what will a man give in exchange for his soul? The brother will not redeem him, nor will the man redeem himself, nor will he appease God, nor pay the price for the redemption of his soul; he will labor eternally and live to the end [Ps 48:8–10]. For we have received your letter through our beloved son, Soffredus, cardinal priest of

174. RI 7:205, 360–63, March 1204

Santa Prassede, presented to our papal office, in which you have taken
care to make known to us that with a contrite heart and sincere spirit, led
to the mandate of Apostolic advice by hope of a general pardon, you have
solemnly taken the vow of the cross and you have intended always to fulfill it fruitfully. But the fact that you followed that youth who said that by
right he ought to hold the Empire of Constantinople was the counsel of
our beloved son Peter, cardinal priest of St. Marcellus, legate of the Apostolic See (and it was not so much human counsel as a pressing necessity)
that the army detour into Romania after the sack of Zara to acquire supplies. But you and the other crusaders, making a virtue of necessity, intended in this way principally to arrange to fulfill the service owed the
Apostolic See and the expected help for the Holy Land that you thought
you had fulfilled completely since the royal city was captured without
shedding of blood. Once the usurper of the empire had fled, and both father and son were restored to the summit of the imperial dignity, you
made them, without coercion, show obedience to the Apostolic See on the
Gospels, having sent an imperial rescript to us for the greater strengthening of the faith that they would fulfill in deeds what they had promised us
in words. And when you were ready to sail to Syria with your forces, the
oaths and agreements were violated by the innate malice of the Greeks.
Your journey was wrongfully impeded not once but often by fire, trickery,
and poison and you were forced, struggling and unwilling, to the occupation of the royal city by their deceit. By the power of God alone you wonderfully triumphed in whatever you did, whether willingly or unwillingly.
After taking counsel with your clergy, you have always held to the vows
so that through you the sons of disobedience might return to the both
owed and devoted obedience of their mother, and the Oriental church
might be united as a principal member to its head. In order that the counsel of the Apostolic See might become better and fuller, the counsel without which all deeds and materials perish, you have awaited until now and
to this point with continuous desires. But because you have received the
sign of the cross, as you say, to destroy the sins of your youth and to eliminate whatever human fragility has contracted from previous times, so
that you might not sin more seriously and freely under the guise of religion and the standard of the cross, you are referring individual things in
all and in everything for the approval of our examination. You are opening yourself to our counsels and mandates, so that if we understand the
situation of Romania and that your delay there would be beneficial to the

Apostolic See and the Land of Promise, and through this you receive the remission of sins. You do not, otherwise, reject dangers or labors, neither with respect to the possessions nor the horrors you may undergo abundantly. But we enjoin it on you to turn aside the wrath of the Divine judge that you abundantly merit.

Of course, you see from what has been written above that we have responded to the tacit objections which can be twisted in such wise against the crusaders. For since you have vowed to serve the Crucified in order to liberate the Holy Land from the hands of the pagans, you are bound under threat of excommunication not to invade the lands of or injure Christians, unless perhaps they should wrongfully impede your journey or some other just and necessary reason should occur by reason of which you would, with the advice of our legate, need to act otherwise. We see that you have turned away from the purity of your vow though you had no power or jurisdiction over the Greeks because you fought not against the Saracens but against Christians, not to reconquer Jerusalem but to occupy Constantinople, preferring earthly to heavenly riches, and what is far more serious, that you spared neither religion, nor age, nor sex, but perpetrating fornications, adulteries, and incests in the eyes of all, not only married women and widows, but also matrons and virgins dedicated to God, exposed them to the filth of the mercenaries. It was not enough to exhaust the imperial treasure and to seize the spoils of elders as well as minors, but you reached out your hands for the treasures of churches and, what is worse, for their very possessions, seizing silver tablets from the altars. You violated the churches, carrying away crosses, icons, and relics, so that the church of the Greeks, so often afflicted by persecutions, refuses to return to the obedience of the Apostolic See, and has seen in the Latins nothing but examples of perdition and works of darkness, so that it rightly abhors them more than dogs.

But you have alleged in your defense, contrary to usurped jurisdiction or power, the counsel of the legate of the Apostolic See, as if he permitted you to set out to restore the aforesaid youth to the Empire of Constantinople, although you could also allege that, since a lack of supplies motivated you, and you could not fulfill your crusade vow without them, it would be licit for you for the now necessary reason to suit your plans to him who seemed to pursue a just cause, especially since, through this you intended finally to aid the Holy Land and benefit the Apostolic See. And when they denied the promised and due reward to you, broke their oaths and agreements, and even attacked you often with arms, fire, trickery, and poison, you were put in a difficult position, so that you had to carry out a just punishment against the schismatics and perjurers unjustly denying you your due. For it seems to have been a Divine judgment that those, so long mercifully tolerated and so often admonished not only by others but also by us, were unwilling to return to the unity of the church and would not give any aid to the Holy Land through those, who were awaiting both equally. They should lose their place and the people, so that, with the evil ones brought to a bad end, the land might be leased out to good farmers and they would bring a harvest at an opportune time [Mt 21:41]. Thus we read in the prophet Daniel, "It is God in heaven who reveals the mysteries and changes the times, and transfers kingdoms. He rules the kingdom of men and he will give it to whom he wishes" [Dn 2:21, 28]. But popular opinion holds that the laws of kingdoms are always violent. Because, however, the judgments of God have never until now been hidden, as the Prophet says: " a great depth" [Ps 35:7], so that the apostle is forced to exclaim, "O the depth of riches of the wisdom and knowledge of God, how incomprehensible are his judgments and mysterious are his ways. For who knew the mind of the Lord or who was his counselor" [Rom 11:33–34]?

We are unwilling to judge heedlessly concerning such a profound judgment, especially before we are more certain about the truth of the business, since they also could be justly punished for sin that they committed against God and you. Nevertheless it would be unjust to punish them for the hate that you bore against neighbors, but if the neighbors are said to be those who refuse to be neighborly perhaps God would give a just reward to you on account of their just punishment as we read in the prophet, "Because you have served me in Tyre, I will give you Egypt" [Ez 29:18–20], whereby Assur calls it "the rod of his anger" [Is 10:5]. We order a clear response to you about this matter, counseling healthfully both for the Holy Land and the Apostolic See as well as for your soul that under fear of the Lord and hope of pardon, you may hold the land you have acquired by divine judgment and you may defend and you may acquire it to be held and defended. You may rule the peoples subject to you in justice, preserving it in peace and conforming to religion, so that you will restore ecclesiastical property to their proper use, doing penance and making satisfaction concerning those things you have done, since an act of this kind can hardly be done without incurring guilt, because he who touches pitch will be stained by it [Sir 13:1]. You should act with a firm commitment to your vow so that you may prudently and effectively support the Holy Land to whose aid you have especially and principally vowed, since it is to be hoped that through this land these things may be easily recovered. Since at the example of the your fathers and brothers who desired always to revere and venerate the Holy Roman Church from a pure heart and good conscience, and with unwavering faith, you are loyal and devoted to us and the Apostolic See, from the fullness of our favor, we render you completely secure. You should know for certain that, as often as opportunity is available, we desire to carry out those deeds which will greatly redound to your honor and profit. Given, etc.[175]

XCIV. But because, by holding the Empire of Constantinople, that by Divine judgment the Latins subjected to themselves, there was hope that the Jerusalemite province might easily be liberated from the hands of the pagans, the Lord Pope began, with a firm commitment to get the support of those who were staying in Constantinople, writing to the archbishops and bishops in this manner:

A man from Rama-theim married two wives, namely, Hannah and Penninah [1 Sm 1]. The offspring of the first was covered with glory, because he was splendid. When the other began to exult in the Lord at the fertility of her offspring, she was enfeebled, as her song shows. We read that these things happened under the shadow of the law, since, according to the apostle, everything that should happen to them spiritually in a figure comes to pass in the people of God at a time of grace so that, with the veil lifted from the face of Moses, through the light of evangelical teaching, the dark water will shine in the clouds of the air and the meaning will appear clearly. For the mediator of God and men, the man Jesus Christ, one entirely, not in the confusion of substance but in the unity of person, calling peoples to himself, namely, the Greeks and Latins, has joined them through the sacraments of faith. But, one of them, namely, the Greeks, who glory in the seventh number of the churches (John makes mention of

---

175. RI 8:134 (133), August 15–September 10, 1205. I wish to thank Christoph Egger for providing me with proofs of this letter and others from the eighth year of Innocent's register. I have also used Andrea, *Contemporary Sources*, 171–76, to check my translation.

these churches and their angels in the Apocalypse) [Rv 1:4], when it saw
the share of the church of the Latins increased, as if agitated by the stimulus of envy, departed from unity, not awaiting what the bridegroom had
promised in the canticles, "there are sixty queens and eighty concubines,
and young women without number," he immediately adds, "My dove is
one alone, my perfect one, her mother's chosen, chosen for my parent, the
daughters of Sion have seen her and pronounced her most blessed, queen
and concubines, they also have praised her" [Sg 6:8–9]. For many daughters collected riches, but she has surpassed all riches. But after the Greeks
broke the chain of peace and departed from unity, they also grew weak,
refusing to confess the faith, that the Holy Spirit, who is the binding force
of unity and equality, proceeds from the Son as from the Father. Because,
therefore, they refused to profess the truth about the procession of the
Holy Spirit, they merited to incur darkness of mind since the Spirit teaches
all truth, as the Son sets forth in the Gospel. For, deprived of the spiritual
intellect because they sinned against the Spirit, they did not throw the
leaven out of the house [1 Cor 5:7], so that they might feast on the un-
leavened breads of sincerity and truth, but having kept the leaven of the
Old, they ate the body of Christ made with yeast. But blessed be the God
and Father of our Lord Jesus Christ, the Father of mercies and the God of
all consolation, who, having desired to console his church, so that Ephraim
might be converted to Juda and Samaria returned to Jerusalem [Is 11:13],
has deigned wonderfully to raise a sign over the same people like a hill
covered with mist and those sanctified to God have entered his gates,
transferring the empire of the Greeks from the proud to the humble, from
the superstitious to the religious, from schismatics to Catholics, from the
disobedient to the devout. For when the Christian army arrived there with
Alexius, the son of Isaac, and after they had captured Constantinople, the
same Alexius received his share, and the army proposed to winter there.
But the things the new emperor desired as benefits for himself would be
too long to list on the present page. Still, that we may list many things
more briefly, when their malice was carried out as if by the iniquity of the
Amorites [Gn 15:16], the right hand of the Lord gave the power and exalted the Christian army, striking down those worthy of punishment and giving their land filled with gold, silver, and gems, abundant with grain, wine,
and oil and flowing with a great amount of all goods, to the army. When
the Greeks were expelled from Constantinople and their land subjugated,
they raised our dearest son in Christ, Baldwin, Count of Flanders and

Hainault, by the common and unanimous will, to the rule of the empire so that there might seem to be fulfilled in him what was said of Cyrus: "I will," he said, "subject the people before his face and I will turn the backs of kings. I will open the doors before him and the doors will not be closed. I will go before you and I will humble the glorious men of the land, I will destroy the bronze doors and I will break iron bars, and I will give you hidden treasures and arcane secrets" [Ps 107:16]. He, therefore, who was so wonderfully raised up humbly asked that we would deign to invite by Apostolic exhortations of the Apostolic See devoted clergy and laity, both nobles and commoners, of whatever condition or sex to come to the Empire to receive from him according as their qualities freely merited riches.

Considering, therefore, that the change of this empire may be a change of the right hand of God and it may have been done by him who alters seasons and transfers kingdoms, since in this way the Holy Land can be aided more usefully, indeed in this way it may perhaps be recovered from misfortune, we admonish and exhort your fraternity in the Lord by an Apostolic letter to you, ordering and commanding that you efficaciously persuade both clerics and laity to approach the emperor, who desires individuals, to use his words, to obtain both spiritual and temporal riches, since it suffices for all whose zeal for the Christian religion lead to him, and he can increase their wealth and fill them with honors according to their status and their difference in birth, so that, after the empire of Constantinople has been strengthened and the church there established in devotion to the Apostolic See, the same emperor with a strong hand and right arm extended may have the power to hasten to fight the barbarous nations who hold and occupy the land in which God our King deigned to work salvation for exigent sinners ages ago, hoping in the Lord Jesus Christ that he who began to carry out this work in a wonderful way may bring it to a even more wonderful conclusion to the praise and glory of his name. We grant that forgiveness of sins to those who, coming to him, work for the support of the Holy Lord that the Apostolic See has granted to other crusaders.[176]

XCV. But after Baldwin was raised to the Empire of Constantinople, he summoned to his presence by ambassadors and by his imperial rescript Peter, cardinal priest of St. Marcellus, legate of the Apostolic See,

176. RI 8:70(69), about May 25, 1205. From proof furnished by C. Egger.

who was then in the province of Jerusalem so that he might establish by Apostolic authority ecclesiastical affairs concerning persons and properties. But, when the oft-mentioned Soffredus, cardinal priest of Santa Prassede, who was also legate of the Apostolic See, was unwilling to remain there after his departure, both left and went to Constantinople, after they had concluded a six-year truce with the Saracens. Such a multitude not only of laity but also of clergy followed them that almost all foreigners and many natives deserted the province of Jerusalem and went to Constantinople. Soffredus, however, made a brief stop there and returned to the Apostolic See by way of Thessalonica where he stayed with the Marquis of Montferrat for a while. But how the Lord Pope wrote about these and other matters to Peter, cardinal priest of St. Marcellus, then in Constantinople, is clear from the content of his letter that follows:

When we heard some time ago that you and our beloved son, Soffredus, cardinal priest of Santa Prassede, legate of the Apostolic See, had left the province of Jerusalem during a period of much need, had arrived by ship in Constantinople, we wondered and were disturbed, dreading the imminent danger to that land. And behold, what we feared has happened and what we were worried about has now come to pass. For in addition to the fact that with the death of the Patriarch of Jerusalem, the church of Jerusalem was vacant, and there was a certain rivalry between Christians from the war that took place between our dearest son in Christ, the illustrious king of Armenia and the count of Tripoli over the principate of Antioch, afterward, due to the unforeseen death of Amalric, King of Jerusalem, of shining memory, and of his son, the Kingdom of Jerusalem was almost entirely without government. And because you, who should rather have sought greater help there, and invited others to aid the same land both by word and example, of your own will went to Greece, not only pilgrims but also natives of the Holy Land went to Constantinople following in your footsteps, with our brother, the Archbishop of Tyre, likewise in your train. Therefore, with your departure, that land has remained destitute in men and arms, and its most recent situation was made worse than its earlier state by your action, since all its friends departed from it in your company, and there was no one to console her from all those dear to her. For this reason, her enemies have gained the advantage, should they wish to break the truce, which also is said by some to have expired with the deaths of the king and his son. Therefore, we are quite disturbed and are rightfully angry with you that you both decided to leave the land that the Lord consecrated by his presence and in which our king long ago wonderfully worked the mystery of our redemption. Although, of course, our venerable brother, the former bishop of Vercelli, was postulated for the Patriarchate of Jerusalem, and we approved his postulation and ordered the *pallium* to be granted to him, still on account of his many occupations, he cannot quickly cross the sea. Therefore, you should have paid heed to and considered carefully the reason for your delegation. Because we sent you not to seize the empire of Constantinople but to defend the rest of the Holy Land and to restore that which was lost, if the Lord should grant that it be restored. Since we and our brothers provided adequately for your expenses, we sent you not to seize on temporal riches but to deserve eternal.

But when we also learned recently from your letter that you had absolved all the crusaders who delayed in defense of Constantinople from the preceding March to the next from their vow of pilgrimage and the burden of the cross, we could not fail to move against you, since you neither should nor could attempt such things in any way, whoever might suggest the contrary to you and however they might seduce your mind. For since they assumed the cross for this especially and principally and vowed particularly to the Lord their God that they would cross over the sea to aid the Holy Land and they later deviated from the path and obtained even until today an excess of temporal benefits, we leave to your judgment whether it was permissible for you to make such a change, nay, rather to pervert such a solemn and pious vow. For behold what we relate with grief and shame. By what we seemed to have profited until now, we are impoverished and by what we were made greater, we are rather reduced.

For how will the Greek church, which has been afflicted to some degree by persecution, be returned to ecclesiastical unity and devotion to the Apostolic See? They look upon the Latins as nothing but an example of perdition and works of darkness, so that now they rightly abhor them more than dogs. For those who are believed to seek not things for themselves but for Jesus Christ ought to use their swords against the pagans, but they are bloody with the blood of Christians, and they do not spare anyone by reason of religion, age, or sex, carrying out incests, adulteries and fornications in the eyes of men and exposing both matrons and virgins dedicated to God to the filth of mercenaries. And it was not enough for them to exhaust imperial riches and seize the spoils of princes and minors, but they reached out their hands for the treasures of churches and what is worse for their possessions, seizing silver tablets from their altars and breaking them in pieces among themselves. They violated sacristies and carried off crosses and relics. Besides, since it was impossible to hide what is believed among so many thousands of men, will the Saracens who, after the capture of Constantinople, were too beaten down by fear not come to know that the crusaders will return to their own land after a year. Divine punishment will now begin to best their iniquities, and already rages against them, and will the Saracens not recover their courage and devour the lambs that you left as morsels to the wolves, if the right hand alone of God does not restore them [1 Sm 17:28]? Also, how could we in the future invite the peoples of the West to aid the Holy Land and defend the Empire of Constantinople when some will argue, even if it is not your fault but the result of your action, that the crusaders, having deserted their pilgrimage, are returning to their homes absolved, and those who despoiled the empire, having left it unfortified, desert it when they are stuffed with spoils? Let not the word of the Lord be bound on your tongue, and like mute dogs, may you be unable to bark, but say this publicly and protest before all so that the more they who found you negligent up to now may find you blaming the more in behalf of God and because of God.[177]

XCVI. But how to proceed to the election of patriarch is made clearer from the letter of the Lord Pope directed to the Emperor in this manner:

After the right hand of the Lord, which is glorified in power, transferred the Empire of Constantinople from the Greeks to the Latins, those who were in the army of the Latins, desiring to provide for the empire a suitable person from the princes of the Gauls, unanimously elected an emperor. But, so that the Venetians who were equal partners in the enterprise might be also partners in the honors, it pleased the laity altogether that a suitable man might be taken from the Venetian clergy to be made patri-

177. RI 8:127(126), July 12, 1205. From proof furnished by C. Egger.

arch of the church of Constantinople. When, therefore, some Venetian clerics were appointed to the service of the church of Constantinople, lest they should appear headless, they met together to discuss making pastors for themselves. They unanimously elected our beloved son Thomas,[178] our subdeacon, as patriarch and postulated confirmation of his election from us through proper messengers, with the noble Doge of the Venetians also making the same urgent request through his messengers. His imperial highness also asked by his letter to us that we should deign to ratify the agreements between him and the pilgrims on the one hand and the Doge and the Venetians on the other, which were entered into before the conquest of the city and fortified with the impression of his seal, and to strengthen them by our Apostolic authority, desiring us to know that we should use his words that he had kept good relations with the Doge and the Venetians and held them loyal and most honest and effective collaborators to the honor of God and of the Holy Roman Church and of the Empire of Constantinople as he had found their deeds witnessed. He was desirous of having their support in the future, since, to conserve the rule of the empire and the aid for the Holy Land and the unity of church, their assistance would be useful and necessary, and without their assistance and love he could not rule the empire competently to the honor of God and the Apostolic See. Also, in the same words, the noble men, Boniface, Marquis of Montferrat, Count Louis of Blois, and the Count of St. Pol made this known through their letter.

We, therefore, ordered the agreement of the emperor, marquis, and the counts to be read before us, and saw that it contained the provision that the clerics of the party from which the emperor was not selected should freely choose the Patriarch for themselves. When, therefore, an election of this kind was presented to us, even though we and our brethren had sufficient information about the person elected from the long stay he had made earlier at the Apostolic See, namely, we knew he was of a noble family, of honest morals, circumspect in outlook and competently educated, we nevertheless examined his election in the usual way. We found it contrary to canonical form not only from the fact that many contradicted it and some even appealed against it, even though later both were withdrawn, and for the fact no layman had the right to intervene in ecclesiastical matters, and no patriarch either should or could be elected in the

---

178. Thomas Morosini, Latin Patriarch of Constantinople.

church of Constantinople by authority of any secular prince. But neither did the Venetian clergy, who call themselves canons-elect of Haghia Sophia, have the right of election in the same church, since they were not appointed in it either by the legates or our delegates, for which reason we have taken care to reject that election in a public consistory with the agreement of our brethren. But since the transgression of persons ought not redound to the injury of churches and the same subdeacon did not act wrongly, since he was elected when absent and did not seek for it, mindful of the prayers of the emperor which seem to suggest not merely utility but necessity and desiring to provide for the same church, whose jurisdiction pertains especially to us, and in hope of showing favor to the Venetians so that they may more strongly lend themselves to the service of the cross of Christ, from the fullness of power granted us we have elected the same individual, our subdeacon and member of the Apostolic See, and confirmed him as patriarch for the same church. We therefore admonish the Imperial Dignity, we also counsel and exhort you that you should receive him kindly as patriarch when he comes to Constantinople, that you should honor and venerate humbly the bishop and pastor of your soul and you should maintain and defend him in his rights as well as the church committed to him so that he will be honored on earth and you may merit to be honored in heaven by him whose minister he was.[179]

XCVII. How he answered the Venetian Doge who was seeking confirmation of the agreements between the Franks and the Venetians, his letter directly to him demonstrates:

We kindly received your messengers, our beloved sons, A., and the noble citizens of Venice, who approached the Apostolic See, and we listened carefully to the matters they took care to propose before us. They stated, therefore, in our presence that certain agreements between you and the Venetians on the one hand and our dearest son in Christ, Baldwin, illustrious Emperor of Constantinople and the Franks on the other, were entered into unanimously, and they were seeking that no one should presume to violate them under penalty of excommunication to be inflicted by the Apostolic See, so that whoever, namely, should act against them would be subject to the sentence of excommunication. But after we held diligent dis-

179. Potthast, *Regesta Pontificum Romanorum*, 1:205 (2383), January 21, 1205.

cussions with our brothers on this first petition, we found three things entirely opposed to it. For, a chapter in these agreements is expressed so that ecclesiastical possessions are divided between the Venetians and the Franks, with a portion reserved for the clergy from which they can be honorably supported. Of course, since violent hands have seized the treasures of churches not without offense to the Creator, they would incur a major fault if they should diminish the possessions of the churches that were despoiled of their treasures and it would not be proper for the Apostolic See to defend those who so offended ecclesiastical dignity. Also, since agreements of this kind should be entered into for the honor of the Roman church and this should be clearly expressed in the chapters, so that all things might contribute to its honor, we ought not, nor can we, confirm what, contrary to the oath sworn by both parties in common, disparages the honor of the Apostolic See. Also, since the power of adding to or diminishing is vested in you and in six of your counselors, and the noble man, the Marquis of Montferrat, and six of his counselors, how can we put our sentence at the judgment of laymen so that they might incur the sentence of excommunication if they do not keep lay constitutions that are unknown to us and inimical to the sacred canons? When our beloved son, Thomas, elect of Constantinople, comes to Constantinople soon, nothing of the possessions of the church of Constantinople must be disposed of by laymen before his arrival, nor must anything be confirmed by us that could redound to the injury of his rights and the expense of his church.[180]

XCVIII. The Lord Innocent therefore ordained the elect of Constantinople to the deaconate on the fourth Saturday of Lent and on the Saturday of the middle week promoted him to the priesthood and on the following Sunday in Rome in St. Peter's consecrated him bishop and then conferred the *pallium* taken from the body of Blessed Peter the Apostle, on him, as a sign of the fullness of the episcopal office, received by him with the oath of fidelity and obedience under that ancient approved form of oath according to which primates and metropolitans are accustomed, on receiving the *pallium,* to swear to the Roman Pontiff and the Roman church, granting the privilege to him under this formula:

180. Potthast, *Regesta Pontificum Romanorum,* 1:206 (2398), January 28, 1205.

The prerogative of favor and grace which the Apostolic See showed to the Byzantine church when it raised it to a Patriarchal See, with the fullness of ecclesiastical power which God, not man, indeed the very God man granted in Blessed Peter to the Roman church is clearly attested and that the Roman Pontiff, his vicar, has thus shown, who makes the first last and makes the last first. Clearly, when the same church, which was then called Byzantine and now is called Constantinopolitan, held neither name nor place among the Apostolic Sees, the Apostolic See created a grand name for it, equal to the name of the great men of earth and raised it as if from the dust, elevated it even to the present so that it might give her preference by privilege of dignity to Alexandria and Antioch and Jerusalem and it might after itself exalt her before others, so that when many daughters gather riches, she alone by the special grace of her mother will excel all. Moreover, although the same church departed from the obedience of the Apostolic See in the past, still because it has humbly returned to her through the grace of God, heeding your requests we have received the same church which God has put in your charge under the protection of blessed Peter and ourselves and we ratify this by the present letter.

In addition, whatever possessions and whatever goods the same church justly and economically possesses in present or in future by grant of the Pontiffs, etc., up to "to obtain," will remain firmly and unimpaired yours and your successors. Also, we have ratified the liberties and immunities of the same church and the reasonable and ancient customs which are not contrary to those established by the Holy See and we permit them to remain in effect for all time. We also grant to your fraternity from the generosity of the Apostolic See, the *pallium,* namely, the sign of the fullness of the episcopal office, which you may use within the churches subject to your jurisdiction on the solemn days of the masses noted below, namely, on the Nativity of the Lord, the feast of St. Stephen the first martyr, on Palm Sunday, Holy Thursday, Holy Saturday, Easter, the second feria after Easter, Ascension, Pentecost, and the three feasts of St. Mary, on the birthday of John the Baptist, on the solemnities of all the Apostles, on the commemoration of all Saints, at the dedications of churches, at the consecrations of bishops, the ordinations of clerics, on the principal feasts of your churches and on the anniversary of your consecration, and at the funerals of the emperor and other magnates and princes. As an indication of fuller favor, we grant you by authority of these presents that you may grant the use of the *pallium* to your suffragan archbishops by authority of the present indulgence. You will receive from them on our behalf and that of the Roman church the canonical promise of obedience. In addition, we impart permission to have the cross, namely, the Lord's banner, carried before you wherever you happen to go save in the city of Rome and in the presence of the Bishop of Rome and we grant you the use of the horsecloth of state in your processions, ordering nevertheless by the present letter that clergy of whatever nation and people obtaining churches or ecclesiastical benefices in the city and diocese of Constantinople should show due and devout reverence to you and the church of Constantinople, saving in all things the authority, reverence, and honor of the Apostolic See.[181]

He also granted these indulgences to the same patriarch:

Just as the Lord distributed his gifts in the Roman Church through the merits of Blessed Peter, so he increased her privileges so that by however much he is liberal to others, she need not fear any decrease of honor or loss of power, rather she takes nothing for herself when she gives the most to others and does not take away what she gives nor does she lose what she gives. For in those things in which he invokes a share of his solicitude, he so disposes of burdens and honors that care for all the churches does not diminish and the fullness of ecclesiastical power adorns rather than diminishes the privilege of Peter.

Since, therefore, you labor personally for the Apostolic See and you have received the diaconate and the priesthood by the imposition of our hands and finally were consecrated a bishop, we wish to do a special favor for you and to honor you personally. Therefore, Venerable Brother in Christ, heeding your petitions, by the authority of these presents, we grant that you, by our authority and as our vicar according to the form of the church, may absolve your subjects who have laid violent hands on clerics and other religious men, unless perhaps the excesses should be so great that you think they should be referred to the Apostolic See. We also commit the absolution of forgers to your fraternity, if perhaps they should commit the vice of forgery on your seal or that of your subjects. Moreover, so that like the bridegroom from the chamber of your mother you may proceed to the bride [Ps 18:6; Jl 2:16], besieged by quarrels and decorated

181. Potthast *Regesta Pontificum Romanorum*, 1:211 (2458), March 30, 1205.

with the mantle of our indulgences, we personally grant you that, if kings in the Empire of Constantinople are to be anointed, as long as the anointing is asked of you and the imperial assent agrees, you may anoint them. Because favor is given freely, that you will not be out of favor with us, an abundance of favor will be poured out over you. Therefore, heeding your requests, we also grant that your fraternity shall have the power to promote suitable persons to the subdiaconate when necessary on Sundays and special feasts. Since none or few have been instituted in the church of Constantinople, you may appoint suitable men for it without any appeal as an obstacle. You should not agree with flesh and blood other than is decent. You should weigh their merits and pay attention to their education, since in all people who do justice this is favorable to God.

Although you have sworn in the form of an oath according to the usual custom on the reception of the *pallium*, it should be stated expressly that you may not sell, give, pawn, or grant in fief possessions belonging to the table of your episcopate, and you may not alienate anything without consulting the Roman Pontiff. Since, however, you have humbly arranged to consult us over these matters, pointing out your newness and the needs of the church of Constantinople and the disturbed situation in the land, in order to avoid having to get in touch with us over every piece of business, we grant by the authority of these presents that in such cases when necessary you may decide from the advice of prudent men what seems to be expedient for the same church and yourself.

By the authority of these presents we forbid anyone, after your death or that of your successors as patriarch of Constantinople, by cunning or violence or deception, to be appointed unless he was elected according to the canonical rules. But when he has been consecrated according to ecclesiastical custom he should send his representatives to the Apostolic See to request the *pallium* taken from the body of St. Peter, namely, the sign of the fullness of the pontifical office. On receiving it, he will take the oath to us and our successors that you have sworn to us when you received the *pallium* according to the custom of the Apostolic See without any contradiction. For this we grant your fraternity that when necessary your subjects may freely appeal to your hearing, unless, when the business has been committed by the Apostolic See, the appeal is set aside. Then you should defer humbly and devoutly to the Apostolic See. Although we do not injure anyone when we use our right, neither should anyone lose anything when we exercise the fullness of ecclesiastical power granted to us. Still we desire to provide for the security of the church of Constantinople and to withdraw any reason for complaint to those with deceitful words and a malignant tongue. Although, therefore, as a result of the cogent necessity and utility of the same church, since, after the Empire of Constantinople had devolved on the Latins, though it was not required because it was our decision, not that of another, we chose you and by election confirmed you as Patriarch of Constantinople. We ordered you to be consecrated, because we were unwilling to take away its liberty of canonical election, but rather to maintain and favor it. We are unwilling that, when it happens to be vacant, anything prejudicial to it should result from our actions, that is not according to canon law.[182]

XCIX. Therefore, the patriarch returned to Venice in order that he might sail from there to Constantinople, but he was forced by the Venetians to enter into certain illicit agreements, and when these came to the notice of the Supreme Pontiff, he ordered them to be cancelled entirely, as is evident from the letter sent to the same Patriarch.

"For this," he said, "God has established the bishopric of the Apostolic See which has the fullness of ecclesiastical power over peoples and kingdoms, so that in the words of the prophet he may root out and destroy, disperse, and ruin those things he finds useless and harmful in his master's field [Jer 1:10], according to what elsewhere he is commanded by his master through the prophet, 'dissolve the bonds of impiety, loose the packets pressing down' [Is 58:6]. We, therefore, understanding that oath that was violently extorted from you in Venice by the Venetians as your information has made known to us, that namely, you would make no one a canon in the church of Constantinople but a Venetian or one who had dwelt in Venice for ten years, and that, in good faith, in all the ways you can, you will work so that the patriarch in the church of Haghia Sophia will always be a Venetian, preserving, however, the right of authority, reverence, and honor of the Apostolic See, although this condition was added by you in such a way that it is not in writing. We, therefore, command you by the authority of these presents and we order strictly in virtue by the Holy Spirit that you in no wise observe that oath since the sanctuary of God must not be possessed by anyone by hereditary right, but is reserved to God in

182. Potthast, *Regesta Pontificum Romanorum*, 1:211 (2459), March 30, 1205.

every nation that does justice. You must guard diligently lest in the future you again fail to observe the command of the Apostolic See in the aforesaid matters. Because, if you appoint only Venetians as canons in the Church of Haghia Sophia or you expend any effort to ensure that there will always be a Venetian as patriarch in the same church, and you appoint no one as a canon in it unless he swears he will never choose or receive anyone but a Venetian as patriarch, you can not be excused about these matters for any reason. But neither may you observe what you say you have promised under oath: that you will not make anyone but a Venetian an archbishop in all Romania. But lest such things are taken for granted for the future either on pretext of an oath or by the obtaining of some kind of promise, by Apostolic authority we invalidate obligations of this kind, prohibiting under threat of anathema anyone to presume to observe them, and we order you to announce to the canons appointed or to be appointed to Haghia Sophia that they must avoid this wrongful judgment. But, although you ought to fear God more than men, and you should not swear anything contrary to God because of men, still if in that oath extorted by force or fear you have shown prescribed caution, so that you have sworn, saving in everything the right, authority, reverence, and honor of the Apostolic See, we grant you for humbly confessing your crime from our special favor that no oath of this kind can cause prejudice to you, as long as you faithfully pursue the command that we have salubriously ordered you to preserve the right, authority, reverence, and honor of the Apostolic See, against whose statutes the things sworn redound. But even if the aforesaid matters are made known to us secretly by your messengers, you should still know for certain that some of these were made known to us earlier in a certain account."[183]

C. When, therefore, the Patriarch of Constantinople had arrived, before he entered the city, he sent messengers and letters to the clergy and the whole people so that proceeding before him, they might receive him with honor. But the Frankish clergy were unwilling to receive him or in anyway to obey him, asserting his promotion had been snatched from the Apostolic See by suppression of truth and the expression of falsity, and they appealed it unanimously in the pres-

183. Potthast, *Regesta Pontificum Romanorum*, 1:242 (2822), June 21, 1206.

ence of the cardinal. The cardinal thought their appeal should be passed on and he was therefore unwilling to force them to show obedience to the patriarch. But they also did not observe the sentence of excommunication the patriarch launched against them, and so they remained in discord until Benedict,[184] cardinal priest of Santa Susanna, the legate of the Apostolic See, came to the city of Constantinople and finally arranged an agreement between them. The Lord Pope appointed him a general legate throughout the empire of Romania, sending him again from his side, both because he intended to send Peter, cardinal priest of St. Marcellus, to the province of Jerusalem and because a recently dispatched legate of the Apostolic See ought to be held in greater reverence and honor as appeared from later events.[185] For his letter sent directly to the Lord Pope showed also how he would proceed and what he would do in this matter: "I remember," "he said, "that I intimated in a letter to your Paternity," etc.

CI. Regarding the possessions of churches, which had come to the Franks from the division made between the Franks and Venetians, the Lord Pope ordered the patriarch and the Franks to observe strictly the agreement between them, as requested by both parties:

Our daily concern, namely, care of all the churches, which is our duty at the order of the Lord, admonishes and persuades us that we should provide Apostolic support for those matters which are established with careful deliberation for the utility of churches so that these arrangements can not be reversed on the quiet by the manipulation of evil men, who envy those in charge of churches and work to their detriment. Since, therefore, an amicable settlement was reached between you and the clergy committed to you on the one hand and our beloved son, the noble Henry, moderator of the Empire of Constantinople, the barons, knights, and people, on the other, about the compensation to be made to the churches concerning

184. Benedict, cardinal priest of Santa Susanna, 1201–1213. Little is known of Benedict beside his leadership of the legation to the East from 1205 to 1207, where he worked to heal the wounds to the Orthodox caused by the Fourth Crusade.

185. This remark is suggestive in light of the pope's later dissatisfaction with Peter's handling of the affair of the succession to Antioch by Raymond Rupin, the nephew of the Armenian king Leo II.

their possessions, we, heeding the necessity of the times, have commanded that the agreement be firmly kept, since it was made without force and
fraud and freely from the certain knowledge of both parties, and was willingly agreed to, because it operated without prejudice to anyone concerning possessions and products of this kind. For better information, we have
ordered the form of the agreement as it is contained in the document
drawn up accordingly to be inserted word for word in this page:

"In the name of the Lord God and our Savior, Jesus Christ, in the year
of our Lord, 1206, in the month of March, in the ninth indiction, at Constantinople. This is the form of the agreement made between Benedict,
cardinal priest of Santa Susanna, legate of the Apostolic See, and the Lord
Thomas Morosini, Patriarch of the Holy Constantinopolitan Church on the
one side and the Lord Henry and the barons and knights on the other on
those things conquered and acquired within and outside of the Empire of
Romania. The Lord Henry, with the advice and consent of all the princes,
barons, knights, and people grants the churches and promises he will give
in compensation of their possessions as it is listed below: outside the walls
of the city of Constantinople, one fifth part and a tenth of all possessions
of cities, *castra, casalia,* fields, vineyards, forests, woodlands, meadows, or-
chards, gardens, salt works, ferries, toll houses on land and sea, fisheries in
the sea and fresh water, and of all possessions even if they are not found
written in solid form in the present document, except that of the lands
they have near the walls of the city from the Golden Gate to the gate of
Blachernae between its wall and the sea, they will not be required to give
the fifteenth. Nor will the Lord Henry and the aforesaid men be required
to satisfy churches from the fifteenth money from *casalia* for whose compensation they will act according to the value of their *casalia* on their first
acquisition. From the commerce that they will receive within Constantinople or outside for the name of the city, they will not pay the fifteenth.

From the commerce that they receive in the city of Constantinople or
elsewhere in the name of the city, they will not give the fifteenth to the
church. But if there will be an agreement for an annual rent with any city
or *castrum,* land or island which the Lord Henry cannot subject to himself
and his empire, they will pay the fifteenth to the church. But if he desires
to make a fief or give or alienate it, he may do this, preserving first of all
the fifteenth share of the churches. Divisions of possessions between the
church and the aforesaid men should be done in this way: that good men
should be chosen by both parties within eight days after the present docu-

ment has been sealed, who, on oath in good faith will divide each land and water possessed into fifteen parts and will cast lots, if they cannot otherwise agree upon which part the lot of the church falls it will be the portion of the church. And this will be done in good faith up to the coming feast of Pentecost. Also all cloisters within and outside the city will be free to the church and not computed in the fifteenth. If question should arise about the number of cloisters, both parties will choose a suitable man within eight days after the question has been raised and those two will choose a third on their oath and what those three or the majority on strict oath within twenty days will decide in good faith should remain decided. If for hard necessity the lands of any *castra* are incastellated, they should be incastellated with the agreement of the lord patriarch or the diocesan bishop, and if they are unwilling to agree with the incastellators, as was said above, the question concerning the cloisters should be terminated. Also they will pay tithes of all the Latins in perpetuity from grain, legumes, and all the fruits of the land and the vineyards which they cultivate or cause to be cultivated at their expense and from the fruits of the trees and gardens, except the fruits of trees and gardens which the head of the house, in good faith, uses for the table or for investitures. Tithes are paid from the raising of four-footed animals, and bees and wool-bearing animals and, if, with the passing of time the church is able to acquire tithes from the Greeks by exhortation or admonition, no impediment will be put in their way. Besides, the clergy and all the churches and their possessions and those remaining on these possessions and churches and religious persons both Greeks and Latins and those dwelling with them and the cloisters of churches and those dwelling in them and those who flee to the church will be free from all lay jurisdiction according to the more liberal customs of the Franks, save for the authority of the Roman church in all things, and the honor and rights of the Lord Patriarch of Constantinople, of the emperor and the empire, and with the exception of the aforementioned chapters.

Of the lands to be conquered in the future, God willing, the church will first have the fifteenth before they are distributed to anyone else. Moreover, the Lord Henry and his barons should consider all these things in good faith and, if possible, take care to hand them over with due effect. No one may infringe on this agreement or pact or dare to go against it. If anyone, etc., The lord Patriarch has promised for himself and his successors that he will firmly observe this agreement. The Lord Henry and his barons and knights and people likewise have promised on their behalf and that of their successors to observe it firmly, except for those things held in common with the Venetians. Given at Constantinople at Haghia Sophia, on the sixteenth of the kalends of April. 'To no one, therefore, etc., to infringe on this our order, etc., If anyone, however, etc. Given at Ferentino on the nones of August in the ninth year."[186]

CII. After this, the patriarch sent solemn messengers with gracious escorts to the Apostolic See on various matters, including quarrels, consultations and petitions, to which the Lord Pope responded in this way:

Among the four animals which are described in the middle of the seat and on its periphery [Rv 4:6], the face of the eagle is mentioned by Ezechial more than the others [Ez 1:10, 10:14], because among the four patriarchal churches, Antioch, Alexandria, Jerusalem, and Constantinople, which are signified by the above-mentioned animals, with the Apostolic See in the middle as if it embraces special daughters to whom those on its periphery are like handmaidens serving it, the church of Constantinople is of preeminent dignity after the Apostolic See. We aspire to increase its reputation so much more joyfully insofar as, embracing it more closely as a more honorable member of the holy Roman church, we recognize more fully that it needs our help in these times. And, Lord willing, we will more happily promote your petitions, you, who are worthy to be in charge of it. To do this is not dishonest, and there is no prejudice against others, since from our action no injuries should arise whereby rights may be derived for others as from a source. Although, therefore, insofar as we can, with God, we desire to bring honor to you and to answer your petitions effectively, still we are not able to give a favorable hearing to the petition by which you sought from us that we would deign to cancel the donations of churches and benefices made by our beloved son Peter, cardinal priest of St. Marcellus, in your presence and entirely without consultation. You point out that he handed over an excessive number of churches, and he handed them over to be held in perpetuity without your consent and that of the chapter of your major church. But the same legate informed us in his letter that, after he received the letter from us about the legation to be exercised in the empire of Constantinople, he transferred certain churches

186. Potthast, *Regesta Pontificum Romanorum*, 1:245 (2867), August 5, 1206.

to various churches and places belonging to the province of Jerusalem, both to some churches which were assigned custody to provide support for the needs of the Holy Land and others to some other religious places whose representatives had approached him at the request of our son in Christ, Baldwin, illustrious Emperor of Constantinople. Having appointed certain clerics, the legate examined the utility that could result from their appointment, taking care to ordain clergy in certain churches. But because it seemed to him that you intended to change what had been arranged by him, he appealed to our court in the presence of our beloved son Benedict, cardinal priest of Santa Susanna, legate of the Apostolic See, and many of the clergy and even yourself, putting everything done by him under the protection of the Apostolic See lest you change anything. That fixed from that time a year as the term for his appeal. Since, therefore, the legate established a reasonable time for his appeal, and he, in such a reasonable case, namely, of good obedience and service of the Holy Land, could delay it for two years, with the appeal pending, according to canonical and legitimate sanctions, as your fraternity is not unaware, in his absence nothing ought to be changed, especially since these matters are assumed to have been done correctly, until the contrary is proved. It would not be valid to act without prejudice to those to whom said churches or benefices were handed over by Apostolic authority, since they were neither cited nor absent by contumacy or convicted but entirely undefended. If we order some of them to be confirmed according to the common form, you should understand that it must be done, namely, as they possess these things justly and quietly, you ought not to wonder about this, as the legate asserts that he conferred the churches and benefices mentioned with you present and not consulted, since you also took care to make arrangements with respect to a much greater church, namely, Haghia Sophia, which was the chief church of the patriarchate as well as the archbishopric and the bishopric in his presence and entirely unconsulted and he was acting as our vicar there. Although, therefore, we have been unwilling to hear your petition, as you desire, for the aforesaid reasons, still we desire to defer to your honor with our honesty as much as possible. Therefore, we have ordered the concession to your fraternity that those who possess those churches or benefices should show due and devout obedience to you, unless perhaps some of those churches were legitimately exempt from the jurisdiction of the patriarch before the capture of the royal city.

But for a twofold reason we did not order a subsequent petition, by which you asked that those churches should be subject to you which prior to the taking of Constantinople answered in no way to the patriarch, to be allowed. For the reason of law demanded that we should ordain nothing in prejudice of those to whom these churches are subject since they were neither cited, nor convicted, nor did they absent themselves through contumacy. Also foresight dissuades us from doing it lest the Pisans and Venetians and some of the others holding churches of this kind in Constantinople should be provoked against the empire at this time. They are better attracted with blandishments until the empire is strengthened by an immovable solidarity. But if you demand your right to be pursued against them, we will, at an opportune time, as the Lord permits, show the fullness of justice to you in these matters.

But you have asked what obedience should be given you by the archbishop and bishops of Cyprus. We have ordered almost the same response to you as in the preceding petition, since they also were exempt before your promotion, since the Church of Constantinople was disobedient and a rebel and we ought not change anything about their status in their absence. But we will not deny justice to you when you seek it.

Additionally, your side proposed before us that some of the bishops of Romania, after being admonished, refused to obey you and they still continued to receive episcopal incomes. But some of them flee their dioceses, deserting their dioceses for they do not heed warnings for six months or more, wherefore you have prayed us suppliantly that, taking counsel with you in a helpful way on this matter, we would deign to write to your devotion how you should proceed about them and their dioceses. We, therefore, heeding the fact that due to the recentness of the change in the empire and the revolutionary character of events it is necessary to proceed with greater mildness, advise your fraternity thus: that you should take care to cite them not once but often, namely, for a first, second, and third time, and if they are not willing to appear but persist in their contumacy, unless perhaps they bring an appeal which may be pursued within the legitimate period, you may compel them to come to your obedience by sentences of suspension and excommunication. But if their hardness cannot be softened, our beloved son, Benedict, cardinal priest of Santa Susanna, legate of the Apostolic See, may remove them from the administration of their dioceses and in cooperation with you he may put suitable persons in charge of these churches, but he should not promulgate a sentence of degradation against them, so that, if it becomes necessary, they can be more easily treated mercifully. In the churches, however, of those who fraudulently absent themselves, so just the citation may not be valid, you may order the edict of a threefold citation to be published, and if they do not take care thus to obey it or also desert their churches for more than six months so that, according to the ecclesiastical canons, they may be properly deprived, the procedure against them should follow the prescribed course. But when the legate returns the property to you, as long as it shall please us and our successors, we personally order that you may proceed in the prescribed manner against the aforesaid rebels as delegated by the Apostolic See.

Your fraternity also asked that, since the number of bishoprics in those parts is too great, we would allow you to reduce their number since too many are poor. We have made provision that since necessity or utility demands it, as long as the legate is in those parts, he will have the power, with your cooperation, to make these changes. He may not unite bishoprics but he may commit as many churches as seems expedient to the one he ordered ordained for one church, so that, if perhaps for the need of the time someone else should be ordained, that deed may easily be changed. When the legate returns to us, however, you shall be delegated by us with the authority to do this if necessary.

You have later asked to be taught by the Apostolic See how you ought to ordain in those dioceses in which only Greeks live and also who you should put in charge of those in which Greeks and Latins live together. To this we respond briefly to your fraternity that in those churches in which there are only Greeks you ought to ordain Greek bishops if you can find such devoted and loyal to you and willing to receive humbly and devoutly consecration from you. But in those in which Greeks are mixed with Latins you should put Latins in charge and prefer them to Greeks.

For the rest, you have humbly asked for our permission to grant those appointed and to be appointed to ecclesiastical offices the staffs, miters, rings, and sandals and to dispense those who presumed to receive major orders without first receiving minor orders. We therefore desire to do you a special favor and by the authority of these presents we give you permission to grant the aforesaid marks of office to those to whom they can be honestly granted according to the custom of the Apostolic See, and you may dispense, on our authority, those who omitted minor orders, but who possess sufficient Latin and a serious demeanor, after they have fulfilled a proper penance.

Your fraternity also consulted us on the question whether you ought to promote to higher orders clerics coming to you without letters from those who ordained them and offering to swear a corporal oath that they have been ordained in some way to ecclesiastical orders. We therefore respond to your enquiry that, unless the matter of their ordination is established for you by suitable canonical arguments, you should neither receive them nor promote them to major orders, especially before their conduct has been proven.

You have also sought to learn from the Apostolic See about the liturgy of the mass and the other sacraments, whether you ought to admit Greeks to conduct these services in their usual way, or force them rather to use the Latin rite. We respond briefly to your fraternity on this issue that you should keep them in their own rite if they refuse to be summoned by you until the Apostolic See has reached a more mature decision on this question.

We order this response to be made to you regarding clerics who, without a just and necessary reason, in this novel circumstance have deserted churches and prebends granted to them, especially without securing your permission. After they have been allowed a fitting period of time, they can be justly deprived unless they return, as long as they have not been prevented by a just impediment.

We also respond to your fraternity in this way about the conversion of Greek monasteries into secular canonries, that, as long as they can remain as established in the hands of regulars, whether Greek or Latin, they should not be transferred to secular clerics, but if regulars are lacking due to their desertion, secular clerics can be established in them.

In addition, you have humbly asked us, since it is difficult for individuals subject to your jurisdiction to labor at the Apostolic See, to agree to put a limit on appeals. Since, therefore, Pope Gregory,[187] our predecessor of holy memory, established that, in lesser matters, which perhaps were within the sum of ten marks, the question might be decided in the courts of archbishops and bishops and should any of the litigating parties consider appealing in a deceptive way, they could compel them to choose judges above suspicion, without right of appeal within the boundaries of their

187. Pope Gregory VIII. See PL, 202:1552d–1553c. "Eapropter universitati vestrae per apostolicam sanctionem praesentibus mandamus quatenus, si forte de modicis rebus, quae infra summam viginti marcarum subsistunt. . . ." (1553a). Perhaps Innocent erred in the amount. Cf. Gress-Wright, 250–51. I follow the reading in Gress-Wright. Keith Kendall kindly looked up this reference for me.

dioceses, but only if suitable men can be found in whose presence the dispute may be put to rest. We understand that there would be too serious an expense for your subjects to approach the Apostolic See because of the risks of the sea and the dangers of the land. Therefore, we grant your fraternity personally that in those cases that ought to be tried in your court, if any of the parties appeal to the Apostolic See and the matter on which the question turns does not exceed the sum noted earlier, notwithstanding the object of the appeal, with justice being equal, you may proceed or force the parties to compromise. You may hear the case without right of appeal and reach a proper conclusion, the same to be done in lesser cases, especially between minor persons, which, since they may be purely spiritual, do not contain a civil question. Moreover, you may compel Venetian inhabitants of the royal city to pay tithes to persons and churches in Constantinople to whom they legally owe them by ecclesiastical censure without right of appeal, notwithstanding the custom that Venetians observe, namely, that they tithe only at death those things acquired in life, so that the church of Constantinople is not on this pretext defrauded of its rights, if perhaps those who live for a long time in Constantinople should return to Venice near the end of their lives. But you should proceed with discretion and maturity in these and other matters, avoiding quick and easy decisions since it is better to move more slowly in matters of this sort than to be blamed for too much haste.[188]

CIII. In the meantime, a certain Burgundian,[189] elected as Archbishop of Patras over the Province of Achaea, approached the Apostolic See, and on his behalf, the nobleman, William of Compiègne, prince of Achaea, and the canons of Saint Andrew of Patras humbly asked the Supreme Pontiff to agree to make him their archbishop, returning him confirmed, consecrated, and with the *pallium*. And how he would proceed in this matter the letter he sent to the Patriarch of Constantinople makes clear:

"Among the four animals," he said, "which are described in the Apocalypse of John as in the middle of the seat and on its circuit [Rv 4:6], even though the eagle is placed after the others, still it precedes the others,

188. Potthast, *Regesta Pontificum Romanorum*, 1:245 (2860), August 2, 1206.
189. Antelmus, perhaps a monk of Cluny, archbishop of Patras, 1205–1241.

since the Roman church is meant by this seat, and it is usually referred to
as the Apostolic See, and the four Patriarchal churches, namely, Jerusalem, Antioch, Alexandria and Constantinople are signified by four animals—namely the lion, the ox, the man, and the eagle—which are contained in the middle of the seat as daughters in the bosom of their mother,
and they are arranged on the circuit of the seat like handmaidens in service of their lady. Although the church of Constantinople may be last in
time among the others, still it is special in dignity among them so that just
as Constantinople is called the new Rome, so the church of Constantinople has been placed second by the Roman through the favor of its mother
with a privilege of dignity over its other sisters, so that according to the
evangelical truth the first may be last and last first.

Therefore, we, who by the grace of the Redeemer have recently restored that church of Constantinople to the obedience of the Apostolic See
as to the bosom of her mother, intend to preserve the entire privilege of
her dignity lest injuries should arise whereby rights would be derived, although, therefore, our beloved son, the noble man, William, prince of the
whole province of Achaea, and the canons of Saint Andrew of Patras in-
stantly and humbly asked that we should agree to appoint for them our
beloved son, Antelmus, elect of Saint Andrew of Patras, who approached
the Apostolic See and who the same canons unanimously elected as archbishop of the same church and [asked us] to ratify with our approval what
was done concerning his person and send him back to them with full hon-
or. Still desiring to allow their petitions in such a way that we do not seem
to take away the rights of others, with the common counsel of our brothers, we have not ordered what has been done by the same canons to be
approved since it was carried out less canonically. Indeed, they also were
instituted less canonically, but after having considered equally the necessity and utility and concerning the truth of the business and the status of
the land, by the oaths of his companions we were more certain of the effect of the election. From the power granted to us by the Lord in Blessed
Peter, we appointed him pastor and ruler of the same church, granting
him full administration both in spiritual and temporal affairs and granting
also for security that he may arrange to be ordained to the priesthood by
any Catholic bishop as needed. Moreover, although from the fullness of
power we possess, at the disposition of the Lord, over all the churches, we
could send him back marked by the gift of consecration and honor of the
pallium to the same church, because we have summoned you to a share of

solicitude, while we have kept for ourselves the fullness of power, and we do no injury to anyone when we use our rights, still desiring to defer to you to whom the church of Patras is known to be subject especially on your recent appointment, we ordered him sent back to you so that he might be consecrated archbishop by you or by another at your orders and receive the honor of the *pallium* from you after he has recognized the Roman Pontiff as his father, giving letters in mandate to our beloved son, Benedict, cardinal priest of Santa Susanna, legate of the Apostolic See, so that he could order the things we set forth about his person to be carried out. For this reason, we order your fraternity by Apostolic letter that you should not delay to mark him with the sign of the gift of his consecration and honor of the *pallium,* so that by your failure, God forbid, he would be forced to have recourse to us."[190]

CIV. After Enrico Dandolo, the Venetian Doge, died at Constantinople, Pietro Ziani was promoted to the dogeship at Venice, and he ordered the Abbot of San Felice of Venice to be elected as Archbishop of Zara and to be confirmed and consecrated by authority of the Patriarch of Grado, sending solemn messengers to the Supreme Pontiff to ask for the *pallium,* which earlier had been denied to him. But, mindful of the offense that the Venetians had committed by the destruction of Zara, the Lord Pope responded to them in this way:

We exercise the office of Apostolic service in a praiseworthy manner, if we correct, comply with, and announce loudly what the Apostle teaches in all patience and doctrine. Because, therefore, the father reproves the son whom he loves and God corrects and castigates those whom he loves, therefore we have paternally reproved our beloved sons, the noble men, R. Permar, and P. Quir., your ambassadors to the Apostolic See, complaining to you in them about the many and great offenses you have wrongfully committed not only against God and the Roman church but also against the Christian people and against us and our neighbors, especially in the attack on the city of Zara, where you deviated and caused the army to deviate from the right way to the wrong, fighting Christian peoples when you

190. Innocent here makes clear that he will not permit the Venetians to control the church in the Latin Empire of Constantinople. See RI 8:154 (153), November 19, 1205. Proof furnished by C. Egger.

ought to have been fighting the perfidious Saracens, repelling the legate of the Apostolic See and rejecting the sentence of excommunication, after you violated your crusade vow to the injury of the crucified. For that, we should be silent about the many evil deeds you perpetrated at Constantinople, seizing the treasure of churches and invading ecclesiastical possessions. You wanted, as if by inheritance, to possess the sanctuary of the Lord, for which reason you have extorted illicit agreements. Tell us when you could restore such a loss to the Holy Land, when you diverted the Christian army—so great, so noble, so powerful, so motivated, and gathered together with such great desire and labor, both with great expenditures and expenses, by which everyone hoped without doubt that not only the promise of Jerusalem should be recovered but also a large part of Egypt would be occupied. For if the army could subjugate Constantinople and Greece how much easier it would be to get Alexandria and Egypt and by this means to snatch the Holy Land from the hands of the pagans. Certainly, even if it is beneficial to us that Constantinople has returned to the obedience of the Holy Roman church, her mother, still it would have been even better for us if Jerusalem was returned to the power of Christian people. And do not think now that you have in no wise sinned because one city or another has been handed over to you and to them more by Divine judgment than worldly power, because the one whipped often pleases God when the action of whipping displeases him, just as is clearly shown by authorities of both the New and Old Testaments.

You should not impute it to our hardness but should ascribe to your offense that we have not agreed to the requests you have made by your ambassadors to send the *pallium* to the Abbot of San Felice whom you call the elect of Zara, because, since from the things which you carried out against Zara, the Christian people has been scandalized against you. We were unwilling to do anything about Zara on your behalf by which the whole church could be more scandalized against us. This would be the case if we should seem to have forgiven you such an offense by granting the *pallium* at your request without any satisfaction, according to the sentence of Solomon, in which the one who sins should be punished in this, although this delay is not so much a punishment as a security by which we intend to provide both for ourselves and you. For even though the people of Zara didn't sin in this matter, still, because the metropolitan dignity was especially granted to them by the Apostolic See in your honor, namely, so that your church would enjoy the Patriarchal dignity not only in name but also in right since the metropolitan of Zara would be subject to it, we want to mark your fault more than their punishment, since it is neither new nor absurd when subjects are punished for their rulers just as the people of Israel was punished without any fault of their own when David sinned in their enumeration [2 Sm 24:15–17]. And so we respond to you through your ambassadors and our letter that you should humbly incline to offer and show satisfaction to God and to us, at least in the example of those who, although they sinned less, still had to make satisfaction for this deed perpetrated by you. But they obligated themselves firmly to us that when you sought pardon from God and us, without excusing but accusing your offense, exposing you to a fitting satisfaction, we would take care to hear you and hope for your salvation and pursue your honor as men, both in these and other matters that you sought. In the meantime, we await your correction in equanimity and we have suspended that censure which universal opinion asserted must be laid on you so that, with the inspiration of the Lord, you should be converted. We not only remit the punishment but we also dispense our favor. And no one should excuse himself on the ground that he was not bodily present when these things were done, if he perhaps consented to these deeds in his heart, because similar blame condemns both doing and approving. Therefore, beloved sons, our words, though sharp on the outside, but sweet within, should please you because just as he, who is ignorant of nothing, knew that they proceed from a pure heart and good conscience and true faith so that, just as the blows of a friend are better than the kisses of an enemy, so the correction of your father delights you more than the adulation of a sinner. Therefore, you should not be ashamed to be humbled under the power of one who with a single nod can humble the proud and exalt the humble, ascribing the victory granted to you not to your virtue but to Divine power, which even though perhaps hidden, still desired to punish others with a just judgment through you, knowing that nothing is more abominable to God than the monstrosity of ingratitude and the enormity of arrogance, both of which proceed from fear of heart. You should also take care to show full obedience and reverence to us with devotion for him whose grace and honor, we, though without merit and unworthy, serve as vicar and hold the place that he may protect and exalt you in the present and glorify and crown you in the future, he, who is king of kings and lord of lords, priest forever according to the order of Melchizedek.[191]

191. Ps 109:4. The inclusion of this letter shows that the author wanted to make

CV. But when the Latins had obtained the larger part of the empire of Constantinople and begun to prosper in all these matters, so that terror of them fell like lightning from heaven not only on the Greeks but also on the pagans, having become insolent from too much prosperity brought on after their vanities, the Latins began freely to decline and to irritate God to wrath by their depraved deeds. Therefore, what happened to them by reason of their sins is made clear in the letter of Henry, the brother of the emperor, sent to the Supreme Pontiff:

To the most holy father and lord, Innocent, by the grace of God, Supreme Pontiff, Henry, brother of the Emperor of Constantinople and moderator of empire, with due reverence, a humble and devout kiss of the feet. Since my brother, the Lord Emperor, related in detail with sufficient clarity the entire progress and series of labors of our pilgrimage to your paternity in numerous letters up to the end of last March, I have ordered that our events from that time on, so unlike what went on before due to our sinfulness, so miserable, be made known to you as to a worthy father and Lord. It happened therefore that the Greeks, who from inborn malice and with their usual perfidy, after every kind of security and caution, showed themselves ever prone to treason. Immediately after the departure of the ambassadors last sent to you, they made manifest the treason they conceived earlier in their minds when they rebelled against us. When my brother and lord emperor discovered this, he left the royal city right away with a small force, since we were mostly scattered in border defenses and fortifications, against the chief center of the rebellion, namely Adrianople, which is a highly fortified Greek city, set in the mountains, near the Vlachs. He intended to attack it. For we were then divided in this way: the marquis of Montferrat was beyond Thessalonica with many men; I was on the other side of the Arm of St. George at Adramyttium with quite a few men; Paganus de Aurelia and P. Bracel towards Nicaea from the same side; R. de Tric at Philipopolis with a fair number; and others scattered elsewhere in towns and forts. Moreover, when the news came to Joannitsa, lord of the Vlachs, that the Latins were besieging the city with such a small number of men, and, at the same time, the Greeks summoned him in secret to help them so that they might inflict more damage, he immediately

---

Innocent's position on the Venetians clear. See Potthast, *Regesta Pontificum Romanorum*, 1:245 (2866), August 5, 1206.

attacked us with a multitude of barbarians, namely, Vlachs, Cumans, and others. Their attack was very unexpected since our men had retreated and were more distant than was helpful to those nearby. Our men were surrounded on all sides by the snares of their enemies. Regretably the lord emperor, the Count of Lodensis, Stephen of Pertico, and some other barons and knights that I cannot mention without shedding tears, overwhelmed by such a great multitude, were captured, but not without loss to the enemy. We do not know, in fact, who were captured, who killed, but we learned from our spies with certainty that the lord my emperor was taken sound and alive, and he is held for the time being, it is said by Joannitsa, with some others, whom we still are not able to name at this time. But you should know that from the day we entered the territories of the Greeks until the day of that unhappy event, as often as the multitude came to meet us, our men, although sometimes quite few in number, still always left the field in triumph and victory. We sorrow over the inestimable loss which then occurred and we weep over the ill-advised audacity of our men, and we believe it happened because of our sins. And so those who escaped the battle eluded the hands of the enemy. After a brief meeting with those who had remained to defend the tents, they departed from the siege without any loss. They marched to the royal city and were so unexpectedly desolated that the Lord suddenly gave a great consolation. As if in a moment, all who had been once scattered gathered in a certain city called Rodestoc as if summoned by the Lord. With the Marquis still happily and victoriously in his Marches, through R. de Trit in his lands, he remained safe and sound by the grace of God. After we inspected our forces there, we immediately began to fortify cities and castles which seemed possible to hold onto against the rebellion of the Greeks and we set out on the road to Constantinople. And so, even though we suffered a grievous loss in persons, we still hoped in the Lord and trusted boldly that we could endure the attacks and assaults of our enemies for a long time with the Lord's help, and also await support and aid from abroad. But now what we feared has happened and we have learned what was circulating by public report, also from the letters of the Vlach, containing his alliance with the Turks and other enemies of Christ, which were intercepted by us with his messengers. We have sent them to your Apostleship in both languages. Even though with more serious expectation, we incur the wound and ruin, whose reception, no one disputes, falls on you as father of all, our patron and lord, especially since we labor only over the reforming of the unity of the church and the aid of the Holy Land, of which the one depends on the other, just as the common assertion makes clear the need of all Christians in the East and especially of the venerable brethren of the Temple and the Hospital, both of whom are with us. Its embodiment not only works its liberation but it seems also to procure most openly in every way the confusion of the pagans and of the enemies of the cross of Christ. The contrary, its destruction, which God averts, not only brings hope of recovering part of the lost Holy Land and returning it in the present to Christian worship, but without doubt it snatches away the hope of holding it. Heeding you as supreme and special, who alone has been appointed before the sons of men and princes in such power to aid us, just as from the beginning our imperfection is insufficient for such a project, we flee to you as the unique refuge of our hope and the foundation, to the feet of your paternity with supplication and devout intention and mind, prostrate with humility and imploring with tears the help of your prayers, so far as we can, that you will not delay to grant the usual effect of your piety to your sons in such narrow straits. Give your counsel and help before all those living to those in need, that we may ask so much more securely from the sweetness of your paternity how much in addition to the vow of our pilgrimage we have given our bodies and our lives for the Roman church in which, beside the common concern of all Christians by which we are held, we also know that we were obligated to your paternity and you to us as your knights and stipendiaries of the Roman church.[192]

CVI. Up to this time, the hand of the Lord did not cease to punish the Latins so that harassment might grant them understanding, just as the aforementioned Henry, brother of the Emperor of Constantinople and moderator of the empire, wrote to the Lord Pope:

"We have ordered," he said, "this worthy man to reveal our situation and rumors of whatever kind for the convenience of the ambassadors to your Holiness. Enough, as we believe, has been made known to you how, because of our sins, our lord emperor, with a large number of his men killed and taken captive, which I cannot speak of without bitterness of heart and the greatest sorrow, was captured by the Cumans in the battle of Adri-

192. Baldwin was captured on April 14, 1205. This letter must be dated in April or May 1205.

anople. Afterward, then, the princes, barons, and knights of the army chose me as regent of the empire. We went out of the royal city with the Christian army and we captured several cities and castles which had rebelled against us, and, after our borders were fortified, we returned to Constantinople around the feast of St. Remigius. But we left the fortification of a certain city which is called Rossa to Theodore of Terramunda, a very active and discrete man, with many knights and sergeants, and while they stayed there, about the feast of the Purification of Blessed Mary they learned that the Vlachs had occupied a certain fortified *castrum* near Rossa. They left Rossa by night with their arms and they killed the Vlachs they found there and, after they destroyed the fortified town, they began to return with the booty and the horses of the Vlachs to that city, and near Rossa a crowd of Vlachs and Cumans hastened from ambush to attack those returning, and, with fighting on both sides, unfortunately, by Divine punishment, almost all of our men were killed or captured.

But those in charge of the defense of the city, about forty knights with their sergeants, returned safely to us under cover of the night, and so the Lord, piling punishment on punishment, rejecting our merits, showed the face of his anger to us who needed him. But because the outcome of battles was, is, and always will be uncertain, and nothing can be done that always ends well for those fighting, and sadness is often mixed with joy, virtuous men ought not despair. For fortune changes in a short time and the Lord looks upon his own and immediately hoped-for joy redeems the desolate. In difficult matters, virtue is tested and these risks make strong men more cautious. For adversity, which is presented to good men, is not an indication of evil but a proof of virtue. Therefore, we, who have found ourselves in these straits, hasten to you, father, indeed as we say, of us all, in this deed, our creator, that you may more mercifully accomplish our need mercifully begun by you, uncovering whatever good ways are needed for the completion of our work.[193]

CVII. The Lord Pope, sympathizing with their misfortunes, therefore, sent a special messenger to the aforesaid Joannitsa seeking freedom for the emperor with a letter of this kind:

---

193. Since this letter does not mention the death of Baldwin, it must be dated to late 1205.

From that special favor by which we have glorified you among all Christian princes, even to the present we have loved you so that we hope for your convenience and honor in the most effective manner, and certainly we hope that you should without cease increase in devotion to the Holy Roman church, your mother, through whose merits you have acquired a glorious triumph over those pressing hard to molest you. Since, therefore, you received the royal diadem and a military standard from us through the legate of the Apostolic See, so that your kingdom may be special to St. Peter, we desire diligently to provide that, freed from the incursions of enemies on all sides, you may rejoice in a tranquil peace. Therefore, you should know, dearest son, that a large army from the west is about to set out for Greece, in addition to that which recently arrived. Therefore, you ought to provide carefully for yourself and your land, so that, while you can you may arrange peace with the Latins, lest they from one side and the Hungarians from the other should desire to attack you. You could not easily resist the attempts of both. Therefore, we suggest to your Serenity and we counsel you with right faith that since you are said to hold captive Baldwin, the Emperor of Constantinople, you should so provide for yourself that by his release you may make a true and firm peace with the Latins so that they will maintain peace with you and your land. For we command by Apostolic mandate to Henry, the brother of the same emperor, who is in charge of the Latin army, that he should work for peace with you in return for the liberation of that emperor and he should cease all attacks on you. And may God so inspire you that you will agree with our advice and counsel, that your kingdom, which you have dedicated to Blessed Peter and the Holy Roman church, may be preserved unharmed. We have longed greatly to accomplish this aim and efficacious work.[194]

CVIII. The aforementioned Joannitsa or Kalojan, King of the Bulgarians and the Wallachians, answered that he had sent messengers and letters to the Latins after he learned of the capture of the royal city in order to have peace with them, but they responded with very great pride, saying they would not have peace with him unless he returned the land belonging to the Empire of Constantinople that he had violently invaded. He responded to these matters that he was more justly

194. Potthast, *Regesta Pontificum Romanorum*, 1:220 (2569), July 20 to August 16, 1205.

in possession of that land than Constantinople was in their possession, for he had recovered land which his ancestors had lost, but they had occupied Constantinople, which in no way belonged to them. In addition, he had received the crown of his kingdom legitimately from the Supreme Pontiff, but he who was calling himself the basileus of Constantinople had inconsiderately usurped the crown of the empire on his own. That empire, therefore, belonged to him rather than to that other person. And so, under the true banner that he had received from Blessed Peter, signed with his keys, he would fight loyally against those who were wearing false crosses on their shoulders. Under provocation, therefore, from the Latins, he was forced to defend himself from them and the Father, who resisted the proud, gave him the unexpected victory; moreover, he gives thanks to the humble and ascribed his victory to Blessed Peter, the prince of the Apostles. But he had not been able to release the emperor at the counsel and mandate of the Supreme Pontiff because he had died in prison.[195]

CIX. After Gregory, the Catholicos of the Armenians, and Leo, the king of Lesser Armenia,[196] had heard about the Lord Innocent's reputation, they sent messengers and letters with gifts to him, presenting themselves humbly for his devotion, and the Lord Pope wrote to them on these matters in this way:

From this we learn that you are rooted [Col 2:7] in the Catholic faith and are Catholic not only in name but also in merit, that recognizing the *magisterium* of the Apostolic See, you confess her to be the mother of all churches and us to be the head of all the faithful, as the series of your letters has informed us. For you have recognized the privilege of Peter that the Lord committed all his sheep to him to be fed when he repeated the words three times, saying, "Feed my sheep" [Jn 21:17], and he conferred the power of binding and loosing over all on him, saying to him, "Whatever you bind on earth will be bound in heaven and whatever you loose on

195. This letter was written in late 1205 or early 1206. Clearly, Innocent's initiative in Bulgaria was in serious trouble.
196. Gregory VI Apirat, Catholicos of the Armenian church, 1194–1203. King Leo II of Armenia. See RI 2:208 (217), 404, n. 2.

earth will also be loosed in heaven" [Mt 16:19]. For you have recognized
the prerogative of the Apostolic See which, by the merits of St. Peter, even
if not in time, still first in authority among the Apostles not by any synodal
decision but by Divine establishment, obtained the *magisterium* among all
the churches, and the primacy, founded on an immobile foundation, of
which Paul the Apostle said: "The foundation has been placed, beside
which no other can be placed, that is, Christ Jesus" [1 Cor 3:11]. And of
this the Truth said to Peter, "Upon this rock I will build my church and the
gates of hell will not prevail against it" [Mt 16:18]. Peter, indeed, after
Christ, can be understood as the one shepherd and the universal church
the one sheepfold, of which the Lord protested in the Gospel, saying: "I
have other sheep who are not of this fold, and I must lead them, and they
will hear my voice, and there will be one fold and one shepherd" [Jn
10:16; Mt 21: 42; 1 Pt 2:6]. Of course, the cornerstone the builders rejected [Ps 117:22] was later put at the top of the corner, making both the Jewish people and the gentile nations one in the unity of the Christian faith,
establishing the church from both, without stain or wrinkle, which, lest it
be divided after his ascension and lest the sheepfold united in his faith
should be divided, he committed its governance to one prince of the Apostles, whom the Lord alone appointed to the office of vicar and successor to
himself. Moreover, your fraternity, diligently heeding this and understanding that according to the apostle we are all one body in Christ, individuals, but members each of the other, you confess us, whom the Lord
desired to be his vicar, though unworthy, successor of the prince of the
apostles, to be head of the church and you recognize yourself and brothers
and cobishops to be part of our body, knowing that, just as a palm tree
cannot make fruit by itself, unless it shall remain alive, so also the member
is lacking in both feeling and the power to act unless it remains in the unity of the body [Jn 15:4]. Therefore, we rejoice not a little that, persevering
in the Catholic faith you piously bear the affection of devotion about us
and denote yourself to be a son of the Apostolic See, while you claim it as
the mother of all, recognizing the *magisterium* of ecclesiastical discipline
from us, which even if received a long time earlier, still you rejoice to have
received it through our venerable brother the Archbishop of Mainz, the
Bishop of Sabina, one of the seven bishops who are at our side in the Roman church, and you desire to observe it.[197] Moreover, it was and is a

---

197. Conrad of Wittelsbach, cardinal bishop of Sabina,1166–1200, and arch-

great indication of your devotion that you have received the same arch-bishop in a wonderful manner and have taken care to honor him quite generously, just as your letter contained and his account to us made clear [1 Thes 4:1; 2 Cor 5:20].

We therefore admonish your fraternity and we exhort you in the Lord and we command you by Apostolic letter that you should persevere [Ps 1:2; 1 Tm 1:10; Acts 18:21] firmly in devotion to the Apostolic See and that you meditate on the law of the Lord day and night and, preaching those things that are consistent with sound doctrine and carrying out those things that you have preached so far as the Lord permits, so that in you works do not contradict your words nor your words your works. Be the teacher of your subjects so that you may teach, a father that you may correct, a mother that you may support; you should teach the less learned, correct the proud, cherish the humble and devout, tempering justice with mercy, and not departing from equity in judgment. But on the subject of aid to the province of Jerusalem, we wish you to know that now, through the grace of God, many, on our advice, have received the sign of the cross and more, the Lord willing, will receive it and at an opportune time will cross over to defend the Eastern province. Also, two of our brothers have assumed the standard of the life-giving cross from our hands and will pre-cede the army of the Lord. Therefore, have confidence and be strong [Jos 10:25] because more quickly perhaps than one thinks, the eastern prov-ince will feel the impact of the awaited help.[198]

CX. To Leo, illustrious king of the Armenians. [God] has set up his church, gathered from the gentiles, not having stain or wrinkle, over peo-ples and kingdoms, he has extended its branches even to the sea and has spread the offspring of his land to its boundaries [Jer 29:14; Eph 5:17; Jer 1:10]. His land is abundant and its fullness, the world, and all who dwell in it. Also, he not only put the Roman church in charge of all the faithful but exalted it over other churches so that the others might not only re-ceive the norm of life and the discipline of manners from her, but they might also receive the documents of the Catholic faith and humbly keep its teachings. For, in Peter, the prince of the Apostles, on whom the Lord conferred more excellently than others the power of binding and loosing, saying to him, "Whatever you shall bind on earth will also be bound in

---

bishop of Mainz, 1183–1200. See Maleczek, *Papst und Kardinalskolleg von 1191 bis 1216*, 67.

198. RI 2:209 (218), 406–8, November 23, 1199.

heaven and whatever you loose on earth will also be loosed in heaven"
[Mt 16:19], the Roman church, its seat and successors, the Roman pontiffs, the successors of Peter and the vicars of Jesus Christ, succeeding one
another one by one through successive changes of times, have received
from the Lord the primacy and *magisterium* over all the churches and the
prelates of churches as well as all the faithful, so that the fullness of power
may reside among them, with other churches called to a share of solicitude. For that privilege has not ended in Peter or with Peter individually,
but the Lord granted it to his future successors even to the end of the
world. Besides sanctity of life and the powers of miracles there is equal jurisdiction in all of his successors, who, even if at different times, the Lord
still desired to preside over the same See and with the same authority.
Moreover, we rejoice that you, as a Catholic prince recognizing the privilege of the Apostolic See, have kindly and enthusiastically received our
venerable brother, the Archbishop of Mainz, the Bishop of Sabina, one of
the seven bishops who are at our side in the Roman church, and been instructed by him in salutary doctrines on which you want your whole
kingdom to be informed more amply according to the content of your letter. You also want to recall all Armenians to the bosom of the Roman
church. Moreover, to the honor and glory of the Apostolic See which you
know was established over peoples and kingdoms, you have received from
his hands the crown of the kingdom, and you have taken care devoutly
and humbly to honor him, and us through him and you have directed
your letter to the aid of the Eastern land [Jas 1:17]. To [God], therefore,
from whom is every fine endowment and every perfect gift, who holds the
hearts of princes in his hand [Prv 21:1], and we can also give thanks to
him who has inspired your mind with such humility. We ask and exhort
your royal serenity in the Lord and we command you by apostolic letter
that, persisting in fear of the Lord [1 Thes 4:1; 2 Cor 5:20], and devotion to
the Apostolic See you desire so much more potently and more effectively
to attack the barbarity of the pagans and avenge the injury to the Crucified insofar as you have understood better because of the closeness of your
location the frauds and stratagems of our enemies. You should trust [Ps
28:7; 1 Mc 3:19] not in the size or power of the army, but in the mercy of
the one who teaches the hands how to fight and moves the fingers to war
[Ps 143:1], who overcomes the bow [1 Sm 2:4] of the strong and girds the
weak with strength. For now by the grace of God many have received the
sign of the cross at our advice and, Lord willing, more will receive it and at

an opportune time will set out in defense of the Eastern province. Also two of our brothers have assumed the standard of the cross from our hands and will precede the army of the Lord. Have confidence, therefore, and be strong because more quickly perhaps than one thinks the Eastern province will get the aid they await. Given at the Lateran VIII Kal. of December.[199]

CXI. After this, the same king sent a certain knight with his letter to the Supreme Pontiff asking and requesting that, since he had appealed to the Apostolic See about injuries which the Count of Tripoli with the Hospitallers had imposed on his nephew, by name Rupin, concerning the succession to the Principate of Antioch, he order that the fullness of justice should be done. The Lord Pope responded to this matter in this way in his letter:

To him from whom is every fine endowment and every perfect gift [Jas 1:17], who holds the hearts of princes in his hands and from whom is all power [Prv 21:1], to whom we can give thanks that he has rooted you in devotion to the Apostolic See even until now, so that not only in spiritual matters but also in temporal [Rom 13:1; Mt 28:18], you hasten to the aid of the Roman church and implore its help in defending your justice by the appeal you have brought. For approaching the Apostolic See, our beloved son, the noble man, Robert of Margate, knight, your messenger, has explained to us fully the depth of your devotion and brought the letter of your royal Serenity to us, which states that when Raymond,[200] the deceased eldest son of the nobleman, Bohemond, Prince of Antioch, married Alice, your niece, and she gave birth to a son, while near death, he begged the same prince to agree to preserve the succession for his only son Rupin by hereditary right. After the death of his son, not unmindful of his prayers, when he had summoned his liege men, he publicly recognized

---

199. RI 2:211 (220), 409–11, November 24, 1199.

200. Raymond, prince of Antioch, was the eldest son of Bohemond III and the godson of Raymond III of Tripoli, who died in 1187 and left the County of Tripoli to him. Raymond III designated his younger son, the future Bohemond IV, to rule in Tripoli. Thus he left as his heir to Antioch, his son, Raymond Rupin, who was the nephew of King Leo II of Armenia. Bohemond IV rebelled against this succession. See Jonathan Riley-Smith, *The Crusades: A Short History* (London: Athlone, 1987), 191.

that said Raymond was his legitimate heir and after his death, Rupin, son of Raymond, was the legitimate heir of that prince and he ordered liege homage to be made to him by all his men, saving the fidelity by which they were bound to him while he lived. Then he invested the aforementioned Rupin with the city of Antioch and the whole Antiochene Principate to be held after his death, save the dowry of Sybil,[201] his wife, and all the gifts he had made and would make in the future and saving his dominion over the whole principate he possessed while he lived, and he called him by the name of his Father, Raymond, as we have seen in the letter you sent us. But the noble man, the count of Tripoli, son of the mentioned prince, considering himself to be deprived of his paternal inheritance in an offensive manner, wanted to attack you together with our beloved sons of the Hospital of Jerusalem and the Knights of the Temple, but looking into whether he could prevail against you, the son, having replaced the prince in the favor of the Antiochene commune, excluded his father and presumed also to heap injuries on contumelies and injuries on his domains. Meanwhile, certain friends of the count of Tripoli, corrupted by money and circumvented by influence, asserting that the count was the legitimate heir of the prince, obtained from the people with false suggestions that, after they had set aside their previous oath, they would show homage to the same count, for which reason your royal Serenity has appealed to the Apostolic See. Also, to the Templars and Hospitallers returning to their loyalty he restored the prince on the princely throne.

But even though we would like to defer to your Serenity as much as possible with God, because, however, we do not wish nor should we, when in doubt, render judgment, since, even if it is consistent with truth in our view, still in the absence of the other party, who has not yet sought judgment, we ought not to proceed to a sentence, we have ordered this case to be reserved to the examination of our legates. They will, Lord willing [Act 14:3], soon make the passage and, to them, we will give both in words and writing a firm mandate to examine it carefully, and to decide it without regard to persons on the basis of reason alone. Nor should they be willing to delegate the case to judges who might be suspect with reason by either party and especially by you [2 Chr 19:7; Rom 2:11; Col 3:25; 1 Pt 1:17]. Therefore, we ask and exhort your Highness more attentively and

201. Sybil, Bohemond III's third wife, was member of a noble Antiochene family. He later married a fourth time. See RI 2:243 (253), 466, n. 11.

recommend by Apostolic letter that you deal with the common case privately and prefer the business of the Crucified to your own convenience, so far as you can. Keeping peace with all Christians, you should direct your efforts to defend the inheritance by our Lord [Ps 126:3] and powerfully attack the barbarity of the Saracens. You ought not go to war against the count or anyone else on account of this matter, especially while the prince who put your nephew in the succession of the principate is still living, as you say in your letter that he has retained the property and dominion for his lifetime. When, however, our legates arrive you should pursue your case not with arms but laws, not vindicating yourself with the sword but pursuing justice before a judge. For we have commanded the same count in our Apostolic letter that he, while preserving his own position, should presume to attempt nothing in this case in prejudice of the right of another, but await the arrival of our legates to whom we have committed jurisdiction and the decision. For this we commend our beloved son your messenger more readily to the Royal Serenity so that from holding him dear you may hold him more dearly in the future. Also we give thanks to your Serenity that you have visited us magnificently and liberally through your same messenger.[202]

CXII. By the same messenger, the Lord Pope sent him the standard he asked for, writing in this way:

To the counts, barons, knights, and all the peoples in Armenia. Even if you received the institutes of the Apostolic See in modern times, serving the Lord according to them in purity of heart and body, still he who paid the workers in his vineyard in morning and evening with the reward of a single denarius, making the first last, and the last first [Mt 20:9–16; 1 Cor 9:24], will grant the prize of eternal victory to you if you have humbly venerated the Catholic church, the bride of the true Solomon, "under whose head" according to the statement in the Canticle of Canticles, "his left hand and his right embrace one another" [Sg 2:6, 8: 3]. Until now the zeal of the Lord has consumed you so that you have exposed your property and persons to avenge the injury of the Crucified and to free his temple and inheritance from the hands of the pagans, thinking with the apostle that in Christ, life and death are a profit to you [1 Sm 10:l; Sir 5:12]. Moreover, we rejoice that, even if you are a new plantation of the Roman

202. RI 2:243 (253), 465–67, December 17, 1199.

church, still newness [Is 16:3] brings an increase of virtue in you and even now renders you fervent in the end, so that, so much more fervently you should rise up to aid all Christians, even of Christ, insofar as you are closer to the enemy. From being closer, you should know and desire to oppose their efforts. Moreover, we send a standard of St. Peter as a sign of our affection, trusting in your sincerity and devotion to him, our dearest son in Christ, Leo, illustrious king of Armenia, at the request of our beloved son, the noble man, Robert, knight, his messenger. He may use this properly against the enemies of the cross and crush their pride, the Lord granting, by the merits of the prince of the Apostles. Therefore, we admonish you one and all and exhort you in the Lord and we enjoin you on the remission of your sins that you should strive powerfully and manfully for the liberation of a share of the inheritance of the Lord from the hands of the pagans and end their audacity and tame their barbarity, just as you have begun well with your king, so that you may be a participant in the remission which we, confident in the authority of the omnipotent God and his blessed Apostles Peter and Paul, have granted to all making that passage.[203]

CXIII. Again the same king sent another knight to the Apostolic See by whom he sent this letter:

We have received the letter of your Paternity, which you sent us by our beloved and faithful messenger, with due reverence and devotion, and we have learned with full understanding its meaning, that you embrace our royal Majesty with the deepest feeling of charity. Also it encouraged us to persist in devotion and love of the Apostolic See, and we have desired and wished always to persevere in this. And the result is the witness of matters, because we appeal to the Apostolic See concerning all our business. Moreover, you have sent a standard of St. Peter by our messenger as a memento of the affection of the Apostolic See, and we will order it always to be carried before us against the enemies of the cross to the honor of the holy Roman church [Phil 3:18]. Our messenger has indeed informed me that he has been received and treated kindly and honorably by your Beatitude and that you have listened diligently and efficaciously to all our petitions, which we have indeed clearly understood from your eloquent letter.

203. RI 2:244 (254), 468–69, December 17, 1199.

We have left the constant concerns on all the aforesaid matters to your Paternity. Moreover, you have desired us to be asked and exhorted to erect a wall against the attacks and violence of the pagans ascending from the other side [Ez 13:15], and we wish indeed to do this, as we believe that until now this is not unknown to your Paternity. And we will in the future oppose the shield of our fortitude in a strong hand and extended arm [Dt 5:15] against the barbarous nations on behalf of our law and the defense of the Christian faith by the favor of your mandate, as long as you send us the desired support. Often and again you have commanded us to keep peace with the count of Antioch and Tripoli and we have observed this well to this time by the grace of your love. But there should be no doubt that by the grace of God we have indeed not been able to restrain the opposition and audacity of the Antiochenes. Moreover, we are not willing to conceal from your holy paternity how and to what degree they have recently taken themselves against us. The count of Tripoli and the Antiochenes sent messengers to Rokn-ed-Din-Soleiman II,[204] enemy of the cross and our adversary [Phil 3:18], and they made an alliance with him against us and plotted together that the most cruel Rokn-ed-Din on the one side and the Antiochenes and Tripolitan Count on the other would not cease to harass us until they drove us from the throne of our kingdom. When we heard this, we sent our spies, who laid in ambush until they captured the messengers. After they brought them before the feet of our power, trembling and in fear, they openly confessed the truth of the matter. Then we approached the boundaries of the Antiochenes and stayed there for three months against our will with much labor and sweat. After this we completed whatever the Antiochenes wished, not in fear of them but carrying out your requests with difficulty. For this reason, we have incurred considerable losses to our kingdom and we have had to withdraw unwillingly from the service of God and Christianity. But when your legates whom we await arrive, preceded by the divine power, we will cause our certitude of the business to be explained by the same messengers in their presence, if the count still lives. We request your Holiness for this reason to send quickly the long-awaited and hoped-for aid. For great discord has emerged among the barbaric peoples and they are tearing one another apart, and if, before they make peace you send help, Christianity will be

---

204. Rokn-ed-Din Soleiman II, sultan of Konya, 1201–1203. See RI 5:42 (43), 79, n. 9.

exalted, and if, God forbid, before the aid comes, they have made peace among themselves, there will be none to prevent their violence and the rest of Christianity could hardly ever or even never resist them.

On what you have written about the business of Rupin, our beloved nephew, that in the absence of the other party you neither wish nor should reach a judgment in an uncertain matter, this is proper for your Holiness; universal law requires it. But we have been moved with considerable joy because you have committed our case into the hands of your legates, with both letters and mandates, not into the hands of persons suspect to us. On this matter, we have given constant thanks to your Holiness and we offer copious praises to the founder of all things. We have asked your most pious Paternity for these things and we press earnestly on bended knees that you please appoint the venerable Archbishop of Mainz, in whom we have great confidence, together with your legates, as judge in our case for the future support of the Holy Land, because there is nothing more by which you can make us happier. Also you have written to us that you have written to the Count of Tripoli that he should withdraw from the right of another, and we have found this gracious and acceptable and we have given great thanks to you. But you should know that nothing has been helpful to us because he lays ambushes like a wolf in hiding [Ps 9:30], and does not stop night and day trying to attract the Antiochenes with bribes and blandishments. Therefore, we are unwilling to conceal from your Holiness that in the month of July we collected our army against the barbarians, and we were hoping to attack them more effectively with God's help [Acts 26:22] because of the discord which emerged among them, and for this business we sent for the Templars dwelling in our kingdom with possessions valued at 20,000 Bezants, to come to our aid for the honor of God and the defense of Christianity. And they came even to Antioch and we went out in our own person to meet them as far as the boundaries of Antioch with joy and exaltation [Ps 44:16; Lk 1:14]. The Master of the Temple sent letters to us for this directed from your side, which we have seen and we received him with due honor. When we had read them, we learned that you requested us to hand over Gaston[205] to them and we immediately sent for the Master and some brethren as you

205. A fortress north of Antioch, held by the Templars since 1160. It was taken by Saladin and retaken by Leo, who returned it to the Templars in 1216. See RI 5:42 (43), 81, n. 21.

asked to speak with them and they came and entered into discussion with us. But after many obscure words we asked the Master of the Temple to carry out your requests that he and the Lord Patriarch of Antioch and ourselves would send our messengers at once to the Apostolic See because we desired to hand over this Gaston, having settled every occasion through your hands with the Templars, and we wanted him to hand over our beloved nephew Rupin to be cared for and guarded in good faith and without evil intent in this castle, and that they should always help the aforesaid boy to acquire his rights insofar as the dignity of their order might permit, and that there should not be any loss in our kingdom through this castle. Until our messengers should go and return with your requests, we wanted to restore the rents of those lands belonging to that castle to the body of our land. And so, we and the boy, our beloved nephew, queried the brothers on what was to be done on this condition and to obtain another castle, called Darbsak,[206] belonging to them and we would aid them likewise with all our people and our strength. But when the Templars saw that I was deceived by such business and they knew that a large pagan army had been collected for war against us, they refused to listen to us, worn down in our humility, and they even ordered the company they had sent to parts of our kingdom to return. And there should be no doubt that they would not conclude a peace agreement about this castle at the request of anyone but you. We again sent to them, asking that, for the love of God, they should come into our kingdom and if they did not want to accompany us against the pagans, at least they should, out of piety for God, keep our kingdom safe until our return. They persevered in their obstinacy and were unwilling to do this. Indeed they left our kingdom to the jaws of the wolf [Phil 3:18] on their own authority. (But we, with God's help, returned safe and sound and, because of your prayers, we found our land safe and uninjured.) Of this we complain to God and you. For what should then be done is not unknown to your Holiness.

Besides, you should not doubt that we are bound for the future to the Holy See. Therefore, if it pleases your Holiness, we neither desire nor should we be bound to any other than the Latin church. This is what we press humbly on your Holiness: that you would please send open letters to us so that neither we nor the Latins of our land of any condition may be

206. A fortress in the Amanus Mountains, northeast of Bagras. See RI 5:42 (43), 82, n. 23.

required to answer to any Latin Church save the Holy Roman church, that it should not have the power to excommunicate us or the Latins of our land or to bring a sentence in our kingdom upon any Latins in any church except as ordered by the Apostolic See. We have sent to the feet of your Holiness our beloved and faithful knight, Garnerius the German, by name, the bearer of the present letter. He will speak to you on these matters on our behalf, as you would not hesitate to believe ourselves. Given at Sis, on the first of the month of October.[207]

CXIV. At the request of the king the Lord Pope sent this letter to him:

The devotion of the Royal Serenity deserves and the sincerity of your charity has demanded that not only should we do a special favor to you but also for your whole kingdom and, on account of the merit of your devotion, we should honor the whole Armenian church. For you more than your other predecessors, whose memory is more special, have persisted in devotion to us and the Holy Roman church, recognizing both the primacy of the Apostolic See and her *magisterium* as you return humbly and devoutly to your mother. For this reason you should reasonably be honored by her. Moreover, we have learned from the letter which your royal Serenity sent us that, since you recognize that the Kingdom of Armenia is bound to the Apostolic See by ties of obedience, you ought not nor do you wish it to be obligated to any other church than the Latin. Wherefore you were asking that an Apostolic letter be granted to you to the effect that no Latin except the Roman Pontiff can promulgate a sentence of excommunication or interdict against you or your kingdom or the men of your kingdom, whether Latins or others of any condition.

Desiring, therefore, to defer to your Serenity as much as we can with God, and to listen with honesty to the royal petitions, we, influenced by your requests, strictly forbid, by the authority of these presents, anyone to dare to exercise ecclesiastical distraint against you or the men of your kingdom of whatever condition they may be. They, with only the same prelates of the kingdom mediating, are subject to the Apostolic See. No one except the Roman Pontiff or his legate, or by his special mandate, should dare to exercise jurisdiction. To no one, therefore, etc., of prohibition, etc.[208]

207. RI 5:42 (43), 78–82, October 1, 1201.
208. RI 5:43 (44), 82–83, June 1, 1202.

CXV. He also wrote to the Catholicos of the Armenians in this way:

We know from the content of your letter how you meditate day and night [Ps 1:2] on the law of the Lord and have decorated it with the varied flowers of authorities from the treasures of your heart, offering new and old [Mt 13:52; Lk 6:45], and intermixing there matters more learnedly with these and those so that once joined fruitfully the flowers may spread their scent. Of course, even if you taught with the word of the Apostle the "we are all one body in Christ each member one of the other" [Rom 12:5] and that all whom the sacred water of baptism regenerates, it makes brothers because "our Father who is in heaven is one" [Mk 23:9], as the Truth states in the Gospel, still you recognize in us who have succeeded St. Peter the *magisterium* of the Christian faith. Wherefore for just this reason you desire to rest in the font of our holy faith and the precepts of the law and of the church and to be nourished [Nm 13:21] so that you may daily suck at our breasts [Is 60:16] and drink in the doctrine of milk flowing from the Apostolic See. And although you are far from us in location still you rejoice that both you and the Armenian church are united in faith with us, since from that fact you are of the sheepfold of which the Lord said in the Gospel, "Other sheep I have which are not of this fold, and I must lead them and they will hear my voice and there will be one fold and one shepherd" [Jn 10:16]. For the Lord committed the sheep of this sheepfold to one shepherd, namely Peter, when he said to him, "Feed my sheep,"[209] signifying by repeating the word three times that whoever has faith in the Trinity in any region of the three parts of the world [Europe, Asia, Africa] and in the threefold order of the faithful, with Noah, Job, and Daniel, whether they are in bed, in the field, or in a mill, they are committed to the *magisterium* of Peter.

Therefore, you have rejoiced that the mother of all churches which enlightens the whole world with its clarity, looking with a good heart, has desired that the Catholic church of the Armenians be consoled, knowing that in this has been fulfilled what Jesus Christ the Lord said to Peter, "I have prayed for you Peter that your faith may not fail you, but when you are converted, you may strengthen your brothers" [Lk 22:32]. You also say that the Armenian church has received the faith from the Roman

209. Jn 21:15–17. See also John C. Moore, "The Sermons of Pope Innocent III," *Römische historische Mitteilungen* 36 (1994): 81–142, esp. 108–9.

church from the beginning and you and your fellow bishops and the flock committed to you and them have not diminished or augmented it in anything but that, even until today, you observe it just as you have received it, keeping its customs according to the ordinances of the earlier holy Fathers. We therefore, who ought to love our neighbors as ourselves [Mt 19:9, 22:39; Mk 12:31–33] rejoice in Christ concerning the purity of your faith; we regard you as a venerable brother and a great member of the church of God in the depths of charity and to honor our dearest son in Christ, Leo, the illustrious king of the Armenians, in various ways and to favor especially the whole church of the Armenians as a daughter of the Apostolic See. Lest, however, the son of the handmaid be heir [Gn 21:10; Gal 4:30] with the free son, indeed lest the son of the handmaid usurp the inheritance of the heir for himself, the handmaid and her son should rather be expelled, we have, therefore, put the "Tau" sign on the foreheads of those weeping and sorrowing [Ex 9:4] so that by the grace of God the army of the crusaders now for the most part has landed in Venice and from there they will board ships to cross over for the support of the Holy Land.

We therefore admonish your fraternity and we exhort you more carefully and we command you by Apostolic letter that, persisting in fear of the Divine name and persevering in reverence of the Apostolic See, you confirm the king and the whole Armenian church in the law of the Lord. You should explain the form of Apostolic remission to them just as we commanded by our other letters and exhort them carefully that to erect a wall for the house of the Lord against those ascending from the other side [Ex 13:5], lest they should hesitate whether it would be necessary to shed blood for him who did not hesitate to undergo the sufferings of the cross for them, since thus they can acquire an eternal kingdom and exchange an earthly for a praiseworthy heavenly commerce. But they should await efficacious help from heaven and quick aid from earth and put their hope in him who is the strength of those hoping in him, who makes success over temptation and after weeping and sorrowing brings joy and exaltation.[210]

CXVI. The letter of the Armenian king to the Lord Pope, however, describes in definite terms how Peter, cardinal priest of Saint Marcel-

210. 1 Cor 10:13; Tb 3:22. See RI 5:45 (46), 87–89, about June 1, 1202.

lus, the legate of the Apostolic See, traveled from Antioch to Armenia and how honorably and devoutly he was received by the king and the Catholicos as well as by ecclesiastical and secular persons, and that all bound themselves to the obedience of the Apostolic See, but in these matters the same king complained about the legate of the Lord Pope and many things were discussed about both the Antiochene business and that of the Templars, which are made clear more fully and plainly from reading about them. Indeed, the king wrote in this way:

Since you, very celebrated father and lord of the whole holy church, administer the care and rule of the Christian religion, the Lord granting, we must resort always to your refuge as to the safest shelter, you, on whom our hope and trust depends, after God, and seek assistance from your Beatitude in necessities. Therefore, most merciful father and lord, having recourse on bended knees to the feet of your Holiness and with all supplication, we complain and we do not cease to complain of the Lord Peter, cardinal priest of St. Marcellus, your legate, that he is suspect in our case and indeed an open adversary. For although when he had arrived in the neighborhood of our kingdom, we, the venerable Catholicos with some of his suffragans and clergy and with our faithful barons and several noble pilgrims also present, received him with as much honor and veneration as we could out of reverence to you both from the legation enjoined on him and for making peace between our nephew and the count of Tripoli. Contrary to justice and our appeal to the Apostolic See for a hearing, he, as we believe, presumptuously approached the usurpers of the Antiochene principate. On the following days, we deliberated concerning the obedience of the Armenian church to the Holy Roman church for which we labored long with the aid of Divine grace, and we induced the Armenian church to this with much labor in the time of your pontificate; by the requirement of your merits, to which our predecessors after much negotiation were unwilling to agree, as Cardinal Peter himself is witness. The Lord Catholicos with due solemnity showing both obedience and reverence to the Holy Roman church and you by the hands of this legate according to the form and mandate of your letter, received the *pallium* sent by your Beatitude in the presence of the aforesaid persons with all humility and devotion, promising, on his order, to visit the Holy Roman church, the mother and teacher of all the churches, every five years by his messengers according to the Apostolic capitularies and to participate in councils on this side of the sea either in his own person or through his representative, and it has been agreed by both parties that ecclesiastical councils should not be celebrated without his presence or that of his messenger.

When these affairs concerning the reformation of peace between our nephew and the count of Tripoli were treated, and when the Apostolic letter concerning the commission was discussed, we represented to Cardinal Peter that he might decide the case, which was delegated to the Lords Soffredus, cardinal priest of Santa Prassede, and Peter, cardinal priest of St. Marcellus, legates, confident that they moved according to your mandates to bring this case to a suitable conclusion by him in the absence of the Lord Cardinal Soffredus, who was in Acre on the business of Christianity. We had found him a lover of equity and justice in the whole case. After we presented the Apostolic letter, as has been said, we committed the case of our nephew to [Cardinal Peter] acting as your vicar and, from the beginning of the case, we always appealed for an Apostolic hearing and we committed this case to his judgement, with the Lord Patriarch of Antioch,[211] the Hospitallers, Templars, and other religious men as witnesses, at Negromonte.[212] But the cardinal and legate Peter, against whom we hoped to harbor no, and I mean no, suspicion, making a private agreement with the count of Tripoli, the Templars and the Antiochenes, fraudulently disparaged our side and aided the other side to our injury and expense, stretching out the hand of counsel and aid to them. And so from the mandates of this legate, in whose hope we were deceived, we approached the Antiochene side for a second and third time to make peace. The count of Tripoli, seeking delay, never came to court on the appointed day. But after the understood and known fraud of the conspiracy was initiated, with Peter the Legate himself under suspicion, indeed, an open adversary, we appealed for an Apostolic hearing and we committed the case of our nephew to your judgment, committing our person, kingdom and peoples under the protection of God and your own which we believed we would obtain by the privilege delegated by your Beatitude. It happened therefore on a certain night, before the arrival of Cardinal Peter, with all our army defending the inheritance of our nephew, with the Antiochene side unjustly attacking, we entered, as it pleased the Lord, within the walls of Antioch

211. Peter of Angoulême, patriarch of Antioch, 1176–1208.
212. Monastic community in the Amanus Mountains northwest of Antioch. See RI 8:120 (119), n. 19. Proof furnished by C. Egger.

with a strong force, and, if we had wished to shed the blood of Christians and set fire to the city, Antioch would have been taken, but out of piety and fear of the Lord and sympathy for Christian suffering, we asked the Lord Patriarch to come to us to be mediator of the desired peace between ourselves and the Antiochenes.

When the peace was being discussed, behold the Templars, whom we honored by your requests and commands, to whom we deferred in all war, with their possessions and holdings safeguarded, whom we were hoping to have as friends, not enemies, sharpened their teeth against us without any excuse, fortified towers, took up arms, and shot their arrows against our army within and outside the walls of the city of Antioch. They prepared a black-and-white standard against us, and what is more serious, set aside the ordinances of religion, and shed Christian blood. They, together with the count of Tripoli and the Antiochenes, united in perfidy, are allied to the Sultan of Aleppo,[213] thus by his machinations, they prevented our nephew, an orphan under your protection and God's, from acquiring his inheritance. Thus we bore a not unexpected wound from the enemy, that we out of vexation have seized the possessions and holdings the Templars possessed in our kingdom, and eliminated them from our land. When these things were done in this way, the Lord Cardinal Peter, leagued with the Templars, asking us to make peace between them and the Templars, forced us to restore immediately the property recently taken from the Templars, first, orally, then, for a second and third time, in writing and by messengers. We responded to him saying that we were prepared out of love for the Apostolic See to restore what was recently taken from the Templars if, at his order, they would promise in the future not to oppose justice and a settlement for our nephew within or outside the walls of Antioch, but act as religious, safe and secure in their houses and possessions. On the contrary, the Templars, supported by the stimulus of arrogance, put themselves to the defense of the walls of Antioch contrary to justice and the settlement for our nephew, having set aside the agreement. But when he could not arrange peace between us and the Templars, the Lord Cardinal Peter, in the absence of the Lord Catholicos, our venerable father, celebrated a council concerning the same case in Antioch and after our repeated appeal for an apostolic hearing, he promulgated a sentence of excommunication on our land, except for the confessions of the

213. As-Zahir I, sultan of Aleppo.

sick, baptism, and the burial of the dead. He sent letters to the Lord Catholicos of the Armenians about this sentence so that the interdict might immediately be promulgated throughout the whole Catholicate. When this came to the attention of the Lord Cardinal and legate Soffredus, he was greatly vexed, and, after he took counsel with the Lord Peter, his colegate, who approached him, because we appealed immediately to your court, they desired to change the mind of Cardinal Peter by holding a council. And so it happened that, from the mandate of the lord cardinals to the illustrious king of Jerusalem and Cyprus and all the noble pilgrims, in the month of September we sent our ambassador, Constantius de Camardesia,[214] our beloved relative, to Acre to make peace between us and the Antiochenes and the Templars and, by the mediating wisdom and discretion of the Lord Cardinal Soffredus, a lover of equity and law, peace was made between us and the Templars, as you can learn from this letter. But we have never departed from the mandates of the Holy Roman church nor will we withdraw from the count, while he lives, although the Lord Cardinal Peter works to eliminate us from these affairs. Therefore we, who by the grace of God and your own favor have been made your new planting in the time of your Pontificate, desiring to produce odoriferous and sweet fruits to the honor of God and of the Holy Roman church, have recourse to the feet of your Holiness, asking and praying on bended knees, that you should not commit the case of our nephew to the judgment of the Lord Cardinal and legate Peter, whom we hold suspect, indeed as an open adversary, and that he should have no power in the future over us and those of any condition inhabiting our land from the legation he enjoys, and that you should order the Templars by Apostolic letter not to be enemies of justice and the settlement of our nephew in the Antiochene matter, just as the Hospitallers and other religious men are not, and you should commit the case of our nephew, about which we have often written your Domination, not to suspect judges, but to such persons who will not turn from the right path but will make a just judgment, on an equal scale, after having heard both parties and who may make a just judgment without exception of persons. We believe from this the Holy Roman church will achieve a building up rather than the extirpation of your new planting [Jer 1:10] and by your favor, your planting may rejoice to have found delightful results in morning and evening.[215]

214. Kostanc Cumardian, lord of Seleucia and Pumar.
215. RI 8:120 (119), September–October 1204. Proofs furnished by C. Egger.

CXVII. The Catholicos indeed sent the following letter:

To the most reverend in Christ, the Lord Innocent, by the grace of God, Supreme Pontiff and universal Pope, John, by the same grace humble Catholicos of the Armenians,[216] devoted and obedient to your Holiness, with due obedience and reverence, full joy of salvation.

From the ineffable providence of our Lord, from whom every good thing proceeds [Jas 1:17], the Armenian church, recognizing the primacy and *magisterium* granted to the Holy Roman church by God himself, has been made her most devoted daughter and I, though her unworthy minister, approaching the Lord Peter, cardinal priest of St. Marcellus, your legate, from the legation enjoined on him in the territory of our Catholicate, meeting him out of reverence for you with the clergy and flock committed to us by God, received him as honorably as we could. We showed obedience and reverence, communicating by mutual looks and conversation through his hands to the Holy Roman church and you according to the content of your letter and, receiving the *pallium* sent by your Beatitude with proper solemnity and with all humility, we promised on our order to visit the Holy Roman church, as the mother and teacher of all the churches, once every five years by our messengers and to be present in councils on this side of the sea. Also, it has been decided by both partners that ecclesiastical councils should not be celebrated on the same matters in our absence or that of our representative. We have received in part the institutions of the Holy Roman church and in part because of the absence of our suffragans we have caused them to be diffused far and wide and because this could not be done without great deliberation of persons. Convening our prelates or the majority of them at set time, we have proposed to receive, with their consent, your institutions with which we are in agreement lest scandal should arise in the church. You will find us faithful and devoted, therefore, in promoting all your mandates.

CXVIII. But the legates wrote to the Lord Pope on these matters in this way:

To the most reverend father and lord, in exceeding fear, Innocent, by the grace of God, Supreme Pontiff of the holy and universal church, Soffredus,

---

216. John II, Medzabaro, chancellor of the kingdom, 1203–1221, Catholicos of Armenia. See RI 8:120 (119), n. 4. Proof furnished by C. Egger.

by Divine permission, of the title of Santa Prassede, and Peter, by Divine
Providence, of the title of St. Marcellus, cardinal priests, though unworthy,
due and ready obedience in all things. While, at that time, when I, Soffredus, came to Acre, there was a truce with the Saracens and a serious war
between the King of Armenia and the Count of Tripoli and the Antiochenes, because, as was said, the count had unjustly occupied Antioch and
with the help of a majority of the citizens had ejected the nobles from
most of the city, because they were unwilling to violate the oath of fidelity
that they had sworn to the firstborn son of their prince. After they held
counsel not once but often with the master of the Temple and of the Hospital, I, at the frequent invitation of both parties, traveled to Antioch to
work for peace and, as much as possible, settle the dispute. Also, I had
written to the count and the commune of Antioch with the counsel of the
Masters that they should come and should send honorable and prudent
men so that I could deliberate with them how I ought to proceed to Antioch. Therefore, when I had entered the city of Tripoli on the feast of St.
Martin,[217] for which day and to which place I had summoned them, no
one came to me, nor were they willing to respond to anything by open letter. But working further, I sent to both parties the venerable men, the
Bishops of Tortosa and Bethlehem, for winter had arrived and I was told
that now it was not a safe season to travel by sea. But I could not obtain
any response until the Feast of Purification. Then, indeed, the Prince of
Tripoli came, not because of me but to promote his own business, as the
opportunity required of him. I was scheduled to have a discussion with
him in person because he had been excommunicated by the patriarchs of
Jerusalem and Antioch and the neighboring bishops, but as he asserted,
unjustly, and so he did not consider himself excommunicated. He was also
unwilling to speak with me through an intermediary. But he worked for
an agreement between himself and the Hospitallers on the matter for
which he had been excommunicated, and after much backing and filling,
he arrived at an agreement in which there was no mention of my name
although the whole business had been encouraged by me and without my
assent the Hospitallers could not make an agreement with him. And so I
remained there until Passion Sunday. And, worn out and disillusioned, I
returned to Acre, for I was awaiting the arrival of a fleet, and I did not
want to be away at its arrival. Many Frankish nobles and the King of

217. November 11.

Jerusalem, the Master of the Temple, and some others, having persuaded me on the difficulty of travel on foot, insisted to me that I should travel by sea with them to Antioch. For if I would go with them, they were prepared to come with me to Antioch to make an agreement. Worn out on foot, I agreed with them immediately, and I and the Master of the Temple, the general Preceptor of the Hospital, Stephen de Pertico, Count Moncia of Hungary and the Ambassador of the Marquis of Montferrat, who had arrived in the land, set sail. We then landed, with the Lord as author, in the port of Antioch. Moreover, the King of Armenia arrived in the lands belonging to Antioch. On the second day, we entered the land of Antioch. And when we heard this, we quickly sent him a messenger and letters so that, out of reverence for the Roman See and ourselves, he might delay injuring the land until we could speak to him. He waited for three days. We came to him on the third day and again we obtained a postponement from him for nine days at which time we expected the King of Jerusalem to come. In the meantime, before all else, we worked to find the road to peace. The King of Armenia offered to go to trial and asked me to commence it immediately, as if by you, and asked humbly on behalf of his orphan nephew and his widowed mother. He agreed to the judgment of the barons who are about to come. He set forth how he has sought justice from the Roman church which you promised him would be carried out by myself and my colleague on our arrival and it would be up to us to use whomever we wished. For he did not refuse to put himself principally to our judgment, even to yours through us. But it happened that a spirit of iniquity subverted their hearts and turned from our unity the one who was believed to have come for an agreement. Indeed, they began to say constantly that this judgment was not ours to make and not the Roman church's either. And he, supported by their counsels, declared constantly who, according to him, should be called prince. And they became so much of one heart and mind on the journey that the said prince hardly did or said anything unless he was informed by their counsel, save for one of them who had come with me, who faithfully and prudently assisted me in the whole business. The King of Armenia also offered 20,000 armed men for the service of Christianity if he could obtain justice for his orphan nephew and his widowed mother. The petition of the king seemed to me to be just and to be granted, the offer also very useful and fruitful for Christianity. But since I had as opponents those whom I was hoping would be supporters, seeing myself almost alone, I departed with the only one who assisted me and I came to Marqab,[218] where I worked God's will even to death. When the lord cardinal came to Cyprus and finally to Acre, I hastened to him, with many letters asked for by him, although at this time I was oppressed by the manifold weakness of my illness. But the lord cardinal, when he took care of his business in Acre, went to Antioch and then to Armenia, where what he did and how malice increased in those lands at the instigation of the devil, he will more prudently relate to you.

I, indeed, Peter, cardinal priest of St. Marcellus, informed your Paternity that in the above events the beloved in Christ father, Lord Soffredus, cardinal priest of Santa Prassede, legate of the Apostolic See, related to your Holiness the matters about this business he himself witnessed and how he proceeded after his return from the lands of Antioch. And when I recently arrived in Acre, having been summoned several times both by the illustrious King of the Armenians and by the count of Tripoli or Prince of Antioch, and the Antiochenes to settle the disagreements described above, I returned to Antioch and attempted a threefold solution to this business. First, if any agreement could be reached from the consent of the parties, for which I labored for a long time, I accomplished nothing. Second, that the parties would submit themselves to the Lord Cardinal and myself so that we might reach an agreement and judge according to justice and equity, and when I had labored on this with both parties for a long time, I did not succeed even after three months. Third and finally, that it did not seem necessary for us to seek from the parties a commitment to the other parties but only to offer from our office to both parties if they wished to propose anything, that we would be prepared to render justice.

For your exoneration of the Roman church, the lord cardinal and myself, I offered the lord king who had presented your letter to me in which you mandated the Lord Soffredus and myself to resolve that business, with justice mediating, that we were prepared, the lord cardinal and I, to carry out and show justice according to the mandate, and he would not sustain any loss through us for attaining justice for his nephew. But the king then responded that he gave thanks concerning this matter that I was offering enough to him and to you and the Roman church and to us two, but he added that the Antiochenes were attacking him. Therefore, he asked that first we should remove said count or prince from possession of the city and the principate of Antioch and afterward we ought to grant

218. Near Latakia.

justice to him. Although I responded that we could not do this justly before a trial, still he might propose this and other reasons which he wanted on his behalf, the king said: "You are vicars of the Apostolic one, I am King of Armenia. I put to you, Lord Cardinals Soffredus and Peter, the business of my nephew and of my niece, and we ask from you and desire to have such justice and to obtain what the Lord Pope would do for us if we were in his presence as a widow and orphan under Apostolic protection. You see the force, violence and injustice that the count works against our orphan nephew and our niece, his widowed mother. You may be sure that, receiving his full power in the matter of Antioch, you should understand that to whichever of the parties you give the judgment, it will remain firm and undiminished." When I responded to him that it was no part of our office to decide on this matter, but he might proceed, if he pleased, in the case, and we would be prepared also to force the other party to assist in the trial upon this fact, he would not proceed even though I explained to him and continued to explain that we were prepared to grant justice. I offered this to the Antiochenes if they wished to lay aside any quarrel. And finally, after I held many discussions with both sides, which are too long to relate, with the counsel of the patriarch, the Archbishop of Tarsus, the bishops, the chapter and abbots of the Antiochene church as well as the Lord [bishop] of Cremona, Sicard, and others who were present with me, I firmly forbade both parties on behalf of almighty God and the Holy Roman church, the whole of Christianity, and ourselves, namely, the legates who were in the land, to wage any war on any of the parties, from whom they were not suffering a lack of justice and we were prepared to show justice to both and that war would be at the expense of the whole of Christianity, especially of the Eastern land. But because the lord cardinal returned to Acre, the Countess of Flanders, who had arrived, and some pilgrims insisted to us that we should not cease again to work for said peace. Afterward, we deliberated about summoning the King of Jerusalem, the Templars, Hospitallers, and the pilgrim nobles who were there, by our messengers and letters and summons, all the aforesaid, to commit themselves to our judgment without any condition. They should demand securities, forts, and holdings to swear in our hands to receive and observe our judgment, and whichever of the parties would not do this, we would pursue that party as an enemy of Christianity both spiritually and temporally. We then sent with our letter the King of Jerusalem and barons, pilgrims, the venerable bishop of Cremona, who admonished the parties presented with our letter to do what we wrote and whoever would not do this, he would promulgate a sentence of excommunication against him on our behalf. And so he approached them and after he had besought each one, as I said before, the King of Armenia offered out of reverence for you and us a truce of forty days which was not accepted by the other party. Even when the messenger who was about to return to us on behalf of the king demanded security to carry out our mandate because he had to cross through enemy lines, this was denied to him. But he returned to us uninjured just as the Lord wished with the mandate of full power that he had received from his lord. In fact, the letter of the king made clear that whatever this ambassador did, the king would hold firm and would observe it as firmly as if it were done by himself. And so concerning the issue with the Templars for which the king was excommunicated and his land subject to the interdict, the messenger swore to keep our mandate as is the custom, upon his soul and that of the king, and he humbly received the mandate that we justly ordered. Finally, concerning the issue of Antioch, the same ambassador offered to do only on behalf of the king what we should think sufficient. And because the count of Tripoli neither came nor sent or even wrote anything that would, as is said, have weight, the king asked that the count should be excommunicated, in order to prevent Christians, especially Templars and pilgrims who until now had sworn aid and favor to him, from assisting him, far different than would be proper and than your statute, made with much deliberation, contained, and that in any case it would not summon the king to obedience to the Roman See, but without doubt lead him to withdraw what he was offering.

To overcome, also, the hardness and contumacy of the count, the ambassador said that when the Bishop of Tripoli and the majority of the tepid and lukewarm canons, and the notary of the same count came, they should have no excuse for any reason, not even the appearance of an excuse, why they had not appeared at our mandates. But we responded that this difficulty did not appear save from a certain unexpected case, namely, because we were on the verge of departing from the land and going to Constantinople for counsel and aid to the pilgrims who labored there for the service of Christianity.

While I would consent in public speech for the honesty of the Roman church to this excuse, in a final sense, I, Soffredus, firmly proposed to the advocates separately, to the Lord Cardinal, the Archbishop of Caesarea, the bishop of Cremona, and the elect of Acre, that I wanted to be excused from this case before God and them, and it seemed to me certain that the position of the aforesaid ambassador was just and must be admitted, and I was prepared, if it pleased the lord cardinal, to do what he asked, because such was irrevocably established and confirmed in our common deliberation by the King of Jerusalem, the Templars, Hospitallers, barons, and pilgrims who were present at Acre, and it was not fitting that what was in such a way and so solemnly decided for the utility of Christianity should be without effect and illusory.[219]

CXIX. Because, indeed, the legates departed from those lands, coming to Constantinople, the Lord Pope committed the case to the abbots of Lucedio, of Mount Tabor, and to the noble men, the count of Katzenellenbogen and Gerard de Furneval in this way:[220]

Even if there should always be mortal hatred between those who are required to love their neighbors as themselves and then love their enemies for the sake of God, still at this time discord among fellow Christians, especially those across the sea, is so much more harmful not only to them but also to the general church, to the extent that the business of the Holy Land is more impeded. For, until now, the enemies of the Christian name who now, because of our sins, hold and defile the temple of God, glory on their sword that they have seized cities and fortified towns from the hands of Christians. They diminish the men and forces which would suffice for the rest of our plan, even if they were carried out by sworn hands with one mind and equal desire against the enemy, if they can in some way avenge the injury of the cross and liberate the inheritance of Christ from the hands of the pagans. But they pay less attention to this than they should as if, having neglected directly the injury of the Crucified, they pursue their own injuries and put their private desires before the common will to the loss of all Christianity. Also, they pursue hate evilly and are thus divided from one another, so that because of their disputes over the Holy Land the word of the Gospel is not properly feared, which says: "Every kingdom

219. After late 1204. See RI 8:120 (119), September–October 1204, to support this date.
220. Peter of Magnano, from Vercelli, abbot of Lucedio, M. Abbot of the Benedictine monastery on Mt. Tabor, Count Berthold of Katzenellenbogen, who came with the Marquis of Montferrat, and Count Gerard I of Furneval, who had accompanied Richard Lionheart on the Third Crusade. See RI 8:1, nn. 1–4.

divided in itself will be made desolate and house will fall upon house" [Mt 12:15].

For behold, by reason of that discord which involves our beloved son in Christ, Leo, King of the Armenians, in the name of his widowed sister and orphan nephew on one side and the noble man, the count of Tripoli on the other, regarding the principate of Antioch, the progress of the Holy Land is much impeded, since their fighting with one another makes them unwilling to fight the enemies of the cross, and with some taking sides with the parties and considering their question their case, the rest labor in vain to bring the disputants to agreement. We, however, having desired to deal with these evils for a long time now, committed the case on this matter to our beloved sons, Soffredus, cardinal priest of Santa Prassede, and Peter, cardinal priest of Saint Marcellus, to be decided. But they, although they avoided neither labors or expenses for sake of this, even when both together and both individually had labored for a long time, they still accomplished nothing with the parties, because it had not been granted from on High. Recently, therefore, the same king stated by his letter to us that he could not obtain justice through our legates, although he had sought it often and was always ready to stay at law. Wherefore, when he finally appeared humbly at the mandate of these legates, who had excommunicated him for a very minor reason, and put an interdict on his lands, he, knocking at the door of the Apostolic See and seeking justice, asked that we not turn him away, since we owe justice to everyone. We, therefore, with the understanding that there ought not to be distinction among persons with us, and that we are required to do justice between man and man, command and order by Apostolic letter to your Discretion that, having convened both parties you should take care to impress upon them that they should agree among themselves about the principate or compromise on arbitrators, who should arbitrate for up to three months after your instruction. Otherwise, when you have summoned the parties, you will hear the views of both and you will decide their case, having removed the obstacle of appeal, if the parties should consent. If not, you will send the case with sufficient information to us, setting a date for the parties, on which they may be represented by suitable plenipotentiaries to receive the sentence. But so that they do not at the same time resort to trial and to battle, you should compel them in the meantime to observe truces by Apostolic authority. But if either of the parties shows himself contumacious, you may, by yourself, proceed against him and all Christians who are in those territories as strictly as you can, both spiritually and temporally; you may forbid our dearest son in Christ, the illustrious King of Jerusalem, the Hospitallers, and all Christians generally to lend support or favor to the contumacious party, but rather to withdraw and to support the party who was prepared to stay manfully and powerfully with the law, but if not all, etc., three of you or at least two, of whom one is a layman, the other a cleric, may execute the Apostolic mandate. Nevertheless, we desire and command that if anyone in the meantime should be appointed Patriarch of Jerusalem, he should participate in this affair with you. Given at Rome, at St. Peter, on the third of the Nones of March, in the eighth year of our Pontificate.[221]

[Peter of Aragon in Rome]

CXX. In the seventh year of the pontificate of the Lord Pope, Innocent III, in the month of November, Peter, king of Aragon, approached the Apostolic See so that he might receive a military girdle and a royal diadem from the same Lord Pope. Moreover, he came by sea with five galleys and landed on the island between Porto and Ostia, bringing with him the Archbishop of Arles, the Provost of Maguélone, with whom were present the elect of Nimes and certain other noble and prudent clerics. He also brought nobles with him: Sancius, his uncle, Hugo of Baucé, Roscellinus of Marseille, Arnold of Fontiano, and many other nobles and powerful men. Moreover, after horses and almost two hundred pack animals were sent to him, the Lord Pope ordered him to come into his presence at St. Peter, sending some of the Cardinals, the Senator of the city, and many other nobles and magnates to meet him. And he ordered him to be received as a guest very honorably in the house of the canons at St. Peter. On the third day, namely, on the feast of St. Martin,[222] the Lord Pope, with the cardinal bishops, priests, and deacons, the Primicerius and the cantors, the Senator, the justitiars, judges, advocates, *scrinarii*, with many nobles

221. RI 8:1, March 5, 1205.
222. November 11.

and a crowd of people, set out to the monastery of San Pancrazio Martire, near Trastevere, and there he ordered the aforesaid king to be anointed by Peter, Bishop of Porto, and afterward he crowned him with his own hands, granting to him all the royal insignia, namely, the mantle and tunic, the scepter and orb, the crown and miter, receiving from him a corporeal oath, whose content follows:

I, Peter, King of Aragon, profess and promise that I will always be faithful to my Lord Pope Innocent and his Catholic successors, and I will faithfully preserve my kingdom in his obedience, defending the Catholic faith and hunting down heretical depravity. I will guard the liberty and immunity of churches and I will defend their rights. I will strive for peace and justice in all the land subject to my power. So help me God and these holy gospels of God.

CXXI. Then the King, having been crowned with much celebration of praise and the applause of favor, returned along with the Lord Pope to the Basilica of St. Peter, on whose altar he placed the scepter and diadem and received the military sword from the hand of the Lord Pope, and he offered his kingdom to Blessed Peter, the Prince of the Apostles, and he established for himself that tribute by a page of privilege, which he handed to the Lord Pope on the altar, whose content follows:

In my heart I believe and in my mouth I confess that the Roman pontiff who is the successor of Blessed Peter is vicar of him through whom kings reign and princes rule, who holds dominion in the kingdom of men, and to whom he wishes to grant it. I, Peter, by the grace of God, King of Aragon, Count of Barcelona, and Lord of Montpellier, desiring principally to be fortified, after God, by the protection of Blessed Peter and the Apostolic See, offer to you, most reverend Father and Lord Supreme Pontiff, Innocent, and, through you, to the holy Roman church, my kingdom, and I establish that tribute to you and your successors in perpetuity, by the inspiration of Divine love, and for the remedy of my soul and our progenitors so that annually two hundred and fifty massamutini[223] should be paid

223. These are Arab gold coins, usually called massamutinus, "[t]he name given

to the Apostolic See from the royal chamber and I and my successors will be held especially faithful and obligated for it. Decreeing by this law, to be kept perpetually, that I hope firmly and trust that you and your successors will defend me and my successors and my kingdom by the authority of the Apostolic See, especially since you have caused me to be solemnly crowned as king by your hands, as if by those of Blessed Peter when I came to the Apostolic See. Moreover, so that this royal concession may obtain inviolable force, I have, with the counsel of the nobles of my court, in the presence of my venerable Father, the Archbishop of Arles, my uncle, Sancius, and Hugo of Baucé and Arnold of Fontiano, my barons, ordered it to be strengthened by the fortification of my seal. Done at Rome, at St. Peter, in the year of the Incarnation of my Lord, 1204, on the third of the Ides of November, in the eighth year of my reign.[224]

CXXII. When all these things were done properly, the Lord Pope ordered him to be led through the city to the church of St. Paul, where, finding galleys prepared, he embarked and, fortified by the Apostolic Blessing, he merited to return to his own kingdom with prosperity. The Lord Pope granted the following privilege on how the coronation of the kings and queens of Aragon was to be carried out in the future:

With such great glory and honor, stomping of feet and applause, you received the crown of kings at Rome from our hand in the monastery of Blessed Pancrazio, after we ordered you to be anointed as king by our venerable brother Peter, Bishop of Porto. Your Sublimity should be aware that we will demonstrate the influence of the affection which we have for your person more clearly by deed. All the royal insignia, namely, the mantle and tunic, scepter and orb, crown and miter, no less precious than beautiful for your work, we ordered to be prepared and we gave them freely to you as a sign of special favor. You, indeed, as a devoted and Catholic king offered your kingdom upon the altar of Blessed Peter to us and through us to the Apostolic See with much expression of devotion by a

---

in Christian Europe to the gold coin (4.45g) of the Almohad dynasty in north Africa and Spain. . . ." See Philip Grierson and Lucia Travaini, *Medieval European Coinage* (Cambridge: Cambridge University Press, 1998), 14, 466.

224. Potthast, *Regesta Pontificum Romanorum*, 1:200 (2322), November 11, 1204.

page of privilege, establishing a perpetual tribute for it, promising firmly on your coronation to observe inviolably the oath of fidelity and obedience given to us and to oblige your successors to give and observe it. Therefore, we, desiring that the favor granted to you by us should be granted to your successors, grant by the authority of these presents that when they decide to be crowned, they should be crowned solemnly by the Archbishop of Tarragona at Saragossa, asking for a crown from the Apostolic See by special mandate, prescribed about these things with suitable security and, because it has been decided by the civil law that women should share honors with their husbands, we grant by the authority of these presents, that the archbishop is permitted to crown them with his own hands. To no one, etc., of our concession, etc. If anyone, moreover, etc.[225]

[The Papal States]

CXXIII. In the tenth year, after the celebration of the feast of the Ascension, the Lord Pope left the city and went to Viterbo. He was received by the Viterbans with great joy, glory, and honor. He began to examine the situation for eliminating the filth of the Patarenes,[226] with which the city of Viterbo was very much infected, so that the Roman church might not be reproached by many that it permitted heretical depravity in its sight and also in its patrimony, and it did not have the freedom of responding about this matter to others who say, "Physician, heal yourself; first, remove the beam from your eye and then you should pull out the mote from your brother's eye" [Lk 6:41–42]. All the Patarenes, however, knowing of his coming, fled. But after he summoned the bishop and clergy of the same city, he ordered that all receivers, followers, defenders and their believers should be sought diligently and carefully described, and finally, all should be brought together by the *podestà* and the consuls to swear an oath, give securities and pledges that they would obey their com-

---

225. Potthast, *Regesta Pontificum Romanorum*, 1:200 (2322), November 11, 1204.

226. This term, used in northern Italy, referred to the Catharist heretics, but was loosely applied by some to other heretical groups.

mands. In the first place, therefore, he ordered the houses in which the Patarenes had been received to be destroyed to the ground, and then he solemnly promulgated generally to the gathered clergy and people a statute as follows:

To eliminate the filth of heretics entirely from the Patrimony of St. Peter, we establish a law to be observed in perpetuity that whenever a heretic and especially a Patarene shall be found in it, he should first be captured and then handed over to the secular court to be punished according to legitimate sanctions. All their goods should be seized so that he who captured them should receive one part, the court that punished them the other, and the third part should be devoted to the construction of walls on the land where [the heretic] was captured. Moreover, the house in which the heretic was received should be destroyed, and no one should dare to rebuild it, but it should become a sordid place of refuge that was the hiding place of perfidious persons. In addition, the believers and their followers should be fined the fourth part of their goods, which should be devoted to the use of the State. But if they are punished again in this manner when they have lapsed into the same fault, they shall immediately be expelled from their homes and never returned to them, unless by the mandate of the Supreme Pontiff, based on worthy satisfaction. Proclamations or appeals of persons of this kind should not be heard, nor should anyone be forced to respond to them in any case, but they should be forced to respond to others. Moreover, judges, advocates, and notaries should not employ their office in behalf of any of them. Otherwise they will be deprived perpetually of that office. Clerics should not administer ecclesiastical sacraments to pestilential persons of this kind and should not receive their alms or offerings; likewise, for the Hospitallers and Templars and other Regulars, otherwise they will be deprived of their office and never restored to it without special permission of the Apostolic See. In addition, whoever dares to give ecclesiastical burial to such persons, namely, believers, followers, receivers, and defenders of heretics, should be punished by the sword of anathema until there is suitable satisfaction. No such persons should be admitted as witnesses, and none may assume any public office or sit on any common council. And he who acts in such a way as a follower of heretics should be fined by the aforesaid penalty. This statute is written in the chapter to which the podestà, consuls, and rectors swear annually, and should never be removed from it, so that they will always swear that this statute will be firmly observed. And whoever refuses or neglects to keep it, after being deposed from office, will incur a penalty of one hundred pounds to be paid to whomever the Supreme Pontiff should order it to be assigned. To no one, therefore, etc., this page of our constitution, etc. If anyone, moreover, etc. Given at Viterbo on the ninth of the Kalends of October, in the tenth year of our Pontificate.[227]

CXXIV. Then he also summoned the bishops, abbots, counts and barons, the *podestà* and consuls of the cities of Tuscany, the Duchy and the March to Rome, and gathered them in a solemn court pertaining to the rights of the Apostolic See. On the first day, he set forth the rights of the Roman church, and received the oaths of all the laymen that they would appear at his order; on the second day, he heard all their quarrels and petitions; on the third day, he promulgated statutes of this kind for preserving justice and peace, which he ordered to be kept under the obligation of the oath they swore:

Since from the requirement of our office we are required to provide by paternal solicitude both for clergy and laity, lest it happen that these or those should suffer injury or cause injury, we condemn and declare completely invalid iniquitous constitutions promulgated against the laws and canons by laymen or also promulgated against churches or ecclesiastical persons, not only by spiritual but also by temporal authority under the obligation of fidelity, and forbid the lifting of anathema so that they may not dare evilly to observe constitutions of this kind. For we have decreed that whatever by occasion of these has been attempted against churches and ecclesiastical persons should be invalid and void, notwithstanding any oath that he may be said to have sworn about the observance of these things, since it should not be observed as illicit. We forbid judges and notaries to dare to exercise their office according to condemned constitutions of this kind, if they desire to avoid the loss of office. Given at Viterbo on the ninth of the Kalends of October, in the tenth year.[228]

227. Potthast, *Regesta Pontificum Romanorum*, 1:271–72 (3187), September 23, 1207.

228. Potthast, *Regesta Pontificum Romanorum*, 1:272 (3188), September 23, 1207.

CXXV. Since the counts, barons, *podestà* and consuls should be sworn to preserve peace and justice and security strictly at our command, we order your community that, preserving true peace you should in no wise attack one another, not the community attacking the community, nor person attacking person, nor person attacking community, nor should the community attack any person, save for robbers and plunderers, and with the exception of those banned and not to be trusted, for whom, having requested punishment from the rector of the Apostolic Patrimony, as often as necessary you should provide help. But if anyone commits an offense, let him not immediately be injured in return, but let him first be advised to amend the offense. And if a disagreement should arise over the amendment, unless it can be settled by another, it should be referred to the judgment of the rector of the Apostolic Patrimony. Otherwise, the person accused should be punished by him as a public enemy. But when controversy arises among some persons, let it be decided by an agreement or a trial, and let him be judge who has proper jurisdiction, save always the appeals legitimately made or even to be made to us or the rector of the Apostolic Patrimony. But if anyone established within the Patrimony of Blessed Peter should refuse to observe this custom, let him be excluded from all according to the mandate of the rector of the Apostolic Patrimony. But if anyone should receive or cause to receive booty by his own authority or if he has stolen anything or caused it to be stolen both he and the one who knowingly buys the booty and stolen goods shall restore them with a twofold penalty. But anyone who buys something stolen or booty of this kind unknowingly should restore it absolutely, having taken no recompense for himself now or in the future, but the buyer should have the right to sue the seller. We enjoin all these things under obligation of the oath sworn by the counts and barons, podestà and consuls to be observed so that they also should keep it faithfully and cause it to be observed faithfully by others throughout their districts. Save always, in all things the mandate of the Apostolic See. Dated as above.

[Papal Concerns with the Churches]

CXXVI. But when he found the monastery of St. Martin de Monte in an extreme situation, so that hardly three monks remained there, with its possessions entirely lost or mortgaged at heavy interest, the Pontiff, intending mercifully to reform it, paid a thousand pounds to redeem its possessions and wrote to the Abbot and convent of Pontigny, which is one of the first four special monasteries of the Cistercian Order, that they should receive the church of St. Martin as a special daughter and send an abbot and a community of monks and *conversi* to it, that they might reform it with a willing mind. Therefore, when they arrived, the Lord Pope blessed the Abbot. So that the religious life might flourish in that place, he granted and donated to them the church of the Holy Savior, which is situated near Orele, with all its incomes and possessions, by far, indeed, greater and better than its other possessions, assisting the brothers in those things needed for cultivating the estates and constructing buildings and granting magnificent privileges to that place.

CXXVII. Meanwhile, a report arrived from the Archbishop of Lund, whom he had appointed as legate for the conversion of the pagans, that the whole of Livonia had been converted to the Christian faith, and no one remained there who had not accepted the sacrament of baptism, and the neighboring peoples were, for the most part, ready for this.

Moreover, when great dissention broke out among the citizens, both major and lesser, of Todi, so that the more noble, having left the city, were attacking the *popolo*,[229] and as a result of this dissention many dangers now arose, namely, fires, murders, plundering, thefts, the slaughter of people, mutilations of limbs, devastation of grain fields, the destruction of houses, and even with many mediators they

229. Term used to refer to nonnoble citizens, but broadly to the popular parties of the communes, composed of lesser nobles, merchants, and craftsmen. Often allied to the church.

could not reach peace, the Lord Pope, having summoned and received corporal oaths from both parties that they would keep his mandate, composed and strengthened a true peace between them, the form of which he ordered drawn up by a public hand in writing and he sanctioned it to be preserved in the future in perpetual law.

During this same period he discussed and settled a case involving the Archbishop of Ravenna and the Commune of Faenza concerning the fortified village of Luci Aureoli and Sanctus Potitus, judging that their church belonged to Ravenna. Still, the Archbishop was laboring in such penury that he did not even have pontifical garb, and the Lord Pope, sorry for him, gave him a chasuble, tunic, and dalmatic of the best red velvet beautifully decorated with gold embroidery and pomegranates, and an amice, alb, girdle, and stoles.

Moreover, desiring to visit in person the patrimony of the Apostolic See located in those lands, the Pontiff came to Montefiascone, where he made a continuing stay of twelve days, receiving there the liege homage of the Count Palatine, Aldebrandinus. Afterward he went to Tuscania and stayed eight days in that city, and he went to Corneto, where he ordered a new palace to be built at St. Nicholas for himself, requiring likewise and demanding the rights which had been invaded by others. From there he set out through Vetralla to Sutri, where he stayed for three days, and he solemnly dedicated the cathedral church, and so he finally returned to the city.

CXXVIII. Through Gregory, cardinal deacon of Santa Maria in Aquiro,[230] the legate he sent to Hungary, he made peace between King Emeric and his brother, Duke Andrew, whose conflict was devastating almost the entire Kingdom of Hungary.

Through Martin, Prior of Camaldoli, a provident and honest man, he restored the treaty of peace between the Milanese and the Pavians, who had now divided into parties and whose ancient rivalry among

---

230. Gregory de Crescentio was cardinal deacon of Santa Maria in Aquiro from 1188 to 1200. See Maleczek, *Papst und Kardinalskolleg von 1191 bis 1216*, 90–92.

the cities of Lombardy was producing a nursery of dissension from which very often great expense and risks for persons occurred. He worked very intensely for six months for this peace.

He sent the Abbot of Casamari to reestablish peace or make a truce between King Philip of France and King John of England. When he had labored at this for a whole year, running back and forth from France to England and from England to France, finally seeing that he could not succeed, he summoned a council of archbishops and bishops and abbots at the city of Meaux, in which the King of France through the same archbishops, bishops, and abbots appealed to the Apostolic See. He was not willing to defer to their appeal unless they swore that they would pursue it in the time limit he would set for their appeal. But the Supreme Pontiff absolved them of this oath, granting them from his special favor the right to come at any time to pursue the appeal on the part of all. Therefore, the archbishops of Sens and Bourges, the bishops of Paris, Meaux, Retymo, and Nevers, and many honorable clergy, procurators for all the others, came at the time fixed. And though they waited for a long time, the king of England sent no one to represent himself, failing to pursue his case. From this negligence, it is sufficiently clear how great a loss came to him, since in a short time he lost almost all of Normandy and Anjou. The archbishops and bishops, after a long wait, professed in a public consistory under the word of truth as bishops that they had not appealed to escape the Apostolic mandate but because they believed it was in their interest, especially since they thought their king to have a just case on his side, but if this was not sufficient and they were in any way suspect by the Lord Pope, they offered a canonical purgation, which the Lord Pope granted them.

CXXX. He appointed prudent visitors to reform and correct vigilantly different provinces and he ordered them to inquire diligently not only about the status and conduct of the churches but also of prelates and he removed from their prelacies those who were found culpable, being unwilling to permit crimes to go unpunished. For who can say how many prelates he deposed from their offices? He deposed the Archbishop of Cologne, the bishop of Worms, the intruder Archbishop of Mainz, the bishops of Hildesheim and Würzburg, Chancellor of the Imperial court, the bishop of Gurk, the vicar of the Archbishop of Salzburg, and the bishop of Nuremberg. In Lombardy he induced and forced the resignation of the Archbishop of Milan, the bishops of Asti and Ivrea and many abbots. In Provence, he deposed the bishops of Toulouse, Béziers, Vence, and Viviers and many other prelates and abbots. In the kingdom of France, he unseated the bishop of Langres and abbots of Vigiliaco, of La Couture, and of Tarascon, and the Bishop of Troia in the kingdom of Sicily, who had assumed the office of Archbishop of Palermo.

CXXXI. Although Blessed Thomas of Canterbury laid down his life for ecclesiastical liberty, still his martyrdom was of little use, because the English church, by the insolence of princes, lay profoundly in the handmaidenship of servitude so that the Apostolic mandate was now kept in England like a concession and the elections of prelates never occurred freely so that one may be silent about other abuses. Moreover, it happened that, at the death of Hubert, Archbishop of Canterbury, a controversy arose about the rights and power of choosing the archbishop between the suffragan bishops and the monks of the metropolitan see of Canterbury, with the former asserting that they were accustomed and ought to be involved with the monks in the archiepiscopal election, and the latter, on the contrary, affirming that the election of the metropolitan did not involve the suffragans at all.[231] The king, however, revealing his abuse, favored the suffragans against the monks. Since the monks did not dare, out of fear, to celebrate a free election, they chose their subprior secretly in chapter under a certain pretense, and at the insistence of the king, whom they dared not resist in public, they chose the bishop of Norwich. The suffragans also

231. See Christopher R. Cheney, *Innocent III and England*, 147–54, 304–56. Also see *Selected Letters of Pope Innocent III Concerning England (1198–1216)*, ed. C. R. Cheney and W. H. Semple (London: Thomas Nelson, 1953).

chose him as a favor to the king. Therefore, both questions were brought for examination of the Apostolic See, both those that involved the right of election of the archbishop between the suffragans and the monks, and those which involved the election of the subprior on the one side and the election of the bishop of Norwich on the other, on which the community of the monks seemed to be divided, with some supporting the subprior, but others the bishop of Norwich, whom the king and suffragans also completely favored. When witnesses were produced and documents revealed sufficiently what was done by both, the Lord Pope, prudently following the *via regia*, not turning to the left or right, decided that the right and power of choosing the archbishop belonged to the monks. He imposed perpetual silence on the suffragan bishops in this case. But he cancelled both elections for lack of justice, refusing completely the gifts, of which it was said that they had been prepared to give more than eleven thousand marks for the sake of this case. But to prevent the most recent error from becoming worse if the monks were sent back to England to celebrate the election, the Supreme Pontiff, to avoid this evil, ordered the community of monks to commit the power of electing the archbishop to fifteen of their brethren, to be sent to the Apostolic See, if perhaps it should happen that both of these elections were cancelled legally, stating this to the king. When, therefore, the monks appeared at the Apostolic command, the Lord Pope, after the cancellation of both elections, enjoined on the fifteen monks that they should hold a canonical election in his presence of a suitable person, and when the wishes of the individuals were examined, several were found to agree on Master Stephen Langton, cardinal priest of St. Chrysogonus,[232] a man famed in life, knowledge, and reputation, whom the Lord Pope in the same year summoned from his teaching chair, which he held in Paris, to be cardinal priest, on whom all the monks finally agreed, but the

232. Stephen Langton, who had taught theology in Paris, was created cardinal priest of St. Chrysogonus in 1206. See Maleczek, *Papst und Kardinalskolleg von 1191 bis 1216*, 164–66.

royal ambassadors took this badly and worked to prevent it in many
ways. When the king heard this news from them, he burned with
such anger, even though the Lord Pope had written to him most kindly imploring him to grant his favor to this deed, that, after the ambassadors returned to him, he did not hesitate to inform the pope by letter that this would not be allowed. But the Lord Pope, as he was
strong and constant, consecrated the said elect with his own hands,
and after giving him the *pallium,* he sent him to carry out his pastoral
care, strictly ordering all suffragans that, unless the king, after he was
advised diligently, should agree, they should subject all of England to
ecclesiastical interdict.

And so this was finally done, with God working in a wonderful
way, that interdict should run at the same time and once and for all
through the whole kingdom of England, that it was to be observed so
strictly everywhere that no divine office or ecclesiastical sacrament
should be celebrated or exercised save for penance for the dying and
the baptism of infants, so that the corpses not only of clerics and
monks or other kinds of regulars but also of bishops should be kept
unburied outside the cemetery. Finally, because of the general complaints, the king, not being able to maintain his position, offered satisfaction by his ambassadors and letters, which he announced to the
waiting archbishop in Flanders in this way:

CXXXII. Our dearest son in Christ, John, illustrious King of England, recently sent a letter of this kind to us through the beloved abbot of
Beaulieu so that we might believe the things he proposed to us from his
side. He set forth that, although he thought he was in many ways aggrieved in the business of the church of Canterbury, still, out of the devotion and reverence he maintained that he had towards the Roman church
and our person, he was prepared to receive and treat you as archbishop of
Canterbury, having granted security both to you and yours which should
seem opportune for this. Promising full restitution both to the persons removed and to churches, he will also permit the monks of Canterbury to
return to the church and to live securely, although this seems to him
rather serious from the fact that he believes that they plotted treasonably

against him in this business. He placed the regalia in our hands through the same abbot that we might confer it at our pleasure. But asked why he would not confer these things himself but rather handed them over to be conferred by us, he answered that his mind was not yet inclined to show favor as a familiar to you. We therefore, after we heard these things, ordered from the counsel of our brothers the matter of the regalia to be carried out in this way: that we would receive the regalia without prejudice to either ecclesiastical or royal rights and would send them to be given to you, so that you may hold them as did your predecessors for their progenitors. Wherefore, we gave letters in mandate to our venerable brethren, the bishops of London, Ely, and Worcester, that, after providing prudently lest any deception should intervene contrary to ecclesiastical liberty, they may receive the offered regalia in the prescribed manner and confer them on you in our place, if perhaps the king, to whom we have written very affectionately about this, cannot be persuaded to confer them on you himself. When these things have been done properly as described above, they may relax the sentence of interdict, causing you, as is expedient, to travel to the church of Canterbury. Therefore, we advise your fraternity and exhort you more carefully, ordering by Apostolic letter that, putting your hope principally in the Lord, you satisfy the king in such a way to show him that you can match the favor of his familiarity and grace to you to better promote the profit of the church committed to you. For we hope in him in whose hand the heart of the king is and however he wishes, he will make it turn out that, just as he has now begun to direct his counsel in part in this business, so he will pursue it to a final result so that he will not infer that handing over care of government which has been received efficaciously by you is not only not an impediment but an aid. Given at Anagni, on the sixth of the Kalends of June, in the eleventh year by our Pontificate.[233]

[Rome, Again!]

CXXXIII.[234] Just as the strength of gold is proved in the furnace of persecution [Prv 27:21], God, wishing to prove the patience of his

233. Potthast, *Regesta Pontificum Romanorum*, 1:293 (3420), March 27, 1208; *Selected Letters*, 106.

234. The following section, from chapter CXXXIII to chapter CXLIII, with the

bishop in the midst of adversity, exposed him as it were as a target to arrows, causing him to be tested with many temptations by his citizens but, as we read in the Psalm: "The arrows of the children are their wounds and their tongues against them are made weak."[235] When he had received the Roman people into vassalage, certain men who, from the discord which they were accustomed to create between the pope and the Roman people, were increasing their profit, realizing that they were not able to fish in clear waters, began to stir up the water so that they might fish in it more profitably. Among them, the first and foremost were John Pierleone and John Capocci, who by their eloquence gained great favor among the people. Therefore, they found this first opportunity of stirring up trouble, saying that the Lord Pope had robbed the city of all its property, just as the sparrow-hawk plucks all the feathers from a bird; because Innocent had recovered the Sabina and the Marittima for the church and had recovered the Senate for the city. But because they profited very little in this way, they conjured up another opportunity, saying that Innocent was not choosing a representative Senate. They claimed that when he was deciding upon senators, he was favorable to his men and hostile to others. Thus, although they tried to rouse the people by many different means and had often encouraged scandal, they were still, however, unable to divide the people completely, especially as they were, as usual, trying to extort money from the pope. But Innocent himself, desirous of abolishing this very bad custom, was unwilling to ransom himself, so that they might cease from their persecution. Meanwhile, those who held the pope in contempt, grew more desirous of persecuting him: but realizing that they could not achieve this alone, they worked to draw the support of many of them and conspired together.

---

exception of chapters CXXXIV and CXXXV, were translated by Brenda Bolton. They are used here with her permission and with only minor emendations.

235. Ps 63:8. See Alanus de Insulis, *Distinctiones*, PL, 210, 930b, the *distinctio* on "sagitta." Referring to this text, Alan of Lille notes that the "sagittae parvulorum" are heretics shooting at Christ. This fits the context here. See also the *Commentatio in VII Psalmos Poenitentiales*, PL, 217, col. 1030c. I owe these references to Keith Kendall.

Thus, they made a long pause while they turned people to their side: some they drew by their simplicity, others they drew by their envy, and some they seduced by appealing to their greed.

In the meantime, the men of Viterbo so oppressed Vitorchiano that they were unwilling to receive the men of that *castrum,* unless, save for their persons and property, they would hand over the *castrum* itself to be destroyed, and, compelled by the greatest necessity, they sent messengers to the Romans and offered to become subjects immediately to their rule together with their *castrum* to avoid the imminent danger. The aforesaid criminals of the schismaticarchy discovered the means to create a disturbance by which they could bring the Roman populace to revolt against the Supreme Pontiff. They said: "We will arrange for Vitorchiano to be received under the protection of the Romans against the Viterbans, and if the Lord Pope is not willing to aid the Romans, the Roman people will revolt against him. But, if he supports them, the Viterbans and their supporters will withdraw from his rule and then war will break out by which we can better fish in troubled waters." Although, therefore, counsel of this kind quite properly displeased wise men, nevertheless, that course prevailed among the commoners so that the Viterbans were held to be hateful and it was agreed that Rome should defend Vitorchiano against Viterbo. But since the Viterbans were unwilling to cease their attack at the command of the Romans, they were denounced by the Romans, and since they gathered an army against them, after they had summoned the rectors of the Tuscan League to help against the Romans, they began to prepare to make a strong resistance. With the approach of the rectors of the Tuscan League with a strong force in support of the Viterbans, the Romans hesitated to proceed and began to complain about those who had advised them to support Vitorchiano. And so the Schismaticarchs were seen to fall into the ditch they prepared for others [Ps 7:16]. What, therefore, did these ignoramuses do, but run to the Supreme Pontiff, humbly begging for his help. But he, not only because of their insistence but also the violence of the men of Viterbo, who never wished to agree to his often-sought advice and commands about the business of Vitorchiano, indeed, even swore to support and favor the men of Narni against him, ordered them to cease injuring Vitorchiano and procure justice in his court. He promised them if they came to grant them full security for their stay and return. But since they were not willing to do this, he denounced them for their contumacy and put them under interdict, enjoining on the rectors of the Tuscan League, who had now come to their aid in Orvieto, that they should swear not to help them against the Romans. In response, they said that since they were bound to aid them by reason of the league they could not desist without committing the crime of perjury. The Lord Pope wrote to them through honorable messengers that, since they had sworn to the league for the honor of the church, they would not, without doubt, be preserving its honor if they lent their assistance to the men of Viterbo, who were condemned to account for their actions at his command and who were denounced and placed under interdict on account of this just judgment. For this reason, the rectors returned home with their army, and the Romans, with those loyal to the Lord Pope, gathered from all placed under his command, faithfully approached Vitorchiano and, fortifying it with foodstuffs and other necessities, proceeded to Viterbo. They set up camp opposite the city towards evening and engaged in battle with the men of Viterbo and were victorious. They did not wait but returned to Rome at the break of day, proclaiming praise for the Supreme Pontiff so that some who had usually opposed the pope said that their tongues would never again speak against him.

CXXXIV. But this situation lasted only for a very short time. For, when the noblemen Lando Collis de Medio and his brothers were engaged in a dispute involving Ptolomey and Jonathan, the Lords of Varni and Gabriano, they appealed to the pope on the ground, namely, that part of the land belonging to them had been seized by violence, and they sought justice from him. Their opponents were unwilling, though often cited, to undergo trial in his court. He issued a peremptory edict to them, to put them in possession of the property they sought with the help of his marshal. Those men, being very disturbed, approached John Leonis Raynerii and John Capocci, and pledged their land to them with a false contract of mortgage, pretending to hold it from them. Moreover, they began to urge the pope to grant them peaceful tenure of the land.

Recognizing their fraud, the Lord Pope ordered that the aforesaid nobles be compelled by the destruction of their crops, the cutting down of trees, the breaking up of their mills, and destruction of their goods. Although these schismatics called on the people against the Lord Pope, saying that he infringed on and took away the liberties, customs and equity of the Romans, acting to create scandal against him, he finally gathered the people together and explained the truth. He sat in judgment and forced the aforesaid nobles with threats and force to withdraw the contract of mortgage and to swear by oath to obey him in all things. They promised to give oath helpers. And so, at length, both parties put an end to the controversy.

The men of Viterbo attacked Vitorchiano and applied so much pressure that the men of Vitorchiano sought the help of the Romans, asserting that, unless they aided them quickly, given their lack of food, they could not hold out. The Senator therefore went out of the city and set up a tent in the field of St. Peter. He ordered the Romans to follow him and summoned all his neighbors and friends to the expedition. But the Romans were few. Departing in disgust, the Senator was hardly able to go to Civita Castellana. Moreover, the men of Viterbo, joined by Count Aldebrandinus, whom they put in charge, with his help and that of some of his friends, gathered a large army, with many mercenary knights and archers and they prepared to meet the Romans. The Romans were few. After they heard about their multiple preparations, they began to be afraid what to do, because it seemed to them ignominious to retreat and dangerous to proceed. But they decided the Senator should seek a loan from the more powerful citizens, with which they might hire sufficient knights and archers. Although he obtained little or nothing from some, Richard, the brother of the pope, lent a thousand pounds to them in their dire necessity, with which they proceeded to hire knights and archers to bring food to Vitorchiano. But the men of Viterbo met them and entered into battle on the feast of the Epiphany, when the pope, celebrating a solemn mass in the church of St. Peter, exhorted the people to pray for their brethren in the army that God would bring them back with prosperity and honor. On that very day, the Viterbans turned tail and fled from the Romans. Many were wounded, killed, or captured in the battle. And so the Romans returned in glory and the Senator with John Pierleonis Raynerii and many others approached the Lord Pope and prostrated themselves at this feet. They offered countless thanks to him, humbly kissing his feet.

But the Senator sent all the captives to the Canaparia to be imprisoned in very miserable conditions.[236] Among them were two elderly men, namely, Napoleon, Viscount of Campiglia, and Burgundius, Protonotary of Viterbo. The pope felt sorry for them and ordered them to be brought from the Canaparia and held in his palace for awhile and finally put in honorable custody at Lariano. Taking pity on the rest, he began to negotiate peace between the Romans and Viterbans. But after Napoleon escaped, the schismatics began to complain against the pope, railing and blaspheming to incite the people against him. Indeed, the populace was much excited by their malign suggestions. The Lord Pope, meeting their furor with a smooth tongue, has proceeded until the present to negotiate the peace and he composed this between them, preserving in all things fidelity to the Roman Pontiff and the Roman Church. So all the captives were freed, and he commanded the Viterbans to restore the bronze doors which they were said to have taken from the basilica of St. Peter and the copper bowls from the holy water font they were said to have taken or broken in the time of the Emperor Frederick.

CXXXV. Although he made this peace with the agreement of the

236. A prison near the Capitol in Rome.

Romans, nevertheless some railed against him, saying that he had made peace to his own advantage. The instigators of these rumors and evils were the Orsini, relations of the former Pope Celestine, and made rich at the expense of the Roman Church, taking advantage of the fact that there were ancient rivalries between the house of Pietro Boboni, from whom they were descended through their father, and the house of Romano de Scorta, from whom the pope was descended through his mother. Because of this they were afraid that he wished to crush them, especially as they held lands from the church, notably Viconario, Burdella and Cantalupo. However, they were able to learn nothing either by deed, word or sign. Therefore, they strove to capture the support of the people from him, under the name of fellowship, and to arouse scandal concerning him and the church, so that the pope, troubled by the people, would not be able to trouble them, and so that they could protect themselves with the support of the people. Meanwhile, therefore, their evil continued, and they awaited the absence of the pope; and when he was staying at Velletri in the summer,[237] they themselves, having laid a trap, unexpectedly and violently attacked Romano de Scorta, and the sons of John Oddolina, relations of the Lord Pope, and expelled them and their wives from their homes. When the pope heard this, he grieved greatly, not so much on account of the wrong that had been done, but on account of the future danger that he feared; and so he hastened to return. The wrongdoers, that is to say, the Orsini, approached him with their relations and friends, throwing themselves upon his judgment in all things. When he had personally received their oaths, they obeyed all his instructions without reservation, but out of fear. He also received similar oaths from the others, and these guarantees were accepted by all sides, and peace was composed between them.

CXXXVI. But Pandolf de Suburra, Senator of the City[238] and a whole-hearted supporter of the pope, was not content with these

237. From September 14 to October 9, 1202. Dates provided by Brenda Bolton.
238. Pandolf was a senator during 1202 and 1203. Information provided by Brenda Bolton.

things, and he compelled each party to swear according to his instructions. When fealty had been received from each, he took their towers into his possession, and forced them to leave the city. He ordered some to stay in St. Peter's and others to go to St. Paul's. For with them out of the way, he could exact punishment more freely and he began to demolish a certain tower of the Orsini, on account of the wrong that had been done.

CXXXVII. Meanwhile, however, Theobald di Benedetto Oddone, a cousin of the Orsini, who frequently went to St. Paul's, talked rather carelessly with the aforesaid Romano de Scorta, his son-in-law. When the sons of John Oddolina heard this, and realized that he was the principal author of all this sedition, anticipating that he was going to do evil to them, they were aroused by an evil spirit, attacked him on the road between St. Paul's and the city and wickedly killed him. When news of this reached the Orsini, they suddenly returned to the city and, supported by the people on account of the enormity of the crime, seized each of the towers that the unsuspecting Senator was holding, and destroyed to the foundations both their towers and their houses, and they carried back the body of the dead man to their home. Their plan was to lay the body with funeral lamentations not only in front of the house of Richard, the pope's brother, but also in front of the papal palace, so that they might rouse the anger of the people against them; but they were hindered and unable to carry out the plan as they had hoped. Fired up to greater enthusiasm by these conspiracies and plots, they thought up whatever evils they could, devising how they might offend the pope, or at least his friends and relations, and they took an opportunity from the fact that Odo de Poli, while his father Gregory was still living and also after his death, began to consider arranging a marriage between his son and the niece of the pope, that is to say, the daughter of the aforesaid Richard. Many negotiations had taken place between them; but at length, through the mediation of Octavian, Bishop of Ostia,[239] his paternal uncle, they

239. Octavian had been cardinal deacon of SS. Sergius and Bacchus and was

came to an agreement. When the aforesaid land, which Odo himself had bound to his progenitors with many obligations, had been freed by Richard from the burden of those obligations, Odo and his brothers, who, as the land lay bound by obligations, were scarcely able to extract a bare livelihood from it, began anxiously to have designs on it. But when they placed their complaint against Richard before the Lord Pope, the same Richard replied time and time again that he was prepared to justify himself before the pope, the cardinals and judges or even to submit himself to the arbitration of good men or a body of people. Furthermore, to show them full justice, the pope promised to bestow compassionately upon Odo and his brothers the necessary expenses for the case. But they themselves, led by wicked motives, began to conjure up falsehoods, not only against Richard but also against the pope himself, in order to excite a clamor among the people, as if in guise of piety, that is to say, that they frequently ran naked through the city to the churches with crosses. Though they had been forbidden by the pope to attempt anything like that against him, nonetheless, from the beginning they were unwilling to desist. Attempting even worse things than previously, on Easter Monday they raised a tumult and unrest among the people so that blasphemous cries having been continuously uttered, they disturbed the Divine Office in the basilica of St. Peter. When, according to custom, the pope, wearing his crown, was reverently walking through the streets, he sustained many great insults and abuse. But he proceeded boldly with a calm expression, showing no sign of concern or worry because his conscience was free and clear. But they were not content with these things, and so their latest error turned out to be greater than their first. When the Roman people had gathered in the presence of the senator on the Capitol, they presumed to give the aforesaid land, which belonged to the property of the Holy See, to the Senate and the Roman people. They gave it as far as it was theirs to give, by word because they could not give it

---

named cardinal bishop of Ostia and Velletri in 1189. He died in 1206. See Maleczek, *Papst und Kardinalskolleg von 1191 bis 1216*, 80–83.

by deed and in writing because they could not give it by law. But when the people had been called together, the pope himself, through certain of his brethren, made the disrespect for their action publicly known. Lest the law of the Church should perish, he recognized their land as belonging to the church and gave instructions to his brother Richard to defend and protect it. But now their daring stretched so far that they besieged the Senator, who was unwilling to conspire in their evils, in his palace on the Capitol, hoping to take him by storm there. But when they were unable to do this, dividing the Roman people from the Senator by lies, they moved against him so forcefully that they took up arms for the conflict, and set fire to his tower and stormed it. They then seized the tower after the senator had escaped with great difficulty, inflicting loss and injury on both him and his supporters. Therefore, the pope, seeing what passion was at large, yielded to the growing furor, and left the city, going into the country-side near Rome. When he had lingered the whole summer at Ferentino, where he had an excellent and very beautiful fountain built, he came to Anagni around the end of September. Here he became so gravely ill, that there was almost no hope of his recovery and throughout the city there were frequent rumors that his last day had come.

CXXXVIII. Meanwhile, in the city, time was drawing near for the re-election of the Senate. Messengers were appointed to seek out mediators to act as electors. For they had persuaded the people that they wanted to have not one but fifty-six senators, so that they would have some supporters, amongst the many. But because a part of them was growing too strong, when twelve mediators from those who were managing the affairs of the Church during the Pope's illness had been assigned to the people, almost all were violently taken into custody by John de Stacio, who compelled them to swear that they would each choose at least two senators from his supporters. When this had been done, the Senator delivered and handed over the Capitol to them or at least to those who favored the pope. When they themselves had sworn an oath according to the old and usual custom, the case was heard concerning the lands that belonged to Gregory de Poli. Some said that, with regard to the land, they might make no contract unless the city held the land previously. In this way, they drew the people in by their machinations. Almost all of them cried that possession of that land was handed over to the city before, and only then to the Church and to Richard. Thus, the land was recognized as being held by the city, according to a law which, however silly and unfair it was, almost everybody knew about. Therefore, when the senators were unable to agree with each other in a vote, they were no longer able to remain in the same place, and those supported by John de Stacio descended to the monastery of Domna Rosa, very close to his house. Thus, with the Senate divided, peace and justice could not be found anywhere in the city. Gradually, therefore, the people began to murmur about the evils which were being committed with impunity, and those people who were of sound mind were aggrieved by those things which were being wrongly done on account of wickedness. So though many solemn messages were sent to the pope, asking him to return to the city and though he himself was unwilling to return, because the matter did not yet seem to demand it, however, finally many more important men were sent on behalf of the people, inviting him to return. He was now, by the grace of God, fully restored to health and so he returned lest he seemed to hold the people in contempt and he was received with great honor.

CXXXIX. Although, however, the disturbance of the many had already begun to subside, nevertheless, the indignation of the malefactors did not cool yet so that, although the Lord Pope spoke kindly and benignly, asking justice for himself, as he himself had been prepared to give justice, that his word would be accepted by them. Therefore, there were consultations with the pope, and when the people had been called together, he had a mediator appointed for them who might choose one senator. But in case there could be any objections against the man that he chose to represent them, he had John Pierleone, a nobleman, appointed. He was someone approved by all the people. When an oath had been sworn, according to custom, he chose Gregory Pierleone as senator. His election seemed to be pleasing enough to the people. But the troublemakers gathered after three o'clock in the afternoon with their supporters at the monastery of Domna Rosa, and, rashly breaking the interlude of peace, which had been confirmed between the Church and the city by an agreement, the troublemakers decided to choose not senators, but their own followers, men who were infamous and criminal for they could not have good and honest men. Thus, this very latest deception was much greater than the first: for they put forward the accusation that the pope deserved to lose the agreement because he had abused it with the power with which he was entrusted. However, Gregory Pierleone, who had legitimately been elected Senator, was a loyal, gentle, and kind man, but not as courageous, vigorous and astute as the evils of the time required. Therefore, with all in confusion, all could do as they pleased. John Cappoci, realizing that he had found the opportunity to achieve what he had been waiting for, began to build up from scratch a tower right next to his house. But as this was not pleasing to Pandolf and his other rivals, they began to consider how they could hinder his plan and sent messages to him to stop building the tower. But despising their prohibition, he began to persevere more strongly with his building. Many warned him not to undertake a private cause as if it were for the common good, because he would for certain lose communal support, and that if the pope chose to support them, he might not be strong enough to resist. But as he was arrogant, he did not turn away at all from such plans, considering only the present and not the future. Therefore, they began to prepare on all sides for war. On that Easter Day, John Capocci, running through the streets, called the people to help him, affirming that on that day he would achieve complete victory over all his enemies. For he calculated that they would not be able to stand in his way, rather he would destroy them in a moment. The aforesaid Pandolf retreated to the hill above his house which is called *Ballea Neapolis,* lest the place itself should be occupied by them. When John Capocci, under arms, had approached with his supporters, Pandolf attacked with a few men and routed them, and he pursued them right up to San Quirico, raining blow upon blow. When on that day there had been fighting in different places on this side and that, Pandolf's side came out best, and many praised God that he had humbled the proud who did not respect the holy day. From that time, their side began to fail and Pandolf's to be strengthened. For Richard, brother of the pope, magnificently came to his rescue with money. They built wooden towers where they did not have stone towers, ramparts, and ditches; and they fortified the baths and the churches. They fought by day and night—and not only the retainers and foot solders on the ground, but also the guards and the servants in the towers who threw down stones and shot arrows. They set up siege engines to fire stones and arrows, hired catapult operators and archers. They fought so bitterly that in addition to the slaughters and the massacres, they lit fires to destroy houses. But as John Capocci did not stop building his tower, Pandolf began to build the "Bean Tower" on top of an ancient monument, which was so close to Capocci's house that stones could be thrown down by the slingers from there onto the other tower. John Capocci was greatly outraged, because, even though he had completed his high tower, men were not able to remain in front of his house on account of the stones being thrown. But the sons of Peter Alessio, supporters of Pandolf, built a high tower on the aforementioned hill and Gilido Carbone, also a supporter of his, erected his three grand towers. But Peter Annibaldi, the Pope's brother-in-law, began to build an opposing tower near all the entrances of the Colosseum. But he was hindered and opposed by James Frangipani and the widow of Raymond Frangipani who, as far as they could, threw down stones and arrows from the Colosseum and Raymond's tower. But he himself did not cease building in spite of all this opposition which has been recounted.

CXL. But John Capocci was anxiously thinking how he might oc-

cupy the "Bean Tower." But he only achieved this after much thought
and effort on the Feast of St. Laurence.[240] After this occupation his
strength grew and, approaching the Lateran, he seized the houses of
Pandolf which were there and destroyed them all, and took possession
of the aqueduct he had there. But Pandolf strengthened the little tower near the Colosseum, close to the church of SS. Quattro Coronati.
But John attacked it violently and such terror filled Pandolf and his
supporters that they were almost on the point of giving up. However,
he overstepped himself in his success and marched against Peter Annibaldi, the brother-in-law of the pope, and began to fight against
him, thinking to destroy him altogether. But many who had supported him, turned from him to the other, because they prized him
more. Thus resisting him, they pushed forward manfully. Then Peter
Annibaldi began to do his duty and, because of this, that side, so revived in strength began to press so hard against him that within a
short time, they violently seized his defended tower, which was com-
monly called "the White Hen" and the tower of Gregory Serraverio.
And they set fire to San Quirico, which was being defended with the
utmost force and destroyed the houses of their enemy on all sides
throughout the whole area. The tower which Baroncello, the leading
supporter of John Capocci, had built, utterly collapsed. Thus, the
courage of the one side grew stronger against the others, so that now
their strength, already weakened, almost failed. For their supporters, burdened for a long time by their efforts and financial contribu-
tions, began to fail them and they were unable to support even themselves. Also, a large number of the people now began to cry out
against them while the malefactors themselves were saying, concerning their failing resources, that the money of the pope was fighting
against them.

CXLI. Many of the people, however, advised the pope to allow
them to be shaken to exhaustion, but he was unwilling to respond to

240. August 10.

them merely to retain their favor, and so, when certain had been called kindly to him, he proposed this formula for peace.

Let four good men be chosen from above the discord and division which has grown up between them and those of the Commune who call themselves good men, and Richard, my brother, to swear to decide and judge within six months what they understand to be just, without bias, hatred, entreaty, bribery, fear, but with good faith and without deceit; unless by any chance they are able in the meantime to bring about peace voluntarily. But before anything else, may they say, concerning the matter of the Senate, that there will be a strict adherence to the boundary between the Church and the city, just as it appears in the agreement. We, for the good of peace, will proceed in this year in the matter of the Senate, according to their advice. Thus, in this way, this will not be able to create an impediment or prejudice for us in the future.

Indeed, this form was pleasing to those who had been heavily oppressed by the war and were now seeking to escape it. But in order that they might hide their evil designs, John Capocci assembled the people and laid before them the form of the peace:

The city has not been accustomed to submit in any struggle, which was undertaken against the Church. It has been accustomed to conquer not by justice but by power. But now, behold, it succumbs altogether. Against the decree of the people and the oath of the Senators, the city is abandoning the land to the church and it is strengthening the support of the Senate for the church. And, if we, who are so many and so great, fail, who from the rest will oppose him? I have never heard such a vile peace made on behalf of the city, nor do I wish to recommend agreement to such a vile peace.

John Pierleone, however, hearing that he who was making peace on behalf of the rest had thoroughly denounced it in accordance with the favor of the people, taking up his cue, began to condemn it in every way. Therefore, peace discussions could not make any progress on that day. But since they were wounded by the barbs of war, now indeed, not being asked but asking, they demanded a peace of this kind. With the common agreement of all, four men were elected who swore according to a prescribed form and immediately said that it was the Pope's right to create the Senate. But since one man could not be found who was acceptable to both sides, they advised the Pope to concede to the people fifty-six senators. But though warning them that the city could not be ruled well through so many senators, because they would quarrel amongst themselves, nevertheless, out of necessity he agreed to their demands for the present. Therefore, fifty-six senators were elected, who all swore fealty or loyalty to the Pope and among them there were quarrels, but they did make a peace of one form or another. In this way, the city began to back away little by little from the strife of war and the above-mentioned troublemakers ceased to speak against the pope and the Roman Church. Therefore, the courage and consistency of the pope did much to lead the church back as if from servitude into freedom, with the result that he was not always having to buy himself off from his persecutors and extortioners. For everyone was of one voice and opinion, that the pope should not be turned aside by wrongs or offenses, but should be aided by obedience and honor.

Meanwhile, while the war raged, two brothers, inhabitants of the Lateran, despite the prohibition of the pope, had built a fortified tower in front of the Lateran Palace alongside the ancient aqueduct which afterwards, when requested by the Lord Pope, they humbly handed over, submitting themselves in everything in accordance with his orders. For a time he held the tower under guard, but then he ordered that it be demolished, in case anyone tried anything similar. It was, therefore, completely destroyed.

CXLII. The aforesaid John Pierleone di Raniero invaded a certain part of the territory of Tusculum. When the pope demanded it back, he claimed that it had been conceded to him by Pope Celestine. But when he could not prove that, after many warnings, the pope threatened to entangle him in the snare of excommunication. But when he heard this, he was very indignant. Since he was arrogant and proud, he thundered that the pope would not dare to attempt against him what none of his predecessors had dared to do for otherwise he would get into a predicament from which he could not easily escape. This was the principle reason why he himself raised the above-mentioned scandal against the Supreme Pontiff. But the same generous pope, lest he should seem to be a dumb dog, not healthy enough to bark, solemnly excommunicated him on the Feast of the Dedication of the Basilica of St. Peter in the presence of a great multitude. Therefore, although there was grumbling, he swore to stand by his contract, and thus stood absolved. And presently, when he was dying, because the pope was not yet satisfied, warned his heirs that if they did not swear to obey his instructions, when he should die, he would forbid him a Christian burial. But when they had sworn oaths and shown him fidelity, he allowed the dead man to be buried according to the custom of the Church.

However, just as the Lord Pope had predicted, the senators behaved so badly in the running of affairs that both within the city and without many evils were committed with impunity by anybody, while peace and justice had been thoroughly banished. Therefore, the people began to curse to such an extent that the pope had to bend to the common petition for a single senator, although it much displeased the troublesome nobles who, at the time of upheaval, were boasting amongst other things that the Lord Pope would never be able to appoint a single senator in the city. But the Senator, presented by the Pope, immediately brought the city back to peace and justice, suppressing rebellions and uprisings. No one dared to utter anything against him, dreading the power of the Supreme Pontiff.

[Works of Piety: The Gift List]

CXLIII. In the meantime, Innocent, trusting in the Lord, was pressing on with works of piety. For when a great famine prevailed with such rumors that a *rublum*[241] of grain sold from twenty to thirty solidi,

---

241. A large dry measure for grain.

he was then staying in Anagni; he returned to the city right away and began to pay out liberally the necessary alms for needy people. Moreover, he ordered them to be distributed so that those who were afraid to beg in public might receive money in secret, from which they might be supported a whole week, but those who were begging publicly would receive bread for each day sufficient for everyone, of whom there was a huge crowd of every condition, that surpassed the number of eight thousand persons. Moreover, some received food in the alms house and so he freed the starving people from immediate danger, exhorting the rich and powerful equally by word and example to give alms. Indeed, how much money he spent on this work, no one knows. From the beginning of his reign, in fact, he set aside the entire income belonging to him from the offerings to the basilica of St. Peter for alms. In addition, he ordered a full tenth of his entire income to be set aside for the work of alms, and from the rest, he very often gave large alms, although in secret. The almoner received all the offerings of those coming to his feet according to the ancient custom and paid them out. He, therefore, ordered the hungry to be fed, the naked to be clothed, poor virgins to be provided with dowries, and exposed children to be nursed. He frequently supported indigent monks and nuns, recluses and hermits, and he often visited religious houses and freed them from their debts. His almoner went about and investigated diligently the poor and weak, especially nobles, and he gave them seals so that each week he might send money for food for those who brought them back, and quite often he was spending fifteen pounds a week for such persons, not counting those who daily received food or money or clothes. The very generous pontiff also allowed poor children to come to the table at the end of the meal for food and he gave them what remained before him. On Saturdays, he made the *mandatum*, washing and wiping, and kissing the feet of twelve poor people and giving twelve coins to each, ordering refreshment for everyone.

CXLIV. Also, at his own expense, he built the hospital of the Holy Spirit at St. Mary in Sassia for the needs of the sick and poor on the public street beside the Tiber in front of the basilica of St. Peter. He enriched and endowed it with buildings, possessions, rents, treasures, ornaments, books, and privileges to the degree that seemed sufficient, and so that religious worship and the favor of hospitality which now flourishes there would always be abundant. Moreover, he established at the same hospital the solemn station for the first Sunday after the Epiphany, on which the Christian people flocked there to see and venerate the *sudarium*[242] of the Savior that they carry in procession with hymns and canticles, palms and torches, from the basilica of St. Peter to that place, to hear and understand the exhortatory sermon, which the Roman Pontiff delivers there about works of piety and meriting and obtaining forgiveness of sins which is promised to those exercising the works of mercy, to which as others he summons them not only with words but by example. For all the needy flocking to those spiritual marriages, he ordered bread, meat, and money to be given, and the most prudent prelate explained the reason for all these things in a homily which he delivered on the Gospel of that day.

CXLV. To what degree he was generous and caring about worship and the ornament of churches the following makes clear. He conferred on the basilica of the Savior, called Constantinian,[243] the church of Frascati in the territory of Tusculum with its holdings, just as it is contained in fixed boundaries, a precious vestment of old velvet with gilt everywhere covering the altar, having on the anterior side the image of the Savior and images of the Blessed Virgin, John the Baptist, the Prince of the Apostles, and wonderfully the sign of the emperor, and a noble dalmatic with gilt, the monastery of St. Andrew in Silice with all its properties, its hospital, possessions in Tusculan territory. Likewise, to the same basilica, a golden cross, worked with precious stones and a gilded silver pedestal for the same cross valued at seven

---

242. The towel with which the face of Jesus was wiped on the way of the cross.
243. The church of St. John Lateran, built by Constantine, the cathedral of Rome, originally called the church of the Savior.

marks, a golden chalice, worth seventeen and a half ounces, and a golden spoon, valued at two ounces and one tarenus.[244]

For the basilica of St. Peter, he granted a fourth share of the offerings of all the ministries and the right of making leaden or tin badges and the income from them.[245] He gave it a golden chalice, worth seventeen and a half ounces, a golden cross with a gilded silver pedestal, two very precious and beautiful texts of the Gospels of gold and enamel, with pearls and gems, a precious red vestment with golden peacocks for the decoration of the altar, a chasuble, a tunic, dalmatic and pluvial of white velvet carefully decorated with pomegranates and gold embroidery, amice and cincture, alb and stole. He also subjected the churches of St. Mary in Sassia and St. Mary in Transpondina to it and donated a royal drape with images wonderfully woven in gold and an ample cloak of German workmanship, one pair of silver basins, worth six marks, and one pair of candelabra, and a piece of gilded cloth of the best German workmanship with two pieces of good gold embroidery. He ordered the apse of this basilica to be decorated with a mosaic and in front of this basilica he ordered the mosaic, which was for the most part destroyed, to be restored.

Also he ordered the walls and roofs of the oratory of St. John ad Fontes repaired.[246]

For the basilica of St. Paul, a tunic, dalmatic, and chasuble of green velvet well prepared and a large woven cloth of purple and gold and an ample cloak; also to the same basilica a noble cloth with images wonderfully made with golden texture for the altar and a golden jar worth four and a quarter and a half ounces decorated all over with precious stones. Also, for the mosaic of the same basilica, one hundred pounds and sixteen ounces of gold. He granted the same basilica Monte Porzio Catone in Tusculan territory.

---

244. A Sicilian gold coin.

245. Brenda Bolton, "Qui fidelis est in minimo: The Importance of Innocent III's Gift List," in *Pope Innocent III and His World*, 113–40, esp. 123–24.

246. Chapel at the Lateran.

For the basilica of St. Mary Major, a red vestment with golden peacocks, an altar cover, bottles, one silver and the other crystal, for the
ministry of the Sacrifice and twenty pounds for the repair of the roof,
and a gilded silver flask valued at six marks less four ounces, and a
chalice worth seventeen and one half ounces of gold, with precious
stones and enamel and a tunic and a dalmatic.

For the basilica of St. Lawrence outside the walls a red vestment
with gold peacocks and an altar cover. Also for the same basilica, one
hundred pounds of revenue, and a cope of red velvet with gold embroidery and a chalice of gold worth sixteen ounces and half, a pair of
silver basins at eight marks less one half ounce, and again for the same
basilica, a hundred pounds for the church of St. Agnes, purple for the
altar, and a vase of silver at three marks, and seventy pounds of revenue for repair of the basilica of St. Constance and the portico of the
church of St. Agnes.

For the basilica of St. Lawrence within the Palace a cope of red velvet decorated with gold embroidery and a cask, worth two marks of
silver.

For the monastery of St. Gregory in Clivo Scauri , a cope of red velvet with gold embroidery, purple, and a canopy and an altar cover for
the use of the altar and a gold ring with precious stones.

For the church of St. Mary on the Aventine, two pieces of velvet,
namely red and violet, carefully decorated with gold embroidery and a
hundred pounds of revenue to buy a mill. Also, at another time, for
the same purpose, thirty pounds of revenue and a large silk cloth woven with gold.

For the monastery of St. Alexis, gilded purple for the altar.

For the church of SS. Sergius and Bacchus, which was in bad condition and threatening ruin, he rebuilt the walls and roof and the altar
with rails and steps. He ordered a columned porch to be built in the
pontificate, giving it a cope of violet velvet with gold embroidery, a
canopy and altar cloth, an ivory chest, corporals and a pyx for the Eucharist, a robe of Limoges manufacture and twenty pounds. Also, for

that church, a silver incense boat and a silver spoon worth seven and one half ounces, and one cloth of red velvet with gold embroidery and gold embroidery for an amice and a large chasuble with gold embroidery and silk thread for the altar and a gilded chalice for eighteen ounces of silver. Also one hundred pounds of revenue.

For the church of St. Mark a thurible of silver, one hundred massemutinas and the same number of solidi, a silk vestment with gild for the altar. Also, one hundred pounds of revenue and a candle of silver worth five marks and two ounces with twelve golden obols and, at another time, a hundred pounds.

For the church of St. Lawrence in Damasus a red vestment with gold peacocks, a cope of red velvet with gold embroidery and a hundred pounds.

For the church of Santa Maria Rotunda a chasuble and a dorsal carefully ornamented with gold embroidery.

For the church of St. Thomas "de hispanis" a chasuble and cope of red velvet with gold embroidery, a gilded vestment for the altar and a cover and ten pounds.

For the church of St. Andrew "de Unda" a cloth of red velvet.

For the church of St. Stephen in the Lateran a cloth of red velvet carefully decorated with gold embroidery.

For the church of St. Stephen "de schola cantorum," a cope of red velvet decorated with gold embroidery.

The church of Santa Pudenziana, three pounds for its repair.

For the church of St. Thomas "de Forma," twenty pounds to buy back a certain piece of its land.

For the church of St. Martin ai Monti, a red vestment with gold borders for the altar.

For the church of St. Marcellus, a black vestment with gold birds for the altar.

For the church of St. Stephen "in Celiomonte," a black vestment with gold birds, for the altar.

For the church of Fossanova, for the completion of the building of the church, a hundred pounds.

For the church of St. Mary "de Roscillo" near Cambiano, a cloth of red velvet with gold embroidery and, at Signi, he granted it the church of St. Simeon with its holdings.

For the monastery of Casamari, for its building fund, two hundred ounces of gold, possessions for a grange near Castrum.

For the church of St. Mary "de Rondineto" situated in the diocese of Como, a chasuble of red purple and another of black purple and a red dalmatic speckled with saffron color and a red tunic marked with certain borders and carefully decorated with gold embroidery and a silk stole with a gold embroidery apparatus.

For the church at Orte, a chasuble of red velvet carefully decorated with gold embroidery, a tunic with heaven-blue borders and a dalmatic and gold embroidery.

For the church of St. Mary "de Campitolio," a chasuble of red velvet decorated in a praiseworthy manner with gold embroidery.

For the church of Holy Cross a chasuble of purple.

For the church at Anagni, silk fabric with gold edges and a silver basin.

For the church of St. Mary of Anagni, a gilded altar cloth.

For the church of Viterbo, a cope of red velvet with gold embroidery and a gold ring.

He sent a chasuble to the Patriarch of the Bulgarians, as well as a tunic of white velvet nicely decorated with gold embroidery and a large ring with five topazes which he had had for his own use, a miter with gold embroidery, a shirt, amice, a manual stole, a cincture, shoes, sandals, gloves, and other ornaments consistent with being a patriarch.

To the Bishop of Branitschewo, who approached the presence of the Pope, a gold ring with an emerald and a miter with nicely arranged gold embroidery.

For the church of St. Mary "in Sassia," an altar cloth, a towel of Germanic workmanship with the whole having gold embroidery carefully placed there, a chasuble of red velvet with gold embroidery, a cloak of red velvet decorated with gold embroidery, a gilded silver chalice, a silver jar for wine and another crystalline jar for water, a pair of candelabras of silver at five marks, and a pair of basins of silver at five marks, a silver thimble at five marks and five ounces, a towel for service of the altar. Also, another shirt, amice, and stole, a silver chest of marks having on the front a gold cross of ounces in whose midst was an onyx stone having a sculpture of Christ despoiling Hell and in the extremities of the extended arm two sapphires and at the top of the erect arm two pomegranates, and in the corners, hyacinth, amethyst, chalcedonium and a sapphire.

For the monastery of Subiaco, a chasuble carefully decorated with gold embroidery and thirty pounds of revenue.

For the rectors of the Roman fraternity, a dorsal and a large towel of German workmanship. Also, a silk cloth with gold stars because he consecrated the altar in their church in honor of the Virgin Mary, for whose use he also gave a fine towel of German workmanship.

For the church of Santa Sabina, a pair of silver basins of two marks and five ounces of silver.

For the restoration of the church of St. Panteleon, which was burned, three pounds.

For the church of the Holy Savior "de Monte Arnisto," near Radicofani, a chasuble of red velvet with gold embroidery.

For the church of St. Lothar in Rieti, whose altar the Lord Pope consecrated, a cloth with lions.

For the church of St. John in Rieti a silk cover with cloth of leopard.

For the church of St. Mary of Spoleto, whose altar he consecrated, a silk cover.

For the church at Ferentino, a chasuble of red velvet with gold embroidery.

For the basilica of the Twelve Apostles, thirty pounds for its repair.

He also ordered an inquiry through all the churches of the city which did not have silver chalices and he gave chalices to each not having one out of reverence for the sacred mystery of the body and blood of Christ. Moreover, their number was one hundred and thirty-three, the weight of one hundred silver marks.

In his chapel he placed all vases of gold, namely, crosses and candelabra, chalice, and thurible, ampules, and water cruets, small chests and basins and others suited for use of the altar, but also gold rings with every kind of precious stones, also pontifical vestments, of all kinds of colors, decorated with gold, pearls, and gems, and very precious and beautiful miters with enamel cleverly worked with pearls, likewise gloves and sandals, so that now the chapel would be seen to be rich not so much in matter as in form.

CXLVI. But because he thought it not only honorable but useful that the Supreme Pontiff should also have a worthy palace at St. Peter, he ordered these buildings to be rebuilt: the chapellancy, the chamber and chapel, the bakery, the butcher shop, and kitchen and stable, the houses of the chancellor, chamberlain and almoner, he ordered the hall to be strengthened and the loggia rebuilt, and the whole palace to be enclosed with walls and towers to be erected on the gates. He also bought a house between the cloister of the palace which he set aside for the dwelling of a physician.

At the Lateran, he also ordered a palace that is above the chapellancy in which the Roman Pontiff had not yet lived, to be prepared, making a roof over the chamber and the entry to the chamber, a toilet, and a small chamber over the apse and elsewhere about the palace, with high and ample candle-holders, which in the vernacular they call *scontros*. He also ordered two chambers to be built at the alms house, also a chamber near the chapel and an oratory before the mirror and a furnace for the oven. He ordered the consistory to be paved and marble steps for ascending to it.

CXLVII. He was very generous to his familiars, conferring benefices and honors on them. For, from his chaplains, he promoted these to offices: Hugolino, cardinal deacon of St. Eustachius, whom he also made Bishop of Ostia; Leo, to cardinal priest of Santa Croce. John, to cardinal priest of Santa Maria in Cosmedin, whom he later made chancellor of the Roman church. Peter, to cardinal priest of Santa Pudenziana; Nicholas, to Bishop of Tusculum; John, to cardinal deacon of Santa Maria in Via Lata; Octavius, to cardinal deacon of SS. Sergius and Bacchus; John, to cardinal deacon of Saint Cosmas and Damian; Paul, to Bishop of Orte; Benedict, to Fondi; Rainer to Bishop of Toscania; John, to Bishop of [actually Forconi] Aquila,[247] whom he later translated to Bishop of Perugia; Egidius, to Bishop of Gaeta; Albert, to Bishop of Ferentino; Peter, to Bishop of Mileto; Saxo, to Bishop of Teramo; Raynald, to Archbishop of Capua; Bartholomew, to Bishop of Trani; Blasé to Archbishop of Torres; Raynald, to Archbishop of Acerenza; Odo, to Bishop of Valva; John, to Abbot of Santa Euphemia. Also he made Peter Ishmael, who had been his teacher in the city, Bishop of Sutri and Peter of Corbeil, who had been his teacher in Paris he made Bishop of Cambrai, and later promoted him to be Archbishop of Sens.

He was especially generous concerning poor, honest, and educated clergy so that without doubt he would order them to be provided with several benefices everywhere in the world, as had been provided for by his predecessors for forty years in the past.

CXLVIII. But because there was too great a superfluity in the world, especially among prelates, he who began to act and teach reduced himself to a modest level so that he could reprove them more freely and correct them by his example, that he changed gold and silver vases into wood and glass, ermine and bear skins to lamb. He wanted his table to be satisfied with the servings and with his two chaplains, employed for the daily ministry of the table religious without laymen, so that he might be served more honestly by regulars, unless a great feast or some other solemnity required more and, with the usual duties, however, limited to nobles who served according to custom on feast days.

CXLIX. He set aside a moderate sum from the treasury and put it in a separate place for urgent needs should any arise. But he paid out al-

247. See RI 2:167 (176), 323, n. 3. Aquila was the diocese after 1256. Perhaps this is a scribal error.

most all the rest in this way: a thousand pounds of revenue he paid out in support of the Holy Land. A hundred pounds of revenues in gold to the nuns of Acre to buy property; a thousand silver marks for the use of the hospital of the Holy Spirit "in Sassia," of which six hundred were in vases and forty in gold plate; for the construction of St. Sixtus for the nuns, fifty ounces of gold of the king and eleven hundred pounds of revenue. For the church of St. Agnes, a hundred pounds of revenue. For the repair of the church of San Quirico, a hundred pounds of revenue. For the monastery of St. Gualgano of Toscania, a hundred pounds. For the monastery of Santa Maria de Faleria, from the denarii the Lord Pope had lent it, he sent back a hundred pounds. For the Monastery of San Pancrazio, fifty pounds of revenue. For the monastery of St. Bartholomew "de Trisulto," for construction, a hundred pounds. For the monastery of Fossanova, a hundred pounds of revenue. For the monastery of Casamari, a hundred pounds of revenue. For the monastery of Marmosolio, a hundred pounds of revenue. For the church of St. Mary of the Aventine, a hundred pounds of revenue. For the church of St. Basil, a hundred pounds of revenue. For the monastery of Santa Maria de Ferraria, ten ounces of gold "de rege." For the church of St. Sebastian, fifty pounds of revenue. For the hospitals of the city fifty pounds of revenue. For the work of St. Vitus "de Macello," ten pounds of revenue. To Brother Guido, rector of the Hospital of the Holy Spirit, a hundred pounds of revenue. To the Hermits of Albano, fifty solidi. For the nuns of Butrino near Viterbo, ten Sienese pounds. For the nuns of St. Leopardus "de Tereto," ten Sienese pounds. For the hospital "de Rigo Saguin-ario," fifty Sienese solidi. For the monastery of St. Martin "de Monte" near Viterbo, a thousand Sienese pounds. For the church of St. Nicholas "de Corneto," a hundred Sienese pounds. For the church of Vetralla, ten Sienese pounds. To Brother William, procurator of the Holy Spirit in Saxia, two hundred pounds of revenue. For the church of St. Peter, a very precious vestment with pearls and gold and a large towel with gold embroidery with pearls. For the church of St. John "de Insula," a chasuble of red velvet. For the church of SS. John and Paul "de Ferentino," a chasuble of red velvet. For the church of St. Lawrence in Viterbo, a chasuble of red velvet and a towel with gold embroidery. For the church of St. Angelo "de Spata" in Viterbo, a cloak of red velvet. For the church of Santa Maria Nova in Viterbo, a cloak of red velvet. For the church of Toscania, one half a cover and a towel. For the church of Santa Maria "de Iuliano," a chasuble of red velvet with gold embroidery. For the church of St. Mary in "Saxia," two large German-made towels. For the monastery of Cassino an ample dorsal for the altar.

For the Bishop of Porto, a chasuble of red velvet. For the Bishop of Ostia, a canopy. For John "de Colonna," cardinal deacon of SS. Cosmas and Damian, a chasuble of black velvet and a dalmatic of white silken cloth. For the Archbishop of Ravenna, a shirt, amice, tunic, dalmatic, and chasuble of red velvet with gold embroidery, with a stole and manciple. For the Lateran church, a large chalice of gold with a paten, weighting sixty-two ounces of gold. For the monastery of Fossanova, a gold cup, forty-two and a half ounces, when he consecrated its altar. For the church of Santa Restituta at Sora, a cloak of red velvet with gold embroidery. For the cathedral church of the same city, purple woven with gold. For the marriages of widows and orphans a thousand pounds.

CL. He removed the sons of nobles, who they call valets, from his court, giving each a sum of money directly from which they could be invested honorably with a military belt. This amounted to almost a thousand pounds. Moreover, he not only gave alms to orphans and widows, to the poor and infirm, but also he showed generosity to domestics and neighbors, both clerical and lay, and this came to more than four thousand pounds.

APPENDIX I. MARTIN OF TROPAU'S LIFE OF INNOCENT III

Innocent, who was born in the Compagna, was consecrated on the feast of St. Peter's Chair and reigned eighteen years, four months, and twenty-four days. Insofar as he was glorious, his works testified to the truth. For he built the Hospital of the Holy Spirit and he renovated the church of St. Sixtus. He composed decretals, sermons, and books *On the Misery of the Human Race* and many other glorious matters. He gave a pound of silver to all the churches in Rome for chalices for each of them not having silver chalices, with the proviso that they could not sell them. He also crowned Otto and deposed him because he did not keep his oath. At this time, Constantinople, a city, indeed one of the greater cities in the world and first in magnificence, was captured by the Franks and Venetians. The inhabitants of the city hardly believed it had been captured even after several days both because of the strength of its fortifications and because of an ancient prophecy they believed. For it had been prophesied that it would be captured by an angel, and so they did not believe that it could be captured by men. But with the enemy entering the city through the wall where an angel was depicted, the inhabitants recognized that they had been deceived by the ambiguity of the word angel. In this period, Livonia was partly converted to the faith. In November of the seventeenth year of his pontificate, in the Lateran Basilica, called Constantinian, a general council for the aid of the Holy Land, for the state of the universal church, was celebrated; many useful statutes were promulgated there. A total of one thousand three hundred and fifteen prelates, with patri-

Appendix I

archs, archbishops, bishops, abbots, and other prelates, took part. During this Council, he consecrated the church of Santa Maria in Trastevere. Finally, when he intended to make peace among the Pisans, Genoese, and Lombards for the sake of the support of the Holy Land, having set out on the journey for this purpose, he died in Perugia. He was buried there in the church of St. Lawrence. And the papacy was vacant for only a day because the Perugians pressured the cardinals very hard for the election to be held.

He condemned Abbot Joachim and the pamphlet he composed against Peter Lombard. He also condemned a certain Amaury of Chartres along with his teaching, as we see in the decretal *Damnamus*. There Amaury asserted that ideas which are in the Divine mind create and are created, since according to Saint Augustine nothing can exist in the Divine mind that is not eternal and unchangeable. He also said that for this reason God is called the end of all things because everything will return to him, so that they will rest unchangeably in him and remain one individual and unchangeable in him. And just as Abraham is not of a different nature from Isaac, but of one and the same, so he said that all things were one and all were God. Likewise, he said that just as light is not seen in itself, but in the air, so God will not be seen in himself by angels or mankind, but only in creatures. He also asserted that if man had not sinned, he would not have been divided into two sexes, and he would not have procreated, but mankind would have been multiplied in the way in which the holy angels are multiplied; and after the resurrection, both sexes will be united, just as, he asserts, was the case earlier at the creation, and he said that this was true of Christ after the resurrection. And all these errors are found in a book entitled *Peri Fiseon*, which is put among the other books condemned in Paris.

Liber Pontificalis, 1:451–52.

APPENDIX II. SIGNIFICANT
EMENDATIONS TO THE EDITION OF
THE *GESTA INNOCENTII III* BY
DAVID GRESS-WRIGHT

The following list of changes in the text of the Gress-Wright edition
is based chiefly on two sources. The first is Ms Vat. Lat. 12111, a fourteenth-century transcript of the original manuscript, long housed in
the Vatican archives. The manuscript was transferred from the
archives to the Vatican Library in 1920. The second is *Die Register Innocenz' III,* edited by Othmar Hageneder, Anton Haidacher, et al. (Graz-
Cologne: Böhlaus Nachfolger, 1964–). Only the first two years were
available at the time Gress-Wright was preparing his edition. The registers have been valuable for comparative purposes.

GW, page:11, l. 7: "seviant" for "serviant"; "subesse" for "prodesse." RI
1:401, 600, l. 22 11, l. 8: "prodesse" for "subesse." RI 1:401, 600, ll.
21–22.

11, l.19: "utrimque grata" for "utrique gratia." RI 1:401, 601, l. 3.

22, l. 25: Insert after "iuramento firmare ut super . . ." the following ". . .
mandatis apostolicis obediret, respondit quod in spirtualibus absolute
pareret, in temporalibus autem iustus mandatis parendi prestaret iura-
toriam cautionem. Quod cum sibi fuisset assertum, quia propter cum
consueta forma iurandi nullatenus mutaretur, promisit tandem in
scriptis quod" . . . and continues ". . . super omnibus pro quibus ex-
communicatus iuraret." Vat Lat 12111, f. 5r, seventh last line to fourth
last line. PL, 24, cap. XXIII, col. xliiid.

68, l. 3: "ad" for "ab." Typographical error.

86, l. 13: "inspiravit, ut" for "inspiraret. Ųt. . . ." RI 2:202 (211), 394, l. 23.

148, l. 18: "mitius et benignius tibi" for "minus etiam benignius. . . ." RI 7:126, 201, l. 29.

180, l. 8: "vertentes" for "vententes." Typographical error.

180, l. 13: "terga" for "tera." Typographical error.

182, l. 4: Insert "quomodo venit in domum Dei et panes propositionis sumpsit et manducavit et dedit hiis qui cum ipso erant" after "cum eo erant . . ." RI 6:102, 168, ll. 10–12.

196, l. 10: "milibus" for "militibus." Vat Lat 12111, l. 22.

204, l. 18: Insert "gloriose coronatum ad imperii fastigia Deo et hominibus amabiles patres memorati pontifices cum universorum applausu et piis lacrimis sublimarunt. Aderant incole terre sancte" after "terre sancte" and before "ecclesiastice." RI 7:152, 259, ll. 17–20.

207, l. 8: "conveniret" for "couniret." Typographical error.

213, l. 13: "Frater non redimet, redimet" for "Insuper non redimet homo." RI 8:134 (from proofs) and Vat. Lat. l2111, ll. 24–25.

216, l. 13: "iurisdictionem" for "justitiam," also in Vat. Lat. 12111, fol. 44r, l. 11.

254, l. 9: Insert "decoratus" after "honore; om. recepto." RI 8: 154 (from proofs); Vat Lat 12111, 53v, l. 24 has "consecratus honore, te post. . . ."

261, l. 13: "iter" for "inter." Typographical error.

275, l. 22: "domus" for "domini."

275, l. 24: "nobis" for "vobis."

291, l. 14: Insert "cum domino collegato ad se accedente quia instantissime vestram appellabamus precellans aurum consilio domino" after "habito consilio" and after "P. cardinalis." RI 8, 120(119) (from proofs). Also, Vat Lat 12111, ll. 16–18.

296, l. 22: "misi" for "nisi."

326, l. 11: "visi" for "nisi."

347, l. 9: "duarum" for "quarum."

APPENDIX III. TERRACINA

by Brenda Bolton

Terracina[1] is situated at the point where the Via Appia meets the coast at the foot of the Ausoni Mountains. It was always of importance to Rome, whether as a Roman colony or as a strategic town where Trajan cut a tunnel through the rocks to allow passage of the Appia. It was equally important in the medieval period as the main point of entry to the Papal States from the south, guarded by the strategic Rocca de Traversa.

The Rocca de Traversa and the nearby stronghold of Circeo were held by the Frangipani family, already declining in importance by Innocent III's pontificate, but still able to cause trouble. The citizens of Terracina likewise had a long history of struggling for their independence, not only against the Frangipani and the popes but also against their near neighbors, the Counts of Fondi. Such rivalries severely tested the loyalties of the local bishops, Fidelgarius or Tedelcarius (?) (d. 1203), who dedicated the church of Santa Maria de Flumine at Ceccano in 1196, and Simon (1203–1238).

In the second half of the twelfth century, the Terracinensi had rebelled against the Frangipani and declared a commune. In 1185, the Frangipani were forced to swear an oath to the commune, renouncing all rights over Terracina, promising to acquire no more towns in the

---

1. Dominico Antonio Contatore, *De Historia Terracinensis libri quinque* (Rome: Apud Aloysium & Franciscum de Comitibus, 1706).

273

area and to form no hostile alliances against its citizens. On their side, the citizens swore an oath to the Frangipani, obliging them to hold and defend Terracina and Circeo, forbidding alliances against them, and restoring all rights and goods usurped during the violence.

The agreement had been broken by the Terracinensi who had occupied both the Rocca de Traversa and Circeo. On June 28, 1203, in his letter "Satis vobis," Innocent ordered the transfer of both rocks to the Frangipani and when, by December 8, 1203, this had not been done, the Terracinensi were ordered to consign the Rocca de Traversa to Peter Annibaldi, the pope's brother-in-law. The commune felt itself threatened by the use the church might make of the strategic rocks, the occupation of which would constitute a threat to the growing communal authority. Furthermore, there was conflict within the Frangipani family. James and Deodato intended to subject the people of Terracina by force of arms to Count Richard of Fondi whilst the other branch, represented by Manuel, Peter, and Odo, was more conciliatory. The problems of the church and the Frangipani family helped the people of Terracina in their quest for independence.

On February 9, 1204, Innocent gave sentence in favor of the Frangipani in regard to the damage they had suffered to their rights over Terracina. On March 7, 1207, Manuel, Odo, and Peter swore an oath similar to that of 1185. They renounced their rights over Terracina, and promised to acquire no more towers in the city and to form no alliances with the Count of Fondi or other enemies of the commune. Other rights, not considered in 1185, were now dealt with: that is, half of the fishing de barciis, half of the income from the port, half of the duty on salt, and many other rights not considered in the oath of 1185.

BIBLIOGRAPHY

Manuscript

Vat Lat 12111, fourteenth century.

Primary Sources

Alanus de Insulis. *Distinctiones. PL* 210.

Ambrose, St. "Contra Auxentium." *PL* 16.

Andrea, Alfred. *Contemporary Sources for the Fourth Crusade.* Leiden: Brill, 2000.

————. *The Medieval Record: Sources of Medieval History.* Boston: Houghton Mifflin, 1997.

Barbiche, Bernard. *Les actes pontificaux originaux des archives nationales de Paris.* 2 vols. Vatican City: Biblioteca Apostolica Vaticana, 1975.

Codex Diplomaticus Dominii Temporalis S. Sedis. Recueil des documents pour servir à l'histoire du gouvernment temporel du Saint Siège. Edited by Augustin Theiner. 3 vols. Rome, 1861–1862; reprint, Frankfurt-am-Main: Minerva, 1964.

Gress-Wright, David [David Wright]. *The "Gesta Innocentii III": Text, Introduction and Commentary.* Ph.D. diss., Bryn Mawr College, 1981.

The Liber Augustalis or Constitutions of Melfi Promulgated by the Emperor Frederick II for the Kingdom of Sicily. Translated with an introduction by James M. Powell. Syracuse, N.Y.: Syracuse University Press, 1971.

Regestum super Negotio Romani Imperii. Edited by Friedrich Kempf, S.J. Rome: Pontificia Università Gregoriana, 1947.

Die Register Innocenz III. Edited by O. Hageneder, A. Haidacher, W. Maleczek, and W. Strnad. 6 vols to date; years 1–2, 5–8. Graz: Böhlau, 1965–.

Selected Letters of Pope Innocent III Concerning England (1198–1216). Edited by C. R. Cheney and W. H. Semple. London: Nelson, 1953.

Stürner, Wolfgang. *Die Konstitutionen Friedrichs II für das Königreich Sizilien* *MGH. Leges, 51* Hannover: Hahnsche Buchhandlung, 1996.

Testi storici veneziani (XI–XIII secolo): Historia ducum Venetorum, Domenico Tino, Relatio de electione Dominici Silvi Venetorum ducis. Edited with translation by Luigi Andrea Berto. Padua: ACoop Libraria Editrice Università di Padova, 2000.

Secondary Sources

Abulafia, David. *Frederick II: A Medieval Emperor.* London: Penguin Press, 1988.

Barone, Giulia. "I 'Gesta Innocenzo III': Politica e cultura a Roma all' inizio del duecento." In *Studi sul medioevo per Girolamo Arnaldi,* ed. Giulia Barone, Lidia Capo, and Stefano Gaspari, I libri de Viella, 24 (Rome: Viella, 2001), 1–23.

Bolton, Brenda. "Qui fidelis est in minimo: The Importance of Innocent III's Gift List." In *Innocent III and His World,* ed. John C. Moore (Aldershot: Ashgate, 1999), 113–40.

———. "Too Important to Neglect: The Gesta Innocentii PP. III." In *Essays Presented to John Taylor,* ed. G. Loud and I. N. Wood (London: Hambledon Press, 1991), 87–99. Also in Brenda Bolton, *Innocent III: Studies on Papal Authority and Pastoral Care* (Aldershot: Variorum, 1995), essay 4.

Brühl, Carlrichard, *Fodrum, Gistum, und Servitium Regis. Studien zu den wirtschaftlichen Grundlagen des Königtums im Frankenreich.* Cologne: Böhlau, 1968.

Cheney, Christopher R. *Innocent III and England.* Stuttgart: Hiersemann, 1976.

Dilcher, Hermann. *Die sizilische Gesetzgebung Kaiser Friedrichs II: Quellen der Konstitutionen von Melfi und ihrer Novellen.* Cologne: Böhlau Verlag, 1975.

Edbury, Peter. *The Kingdom of Cyprus and the Crusades, 1191–1374.* Cambridge: Cambridge University Press, 1991.

Elkan, Hugo. *Die Gesta Innocentii III. Im Verhältniss zu den Regesten desselben Papstes.* Heidelberg: Buchdruckerei von J, Hörning, 1876.

Eubel, Konrad. *Hierarchia Catholica Medii Aevi.* 2nd ed. 6 vols. Münster: Regensberg Library, 1960.

Fliche, Augustin, and Victor Martin. *Histoire de l'église.* 34 vols. Paris: Bloud et Gay, 1934–1960.

Foreville, Raymonde. *Innocent III et le France.* Stuttgart: Hiersemann, 1992.

———. *Latran I, II, III, IV.* Paris: Editions de l'Orante, 1965.

Grierson, Philip, and Lucia Travaini. *Medieval European Coinage, with a Catalogue of the Coins in the Fitzwilliam Museum, Cambridge: Vol. 14. Italy III (South Italy, Sicily, Sardinia).* Cambridge: Cambridge University Press, 1998.

Hagedorn, Gerd, "Papst Innocenz III und Byzanz am Vorabend des IV Kreuzzugs." *Ostkirchliche Studien* 23 (1974): 3–20, 105–36.

Hageneder, O. "Das Sonne-Mond-Gleichnis bei Innocenz III." *Mitteilungen des Instituts für österreichische Geschichtsforschung* 65 (1957): 340–68.

Imkamp, Wilhelm. *Das Kirchenbild Innocenz III (1198–1216).* Päpste und Papsttum 22. Stuttgart: Hiersemann, 1983.

Initienverzeichnis zu August Potthast Regesta Pontificum Romanorum. Munich: Monumenta Germaniae Historica, 1978.

Innocenzo III: Urbs et orbis. Edited byAndrea Sommerlechner. 2 vols. Rome: Società Romana di Storia Patria, 2003.

Laufs, Manfred. *Politik und Recht bei Innocenz III.* Cologne: Böhlau Verlag, 1980.

Lefèvre, Yves. "Innocent III et son temps vus de Rome: Etude sur la biographie anonyme de ce pape." *Mélanges d'archéologie et d'histoire de l'école française de Rome* 61 (1949): 242–45.

Maccarrone, Michele. "Innocenzo III prima del suo pontificato." *Archivio Romano di Storia Patria* 66 (1943): 59–134.

———. *Nuovi studi su Innocenzo III.* Edited by Roberto Lambertini. Rome: Istituto storico italiano per il medio evo, 1995.

———. *Studi su Innocenzo III.* Italia Sacra 17. Padua: Antenore, 1972.

Maleczek, Werner. *Papst und Kardinalskolleg von 1191 bis 1216: Die Kardinale unter Coelestin III und Innocenz III.* Vienna: Verlag der Österreichischen Akademie der Wissenschaften, 1984.

———. *Pietro Capuano, patrizio amalfitano, cardinale, legato all quarta crociata, teologo (1214).* Amalfi: Centro di cultura e storia amalfitana, 1997.

Matthews, Donald. *The Norman Kingdom of Sicily.* Cambridge: Cambridge University Press, 1992.

Moore, John C. *Pope Innocent III (1160/61–1216).* Leiden: Brill, 2003.

———. "The Sermons of Pope Innocent III." *Römische historische Mitteilungen* 36 (1994): 81–142.

Morris, Colin. *The Papal Monarchy: The Western Church from 1050–1250.* Oxford: Clarendon Press, 1989.

Paravicini-Bagliani, Agostino. "La storiografia pontificia del secolo XIII: Prospettive di ricerca." *Römische historische Mitteilungen* 18 (1976): 45–54.

Pennington, Kenneth J. *Pope and Bishops: The Papal Monarchy in the Twelfth and Thirteenth Century.* Philadelphia: University of Pennsylvania Press, 1984.

Pfaff, Volkert. "Die Gesta Innocenz III. und das Testament Heinrichs VI." *Zeitschrift der Savigny-Stiftung für Rechtsgeschichte* 81 (1964): 78–126.

Potthast, August. *Regesta Pontificum Romanorum.* 2 vols. Berlin: Decker, 1874.

Powell, James M. *Albertanus of Brescia: The Pursuit of Happiness in the Early Thirteenth Century.* Philadelphia: University of Pennsylvania Press, 1992.

———. *Anatomy of a Crusade.* Philadelphia: University of Pennsylvania Press, 1986.

———. "Innocent III and Petrus Beneventanus: Reconstructing a Career at the Papal Curia." In *Pope Innocent III and His World*, ed. John C. Moore (Aldershot: Ashgate, 1999), 51–62.

———. "Innocent III and Secular Law." In press.

———. "Innocent III, the Trinitarians, and the Renewal of the Church, 1198–1200." In *La Liberazione dei "captivi" tra cristianità e islam: Oltre la crociata e il Gihad: Tolleranza e servizio umanitario*, ed. Giulio Cipollone (Vatican City: Archivio segreto Vaticano/Gangemi Editore, 2000).

———. "Myth, Legend, Propaganda, History: The First Crusade, 1140–ca. 1300." In *Autour de la première croisade* (Paris: Publications de la Sorbonne, 1996).

———. "Pastor Bonus: Some Evidence of Honorius III's Use of the Sermons of Pope Innocent III." *Speculum* 52 (1977): 522–37.

———. "Pope Innocent III and Alexius III: A Crusade Plan that Failed." In *Experiencing the Crusades*, 2 vols. (Cambridge: Cambridge University Press, 2003), 1:96–102.

Riley-Smith, Jonathan. *The Crusades: A Short History.* London: Athlone, 1987.

Robinson, Ian S. *The Papacy, 1073–1198: Community and Innovation.* Cambridge: Cambridge University Press, 1990.

Röhricht, Reinhold. *Regesta Regni Hierosolymitani.* 2 vols. Oeniponti, 1893–1894; reprint, New York: Burt Franklin, n.d..

Sayers, Jane. *Innocent III: Leader of Europe, 1198–1216.* London: Longman, 1994.

Schedario Baumgarten. *Descrizione diplomatica di bolle e brevi originali da Innocenzo III a Pio IX.* 2 vols. Vatican City: Archivio Segreto Vaticano, 1965.

Schimmelpfennig, Bernard. *The Papacy.* New York: Columbia University Press, 1992.

Takayama, Hiroshi. *The Administration of the Norman Kingdom of Sicily.* Leiden: Brill, 1993.

Treadgold, Warren. *A History of the Byzantine State.* Stanford, Calif.: Stanford University Press, 1997.

Twyman, Susan. "Papal Adventus at Rome in the Twelfth Century." *Historical Research* 69 (1996): 233–53.

———. *Papal Ceremonial at Rome in the Twelfth Century.* Woodbridge: Boydell and Brewer, 2002.

Van Cleve, Thomas C. *The Emperor Frederick II of Hohenstaufen: Immutator Mundi.* Oxford: Clarendon Press, 1972.

———. *Markward of Anweiler and the Sicilian Regency.* Princeton, N.J.: Princeton University Press, 1937.

Waley, Daniel. *The Papal State in the Thirteenth Century.* London: Macmillan, 1961.

INDEX

The Deeds of Pope Innocent III by an Anonymous Author was designed and

composed in Meridien Roman with Cataneo display type by

Kachergis Book Design, Pittsboro, North Carolina;

and printed on 60-pound Glatfelter and bound

by Edwards Brothers, Inc., Lillington,

North Carolina.